A Prehistory of Australia, New Guinea and Sahul

J. Peter White

Reader in Prehistory
University of Sydney

with

James F. O'Connell

Associate Professor of Anthropology
University of Utah

Illustrations by
Margrit Koettig

ACADEMIC PRESS
A Subsidiary of Harcourt Brace Jovanovich, Publishers

Sydney   New York   London
Paris   San Diego   San Francisco
São Paulo   Tokyo   Toronto

603268

ACADEMIC PRESS AUSTRALIA
Centrecourt, 25–27 Paul Street North,
North Ryde, N.S.W. 2113

United States Edition published by
ACADEMIC PRESS INC.
111 Fifth Avenue
New York, New York 10003

United Kingdom Edition published by
ACADEMIC PRESS, INC. (LONDON) LTD.
24/28 Oval Road, London NW1 7DX

Printed in Australia

National Library of Australia Cataloguing-in-Publication Data

---

White, J. Peter (John Peter), 1937–.
  A prehistory of Australia, New Guinea and Sahul.

  Bibliography.
  Includes index.
  ISBN 0 12 746750 5.
  ISBN 0 12 746730 0 (pbk).

  1. Man, Prehistoric—Australia. 2. Australia—Antiquities.
  3. Man, Prehistoric—Papua New Guinea.
  4. Papua New Guinea—Antiquities.
   I. O'Connell, James F. (James Francis).
   II. Koettig, Margrit. III. Title.

994

Library of Congress Catalog Card Number: 81–71781

To Moira and Laura

But Scientists, who ought to know,
Assure us that they must be so . . . .
Oh! let us never, never doubt
What nobody is sure about!

—HILAIRE BELLOC

Contents

List of Figures and Tables   ix
Acknowledgments   xi
Explanatory Notes   xiii

1
Perspectives   1

1.1   About Prehistory   1
1.2   About this Book   3

2
Land, People and Research   5

2.1   Sahul   6
2.2   Traditional Societies and White Contact   17
2.3   History of Archaeological Research   22

3
Sahul: Early Prehistory   31

3.1   50,000–25,000 Years Ago   33
3.2   Sahul Settlement: Background and Process   42
3.3   25,000–10,000 Years Ago   54

4
Intermission: Three Problems   73

4.1   1, 2, 3, . . . , n Groups of Settlers?   74
4.2   Flaked Stone Tools   83
4.3   Megafauna: Dying and Dwarfing   88

5
Australia: The Last 10,000 Years   97

5.1   Introduction   97
5.2   Stone Technologies   105
5.3   Local Subsistence Patterns   133
5.4   Tasmania   157

6
New Guinea: The Last 10,000 Years   171

6.1   Introduction   171
6.2   Highlands   174
6.3   Lowlands and Coast   194

7
Sahul: Internal Patterns and External Comparisons   213

7.1   Change in Prehistory   213
7.2   Sahul in World Prehistory   215

8
Update   221

Appendixes   225

I.   Uses of the Past: Tasmania   227
II.   Journals Concerned with Sahul Prehistory   236
III.   Selected Bibliography   237

References   239
Index of Names   269
Index of Places   275
Subject Index   281

List of Figures and Tables

Figures

2.1	Sahul mirror-imaged onto northern hemisphere lands. 7
2.2	Sahul: altitudes. 9
2.3	Sahul: annual rainfall. 10
2.4	Sahul: seasonality. 11
2.5	Sahul: vegetation. 13
2.6	Excavations at Shea's Creek, 1896. 25
2.7	Ballina: Statham's section, 1892. 25
2.8	Devon Downs: plan and section. 26–27
2.9	Lapstone Creek: plan and section. 28
3.1	Sites referred to in Chapter 3. 32
3.2	Willandra Lakes: plan and stratigraphy. 34
3.3	"Horse-hoof" cores. 38
3.4	Devil's Lair: stratigraphy. 41
3.5	Wallacea. 44
3.6	Sea level changes during the last 150,000 years. 45
3.7	Sahul: model of settlement. 51
3.8	Kosipe: excavation. 56
3.9	Kosipe: stratigraphy and dates. 57
3.10	Waisted and tanged tools. 58
3.11	Ground hatchet heads. 60
3.12	Miriwun: section. 61
3.13	Devil's Lair: bone points. 62
3.14	Devil's Lair: bead. 62
3.15	Koonalda: plan and section. 63
3.16	Tanged blade from New Guinea. 69
4.1	Sites referred to in section 4.1. 74
4.2	Reconstructions of some megafauna. 89
5.1	Sites referred to in sections 5.2 and 5.3. 98
5.2	Cultural areas of Aboriginal Australia. 101
5.3	Backed blades. 107
5.4	Backed artefacts. 108
5.5	*Elouera*. 109
5.6	Unifacial points (*pirri*). 110
5.7	Unifacial points (*lelira*). 111
5.8	Bifacial points. 112
5.9	Bifacial points. 113
5.10	Glass point. 114
5.11	Backed points from Miriwun. 115
5.12	*Elouera* from Cannon Hill I. 116
5.13	Backed blades and points from Sulawesi. 122
5.14	Ground hatchet heads. 126
5.15	Adzes and adze slugs. 127
5.16	Edge-ground chisel. 128
5.17	Distribution of hatchet heads, northern NSW. 130
5.18	Distribution of hatchet heads, Victoria. 132
5.19	Subsistence models, south coast, NSW, and south coast, Queensland. 135
5.20	Lake Condah fish traps: plan. 139

5.21 Malangangerr: excavation. 142
5.22 Currarong 1 and 2: sections. 144
5.23 Bone bipoints and unipoints, NSW. 146
5.24 Durras North: plan and section. 149
5.25 Fish hooks, blanks and files. 152
5.26 Sites referred to in section 5.4
          (Tasmania). 158
5.27 Rocky Cape North: section. 159
5.28 Tasmania: stone tools. 164
5.29 Tasmania: stone tools. 165
5.30 Mt. Cameron West: engravings. 167
6.1   Sites referred to in Chapter 6. 172
6.2   New Guinea: population densities. 174
6.3   Kuk: main drains. 178
6.4   Kuk: excavations. 179
6.5   Mugumamp Ridge: plan and section. 180
6.6   Kuk: modern garden system. 181
6.7   Prehistoric gardens. 185
6.8   Swimming pigs being hunted. 188
6.9   Mortars from New Guinea. 191
6.10 Club head from Papua. 192
6.11 Club heads from New Guinea. 193
6.12 Repainting rock art, Aibura. 194
6.13 Modern New Guinean rock art. 195
6.14 Motupore: chert drill-points. 207
6.15 Wanigela: pedestaled bowl. 210
6.16 Wanigela: engraved conus shell. 211

Tables

3.1   Willandra Lakes history. 36
3.2   Distances between Wallacean islands. 45
4.1   Human skeletal remains older than 6000
          years. 78
4.2   Flaked stone tools used per capita. 88
5.1   Northcliffe: distribution of excavated
          material. 118
5.2   Bass Point: stratigraphy. 147
5.3   Durras North: fish. 148.
5.4   Rocky Cape: analytical units and
          dates. 160
5.5   Rocky Cape: minimum numbers of
          animals. 161
5.6   Rocky Cape: meat weights. 161
5.7   Rocky Cape: fish bones. 162
5.8   Rocky Cape: bone tools. 162
5.9   Rocky Cape: stone tools. 163
5.10 Rocky Cape: exotic stone. 163
6.1   Manim Valley shelters. 176
6.2   Kuk: drainage phases. 178
6.3   Aibura: fauna. 186
6.4   Aibura: mandibles. 186
6.5   Highlands sites: pig bones. 187
6.6   Nebira 4: distribution of ceramic
          decoration. 201

Acknowledgments

Although this book was written between 1979 and 1981, it contains ideas and opinions tried out on students, colleagues and friends, especially in Sydney and Canberra, over a number of years. We cannot now identify all who helped us, but wish to offer our thanks to all who have done so.

For more specific assistance, in the form of advice, information, discussions, illustrations, permissions and other forms less acknowledgeable, it is only fair to name and thank the following: Jim Allen, Wal Ambrose, Val Attenbrow, Jane Balme, Sandra Bowdler, Jim Bowler, Pat Carter, John Chappell, John Clegg, Peter Coutts, Frank Dickson, Charlie Dortch, Neale Draper, Brian Egloff, Roland Fletcher, Jack Golson, Pawel Gorecki, Shelley Greer, Chris Haigh, Ed Harris, Brian Hayden, Peter Hiscock, Jeanette Hope, Phil Hughes, Nancy Howell, Ian Johnson, Lucy Lewis Johnson, Rhys Jones, Jo Kamminga, Ron Lampert, Peter Latz, Roger Lennon, Roger Luebbers, Isabel McBryde, Fred McCarthy, John Meaney, Betty Meehan, Duncan Merrilees, Tony and Jenny Minson, Theya Molleson, Mary-Jane Mountain, John Mulvaney, Win Mumford, Peter Murray, Bob Netting, Henry Nix, Gretchen Poiner, Winston Ponder, Jocelyn Powell, Bill Rathje, Jim Rhoads, John Roberts, Bob and Judy Rodden, Ed Roper, Annie Ross, Mike Schiffer, Carmel Schrire, Jim Specht, Alan Thorne, Norman Tindale, Ron Vanderwal and Doug Yen. Special thanks to Geoff Irwin, Ruthann Knudson and Harry Lourandos for commenting so cogently on parts of the manuscript. Also, to Richard Wright for allowing us to draw on Margrit Koettig's time and cartographic talents, and for helping as only a good colleague and efficient administrator can.

Margrit Koettig's name is deservedly on the title page, for her skilled work as illustrator and research assistant has been a major contribution.

For those of us who write in longhand, typists are essential in the move from manuscript to book. We thank Debbie Hegedus, Ruth Turner, Ann Broughton, Jayne Munro, Rhonda Porada, and especially Departmental Secretary Robyn Wood, who, like all people in her position, is a god, and in her case a kind one.

We also gratefully acknowledge assistance from the following institutions: the Universities of Sydney, Arizona and Utah; the Anthropology Library of the University of Cambridge; the National Parks and Wildlife Service (NSW); the Australian Museum; and the Australian National University.

The following journals, publishers and institutions have permitted the use of material in their care, the re-publication of material, or have helped in other ways. We thank them all: *Asian Perspectives; Archaeology and Physical Anthropology in Oceania; Mankind; Artefact;* Royal Society of Western Australia; Australian Museum; University of Sydney; Australian Institute of Aboriginal Studies; Tasmanian Museum and Art Gallery; Western Australian Museum; Australian Consolidated Press; W. Junk; Academic Press; Australian National University Press.

Finally, our sincere thanks to Bill Woodcock and Grant Walker of Academic Press for asking us to write the book, and to Dallas Cox for editing it with an acumen which we can now appreciate.

J. Peter White
James F. O'Connell

Explanatory Notes

All the large-scale maps are drawn on an azimuthal equal-area projection. This minimizes the latitudinal distortions.

In all artefact drawings, the side of the cross-section closer to the plan view is the one drawn in plan.

The term "New Guinea" is used to refer to the whole island and in other geographical contexts; the political divisions Irian Jaya, New Guinea, Papua, Papua New Guinea and subdivisions of these are used only where necessary. The montane regions generally are referred to as "the highlands" and their inhabitants as "highlanders"; the terms "Highlands" and "Highlanders" are restricted to approximately the Highlands political districts of Papua New Guinea and their inhabitants, following the usage of Paula Brown (1978) and J. B. Watson (1964).

Since Australia has no single site-numbering scheme, and the numbering systems of the various states are neither widely known nor commonly used, we have continued to use the names bestowed by investigators. For Papua New Guinea, where a national scheme does operate but the designations have not been widely adopted in the literature, we give both names where these are known to us.

Chapter 1
Perspectives

1.1   About Prehistory

Sciences of the past draw on a body of theory derived from recent observations in order to explain past events. They depend on the belief that the physical laws of the universe, and their workings throughout time, have not changed. Water runs downhill and moves clay, sand or boulders, depending on what the hill is made of, the volume of water and the steepness of slope. Living organisms evolve through the operation of natural selection, drift and other mechanisms on genes, affecting individuals and populations. For a geologist or biologist these and other uniformitarian principles are basic to the way that the past is explained: every event in the past can be analysed through them, although the principles themselves are insufficient for predicting a past event. Even a catastrophe is not a suspension of these laws but another facet of them: it is not a miracle.

Archaeology is also a science of the human past, and, like other sciences, must depend on uniformitarian assumptions in order to study particular interesting events, explain the characteristics of past cultural systems and write prehistory. Prehistory is simply the result of attempts to give meaning to observations on a particular archaeological record, using general principles about the relationship between actual human behaviour and the material remains now visible to us (L. R. Binford 1981: 22). For some scholars, such as Binford and D. L. Clarke, it is the development of general principles — middle-range or interpretive theory — which is of critical importance at this time. For others, it is the application of such principles as we already have to interpret particular aspects of the human past. But both groups focus on understanding the material record of the human past.

We do not here deny the critical importance of developing interpretive theory. One of the greatest weaknesses of current prehistory lies in its dependence on a limited understanding of relationships among the manufacture, formal patterning, use and discard of material objects and other aspects of human behaviour. Through studies of present-day activities, such as tool-making, where and how people lose things, hunting and butchering, human and animal scavenging, the size and spacing of houses, villages and towns, and destruction and decay of all kinds, some clues have been gained and some useful generalizations formulated. But further development of these is required. The study of modern material behaviour (Rathje 1979) and of site formation processes (Schiffer 1976) is crucial if we are to investigate and explain the archaeological record of particular events within human history. We do not, however, think that interpreting the past should be renounced until what we judge as "adequate" or robust generalizations have been formulated. We think it important now to approach the past with the principles and generalizations we have, to see how they operated in a particular situation or whether there are aspects of past behaviour reflected in the archaeological record with which they are not congruent. Our interpretive theory must be constantly tested against the archaeological evidence and, if it fails, refined in the present. As L. R. Binford says (1981: 29), "only in the present can we observe the bear and [its] footprint together, the coincidence of the dynamic and the static derivatives." The purpose of refining our theory is to write better prehistory.

A necessary consequence of this view of prehistory is that every account of the past is totally an *interpretation.* Too many archaeological reports suggest that "the data" can be

recorded objectively and then interpreted. This is nonsense: what you see is what you get. And what one "sees" depends on the problem being investigated, the theories and techniques one uses, one's personality, training and experience, the time, money and equipment available, and on what one expects the answer to be. These factors operate to ensure that every account of the past is as much the result of interpretation as the Guide to Collections of the Metropolitan Museum of Art or the story of the Lightning Brothers.*

Why are we interpreting the past, and what do we learn from it? The rationale of prehistory, as of history, is a social one. Historians have long recognized that the problems they investigate in past societies relate closely to major problems of interest in their own time (e.g. Carr 1961; Geyl 1955). A similar situation can be seen throughout the history of prehistory. Its first concern was human antiquity, proper in a world which Lyell had recently shown to be millions of years old rather than the Biblical 6000 years. From this it turned to a study of technology and its changes, appropriate and important in the industrial societies. The mechanisms of change which were invoked — external "influences" or migrations — paralleled those in a world wherein the colonized majority changed at the dictates of imperial powers, and large numbers of people moved across the world to colonize new lands, dispossessing the older inhabitants. The more recent concerns of economic change, independent developments in different parts of the world and the possibility of prehistoric environmental degradation are, of course, current social concerns. We do not wish to suggest a simple link between the concerns and interpretations of researchers and those of the society in which they live. In fact, many analyses of history and prehistory caution *against* the easy and over-simple interpretations of our own situation. But it can hardly be doubted that there is a social purpose to our endeavour. Why else is it worth doing? Professionals might argue simply that archaeological research is fun or satisfying intellectually, or that it keeps people off the

---

* The Lightning Brothers, Yagdjabula and Tjabuindji, are spectacularly painted in a cave at Delamere, NT. They were Wardaman tribal brothers in dispute over a woman, and their story has been recorded by Arndt (1961).

streets. None of these provides a reason for society to support it except as a fad, akin to chess or yoyos. We believe that prehistory, like history, is useful within our society for the perspective it gives, the alternatives it demonstrates can exist, and the wisdom it allows people to gain. Wisdom, not knowledge. Prehistory will not provide formulas for action or answers to specific problems, but perspectives. It is a mirror within which we can view ourselves and our concerns, but, like all mirrors, we have constructed it and its reflective properties.

Within the Pacific region the social purpose of prehistory is particularly strong. Here, prehistory is the history of the colonized and dispossessed, people either still disadvantaged by that experience or newly politically (but not economically) independent. Prehistory may be used by them as a charter, but its value is probably as great for the colonizers and conquerors, still incorrigibly racist and technologically dominated. "Why did these savages never develop?" is still the most common question asked of prehistorians. The demonstration that these "savages" also crossed the sea and colonized a continent, became as good agriculturalists as we are, altered the balance of nature and, in short, acted like all other humans will, we hope, help us to think of them as such (see Appendix I).

1.2   About this Book

The use of the word "Sahul" in the title of this book indicates that it will focus on the similarities, as well as the differences, between Australia and New Guinea. Because these are now two islands, and separate political entities, they are usually studied by different people, from different perspectives and using different methodologies. At the simplest level, maps of the two countries are drawn to different scales and present their data in different forms and units. But for at least 80% of the time during which humans have occupied the area, Australia and New Guinea were subsumed into the single continent of Sahul. For about the first 40,000 years, the people of Sahul have a common history. Traces of this may be observed in many aspects of their societies as recorded at the time of

European contact, but the full expression of this commonality can be seen only in prehistoric times.

Our intention in writing this book is to outline the prehistory of the area by focusing on some major problems. In doing so we avoid presenting "the data" as anything other than totally dependent on the framework of interpretation. This book is not a compendium of things and data. It is written as much as possible from the inside of current arguments within the field — here is the situation as we see it, these are what we see as appropriate data and what we think of them, here are some views about the problem. This is a book about the questions we have been asking of the past and how we have gone about investigating them, rather than a series of detailed answers to well-defined problems.

In researching, we have relied primarily on the literature and museum collections. Except for theses, we have endeavoured not to use unpublished material or unpresented field data, for two reasons. First, we wish to allow readers to be able to restudy these analyses and form their own conclusions; second, it demonstrates how much of Sahul prehistory is based on appallingly small samples, and makes it clearer in what ways these need to be increased.

The fact that our samples are so small has increased the problems of writing. Almost every one of our current propositions about Sahul's prehistory can be challenged on the basis of a poor relationship between hypothesis and the sample studied, and it has been necessary to elucidate this before tackling the actual hypotheses. Further, because the total field is so small, each new discovery, site or worker can be expected to have a more significant effect on the discipline than in areas where much more is known. Since we started writing in 1979, at least two aspects of Sahul's prehistory have radically altered, and we expect more to do so before publication; hence the provision for an up-date section (Chapter 8).

The arrangement of the book is primarily chronological, and secondarily regional, with some problems that do not fit this framework being treated separately (e.g. Chapter 4). A chronological arrangement, though it posed difficulties in dealing with sites which span more than one of the divisions made here, seemed the easiest for people not directly involved with the field and certainly cut down on the repetition of data which would otherwise have been required. In presenting chronologies, we have used uncorrected radiocarbon years (determinations) throughout. Since Sahul came into contact with Christian-based time only within the last 200 years, and very little of our account is comparative with the rest of the world, radiocarbon years seem to be the appropriate framework. Those who wish to translate them will no doubt do so.

Finally, this book is selective, but we hope unbiased. We have tried to select the material without deliberately distorting or omitting evidence and interpretation which is relevant to the problem being discussed. It would be specious to deny that the book is opinioned, some may say opinionated: one cannot be involved in a field of study without being so. However, in forming opinions we have tried to be as unbiased as we can. The world's knowledge of the prehistory of Sahul is recent, and some of the discoveries form an exciting challenge to current interpretations of archaeological data and of prehistory. Those discoveries become important, however, only because they are interpreted through certain theoretical perspectives. What we have tried to do is make those perspectives clear, explain why we have adopted them and elucidate their implications. This results in *a* prehistory of Australia, New Guinea and Sahul, not *the* prehistory.

Chapter 2
Land, People and Research

This chapter sets the physical and intellectual scene for the prehistory of Sahul. First, we look at the land itself, the folded, tropical monsoonal north and the flatter temperate zone with its highly erratic rainfall. In these environments live the unique flora and fauna of Sahul, not only visually strange to Old and New World eyes, but adapted in unexpected ways to the environment. These environments have not been stable. Tectonic movements in the north and climatic changes during the Pleistocene have been documented. Humans too have made their mark by firing and clearing the land, with the effects of the last two centuries of White migration being on the largest scale.

The people who inhabited Australia and New Guinea when Whites arrived are next described. We stress the importance of recognizing how rapid the impact of White colonization was and the implications this can have for our descriptions. Despite this, however, continent-wide similarities do occur, with the most notable contrasts being between the formalized gardens and higher population densities of parts of New Guinea and the more areally extensive subsistence patterns elsewhere. This ethnographic record tells us what recent societies were like and will later be helpful in interpreting the archaeological data; but we must recognize that major changes have occurred in prehistory and not project the present into the past simply because we know it better.

Finally, we look briefly at the history of archaeological research. It is clear that the underlying question has always been the antiquity of occupation, with questions of subsequent changes and subsistence variation being of secondary interest. The major question is now close to being answered, and with the growth of the discipline other issues are now ripe for further exploration.

2.1 Sahul

Almost two-thirds of the world's land surface is one continent, Aseurica we might call it, and on it humans have evolved during the last five million years. Escape from it to the other major continent, the Americas, was sometimes possible by land, but the route was then so guarded by ice and cold climates as to be impassable for early humans. The other continent, Australia, along with New Guinea, Tasmania and the smaller islands of the Pacific, was guarded by the sea. Throughout human history, these lands have been accessible only to people with the technology to carry them over tens or hundreds of kilometres of ocean.

The continent with which this book is primarily concerned has no single name. Biogeographers, who most frequently treat it as a unit, call it Sahul-land, meaning by this the area of biotic similarity encompassed by the present large islands of New Guinea, Australia and Tasmania. Greater Australia, a term sometimes used, draws attention not only to the land but also to the parts exposed at various times in the past by lowered sea levels. It does, however, tend to subsume the whole into one part, Australia, which although the largest, is, and has been, climatically and biotically distinct from its northern quarter, now New Guinea. We prefer the biogeographic term, Sahul, for the times when one land mass was present, and the better known New Guinea, Australia and Tasmania for the more recent, separate islands. We shall, however, also have to use these latter terms to refer to regions within the earlier larger continent. This

may seem confusing initially, but it is important for prehistorians constantly to keep in mind that not even the lands upon which the human drama we study is enacted are entirely static. The fact that the stage and its biological scenery alters through time is an essential factor in the play, and for the players.

Of necessity, the biogeographic description in this section is of the land masses as they are known today (Brookfield with Hart 1971; Jeans 1978; Keast 1966, 1981; Keast *et al.* 1959). It would be appropriate if we could start our account with a description of the environment at some point in the past and then show what changes have occurred between that time and the present. But although environmental changes during the last few tens of millennia have been the focus of much recent research, we are not yet able to describe any palaeo-climate. Therefore, we will start with a broad outline of the current geology, climate and biology and then make some reference to changes during the later Pleistocene.

Geology and Climate

Sahul is located in the south-western part of the Pacific Ocean, from the equator to 44°S, and between 112°E and 152°E. The northern end reaches to the same latitude (0°) as the mouth of the Amazon River and the lakes which form the source of the Nile; the southern tip is as far south of the equator as New England, northern Japan and northern Italy are north of it (Fig. 2.1). Its maximum extent, at times of lowest sea level, was about 10.6 million km^2; the area of its three main islands is now about 8.5 million km^2. Sahul consists of the Australian continental plate, with a series of trough sediments and volcanics welded to the northern edge. This folded area, basically modern New Guinea, consists of a series of massive mountain chains running west-north-west to east-south-east, with maximum altitudes up to 5000 m. Within the chains are some large inter-montane valleys, mostly around 1600 m altitude, which are now important to human populations. The landscape throughout the area is very steep and the slopes are subject to continuous and heavy erosion, the products of which have built up so rapidly in larger valleys

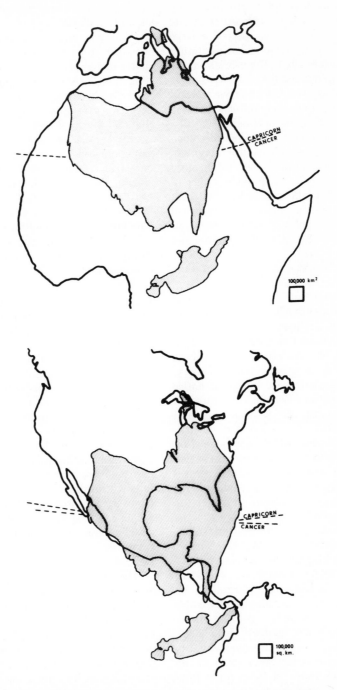

FIGURE 2.1. Sahul mirror-imaged onto northern hemisphere continents, with the Tropics aligned. Currently, White populations in Australia are concentrated in the south-east quarter of the continent, indigenous populations in northern Australia and New Guinea.

and lowland areas that these are frequently swampy. Vulcanism, which with uplift during Tertiary and Quaternary times played a large part in forming the present landscape, continues to be important, especially in the islands east of New Guinea. Throughout the area, erosion is increased by earthquakes which remove soil and rubble in mass from steeper mountain slopes. As might be expected along the crumpling edge of a continental plate, the area is geologically complex. Particularly along the central mountain chain, limestones, shales and other sedimentary rocks are intruded into by a wide range of volcanics with the result, for humans, that high quality stone useful for a variety of technological purposes is fairly readily available. Lowland areas, with their heavy alluvial cover are not always so well endowed.

The contrasts between New Guinea and the rest of Sahul (that is, modern Australia and Tasmania) are extreme (Fig. 2.2). Only 6% of this latter region is over 600 m in altitude, and most of these areas are high-level plateaus that are now heavily dissected, rather than steep mountain chains. The western two-thirds of the continent is a shield of very ancient rocks now much planed and weathered. Along the entire eastern coast, from Cape York to Tasmania, is a belt of higher ground, 150–450 km wide and highest in south-east Australia. It is geologically complex and generally deeply incised by rivers east of the watershed. Between these two major geological provinces lies the central basin, a landscape of rolling lowlands of sedimentary rocks. This region, much of the western shield and the western slopes of the highlands are all areas of internal and often uncoordinated drainage. The Murray–Darling River system, draining the south-eastern highlands, is the only major internal river system to reach the sea. It is also significant that the eastern highlands are everywhere sufficiently rugged to cause the major rain-bearing winds from the Pacific Ocean to drop their loads before reaching far into the interior, which is therefore semi-desert. Over large areas of the continent, silcretes (some of them quite fine-grained) and sandstones are the rocks that are readily available for human use. True flint is restricted to the southern coasts, while cherts

and volcanics occur mostly along the eastern mountain chain.

The geological and altitudinal contrasts between the New Guinean and Australian parts of Sahul carry through to their climates (Fig. 2.3). New Guinea and the islands to the east of it lie within the humid tropics. Rainfall is heavy throughout the area, especially along the southern slopes of the larger islands. Annual falls of more than 2500 mm are common, and only in a few small areas is there a seasonal bias in its occurrence. Otherwise, rainfall is regular and, except for small areas on the south coast of New Guinea, frequent. Only two or three times a year are there spells of more than ten days without rain in most areas. The highlands and inter-montane valleys generally have their own weather pattern, strongly influenced by local air circulation, with heavier and more regular rain on higher ground. Highland temperatures are lower than elsewhere, and there is greater diurnal variation. Elsewhere there is little daily or seasonal influence on the climate, which has the effect of moderating variation and increasing rainfall.

Within the present Australian continent only the extreme northern and north-eastern fringes can be called humid tropics, and they receive rainfall equivalent to that common in New Guinea. The 1500–2500 mm annual rainfalls in Australia occur in very restricted areas and on a highly seasonal basis. Resulting entirely from the north-west monsoon, all rain falls within the hottest five months of the year (November–March). As there are no mountains which can keep water locked up and release it slowly, many rivers are not perennial. Inland from the coastal fringes rainfall decreases rapidly.

The rest of the Australian continent is best envisaged as a series of climatic zones concentric around the western and central deserts. In these deserts, which comprise two-thirds of the country, mean rainfall is less than 500 mm per year and is highly erratic in its occurrence (Fig. 2.4). Port Hedland, on the west coast, for example, has an annual mean of 275 mm, but variations range from 32 to 1019 mm. Even on the north-east coast, outside the desert area, Townsville's mean is 1214 mm, but within one eight-year period annual falls ranged from 280 to 1803 mm. In the country as a whole, rainfall averages 470 mm per year, and this exceeds evaporation by only 50 mm a year. In 70% of the entire area potential evaporation exceeds precipitation throughout the year. It is the south-eastern coastal strip, only a few hundred miles wide, which, along with the south-western corner and Tasmania, has both reasonably high and reliable rainfall. But even in these areas only the short rivers that flow from high country directly to the coast are truly permanent; the Murray–Darling, Australia's largest river system, draining one million km^2, has more than once in the last two centuries ceased to flow entirely for months, and the northern branches are especially liable to be reduced to a series of pools or less.

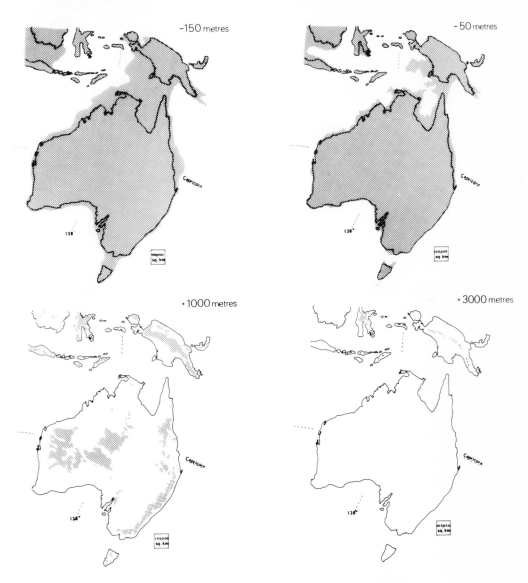

FIGURE 2.2. Sahul: altitudes above and below present sea level.

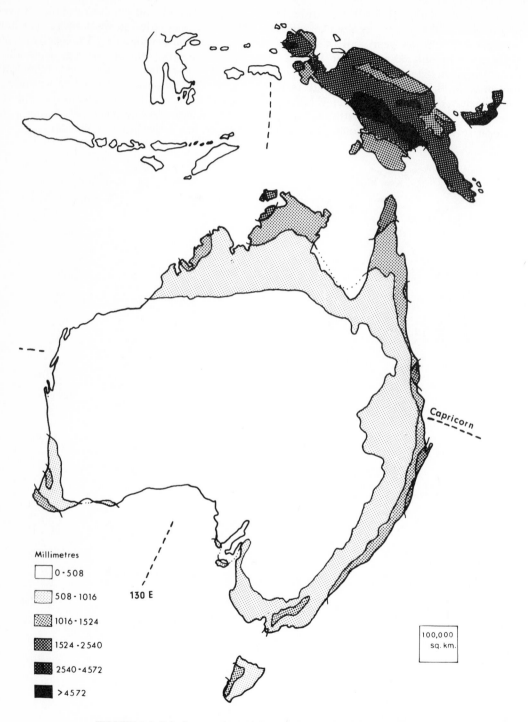

FIGURE 2.3. Sahul: annual rainfall. Wallacean data not included.

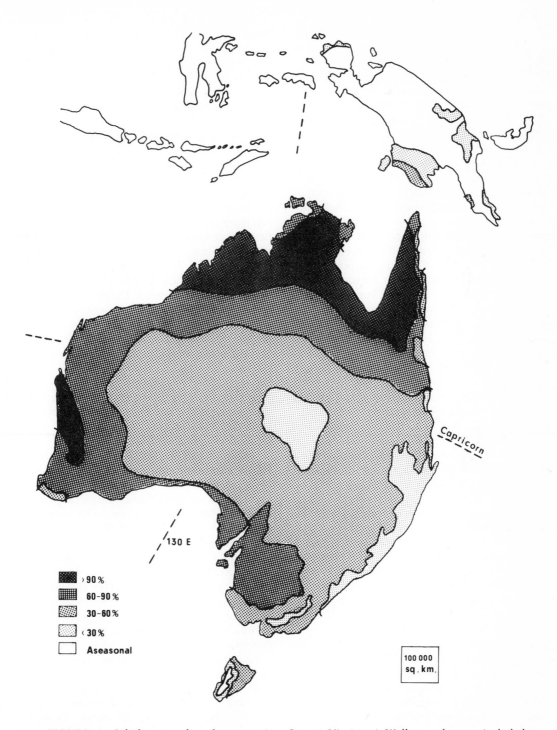

FIGURE 2.4. Sahul: seasonality of water regime. Source: Nix (1981). Wallacean data not included.

Fauna and Flora

The best-known aspect of the uniqueness of Sahul is undoubtedly its fauna and particularly its mammals. The sea barrier between Sahul and Asia is more than 50 million years old, and its effect has been to allow the Australian fauna to evolve independently of that in the rest of the world. First recognized and recorded by Alfred Russel Wallace in 1860 as a boundary line, the division between the two areas is now generally recognized as a transition zone (Wallacea) within the eastern Indonesian islands (Simpson 1977). The Asian fauna consists of eutherians, including ungulates, felids, elephantids and primates. These are absent from Sahul, and their places are filled by marsupials — macropods (kangaroos and wallabies), phalangerids (cuscus, "possums"), a range of browsers, burrowers and scavengers, and a few predators. More modern animal forms are represented only by bats and rats. The latter have been present long enough to evolve a wide range of species which, interestingly, are very different in Australia and New Guinea. Fresh-water fish and frogs are also Sahul-specific, but reptiles and birds in particular display closer connections with Asian forms. Sea life, including fish and molluscs, shows much less in the way of contrast, the major differences being between the tropics and the southern regions. Indeed there is more similarity in the marine faunas from both sides of Wallacea than there is between those of northern and southern Sahul. These differences are enhanced by the fact that on coasts south of the Tropic of Capricorn wave energies are high and tidal amplitudes low (1 m or less), whereas the reverse is true north of here (Davies 1978: Fig. 7.2). There are also almost no large tidal plains in the south. Marine and littoral fauna and flora of the two areas are thus very different.

Within Sahul there is some faunal contrast between Australia and New Guinea, the result of adaptations to the very different environment and flora. Compared with other areas of the world, the number of animal and bird species is low in Australia but high in New Guinea, the latter probably reflecting diversity in relief and habitats which encourages speciation.

The botanical boundary between Asia and Sahul is not as clear as the faunal one. The floras of New Guinea and tropical monsoon Asia are sufficiently similar for them to be grouped within the Oriental botanical realm and their origin seen in a common palaeotropic flora. However, the presence of some eucalypts and other Australian forms within New Guinea can be used as a distinguishing characteristic (Walker 1972).

More than 90% of New Guinea is forested, and much of this is lowland rainforest (Fig. 2.5). Various vegetation zones may be distinguished, but they are more closely related to altitude than rainfall (Paijmans 1976). In the flat coastal plains, extensive nipa or sago swamps lie behind sandy beaches or mangrove mud-flats. Lowlands and mountains are covered with rainforest with buttressed trees, rattans, creepers and tree ferns. At higher altitudes, stands of single species, especially of beech (*Nothofagus*), pine (*Araucaria*) and pandanus are noticeable. Alpine shrubland occurs only on the highest peaks. Savannah woodland is restricted to the two areas of seasonal rainfall on the south coast. Grasslands, which are now extensive in the Sepik and Markham valleys, and in the eastern highlands, may well be anthropogenic but are maintained by low or seasonally variable rainfall, local soil conditions and frequent firing (Brookfield with Hart 1971: 51–53).

Within Australia, rainforests like those in New Guinea exist only in small patches near the far north-east coast. Other types of rainforest occur in patches along the eastern highland chain (O'Neill 1980; Webb 1968). The dominant vegetation types are sclerophyll open-forest and woodland savannah grading into open scrub and grassland. Rainfall zones are key determinants of the flora. The central and western desert areas are covered by hummock spinifex (*Triodia*) and tussock (*Astrebla* and others) grassland, along with some trees (e.g. mulga, *Acacia aneura*) and shrubs. To the south there is a broad belt of low scrubby trees (mallee), while east and northwards denser savannah woodland is encountered. This only grades into open-forest, consisting mainly of eucalypts and acacias (wattles), in well-watered south-western, eastern and southern regions, including Tasmania (Carnahan 1978).

For many ecologists, the contrast between

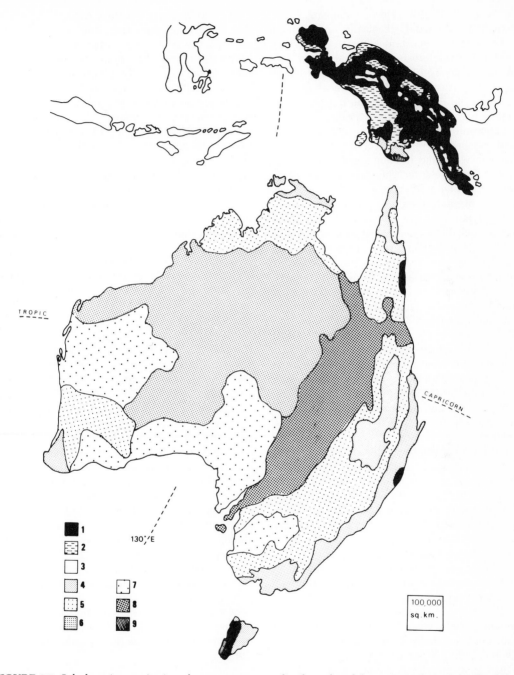

FIGURE 2.5. Sahul: major vegetation classes, very generalized. 1: closed forest ("rainforest"); 2: floodplain forests and swamps; 3: montane forest and Alpine vegetation, including some grasslands; 4: open forest, much of it *Eucalypt*-dominated; 5: woodlands, much of it *Eucalypt*-dominated; 6: shrublands (much *Acacia*) and woodlands with hummock grass understory; 7: shrublands, much dominated by *Acacia*; 8: open shrublands and herblands, with tussock grasses; 9: mangroves. Based on Brookfield with Hart (1971), Carnahan (1978). Wallacean data not included.

rainforest (basically New Guinean) and sclerophyll woodland (basically Australian) marks a more important division than that between the rainforests of tropical Sahul and Asia (van Balgooy 1976; Walker 1972). It is not simply the presence of distinctive eucalypts and acacias in the Australian region, but the entire range of plant types and their associations that are important. This is best seen by comparing the small patches of rainforest in Australia and savannah woodland in New Guinea with their surrounding vegetation types. In each case, there are much greater differences in content, structure and organization than can be seen between similar types that are considerable distances apart. For smaller fauna, such as insects and land snails, the floral difference also marks a major boundary, with nearly all forms being adapted to one type only. Even among birds and animals, Australian forms are largely woodland adapted and differ markedly from the rainforest adapted forms in New Guinea. We might expect also that this basic contrast would have affected human subsistence strategies and technologies, and that there will be greater similarities between those of the east coast of Australia and New Guinea than between the former and those of arid Australia. There are already some suggestions of this (Golson 1971), but its prehistory has not yet been explored.

Within Australia, the long-term adaptation of both plants and animals to the major environments is well recorded, with different species occurring in each. The clearest cases of adaptation are to desert environments and their highly variable rainfalls. Among the plants, many seeds lie dormant for years, to sprout only when rain occurs. Most animals, including amphibians, fish, birds and marsupials, are opportunistic breeders, able to reproduce whenever conditions are appropriate. Some desert macropods even enter a state of anoestrus during prolonged drought periods, while both these animals and zebra finches actually begin to breed when rain falls rather than in response to subsequent feed. By contrast, in climates with more reliable seasons animals breed seasonally. The occurrence of these patterns confirms both the long-term presence of major environmental zones and the local evolution of animal behaviours (Keast *et al.* 1959; Tyndale-Biscoe 1973).

A striking characteristic of Australian flora is the important role that fire plays in its maintenance and regeneration. Except for the rainforest, where the evidence is unclear, it seems that periodic, naturally occurring fires are a normal constituent of most environments and a key requirement for vegetation regeneration in many areas (e.g. Anderson 1941; Howitt 1890; A. G. McArthur 1973; Mount 1969; Stocker 1966). Recent surveys (A. M. Gill *et al.* 1981) suggest that the fire-adaptedness of the flora is highly variable, and the susceptibility of regimes depends on a number of factors which differ for each vegetation type and region. For one of the better-known areas, Tasmania, Mount (1979: 185) points out that:

> except for some of the lowland rainforests, fire comes eventually to practically all Tasmanian vegetation types and, without man's interference, generally regenerates them — i.e., the pattern is one of stable fire cycles rather than one of succession.

He shows that in both the wet and dry sclerophyll forests of this area, eucalypt re-generation is best accomplished by wide-ranging and intense fires which establish optimum conditions for sprouting and growth. The result of this is that in some regions the naturally occurring forest is even-aged, and this is self-perpetuating. Similar patterns apparently occur in many eucalypt forests. Species of many other genera, such as *Hakea* and *Acacia*, are also fire-adapted, their seeds being resistant to fire and sprouting only after it has passed through an area. Many species also have lignotubers, which readily re-sprout after fire has killed off the above-ground part of the plant (A. M. Gill 1981). The fire-adaptedness of the Australian flora has been used by human settlers to their advantage in a number of ways, although the differences between naturally and humanly induced fire regimes may well have altered the vegetation structure in many areas (R. L. Clark 1981; A. M. Gill *et al.* 1981).

Environmental Change

A critical aspect of the environmental picture is that it is not static. Over the period of human occupation, say the last 50,000 years, there have been two major causes of environmental change: non-human and human. Both will be touched upon here.

During the last 50,000 years, there has been one long-term cycle of climatic change — in colloquial terms, an "ice age". Whatever the causes of an ice age (variations in solar radiation currently seem the most likely: Imbrie and Imbrie 1979), its effect is felt throughout the world. The most important change in the Sahul area was a lowering of sea level. A drop of only 30 m from present levels would join New Guinea and Australia, and the sea was lower than this throughout the period 80,000–6500 years ago (Chappell, 1976). Australia and Tasmania were joined when the sea dropped more than 65 m, which it did perhaps three times during this period, most notably between about 25,000 and 12,000 years ago. The lowest sea level during the last 80,000 years was around -160 m. This occurred only for short periods around 53,000 and 17,000 years ago and enlarged the land area of Sahul by about one-quarter, most of this being in the area between Australia and New Guinea. The impact of these changes throughout the region is not yet fully understood. Palaeo-climatic and environmental investigations have been particularly concerned with the most extreme changes some 20,000–15,000 years ago. At that time, ocean currents were diverted, especially in the north, and rain-bearing winds probably dropped more of their moisture over what is now sea. In lowland tropical areas, present-day coasts were then far inland and probably considerably drier than at present. For all coastal areas Chappell and Thom (1977) argue that fluctuating sea levels throughout the period would have created an unstable environment with generally lower numbers of plant and animal species. Many shore communities now present may not have existed for much of the time, and most coasts would have been less attractive environments for people than they are today, when sea levels have been stable for several thousand years. Inland, there is evidence that some areas, such as the Murray–Darling drainage area, experienced increased effective precipitation around 40,000–25,000 years ago, but while the area of extreme desert may have shrunk somewhat, it does not appear to have changed to any

major extent (Bowler *et al.* 1976; Mabbutt 1971). Concomitantly, in the higher country of southeast Australia and New Guinea mean temperatures declined by as much as 5°C, so that vegetation zones moved downhill. At the time of extreme climatic difference, much of the area of New Guinea presently covered by lowland rainforest may have been open forest (J. Hope and G. Hope 1976; Nix and Kalma 1972).

Humanly caused changes to the environment have also been important. The best documented effects are in New Guinea where forest clearance in the inter-montane valleys of the highlands during the last 10,000 years or so has led to increasing areas of secondary bush and grassland. By the twentieth century these changes had led to a totally managed landscape in some areas. Even where this did not occur, fire and clearance served to maintain large areas of grassland. Some of these changes are discussed in more detail later (6.2).

Within Australia, humanly caused fire seems to have been the most important prehistoric agent. Ethnographic records from many parts of the country and the increased frequency of charcoal particles in some pollen cores suggest that the arrival of humans meant an increase in the firing of the countryside (e.g. Hallam 1975; Jones 1980). The ethnographic records also suggest that this firing was normally frequent and light in effect, being sufficient to clear out grass, underbrush, bark litter and many smaller eucalypts and other seedlings (e.g. Latz and Griffin 1978). It might be anticipated that firing of this type would, in the long-term, sometimes create a more open savannah environment. This is confirmed in many parts of the eastern highlands (from Tasmania to northern Queensland) and in the south-west where a much denser forest has grown up following the cessation of firing by Aborigines during the last 150 years. This was also noted by the commandant at Port Essington, near Darwin, during the 1830s. It is worth mentioning that, although ethnographic accounts show that fire was used as a sophisticated tool, in the long-term it was not conservation oriented, and almost certainly has been responsible for major changes in the representation of particular plants and the overall vegetation structure of large regions. Geographers (e.g. Carnahan 1978; R. L. Specht 1970) have tended to dismiss the Aboriginal impact on vegetation as minor. While it is true that the relative effects of non-humanly and humanly caused changes may be hard to distinguish, it seems likely that millennia of constant firing by the Aborigines would have had significant effects in many areas. In time, this will be confirmed by palaeo-environmental records (e.g. Singh *et al.* 1981).

The other agents of prehistoric environmental change have been the animals introduced by man. The impact of pigs in New Guinea has still not really been assessed, but the introduction of dingoes into Australia some 4000 years ago soon resulted in the extinction of a marsupial predator (*Thylacinus cynocephalus*) and a scavenger (*Sarcophilus harrisii*) (Milham and Thompson 1976). Its other effects are not known.

Humanly caused changes to the environment have been much greater during the last 200 years than in any preceding period of Australian prehistory. Due to over-grazing, the drier areas are now more desert-like than 150 years ago, while in many better-watered areas forest clearance or logging has increased run-off, erosion, the build-up of silt in streams and estuaries, and the incidence of floods. In one small swamp at Lancefield, for example, about 70 cm of silt built up between 1840 and 1970, whereas the previous 70 cm had taken about 6000 years to accumulate (Gillespie *et al.* 1978). At Roonka on the Lower Murray, 4 m of riverside dune has been eroded within a century of the clearance of vegetation (Pretty 1977). Only in the northern and north-western parts of the country has the effect been less, for fewer Whites have lived and worked there. The other aspect of the impact is the introduction of exotic flora and fauna. Blackberries, prickly pear, Paterson's Curse, St. John's Wort and many other plants introduced originally for decoration or fruit have adapted so well to parts of Australia that they are now classified as noxious weeds. Among the animals, rabbits, foxes, cats, pigs, camels, buffalo and a range of birds are now all common in some or all of the country, altering its flora and challenging or extinguishing the existence of many native animals. In Arnhem Land, for example, Indian buffalo have so trampled and wallowed in the swamps that many birds can no

longer find food there, and in Cape York pigs have had much the same effect, while throughout the country feral cats are primarily responsible for a marked decline in small marsupials (Anon. 1977). As Adamson and Fox (in press) point out: "man is creating fundamentally new ecosystems and new vegetations in Australia". Equally extreme impacts have not been observed in New Guinea where dispersal of resources and the absence of seasonal climates have been sufficient to keep at bay even such potential dangers as feral pigs.

Discussion

This account of the environment of Sahul is perforce on a grand scale. Even within the most carefully researched localities, among which the Willandra Lakes (Bowler *et al.* 1976) must rank highly, there is almost no understanding of the environment on the time scale and at the level at which groups of prehistoric people reacted to it. As Brookfield and Hart (1971: 43) say of New Guinea:

> Melanesians are usually well aware of short-term dynamic variations in environment: vulcanism, earthquakes, storms, climatic seasonality and mass movements of soil. They are rather less aware of dynamic variations that operate over periods of tens to hundreds of years ... [and] are hardly at all aware of the slowly varying dynamic changes of soil formation, gross vegetational changes, slope and valley formation and sea level changes ... It is therefore the immediately observable features such as the biota which play such an important part in the perception ... of environment.

And yet it is precisely the longer-term changes which are best observed by the palaeo-environmentalist. Human groups perceive and react to short-term environmental variations, and individual archaeological occurrences will reflect these local adaptations to seasonal, annual and occasional variability. The link between the short-term and long-term evidence can only be made when we have sufficient samples from any area, so that the gross pattern, as well as the individual variations within the system, will be distinguishable. Only by knowing the general pattern can we understand the basic constraints within which the people of a particular time and area lived. To return to our original metaphor, the long-term environmental pattern constitutes a slowly changing stage; the theatrical sets within which the players act vary quite markedly from place to place and from time to time. Human actors are not only constrained by that stage, but even more so by the short-term environmental set within which day-to-day life occurs and with which they interact positively.

2.2 Traditional Societies and White Contact

The first encounters between Europeans and the people who lived in New Guinea, Australia and Tasmania occurred between AD 1600 and 1950. Europeans had never before encountered anyone so unlike themselves. Thus our knowledge of nearly all of the traditional societies comes exclusively from White observers, most of them writing between 1750 and 1930. Both the nature of the contacts and the White observers' a priori views of these societies must be understood and evaluated if we are to reach through them to see the Aborigines and New Guineans as they were.

The earliest meetings, between Dutch navigators who missed their way to the East Indies (Indonesia) and Western Australian Aborigines in the seventeenth century, are barely reported. Tasman, who discovered the island that bears his name, did not even see any people. Only the Englishman Dampier, who twice visited the west coast of Australia (1688, 1699), described the inhabitants, and his accounts were not encouraging: "the miserablest people in the world ... differ but little from brutes ... of a very unpleasing aspect ... no sort of cloaths ... no houses ... their only food a small sort of fish ..." and so on (Dampier 1688 [1906]:453–54).

Almost a century later, on the other side of the continent, Cook's account was rather different, and much more sympathetic: "in reality they are far more happier than we Europeans ... they live in a Tranquility ... they covet not ... they live in a warm and fine climate ... in my opinion ... they

think themselves provided with all the necessarys of Life" (23 August 1770, Beaglehole 1955:399).

Cook's description of the country and of the material culture of the inhabitants was less enthusiastic, though he and Joseph Banks between them said enough to encourage later British settlement. Cook's enthusiasm for the "hard primitives" (B. Smith 1960:125) was excelled only by some French explorers who in the next forty years thought they had encountered the originals of Rousseau's noble savages in Tasmania.

In general, subsequent White attitudes towards Australians and Tasmanians owe more to Dampier than to Cook. During the first few years of White settlement at Sydney (settled 1788) diaries and official reports speak with some curiosity, kindness and even admiration of Aborigines. Journals of the early governors, Philip and Hunter, were published in England with engravings of classicized savages (B. Smith 1960:128). Manly, on Sydney Harbour, was so named because of the bearing of one Aboriginal man, while another, Arabanoo, was considered grave, steady and independently minded by Captain Tench in 1793 (Fitzhardinge 1979:150). While relics of this attitude persisted, for example in early Australian poetry (Webby 1980), day-to-day interactions soon became very different (Stanner 1977). Although official policy generally continued to proclaim that Aborigines had rights, at least that of not being shot on sight, the actions of most White settlers were such as to put even this in doubt. By 1840 most Tasmanian Aborigines were dead; the remaining few were confined on a small island or were cohabiting with the least literate and most lawless of the White population (Plomley 1966; Ryan 1972, 1981). A similar process took rather longer on the much larger Australian mainland, but within a century Aborigines throughout the better-watered, temperate parts of the country were either dead from smallpox, lead bullets and poisoned flour, or dispossessed, replaced by sheep, wheat and towns (Christie 1979; Evans *et al.* 1975; Rowley 1970). Most White Australians thought, as many still think, that this was a good thing or at least inevitable (Tatz 1980). Few thought that Aborigines were of much interest or their knowledge of the country of any value. One consequence of this was that many early White explorers struggled and died in environments where the Black inhabitants had lived well for thousands of years (see Reynolds' brilliant article, 1980).

Along the north and north-west coasts of Australia, Aborigines had been accustomed to foreign visitors since at least the eighteenth century and probably for many hundreds of years before (Macknight 1976; Schrire 1972). However, the Indonesian fishermen who came there seasonally left few written reports, and the impact of their genes and technology was quite limited. The Whites who replaced and excluded them late in the nineteenth century were relatively few, and their cattle-herding activities could not draw on the cheap White convict labour available earlier in the south of the continent. They therefore turned to Aboriginal labour, so that in this region Aborigines were allowed to live, and their traditional life was allowed to continue after a fashion.

New Guinea, more tropical and much more populous, was even less suited than northern Australia for large scale White occupation. Occasional contacts occurred from the early seventeenth century, but not until the early nineteenth century did any area participate even marginally in the industrial world's economic activities. Most coastal regions were drawn into a colonial economy only about 1880–1900. The highlands first became known to the European world only in the 1930s (Leahy and Crain 1937; Souter 1963). Throughout the area many early accounts are by administrators, and it is they and missionaries, not settlers, who established the context of contact. The few settlers relied on New Guineans for labour rather than wanting them cleared away as dangerous competitors.

The history of contact and of White attitudes to local inhabitants is, of course, much more complex than this. But knowing that this history exists is essential to an evaluation of any account of traditional societies. Not only was there a range of attitudes among the Whites, which coloured their perception and their record (Burridge 1973; Howe 1977; Mulvaney 1958, 1971a; B. Smith 1960), but also the traditional societies were themselves changing, often catastrophically, and attempts to portray them as they

were before White contact can be made only after detailed historical analyses (e.g. I. Hughes 1978; McBryde 1978a).

The following brief outline of the traditional societies of Sahul refers primarily to their material technology and environmental adaptations, these being of most direct relevance for the elucidation of prehistoric data. Some reference will also be made to exchange systems and other socio-political aspects of society which influenced their economies and subsistence activities. For fuller accounts of Australian societies, see Berndt and Berndt (1964), Lawrence (1969), Maddock (1972); for New Guinea see Chowning (1973) and Paula Brown (1978).

At the time of White contact, societies throughout all three islands depended on tools made of stone, bone, shell, wood and other organic materials; metals were known, if at all, only along the north coast of Australia where occasional examples were introduced. These tools were used to make a range of other artefacts, nearly all of organic materials, including houses, carrying bags and baskets, traps, nets, weapons, ornaments and ceremonial pieces. The number and kinds of artefacts varied, but was generally greater in New Guinea than in Australia, with the Tasmanians having fewer still (Jones 1977a; Satterthwait 1980). Some folk on the coasts and in the lowlands of New Guinea made pottery, but no one else did so. In the New Guinea rainforests substantial houses were often built, insulated against the cold at higher altitudes; the same precautions were frequently taken in southern Australia and Tasmania. Another similarity was in women's tools, for digging sticks, the occasional shovel and a carrying bag, basket or tray served them throughout the area. In the drier parts of Australia, grindstones for seeds were also critical. Carrying bags and baskets were made of string, sheet bark and wood, depending on the area. It is in artefacts like these that the consequences of settled life become apparent — New Guineans usually had more and a greater variety of utensils. New Guineans made more kinds of animal traps, but nets were used for fishing, hunting and birding in both areas (except Tasmania). In many areas Australians built fish weirs, which were operated by the tide or fresh-water flows. Tasmanians did not eat bony or cartilaginous fish. One clear contrast is in the weapons of chase and fight. No New Guinean man was for long without a bow and a clutch of unfletched arrows, and many also carried stone-headed clubs; Aborigines relied on spears, thrown with a spear-thrower in most parts of the Australian mainland, and sometimes on wooden clubs. Tasmanians used hand-thrown spears and clubs only.

The most widely recognized contrast between Australia and New Guinea is in subsistence behaviour. Noticed first by Cook (23 August 1770, Beaglehole 1955:398), it was commented on in 1876 as follows (Moresby 1876:18):

> It is strange that these people [Cape York Aborigines] have never learnt to cultivate the earth and build houses, but remain content to wander about, living precariously on wild fruits, grubs, a little chance fish, and such animals as they can spear, whilst their Papuan neighbours in the near Torres Straits islands build good huts, supply themselves with constant vegetable food, and have fine canoes for fishing.

The Torres Strait is usually seen as the boundary between agriculture and its absence (Baldwin 1976; Walker 1972; J. P. White 1971), but as D. R. Harris (1977) firmly points out, the closer one looks the less the apparently clearly marked demarcation can be seen. Our belief is that the primary contrast between the two areas was not in the ways environments were changed to improve plant yields, but in terms of the spatial reorganization of plants into fields or gardens. Most New Guineans made gardens, while Aborigines did not. At the boundary, Torres Strait, the situation was fluid. Islanders might make no gardens if collecting was good that season; only in bad seasons would they become agriculturalists (Moore 1979:279).

On the New Guinean side, a very wide range of subsistence practices is known (Brookfield with Hart 1971:94–116). In some coastal areas, sago provided the basic starch in return for no more than occasional care of the palms (Ohtsuka 1977; Rhoads 1980, 1982). By contrast, in some highland areas elaborate water-control systems, mulching, tilling and mounding produced continuous harvests of root crops, especially sweet potato, which allowed densities of up to 200 people per square kilometre, one of the highest in non-industrial societies anywhere. Between these

two extremes lies a gamut of systems of varying intensity, utilizing both roots (taros, yams) and fruits (bananas, breadfruit) as basic crops. Settlement patterns also vary from villages inhabited for hundreds of years, for example Mailu (Irwin 1977), to dispersed houses occupied for several years and basecamp villages occupied only seasonally or irregularly.

Within Australia, all groups seem to have been nomadic or semi-nomadic, gathering seasonally available plant and animal foods from across a known territory. Unlike New Guinea, year-round staples were unknown, and in the more erratic Australian environment it was usually more efficient to move between resources than try to centralize them. In the richest and best watered areas of Australia, such as the north coast, east coast estuaries and Murray River mouth, distances moved might have been only a few hundred metres, with only a few moves being made each year. From this extreme, densities decreased, and the extent and frequency of movement increased as one moved towards the central desert, where population densities were about one person per 100 km^2. Roughly speaking, population density away from riverine and coastal areas was inversely correlated with annual rainfall (Birdsell 1953).

Many early observers of Aboriginal life referred to their villages, especially in the colder or wetter parts of the country, and collections of well-built houses, sometimes partly dug into the ground, are well recorded (H. Allen 1972; Koettig 1976). These villages were used for weeks or months, and people returned to them either seasonally or irregularly (e.g. Lourandos 1976, 1977). In such situations, the contrast between some Australian and many New Guinean societies is less pronounced.

Trade and exchange systems, which sometimes leave evidence in the archaeological record, were common to both areas. In New Guinea, a majority of social groups were both differentiated and bound together by elaborated exchange networks which moved a range of resources (from food and tools to paint, feathers and ceremonial objects) around the countryside (e.g. J. Allen 1977a; Brookfield with Hart 1971:314–34; Harding 1967; I. Hughes 1977; Malinowski 1922). Exchange often served as a mechanism of competition for power and prestige within groups. Within Australia, networks of exchange covered large areas, and objects could be moved long distances (Mulvaney 1976), but a considerable percentage of the resources moved seems to have been religious and spiritual knowledge. There is little evidence that personal competition played much of a role in these exchanges, although competitiveness at both the individual and group level has recently been more widely recognized as a common part of Aboriginal life (e.g. Barker 1976; Bern 1974; Lourandos 1977:217–18). Trade did occur between New Guinea and Australia, with objects and knowledge moving in both directions (Moore 1978; Thomson 1933, 1934), but only the inhabitants on both sides of Torres Strait were beneficiaries.

Generally speaking, the contrasts which are usually seen between New Guinea and Australia have been over-emphasized. Of course there are differences — of environment, local population density, language and material culture. But these are most noticeable if extremes are considered, for example by contrasting the Highlanders of New Guinea with the Aboriginal people of the Western Desert. As we look more closely at the range of ethnographic data from both islands, the differences diminish and, especially in such features as subsistence behaviour, population density and even social and political organization, a continuum of practices is evident. The exposition of these continuities has yet to be undertaken: so far only hints of them occur (e.g. H. Allen 1972; D. R. Harris 1977; Lourandos 1980a; E. Williams 1979). To some extent they have been masked by our own perceptions of the differences between Aboriginal "hunter-gatherers" and New Guinean "horticulturalists"; they have also been masked by the effects of White contact, which in Australia may well have increased Aboriginal mobility and flexibility and decreased the power of age-related hierarchies through dispossession and genocide. The ethnographic data from Sahul is in great need of re-evaluation from this perspective.

This re-evaluation must include an internal analysis of the ethnographic records themselves, treated as historical documents, in order to assess the nature of their content. Historians are well used to this source criticism, for it is a basic method of evaluating the reliability of data. Part of this process involves understanding the generational status of the record. Is it a field diary written after an eventful day when incidents and impressions are still fresh? Is it a report from those notes, designed for superiors, an account likely to stress certain matters and gloss over others? Or is it a later compilation for publication? The distortions which can creep in, even unintentionally, during the writing and editing process are considerable.

Another aspect of any ethnographic record to be evaluated is its date in relation to contact. The records that we have are the result of interactions, and the very fact of these interactions cannot but have changed both participants. We must remember also that interaction and change started well before the first recorded contact. The finding of a few old steel tools in the New Guinea highlands or the Central Australian desert by the first White explorers is not, perhaps, surprising; but we also suspect that there was, in New Guinea at least, a substantial but unrecorded traffic of people. To them the Whites were not as they saw themselves, a frontier, but more of an interesting addition to the traditional landscape. For example, Hallpike (1977:27) records that Tauade men from the Aibala valley carried goods for a naturalist's expedition in an area 30 km away from their home 5–10 years before any missionary or government officer visited them. Duna men acquired steel axes by working on an airstrip prior to any government patrols through their homeland (C. N. Modjeska, pers. comm., 1973). I. Hughes (1978) suggests that the rate at which sea shells were moved into the New Guinea Highlands appears to have increased for several decades before the first White exploration of the area.

A most surprising aspect of traditional societies' reactions to White contact is the rapidity with which changes in basic aspects of peoples' lives can occur. For instance, Sorenson (1972:362) claims that the Fore of the eastern New Guinea Highlands stopped fighting as soon as the first government officer arrived, "almost as if they had only been awaiting an excuse to give it up ... They looked to his arrival as the beginning of a new era". Similar examples are common. At the other end of the central Highlands, C. N. Modjeska tried to study traditional religion only four years after the first missions had been established in the area. He found it quite impossible, for people had taken to the "new way" with such enthusiasm that he could not collect enough information for a PhD thesis, and eventually undertook an investigation of gardening (Modjeska 1977).

On a broader scale, I. Hughes (1978) has elegantly documented the changes to all Highland societies brought about within a few years of the Whites' arrival. While the first explorers of the Highlands were gold prospectors (Leahy and Crain 1937), they were rapidly followed by missionaries and government officials. These people contacted a series of small-scale societies in which sea shells, traded from group to group from the coast, were everywhere more valuable and performed the functions of money more often than any other commodity. In an affluent area, an average family might possess 100 cowries, 20 dog whelks and a few pieces of pearl or cone shell. In 1933 a camp, a government station and a mission were established in the central Highlands. All used sea shells to buy food and pay for labour in building houses and airstrips. Within a few months, so many shells had been passed out that their value had greatly declined. The exact number of shells used is hard to determine, but by 1934 there were seven mission stations in one area using shell money flown in from the coast. By the end of 1936 government officers needed 250,000 small cowries a month to buy food and labour. Hughes estimates that in the first seven years of contact 5–10 million shells were passed out, and more were used in later years. Within a decade, the number of shells in the central Highlands had at least tripled.

The overall effect of these new shells is clear: they caused inflation. Bride-prices increased, and pigs, stone axes and other valuables tended to flow towards the new wealth. Groups living away from the new sources of wealth were socially and politically weakened. Trade routes out of the Highlands, along which axes, feathers and oil had moved against shells for thousands of years, became one-way streets, for all key goods were now found in greatest numbers within the Highlands and especially within those groups with privileged access to the White settlements. Thus the "ethnographic record" of the 1950s, written within 20 years of contact, is absolutely not one of "pristine societies", traditional in all their ways.

We have stressed the New Guinea Highlands case because it is the most recent and best documented, but similar processes occurred earlier in all societies in Sahul. Within a year of the first White settlement at Sydney Cove, disease, and technological and economic pressures had dislocated local Aboriginal societies, as Stanner (1977) so movingly shows. White contact always meant rapid and immediate changes, and until archaeologists understand the nature of those changes, the picture of the traditional societies which provides so many of our guides to the past will be flawed.

A final bias to the ethnographic record which is rather more widely recognized is its selectivity. It usually stresses the different, the unusual, the bizarre: the occasional poor old mother being eaten gets more space than the daily digging of roots; religious beliefs and mythical charters are preferred to the hard facts of trade; ground stone axes are better recorded than flaked tools. More recently, the skew towards male activities has been realized. Almost without exception, explorers, government officers, missionaries and anthropologists have been male, as were their interpreters, informants, servants and opponents. Male activities and ceremonies, or the male role in these, has thus dominated our writings (cf., e.g., Bowdler 1976; Feil 1978; Weiner 1976). A similar selection of information, but even less corrected, occurs in relation to pre-adult activities. Studies of children's behaviour, and especially of their learning processes and the artefactual components of these, are almost unknown. Yet both women's and children's behaviour may be expected to be incorporated into the archaeological record, and must therefore form part of our ethnographic knowledge.

To sum up this section, we stress that the ethnographic record must be employed judiciously, after researching it as a phenomenon in its own right. Ethnography is the first evidence to which we turn in tackling prehistory, and it is critical that our understanding of it be as informed as possible. Three considerations are involved in this. First, we need to know about the observers as people, and under what circumstances each observation was made. Second, no matter how careful and sympathetic an observer may have been, we must evaluate, from as many sources as possible the situation being observed.

How much, for instance, was it likely to have changed from pre-European times? Finally, and critically, prehistorians must constantly recognize that even the best ethnographic accounts cannot be taken as descriptions of societies that existed millennia in the past. To use them in this way, especially in the form of direct historical analogies that are so seductive in Sahul, will inhibit the recognition of changes in human behaviour in prehistory. It is only too easy to obscure precisely those phenomena and beg precisely those questions which we should be most concerned to investigate. Ethnographic accounts must be used to help us reconstruct the past, but they must be used as building blocks, not as blankets.

2.3 History of Archaeological Research

European speculations about the origins of Sahul's inhabitants began with the eighteenth century explorers, and the problem has remained of continual scientific and popular interest until the present day. Australian Aborigines have often been seen as refugees from "higher" cultures, or as savages (in the Tylorean sense) who migrated from some imprecisely defined homeland in South-East Asia. In either case, it was assumed that most of their culture was acquired by contact with, or diffusion from, more advanced societies (McCarthy 1977; Mulvaney 1958). Tasmanian Aborigines, who had been isolated on their island for thousands of years and thus failed to acquire any recent aspects of Australian culture, have therefore exemplified the original Pleistocene savages (Jones 1971a; Sollas 1911), or at least been seen as the most direct heirs to the culture of Pleistocene Australia (Jones 1977a). New Guineans have been more defiant of explanation, the complexity of their languages and cultures defeating all but the most simplistic attempts at organization and definition (e.g. Riesenfeld 1950), and their origins therefore being left uninvestigated. The history of scientific speculation of this topic remains to be written.

Archaeological research in Sahul has a history nearly as long as that of White settlement on the continent. On 15 May 1788, the day the foundation stone of the first stone building of the new colony was laid, Governor Arthur Philip wrote to the Colonial Office that he had found some earth mounds like those heaped over the dead English poor (Historical Records of Australia I (1):28–29).

> I had one of these graves opened, and from the ashes had no doubt but that they burn their dead. From the appearance of the ashes, the body must be laid at length only a few inches below the surface and is ... covered lightly over with mould, fern and a few stones.

However, there is no record of further burials being uncovered, and the history of archaeology from then until 1929 is almost completely unstudied. Mulvaney has made a number of perceptive but scattered observations (1958, 1966a, 1971a, 1971b, 1977; see also Horton 1981a), but no one has looked extensively into the archaeological investigations undertaken during those 140 years or at the questions asked by those researchers. To undertake that task properly would require a book of its own, but we will try briefly to identify some of the main preoccupations apparent in the period. This is an essential background to understanding the nature of archaeological studies in Sahul today. We will look first, and more intensively, at Australia, for New Guinean archaeology is a later development, on a smaller scale, and until recently derivative from Australia (T. Murray and White 1981).

As a background, the European situation needs to be understood (Daniel 1962, 1975), for it provides the paradigms and intellectual milieu within which most of the research was organized. Even today, much Australian research is Eurocentric in its approach, and that attitude was much more common before 1945.

The most influential concept was that all human societies (both present and past) could be classified and ranked like so many Linnean species. This is expressed both in the Three Age system and in the more culturally oriented stages of savagery, barbarism and civilization. This strategy for organizing knowledge was employed by scientists for several decades in many parts of the world. As Daniel says (1962:77):

> the late nineteenth century prehistorians were really only elaborating the basic concepts which had been hammered out before 1859 ... between

1865 and 1913 it is surprising how little change there really was; and I mean here change in fundamental outlook ...

The effect of this concept was to make Australian prehistory seem of marginal importance. By the 1800s most scientists thought that human development occurred in a series of stages through which all societies must move, even if the mechanisms of progress were unclear. Aborigines, as was widely recognized both by overseas scholars such as E. B. Tylor and J. Lubbock and, less politely, by the White Australians who newly occupied their lands, were still in the lowest stages. As representatives of Neolithic or even Palaeolithic man, but in either case clearly savages, they were more interesting in the flesh than in the ground. Why dig up remains when the living fossils were there to be inspected? Until questions of some scientific strength could be phrased, ethnology would obviously remain of more importance than archaeology.

This attitude has dominated Australian Aboriginal studies until the present. From the early French encounters with "noble savages", through the nineteenth century observations by explorers (e.g. Eyre 1845) and the later amateurs and scientists (such as R. H. Mathew, H. Ling Roth, L. Fison and A. W. Howitt, Baldwin Spencer and F. J. Gillen), to the early twentieth century scientists, concern has been with living Aborigines and what they can tell us about the early history of man (and it usually was man, not humans). In 1963 one of the most perceptive heirs to the nineteenth century, N. B. Tindale wrote (1963: vii):

> In the first Australians we see, preserved almost miraculously into the second half of the twentieth century, some of the ways of life of hunting men of the Old Stone Age. Their beliefs, behaviour and customs help us to visualize and illustrate the general patterns of simple living which must have been practised by Old Stone Age man, and they do it far more vividly than all the bones and stones dug up by the archaeologists.

Even a mid-twentieth-century scholar can see in nineteenth-century Tasmania "the cultural inheritance of Late Pleistocene Australia" albeit in a simplified form (Jones 1977a:196).

Another important aspect of the "stage" view of human history was the credibility it gave to the view that because Aborigines appeared physically similar, and their subsistence patterns did not utilize fields or domestic animals, they could be treated as equivalent throughout the continent. Mulvaney (1966a:300) quotes von Blandowsky in 1862: "the Aborigines are of the same type over the whole continent, together with the same customs, the same weapons". And the predeliction to mingle together data from all parts of the continent in order to build up a picture of "Aboriginal" technology, religion or whatever runs constantly through Aboriginal studies. Indeed, one can see a continuation of this phenomenon in Tindale's (1959, 1968) and McCarthy's (1948) claims that artefact types from one area should be found throughout all (or most) of Australia. The idea that Aborigines are "all the same" is still widespread among White Australians.

Stronger support for the direct study of prehistory came from geological concepts. It is clear that by the middle of the nineteenth century the uniformitarian nature, and hence considerable antiquity, of the world was widely accepted by geologists. The long prehistory of humans was also established by their association with extinct fauna, which were themselves clearly of great age because of their contemporaneity with glacial climates. Attempts to document a similar association lay behind many Australian studies. Probably the best recorded of these were carried out in New South Wales in the 1890s. Perhaps not surprisingly, the researchers were natural scientists rather than anthropologists (in any sense of that term), and publications occurred under the aegis of the Geological Survey and the Linnean Society, as well as the Royal Society of NSW and The Australian Museum. In 1889, T. W. Edgeworth David and R. Etheridge Jr. reported finding a skeleton along with some marine shells and two stone tools at Long Bay (NSW). Although believing they could trace these remains back to a very early period of man's occupancy of this country (1889:15), they concluded that "it is hardly possible to assign even an approximate date to the burial". Their account goes on to make a plea for archaeology on geological rather than archaeological grounds:

The advent of man on this continent is still wrapt in obscurity, and probably will remain so — certainly until we possess more definite geological evidence of his presence than we at present have before us. So little general interest has been manifested in the natural history of the aboriginal inhabitants of this part of Australia as almost to amount to a national disgrace. Their burial-mounds, "Kitchen-middens," and other traces likely to become geologically interesting, are disappearing so fast through the rapid march of "improvements" that ere long few or no traces will be left. It is, therefore, much to be regretted that some systematic and scientific method of investigation of the early history of this fast disappearing and ill-used race be not forthwith established.

In 1890 Etheridge discussed "Has Man a Geological History in Australia?" with the Linnean Society and, considering only a clearly Pleistocene age to attain "antiquity", answered his question negatively. A year later, he amplified his answer to state, "there is however no evidence whatever of cave or cave-shelter tenancy by man alternating with that of either a living or extinct lower mammalian fauna, similar to that found in other quarters of the globe" (1891:173). Here, it is apparent, is the nub of the problem — time. Within Australia, neither the animals nor the artefacts were like those of Europe, and in neither case could clearly different suites of material be discovered. Since changes did not exist they could not be geologically certified so that no basis for antiquity of Aboriginal humanity could be ascertained. However, the possibility that they had been in Australia at least long enough for environmental change to have occurred was explicitly recognized when dugong bones which had been cut with a stone axe were found at Shea's Creek (NSW) in 1896, leading to "the somewhat startling conclusion that Neolithic man may have inhabited Botany Bay when the ocean level was about five feet lower than at present" (Etheridge et al. 1896:180) (Fig. 2.6). That this might not have been very long ago was the general opinion as the rate of surficial environmental change in Australia was thought to be much greater than in Europe.

The other possible method of determining antiquity through the detection of cultural change as recorded in archaeological sites did not

seem feasible. Around 1900 Whitlegge recognized and collected many "chipped-back surgical knives" on coastal sandhills near Sydney. The report (Etheridge and Whitlegge 1907) states that these tools were similar to those found in America, India, England and Ireland and that the Aborigines no longer manufactured them, but no implications were drawn from this about possibilities of future research. Indeed, it seems that there was little idea of how archaeological material might be used to write culture history. The contents of shelters were "simply refuse heaps, thus resembling those of France and Belgium" (Etheridge 1891:173), and although it was claimed that the study of these could be informative of the "habits and manners" (Etheridge 1905:19) of earlier inhabitants, this information was not, in fact, derived.

One interesting suggestion to this end was made in 1892. E. J. Statham, who had for some years been investigating shell beds in coastal areas several hundred miles north of Sydney, proposed a "detailed and systematic" study of shell mounds at Ballina (1892:313–14):

> After determining which are natural and which are artificial deposits, the first essential would be to trace the position and extent of the old shell banks from which the heaps are derived and the area of gathering ground they afford at a depth not exceeding four feet. Then the Fisheries Department may be in a position to state or ascertain the maximum and average yields per acre of the beds already worked, so that by this means co-efficients may be arrived at by which the length of time required to provide sufficient material for the building up of the heaps referable to these sources, can within definite limits be more accurately ascertained.

There is no record of Statham himself, or anyone else, acting on this proposal until the 1970s (Bailey 1975). Statham's published section (Fig. 2.7) suggests that he would have been capable of following up his own proposal.

Mulvaney (1958, 1975:118) has argued that it was only in 1929 that excavations at Devon Downs on the lower Murray River introduced the concept of "culture" and culture change into Australian prehistory through the recognition of stratigraphy (Fig. 2.8). This is not entirely true.

FIGURE 2.6. Excavations at Shea's Creek, NSW, 1896. Standing: right, R. Etheridge Jr. (Australian Museum); left, J. W. Dun (government paleontologist). Courtesy: Trustees of the Australian Museum.

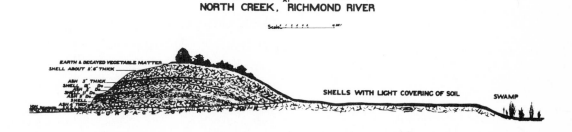

FIGURE 2.7. Statham's section through a shell mound at Ballina, NSW. Source: Statham (1892).

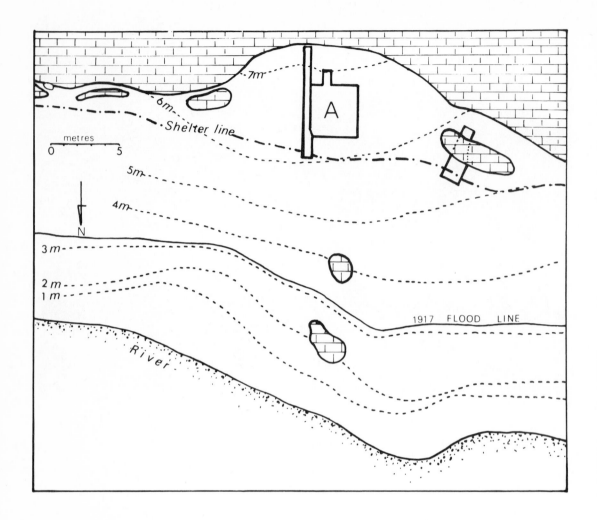

FIGURE 2.8. (a). Plan of the Devon Downs, SA, excavation 1929. "A" is the major trench excavated. Source: Hale and Tindale (1930).

(b). Section through the Devon Downs excavation, 1929. Specific features noted were:

a:	infant burial;
b:	child burial from land surface in middle layer III;
c:	limestone block used as grave capping;
d:	pocket of debris originally from layers V–VII;
e, f:	roof fall and its original position;
g:	grave excavated from layer IV;
h:	capping stones for grave g;
i:	broken skull and bones of child in grave;
j:	blocks used as grave lining;
k:	lower jaw of 5-year-old child disturbed and re-buried;
l:	teeth of 5-year-old child, apparently undisturbed;
m, n:	upper and lower limits of tool sharpening marks on wall;
o:	bone implement cached in small hole in wall;

Source: Hale and Tindale (1930).

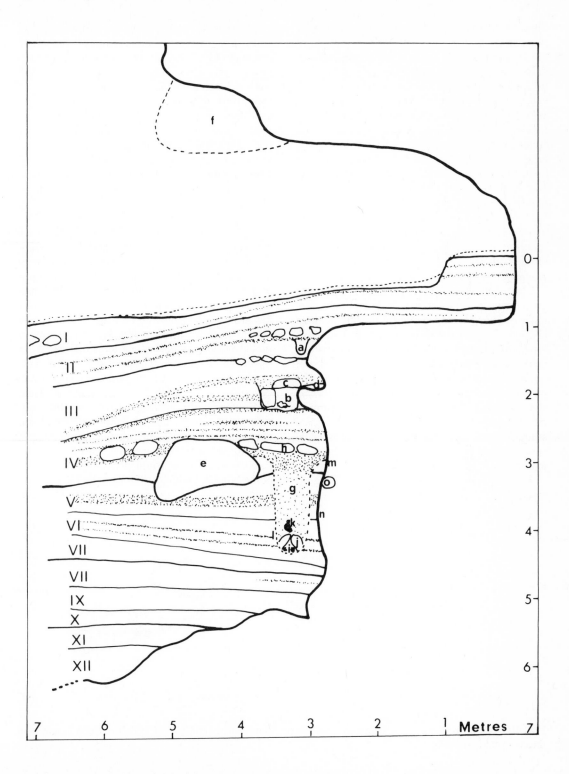

Throughout the nineteenth century, the idea of two culture periods in Australia was implicit in the recognition of Tasmanian Aborigines as Palaeolithic and the Australians as Neolithic (e.g. Etheridge *et al.* 1896; see also Horton 1981a). It was even given explicit recognition on occasion, such as in E. Kennedy's one-page account of a rock-shelter excavation, which concludes that "there was only one culture period during the occupancy of the shelter ... [and] no Tasmanian [tool] types were found" (1934:201). What Hale and Tindale (1930) did at Devon Downs was to demonstrate that particular artefacts occur in sequence and can thus act as "fossiles directeurs". They also asserted that these changes occurred as a result of migrations, though they did not identify any of these as being of the Tasmanians.

The extent to which the problem of sequence and change was important to Hale and Tindale is unclear. They developed none of the implications of their claim. Similarly, when a two-stage artefactual sequence was excavated at Lapstone near Sydney, in 1936, the excavator did not publish it for 12 years (McCarthy 1948, 1978). The plan and section provide poor support for his claim anyway (Fig. 2.9). The report attempts to date the industries by reference to technological equivalents in South-East Asia and to geological considerations: it does not refer to the Tasmanians.

Despite the occasional insight, archaeological research in the first half of this century was of little moment. Having failed to find Aborigines and extinct fauna in association, or any other evidence of high "antiquity", geologists and other natural scientists seem to have dropped the subject, leaving it to amateur collectors, weekend excavators of artefacts and untrained but perceptive museum curators. For the most part, these people had little idea of what to do with prehistoric evidence. The purpose of their collections seems to have been to accumulate a very large number of objects, some of which were more finely made, better coloured or more displayable than others. It is probably true to say that during this period all major surface sites within the better watered temperate areas of Australia were picked over, and many were totally removed. The few collections which have made their way to museums are almost certainly only a tiny fraction of the total, most of which has now served its recreational purpose and been discarded, unlabelled and unloved. The one clear benefit from all this activity was a recognition that Australian flaked stone tools differed from those in other parts of the world and needed their own classificatory system. Mulvaney (1977) has described some of the schema, most of them distinguished by their ignorance of the technology of stone flaking and by simplistic assumptions concerning function. Nonetheless, in 1946, McCarthy and Bramell, with the visiting Englishman Noone, could produce a manual of stone typology which still forms the basis of the "generally shared recognition ... for the way

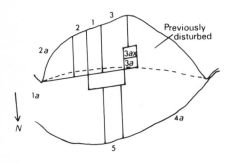
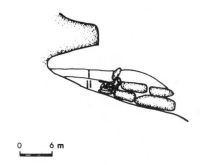

FIGURE 2.9. Plan and section of Lapstone Creek excavation. Source: McCarthy (1948). Courtesy: Trustees of the Australian Museum.

qualitative attributes are combined when artifacts are sorted into groups" (Gould 1977a:79–80), even if it is now in need of substantial revision, which no one has been brave enough to undertake.

As well as Devon Downs, several sites excavated in the Northern Territory also demonstrated that there was some variability in artefact sequences over time and across the country. In 1930 Davidson excavated at Delamere and Willeroo (D. S. Davidson 1935), and Macintosh dug up similar materials at Tandandjal, 200 km further south eighteen years later (Macintosh 1951). But in neither case was the analysis pushed beyond the simple fact of sequence.

One major difficulty was that a sequence, although implying some antiquity, could not measure it. On the basis of the occurrence of stone artefacts on Kangaroo Island (South Australia) and the total absence of Aboriginal use of the island in the nineteenth century, Tindale (1957) could argue that occupation of the area must date back to the Pleistocene period of low sea level. A similar argument clearly applied to the Tasmanians. But until the development of some technique of absolute dating there could be no independent validation of this antiquity.

The first radiocarbon determinations bearing upon Australian prehistory were published by E. D. Gill (1955:51) and dated charcoal from two Aboriginal middens in Victoria. Within five years, dates on Aboriginal materials were known from three states, the oldest being 8700 $\pm$ 120 (NZ-69) from South Australia (Mulvaney 1961). In 1962 radiocarbon dating demonstrated human occupation of Australia during the Pleistocene (conventionally defined according to the European schema as ending around 10,000–11,000 years ago: Mulvaney 1962a), and since that time the dating of archaeological materials has rarely been a problem in Australian prehistory, although the oldest finds now push threateningly close to the limits of its effective operation.

The professional development of Australian archaeology goes almost hand-in-hand with radiocarbon dating. The first Anthropology Department in an Australian university was founded in 1925 at Sydney, and it remained the only one for nearly three decades. It was primarily intended for undergraduate training, with particular emphasis on administration. Its first professor, A. R. Brown was a strongly functionalist social anthropologist, and his long-term successor, A. P. Elkin, always stressed the practical uses of cultural anthropology and linguistics to missionaries and administrators. There was no place for archaeology in this milieu.

The first professionally trained archaeologist was in fact appointed to a History Department (Mulvaney, University of Melbourne, 1953), but further university cognizance of the subject did not occur until the early 1960s when several appointments were made at three universities. Among these was the Australian National University, which was then a post-graduate research institution. The impetus to major projects that its students and staff have given over the years has been considerable, and it awarded the first PhD in archaeology (to J. Matthews, in 1965). By 1980, prehistory was being taught in eight universities, and public archaeology programmes had been initiated in all states (T. Murray and White 1981).

There are several important aspects to the development of archaeology during the last twenty years. First, it has not been as closely tied to other branches of anthropology as has been the case in the United States, although it is closer than in the United Kingdom. Archaeologists have worked in History and Psychology departments and, in the last ten years, in their own separate departments of Prehistory. Only one has been attached to earth science disciplines. That this is so has been in part a reaction to the more narrowly "social" nature of Australian anthropology, many of whose practitioners still echo to some extent A. R. Brown's ahistoric attitude.

This split between social anthropology and prehistoric archaeology derives in part from the continuance of British traditions within Australia. Nearly all archaeological appointees in Australia until the last five years have been British, or at least trained in the UK, particularly at Cambridge University. Perhaps this is less true for social anthropologists, but a strong British tradition is still evident. The split between these fields, which developed in England from the 1920s onwards, has manifested itself in Australia also.

The dominance of the English tradition in

prehistoric archaeology has directed archaeological research in Australia towards "a regional approach ... and dated stratigraphic sequences" (Mulvaney 1964:42). Although the definition of other problems is now becoming more important (e.g. J. P. White and O'Connell 1979), a dated, regional technological sequence is still the aim of many investigations.

The reliance on radiocarbon dating and the stress on stratigraphy has meant that studies during the last two decades have been able to ignore almost all the archaeological research undertaken prior to 1950, with the exception of some typological studies. The previous failure to establish a Pleistocene antiquity or to seriate stone artefacts in any way that could be meaningfully related to the products of later research has meant that the culture histories of Australia written over the last two decades have been written almost without historical background (e.g. Blainey 1975; Gould 1973; Mulvaney 1969, 1975). Mulvaney's (1961) critical analysis of previous work is certainly partly responsible for this attitude. In some respects this has been helpful, particularly as it allowed new approaches to the past to be readily developed. The massive increase in trained young personnel during the 1960s has also meant that the results of radiocarbon dating could be accepted with much less impact on archaeologists' egos than in other parts of the world. Not only did the new arrivals have the numbers but, as we have tried to show, established workers had fewer intellectual positions to defend (but cf. Tindale 1968). They too could welcome the new technique and its consequences.

Nevertheless, ignorance of the history of Australian archaeology among its current practitioners is not totally healthy. Even if the major concerns of the past are no longer ours, earlier remarks concerning the quantity and distribution of prehistoric materials and their destruction throughout the period cannot fail to be relevant to anyone interested in site location and spatial ordering (e.g. M. E. Sullivan 1981). Similarly, anyone attempting to study the distribution of particular lithic resources must face the fact that only sealed stratified sites contain the full component of materials originally present: it is absolutely clear that we are not investigating an archaeological scene any more "pristine" than the ethnographic one. In this situation it seems at least possible that technological and economic data relevant to current questions can be extracted from the older literature. This may well occur as the discipline matures.

The history of archaeological research in New Guinea, the eastern part of which was controlled by various colonial powers until 1977, the western half being incorporated into Indonesia in 1971, is, until 1959, basically one of scattered, uncoordinated and undated collection and excavation of archaeological material, some of it presumably prehistoric. Excavations by Meyer (1907), Pöch (1907a, 1907b) and Leask (1943), and surface collections described by Seligmann and Joyce (1907), Casey (1939) and others, produced pottery and other artefacts, some of which were used by Riesenfeld (1950) to support a completely diffusionist prehistory. Stratigraphic excavations by S. Bulmer in the highlands in 1959 (S. Bulmer and R. Bulmer 1964; S. Bulmer 1966) set a pattern of research into regional sequences which has been largely followed until the present, perhaps not surprisingly since most workers have come from Australian institutions or been trained in them. It is the case, however, that economic and some technological change has been a more obvious factor in New Guinea's prehistory than in Australia's, and some research projects have been particularly directed towards these problems (e.g. J. Allen 1977a, 1977b, 1977c; Golson 1976, 1977a, 1977b). Almost no stratigraphic excavations have been undertaken in Irian Jaya, and apart from some interesting bronzes found on the north coast thirty years ago, and deriving apparently from South-East Asia, almost nothing is known of prehistoric materials (Solheim 1979).

Although limited, this account of archaeological history has sought to follow Collingwood's suggestion (1946) that an historian must try to see what problems a past individual faced and how these were solved. The history of science is particularly amenable to this procedure, and a fuller appreciation of the nature and uniqueness of Sahul's prehistory will derive from watching our predecessors solve, and fail to solve, their problems.

This chapter reviews the evidence of Sahul prehistory during the Pleistocene, from earliest settlement until about 10,000 years ago. While actual dates go back no further than 35,000 years, we outline reasons for believing that colonization occurred at least 50,000 years ago, although probably not much before then.

We start with the evidence from the earliest dated sites, which include both open campsites and rock-shelters. From these we gain some impression of technology, subsistence, and social and spiritual life, especially in southern Sahul. We next turn to the prehistory of South-East Asia and Wallacea from whence all Sahul settlers came, and note that water-craft of some kind must have been used there for many tens of millennia. It seems likely, then, that even if the settlement of Sahul was accidental, the accidents occurred to people used to living by and from seas and coasts.

Following initial settlement, the population grew to occupy the continent. While there is no record of this process, it is possible, by using our knowledge of present-day societies as a guide, to model both population growth and the advance of settlement. We argue that both processes occurred quite slowly and probably unevenly. Although some coastal areas were undoubtedly occupied first, we suggest that inland resources

Chapter 3
Sahul: Early Prehistory

FIGURE 3.1. Sites referred to in this chapter. The Australian states are shown for convenience.

were used at an early stage. However, the desert core may have been settled only during the last 20,000 years. Although many aspects of our models are archaeologically untestable, they play a critical role in interpreting available data. This is why we try to make them explicit. As part of this process, we compare our Sahulian model with the most widely accepted, but very different, American one.

In Section 3.3 we look at technological and subsistence patterns found in sites 25,000–10,000 years old. During this period there was considerable environmental change, and the effects on human populations must have been considerable, even though we can only hint at them. During this period also there is greater evidence of artistic and spiritual life.

The limited quantity and range of evidence means that we cannot draw a very clear picture of early Sahul prehistory. Despite this it is apparent that the environments, technologies and subsistence patterns then were so different from those found in modern times that we must consciously recognize that direct historical analogies will be misleading. The people who settled Sahul during the Pleistocene must not be thought of as modern Aborigines and New Guineans living in past times. They were indeed ancestors but not doppelgängers.

3.1   50,000–25,000 Years Ago

On 5 July 1968, geomorphologist Jim Bowler was walking along the southern end of the sand dune which curved around the eastern shore of the now dry Lake Mungo in western New South Wales (Fig. 3.2). He knew already that the dune had been built up in several stages during later Pleistocene times and had noted stone artefacts lying on the eroded surfaces. But on this morning he encountered something different — a small cluster of broken bones embedded in a part of the dune he knew to be more than 20,000 years old. He suspected that these bones were food bones remaining from human activities, and they appeared to have been buried during the time the dune was forming.

At the same time as Bowler was tracing out the Late Pleistocene history of Lake Mungo and the

climatic implications of this, Harry Allen was starting to look for prehistoric sites in southwestern New South Wales. From an analysis of nineteenth century explorers' journals, climatic records and other data, it was clear that Aborigines then concentrated their summer activities around major water sources such as the Darling River, but dispersed over the plains and into the low hills in the cooler parts of the year when standing water was more available (H. Allen 1968). The main difficulty with tracing this pattern back into the past lay in the fact that most Aboriginal encampments resulted in single-level sites, and the artefacts they contained were insufficiently distinctive and time-specific to be useful in dating or even temporally ordering them. Apart from one small and only recently used rock-shelter, stratified material was at a premium in the late 1960s. Therefore, when Bowler recognized that his find was within dated sediments and asked Allen and other prehistorians to investigate it, he opened up a research field of some potential. Not only were the bones human, but it now seemed possible to order prehistoric material in sequence, give it a firm chronology and look at it in relation to changing local environments (Bowler *et al.* 1970). The potential of Lake Mungo and similar sites in the area is only just beginning to be realized, even after more than ten years' work. In part, this is because of the nature of the data and the scale on which research needs to proceed (Shawcross and Kaye 1980).

The majority of archaeological remains throughout Sahul's prehistory derive from small, short-term, open-air encampments and special activity areas. These sites provide little persistent data beyond a hearth, some stone artefacts and food remains. Once abandoned, this material was usually disturbed, attacked and transported by scavengers, wind and water before being buried. The remains of any activity could be spread over a considerable area, partly preserved in sand or water-lain clay, or partly rolled into creek beds and other natural traps. Further, each small cluster of remains is likely to represent only one part of a much larger camp that was discontinuously spread over perhaps 100,000 m^2. Some of the whole might be preserved, but probably most will not. In any case, the whole site will

FIGURE 3.2. (a). The Willandra lakes system, a series of extinct overflow lakes formed by the Lachlan River. Source: Bowler (1971:57). Courtesy: Australian National University Press. (b). The present surface stratigraphy of the southern end of Lake Mungo dune. 1 and 3 are the sites of reported skeletons. Z: Zanci; UM: Upper Mungo unit; LM: Lower Mungo unit. Scale in metres. Source: Bowler and Thorne (1976:133). Courtesy: Australian Institute of Aboriginal Studies, Canberra, Australia.

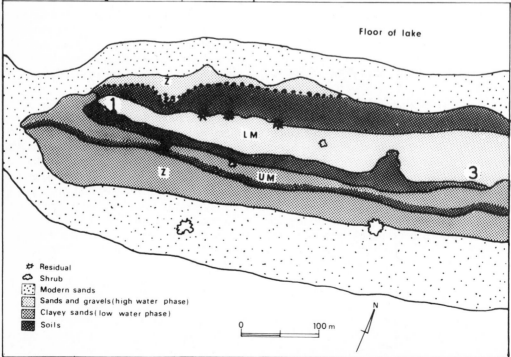

certainly lie on and in many locally different geomorphic units, the exact correlation of which will range from difficult to impossible. And people did not camp only on the shores of Lake Mungo, but alongside many or all of the hundreds of other lakes in western New South Wales, and probably in the country between, moving from one locality to another as natural and social environments suggested.

The other part of the problem is the number of scientific researchers who have been involved. No more than a dozen people, often working alone, have studied aspects of Lake Mungo prehistory, and only a handful have been able to make major projects out of it (i.e. PhD level studies and above). In every case, the work has had to start with only the most general background data: the present geology, geomorphology, flora, fauna and ethnography were all almost unknown fifteen years ago, and this has indeed been the case with most research on Sahul.

At the time of writing, Lake Mungo is the oldest clearly dated focus of human activities in Sahul, with a radiocarbon date from hearth charcoal of 30,780 ± 520 years (ANU-680). Dates on humanly transported freshwater shells go back to around 32,000 years, while dates on other carbon and shell in similar geological levels range back to 35,000 years but are less certainly associated with human activity. It is also the most comprehensively described early site, and it is thus appropriate to start our prehistory of Sahul at Lake Mungo (H. Allen 1972, 1974; Bowler and Thorne 1976; Bowler *et al.* 1970, 1976; Kefons 1977; McIntyre and Hope 1978).

Lake Mungo: Environment

The Mungo dune (or lunette) has three main members. From oldest to youngest these are Golgol, Mungo and Zanci (Fig. 3.2b). Each of these can be related to a period of dune formation, and each consists of a series of layers of clay, sand and humus. Bowler's studies (1971; Bowler *et al.* 1976) demonstrate the different mechanisms responsible. Quartz sand was added to the dune when the lake was full and wind-caused waves moved particles along the lake

floor and into a beach formation. This is primarily how the Mungo unit was formed. Clay was added when the lake's water level was fluctuating and the lake floor was exposed from time to time, allowing the prevailing westerly to south-westerly winds to blow clouds of fine particles off the floor and deposit some of them on the dune. Much of the Zanci unit was thus formed. Note that whenever lakes are low, salinity is high, and this does not provide a good environment for much animal life. When these lakes are empty, humus forms and vegetation can grow over the static dunes. Full or high lake levels will encourage fish, shellfish and bird life, and we may expect Aborigines to have made fuller use of the lakes at such times.

Lake Mungo is part of a network of lakes — the Willandra Lakes — which were filled from the Lachlan River. When they filled, the river was in flood, because the lakes were overflow catchments. They have never filled during the last 100 years or even, as far as we know, for the last 10,000. For some time during the Pleistocene, however, enough water flowed down the Lachlan to keep the lakes permanently full. Several factors may have helped cause this, and their disentangling is no easy task. One obvious explanation would be increased rainfall, especially in the Snowy Mountains where the river's catchment lies. There may also have been decreasing evaporation which increases "effective" rainfall: increased cloudiness and lower wind velocities, or minor fluctuations in solar radiation leading to lower temperatures, could all cause this. Equally, changes in sub-surface water-tables may have allowed more water to remain on the surface. These events, of course, would have been linked to larger scale climatic changes which we know occurred throughout the world (CLIMAP Project Members 1976). Whatever the larger picture, the Willandra Lakes experienced a number of changes during the human occupation of the dune, which stretched throughout the period of Mungo and Zanci formation (Table 3.1).

The Golgol unit, like those above it, was formed during times of full and fluctuating lake levels, dated at present to about 150,000–120,000 years. No remains of human activity have been found in it. Then, for many thousands of years, the lake was dry and soils formed on the surface of the Golgol unit. There may also have been erosion or deflation (by wind) of some areas. About 45,000 years ago, Lake Mungo started to fill up again.

As well as the Willandra Lakes, many other Pleistocene lakes as far north as Lake Yantara (Dury and Langford-Smith 1970) have similar fringing dunes, suggesting that during the later Pleistocene (45,000–15,000 years ago) an abundance of water made this area a much easier place in which to live than it is today, with more fish, shellfish, animals and food plants being available. It is worth repeating that we are dealing here with the effects of precipitation, not necessarily greatly increased rainfall. Although there is some dispute about the relative importance of various effects, pollen analyses in the southern highlands clearly indicate cooler conditions, which would have resulted in increased run-off, though higher rainfall may also have been involved (Bowler and Jones 1979; Bowler *et al.* 1976:385).

Lake Mungo: Archaeology

Excavation of Bowler's original discovery took place in March 1969 when the carbonate encrusted bones were removed and identified as human (Bowler *et al.* 1970). Survey of the surrounding area showed that 27 stone artefacts and 16 roughly circular patches of concentrated carbon were eroding out of the Mungo unit over a distance of 150 m, and about 18 m back from the Pleistocene beach. All tools and bones within the carbon patches were encrusted with calcium carbonate, and the occurrence of this encrustation on tools found on the surface has been used to attribute them to the Mungo unit.

The carbon patches, 60–90 cm in diameter and 5–10 cm deep, appeared to be hearths. Their contents were varied. Most (12/16) contained fish bones, all but two contained mammal of some kind, and a few, bird, freshwater shellfish or emu eggs. Four also held a stone tool. The immature specimens of golden perch fish, in particular, may suggest that some hearths were made in the late spring, around October–November. Emu eggs suggest an occupation earlier in this season too. Kefous' (1977) detailed analysis of the fish remains has also suggested that, because of the restriction to one species and to a particular size range of fish, these were probably netted rather than speared or hooked.

Following the original discovery, further surveys were made around the shores of Lake Mungo. Discoveries have included: artefacts and freshwater mussel shells eroded from the Mungo unit (dates on the shells range back to 32,750 $\pm$

TABLE 3.1
Willandra Lakes history.

Phases (Lake Mungo only)	Years bp	Conditions
	present–14,000	Lakes dry apart from ephemeral flooding to the lake furthest upstream.
	14,000–15,000	Minor freshwater return to upstream lake.
Zanci	15,000–18,000	Lakes becoming dryer and drying out.
	c. 18,000	Brief high water levels.
	19,000–26,000	Lower levels and some salinity; saline clays blown into shoreline dunes.
Mungo	26,000–45,000	Lakes filled with fresh water and overflowing. Minor fluctuations in levels.
	45,000–>70,000	Long period of dry lakes; soil formation.
Golgol	>70,000	Quartz sand accumulation.

Source: Bowler *et al.* (1976).

1250: ANU-331); a series of ovens, each a shallow depression filled with ash, charcoal and artificially moulded clayey lumps (probably substitute cooking stones in the absence of many pebbles or cobbles in the area); some fireplaces (burned and blackened earth 30 cm in diameter and containing ash and charcoal); a few pieces of ochre with facets ground down by use; and a thin shell midden, 10 m long, containing many pieces of charcoal. All of these pieces of evidence are from within a unit which consistently gives dates of 33,000–24,000 years ago.

The flaked stone tools found in and on the Mungo unit in 1969 are not very diversified in form and are similar to tools found throughout Pleistocene Sahul. They comprise two major groups: tapered, multi-faceted cores, often as long as they are broad, with flakes removed from around the periphery; and flatter flakes or pieces with wear or intentional chipping along one or more edges. The angle of each edge is either steep or acute, and it is probable, though not proven, that each type was used for a different range of tasks. The acute-angled edges on tools are either straight or concave in shape, and again a functional difference is possible: the concavities might have been good for, or the result of, scraping rounded shafts of wooden tools. The tapered cores are often called "horse-hoofs" because of their shape, and are assumed to have been used for heavy-duty scraping, planing or pounding (Fig. 3.3). However, there is little evidence that these tools are more than just cores that were used to produce flakes, these being often used in their raw form when they would be sharpest. It is worth noting that all the collections so far described from Mungo contain about the same number of flakes as retouched tools and cores. This implies that no workshop sites where flaking was regularly undertaken have yet been found, because there would be many more flakes, especially very small ones. People probably flaked stone at the source outcrops, which are not far away, but natural processes may have also removed some smaller flakes from these sites.

There is little variability in the material collected from the exposed surfaces of the Mungo unit, but this does not mean all tools are contemporary. A haphazard scatter of stone tools over a large area implies that the activities of which they are the end result happened there a number of times. The tools found within the Mungo unit were also not clustered but scattered. Some scatters might have resulted from one individual moving a work-place during the day, or between days, but unless pieces fit together there is little chance of checking this. As the hearths also suggest, we have here the remains of penecontemporary use of an area over a period which may range from a few weeks to a thousand years or more.

Lake Mungo: Human Remains

Following the original report of human bones, several other sets of skeletal remains have been recovered from the area, but a description of only one of these has been published (Bowler and Thorne 1976). The original Mungo I skeleton, dated to 24,500–26,500 years, consists of the charred and broken up fragments of a woman about 20–25 years old (Bowler et al. 1970). The skeleton was so broken following the cremation that even the cranium has not yet been fully reconstructed. Nonetheless, on the basis of the 21 cranial measurements that can be taken, Thorne has been able to conclude that the dimensions of the posterior and basal portions of the cranium lie outside the range of recent Aboriginal populations living in the same area. Further, Mungo I is smaller overall than the average of recent Aboriginal females, and in technical terms "extremely gracile" (Thorne 1971). Mungo II, found with Mungo I, consists of 30 cranial and vertebral fragments.

Mungo III was an extended burial discovered by Bowler on 26 February 1974 under similar circumstances to Mungo I (Bowler and Thorne 1976). Mungo III is apparently an adult male with somewhat worn teeth. The skeleton is fragile and eroded, but the parts of the cranium and mandible available for study show the same "gracility" as Mungo I. Indeed, Thorne has suggested (1976) that, in terms of its overall cranial characteristics, Mungo III is more like recent Aboriginal females than males. It is dated by its position within the Mungo unit to 28,000–30,000 years ago.

The penecontemporaneity of these early *Homo*

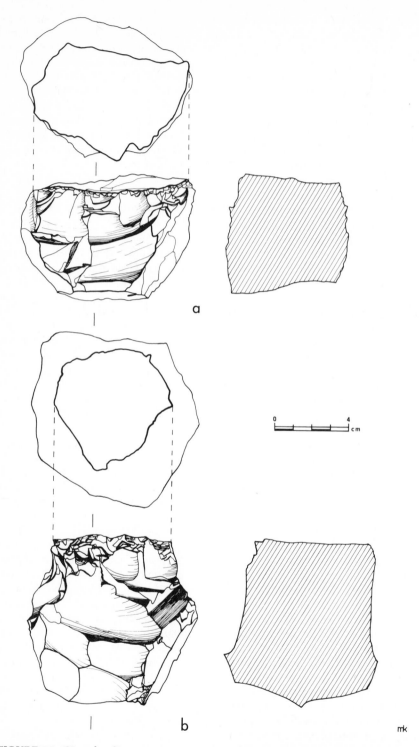

FIGURE 3.3. "Horsehoof" cores. a: provenance unknown; b: Tambar Springs, NSW.

sapiens is in sharp contrast with the very divergent manners of their burials. The Mungo I burial was complex. Because bones of the left side were more intensely burned, Thorne believes that the body was burned while lying on its left side on a pyre. After fairly complete burning (for some of the bones were calcined) the remaining material was gathered up, broken into small fragments and placed in a shallow pit either adjacent to or under the pyre. Mungo III, on the other hand, was an extended burial of a fully or partly fleshed corpse, probably within a grave which could not be observed stratigraphically but which was outlined with pink ochre powder scattered over the upper part of the skeleton. No grave goods were deposited with either skeleton.

It is difficult to say whether this is evidence of a sequence in burial form — for the two *might* be as much as 5000 years apart in time — or of a difference based on sex, status, totem or some other sociological parameter. Since, in later periods, many techniques for disposing of bodies were used within one area (Meehan 1971), a sequence is perhaps less likely than some other explanation, but more data are needed.

There are no other human skeletal remains in Sahul anywhere near as old as those of Mungo. The Keilor cranium, well preserved but encrusted with carbonate, was found in 1940 in a river terrace, the stratigraphy of which was not well understood (E. D. Gill 1966). Reconstruction of its probable location allows for it to be as much as 15,000 years old, while there is only a minimum date of just over 7300 years for the carbonate crust around it. It, like the Mungo remains, is of modern type though rather smaller than most modern specimens.

Lake Mungo: Discussion

Lake Mungo gives us evidence — hearths, cooking places, stone tools, food remains, ochre, burial and cremation — of a wide range of late Pleistocene activities. It is possible, of course, to treat all this evidence as contemporary, and to reconstruct a way of life in a 30,000-year-old environment, fleshing out the details by analogy with the nineteenth century (e.g. Blainey 1975). But even if we overlook the fact that the evidence from Lake Mungo is likely to span a period of

several thousand years and thus be subject to internal changes, the nineteenth century patterns cannot be analogous in all respects. We know, for instance, that tribes living along the Darling River and its near tributaries during the nineteenth century organized their economic life on a semi-seasonal basis, moving away from the rivers in wetter times (usually winter), concentrating on the rivers when floods brought on large stands of edible grasses (*Panicum decompositum*) or when very dry seasons made all other water sources marginal. No one has yet produced a convincing argument that life around the late Pleistocene lakes was so seasonally differentiated. It is clear, also, that the technology used recently to process grass seeds, mullers and grindstones, was not known in the area before about 14,000–16,000 years ago (H. Allen 1972), so that the economy of the nineteenth century, which relied on this resource heavily if seasonally, *cannot* have been the same as the earlier one. Thus, although we can argue for a hunting and collecting aspect to an economy, delineate a stone technology and probably a semi-sedentary or even more mobile settlement pattern, we probably lack data on the full range of sites and thus cannot fully reconstruct the Pleistocene economic system. As well as workshop sites, we argue in more detail later that killing, butchering and game-cooking sites should be present. Although our evidence is limited, we can see already that human life in this area was very different from anything known in the recent past.

Other Early Sites

Another site which is probably within the same age range as Lake Mungo is at Keilor, on the Maribyrnong Creek near Melbourne (Bowler 1976; E. B. Joyce and Anderson 1976). There, a complex series of alluvial clays and soils (the whole usually called the D Clay and deposited by overbank flow) contained several discrete, approximately horizontal levels of quartzite flakes. These flakes were the only large pieces of stone within the deposits, and they all show clear evidence of detachment from cores. No other clearly humanly created remains were found in these levels. The relationship of the levels to periods of soil formation between episodes of deposition has not been precisely defined. The flakes are not rolled, suggesting little post-depositional movement. However, the assemblages do not include large numbers of very small flakes as would be expected if they were debris from human flaking. These may therefore simply be assemblages resulting from the occasional use of a land surface, possibly re-sorted by river flow. So far, these records tell us little more than that people used the area.

The date over which the D Clay accumulated has been estimated on the basis of carbon dates for a later terrace and rates of soil formation and silt deposition. A minimum date for the earliest artefact-bearing horizons is given as 36,000 years with a maximum of around 45,000 (Bowler 1976). The processes of river-terrace formation in the area and the artefacts themselves are still under close study (E. B. Joyce and Anderson 1976), and the site has recently been made the focus of a major project (Coutts 1978a; S. Simmons and Ossa 1978; Witter and Simmons 1978). Over the past two decades, Gallus has claimed that humanly made artefacts occur in other horizons equivalent to, and much older than, D Clay (Gallus 1967, 1971, 1972, 1976), but neither his description of the artefacts and their stratigraphic locations nor inspections of the artefacts themselves have yet convinced most other prehistorians. A good review of the data and claims made about the Keilor site to 1974 is given by Bosler (1975).

Other sites reported to contain evidence of very early human occupation occur in Western Australia. In the south-west, Devil's Lair is a small limestone cave containing at least 6.5 m of naturally and humanly accumulated deposits (Balme 1980; Balme *et al.* 1978; Dortch 1979a, 1979b; Dortch and Merrilees 1973) (Fig. 3.4). A series of thirteen radiocarbon dates stretch back to 35,000 years ago, with the pooled mean of the three lowest being 33,150 ± 840 years. Below about 3.5 m (layer 31) sedimentation occurred in rapid bursts. There, deposits contained some stones which may be artefacts, mostly made of calcrete and quartz, and three probable bone artefacts. The clearest indication of human presence is two tiny chips of exotic stone, one from the top of layer 30, the other from 34. Suggestion of human use of the area even earlier

is made on the basis of carbonate encrusted and re-deposited stones and bones which may be artefacts.

There is clear evidence of human presence at the time of the change in sedimentation in layers 28–30, which date to 24,000–27,000 years ago (SUA-31, -539). These levels contained 3 g of charred bone and twelve stone artefacts for each litre of deposit removed. The artefacts consist of retouched and notched flakes, some made with a bipolar technique, and some bone points. There are also many animal bones. There is evidence that a variety of predators may have contributed to the bone accumulation, but the fact that charring is selectively concentrated on the remains of larger animals, whose bones are virtually absent from earlier deposits, is a strong reason for believing in their human derivation. At the time of its earliest use, the cave was 10–20 km inland, and it is clear that the inhabitants were hunting available large animals. It is interesting to note that no bones of large, now-extinct animals are among those charred: a few bones of these animals occurred in the deposit, but they appear to have been re-worked from older levels.

Another site often mentioned as containing early evidence of human use is Mammoth Cave, 11 km north-west of Devil's Lair. Most of the material was excavated early this century without good stratigraphic control, and the provenance of some of it has since been mislaid. The material has been re-studied by Archer *et al.* (1980). Stone artefacts were neither found among the material nor recorded in the early notes, but they report one bone damaged by sawing and battering, more than thirty bones wholly or partially charred, and some femurs broken in a fashion best replicated by knocking them on a sharp rock. Among the thousands of bones collected from this site are many from extinct giant marsupials, and their bones are among those altered. Two dates on charcoal collected recently are >37,000 (O-657) and >31,500 (Tx-31). In our view, while this site is suggestive it cannot be taken as conclusive proof of human occupation more than 40,000 years ago (cf. L. R. Binford 1981; Horton and Wright 1981).

Areas with a clear potential to produce data in this age range occur some 700 km north, in the Quaternary alluvial deposits of such rivers as the

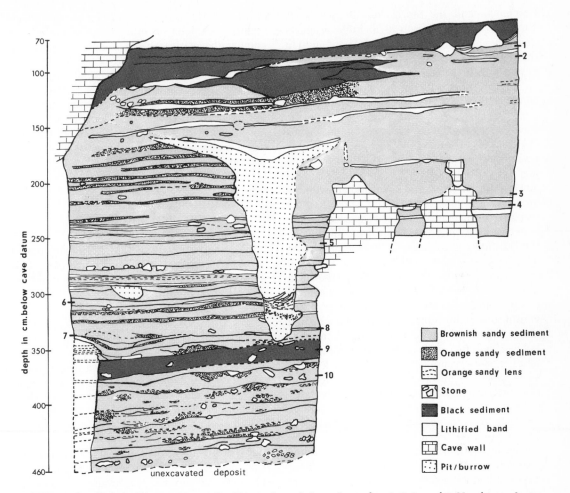

FIGURE 3.4. Devil's Lair, Western Australia. Nominal south face of trenches 2, 5, 8_2 and 9. Numbers refer to radiocarbon dates as follows:

No.	Level	Lab	Date
1	K	SUA-103	12,050 ± 140
2	M	SUA-102	11,960 ± 140
3	7	SUA-101	19,000 ± 250
4	9	SUA-33	19,250 ± 900
5	10c	SUA-32	20,400 ± 1000
6	18	SUA-457	31,400 ± 1500
7	28	SUA-539	27,700 ± 700
8	28	SUA-31	24,600 ± 800
9	30	SUA-585	32,480 ± 1250
10	31	SUA-586	35,160 ± 1800
11	38	SUA-546	31,800 ± 1400

The 2 m deep pit (or burrow) may be man-made. Source: Balme *et al.* (1978:37). Courtesy: Royal Society of Western Australia.

Greenough and the Murchison (Bordes *et al.* 1980; Wyrwoll and Dortch 1978). Stone artefacts and bones of extinct animals have been found in these Late Pleistocene sediments: the problem now is to date them accurately.

The only other evidence of human occupation contemporary with that from Mungo and Devil's Lair comes from Kuk near Mount Hagen in the New Guinea highlands where carbon and some fire-cracked rocks, which had been humanly transported, are dated to around 30,000 years ago (Golson and Hughes 1977). The altitude of this site is around 1600 m, and its location is within a large swampy valley, but nothing other than the one large burned area has been reported.

A case for human occupation occurring during the last interglacial (some 125,000–70,000 years ago) has been suggested by Singh *et al.* (1981) on the basis of an increase in firing of the bush around Lake George, near Canberra, as evidenced by increasing numbers of charcoal particles within the sedimentary profile. That human action is the only explanation for this increase is not demonstrated, and such a claim runs counter to other, more secure data given by Clark in the same paper (see also R. L. Clark 1981). No other evidence currently supports such an early date.

There have been remarkably few serious attempts to claim that the prehistory of Sahul is several hundred thousand years old. Prior to the advent of radiocarbon dating there were some claims for Tertiary Man and the like, but these have not had any lasting influence. Nor has any credence been given to more sensational claims, such as that the Ayers Rock area was the original Garden of Eden or that Australopithecines have been found near Sydney. It is true that within the last three decades the known antiquity of humans in the continent has more than quadrupled, and it has sometimes been assumed, as with many other growth rates in our era, that this one will continue (e.g. Jones 1979). Although there is no basis for saying it will not rather than it will, our own guesstimate is that human presence in Sahul is likely to be no older than 50,000–70,000 years. This has already been called "a conservative guess" (Jones 1979), but we can see no reason to go beyond it.

In direct support of this guess we can offer only the absence of archaeological material from the Golgol unit at Lake Mungo and other units in similar positions on other lakes, along with a similar absence from dune series of this age along the NSW coast (Bowler 1976:66) and from many Late Pleistocene sites containing megafaunal remains. Negative evidence is, or course, about the weakest there is, and any single, properly documented discovery will destroy this guess. Nonetheless, at present it seems about the best bet: even occupation as old as 50,000 years has not been demonstrated.

3.2 Sahul Settlement: Background and Process

We can now look at the wider questions of where the original population came from, how they got here and what evidence there is of their spread throughout the continent.

South-East Asia and Wallacea

The ultimate origin for Sahul's people, as for all Pacific populations, must be South-East Asia, part of the old Aseurican world within which humans evolved. The land area of South-East Asia includes the Vietnam and Malayan peninsulas, the countries lying between and to the north of them and the Indonesian islands as far east as Bali and Kalimantan. This region, joined at times of lowered sea-levels into a major continental mass, is known to biogeographers as Sunda-land. Its fauna and flora are Asian, with minor variations now occurring between various islands.

The earliest record of human presence in Sunda-land comes from Java. The geology of the area is extremely complex and includes records of a number of phases of volcanic activity, which provide potential for detailed dating and correlation. However, all discoveries so far have been made in sands, fine gravels, silts or other water-lain deposits, where each relic has been washed into its find-spot rather than being originally deposited there (see van Heekeren, 1972, and the journal *Modern Quaternary Research in Southeast Asia*).

At present, it appears that the lowest levels of

interest are the Putjangan Beds, which contain the Djetis fossil fauna. This consists of early forms of ungulates, carnivores and elephantids, with which have been found seven skulls and mandible fragments of *Homo erectus* (*H. modjokertensis*, Boaz 1979). A similar fauna, along with a child's skull, comes from Mojokerto, and in 1969 a sample of volcanic rock below this skull was dated by the potassium-argon technique to 1.9 ± 0.4 million years (Ninkovich and Burckle 1978).

The Kabuh Beds, at least 100 m thickness of muds and fragmentary volcanic sediments, lie above the Putjangan Beds and contain the Trinil fossil fauna. This includes more modern forms of the same range of animals, among them more than twenty human fragments. Pumice above and below two of these has been dated to around 0.75–1.0 million years. Several stone artefacts were found in sediments of the same age in 1975 (Jacob *et al.* 1978).

Younger finds include chert and jasper flakes and cores from the Notopuro Beds, which are not directly dated. The fauna is described as being like Trinil though more modern, and the human skulls have a larger cranial capacity than those from the Kabuh Beds below. It is likely that this material is at least 300,000 years old.

Probably younger than this are the eleven calvaria and two tibias found on a supposed Upper Pleistocene river terrace of the Solo River near Ngandong in central Java. The dating is based on the faunal remains said to be associated with the humans, but the stratigraphic and chronological relationships are quite unclear. As the major researcher in this area reported (T. Jacob, quoted by I. Glover 1973:119):

> The work at Ngandong was mostly carried out by untrained geological assistants, and subsequent information suggests that none of the associations can be relied on; even the find spot of the skulls may have been misrepresented.

The most important aspect of this South-East Asian material is that it establishes more than a million years of human presence in the region from which Sahul is most readily accessible. The Javanese humans were part of the Aseurican evolutionary pool, at least whenever the sea-level was lowered. They were clearly at home in a tropical environment, which would have been heavily forested for most of the time. Their use of the sea and its resources is unknown, but we must believe that over the last million years the frequent changes in shorelines and the presence along these of abundant, easily exploited food resources gradually allowed and encouraged human exploitation. When and how people learned that the sea, like the land, could be used to advantage we do not know. In other parts of the Old World we know this process was in train more than 50,000 years ago (McBurney 1967; Volman 1978) and, as Carl Sauer (1952) pointed out, the tropical, closely packed islands of Sundaland would be a prime environment for human development of this kind. Some indication of it will be gained as we date the human occupation of Wallacea.

Wallacea is the zone of islands lying between Sunda (mainland and island South-East Asia) on the west and Sahul on the east (A. R. Wallace 1860) (Fig. 3.5). Within this zone, channels between islands are too deep to have been emptied by lowered sea levels at any time during the last 50 million years or more. Many of the islands are separated by only a few kilometres and most are high volcanic lands, one clearly visible from the next. Nonetheless, some form of water transport, however primitive, would have been required to move humans from one side of Wallacea to the other.

We can say this because apart from those hardy survivors, rats, humans are the only land-based animals to have crossed the entire stretch of Wallacea in either direction during Pleistocene times. Some other animals are found on a few islands, most importantly elephants, which got as far as Sulawesi and Timor, most likely as a result of accidents combined with their strong swimming ability (D. L. Johnson 1980). But if accidents, such as being carried out to sea by floods, were a major mechanism of mammalian dispersal, we would expect to find more smaller mammals within Wallacea, and to find them further away from their homelands than is the case. The fact that humans did spread right through Wallacea, eventually to find Sahul, is a strong argument for their relative familiarity with the sea.

Human migration through the region is likely

to have been largely the result of accidents. Once some simple forms of water craft were in use, the chances of accidents would have risen steeply. The craft could have been, and probably were, very simple, such as logs or reed-bundle rafts, normally used for crossing river mouths or making trips of a few hundred metres to off-shore islets and reefs. Accidents involving off-shore winds or unexpected currents could then have occurred from time to time, and only some of these would have been recoverable in the sense that a return to a home island would have been possible. Some measure of this possibility of accidental voyages may be gained by looking at the operating abilities of more recent simple watercraft, and the uses to which they were put.

Within Australia during the last century, rafts and canoes were widespread (Holland 1976). The former were made of logs or reed bundles, the latter frequently of bark either tied at the ends or even sewn together (Akerman 1975; Jones 1976; Tindale 1977a). The largest and most sophisticated craft appear to have been the sewn bark canoes of Arnhem Land, which were up to 5.5 m long and could carry 6–8 people (Holland 1976). Even these, however, seem to have been used for voyages of only a few kilometres (B. Spencer 1904), as was the case with more primitive craft. In all situations, continuing buoyancy appears to have been a major problem (Jones 1976; Tindale 1977a:268). Looking at the problem in another way, Jones (1977b) studied

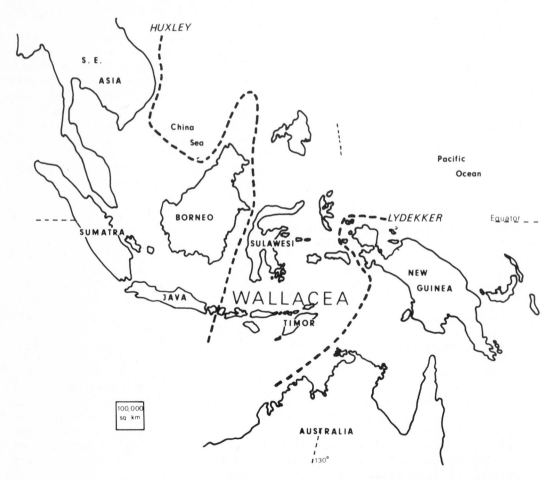

FIGURE 3.5. The location of Wallacea. The lines of Huxley and Lydekker mark the most western and eastern locations of attempts to draw a single line of division between Sunda and Sahul. Data from Simpson (1977).

Aboriginal use of the small islands lying off Tasmania's shores. He argued cogently that all regularly visited islands lay well within a voyaging range of 10 km and that risks were too great for longer trips to be made regularly or intentionally. As far as we know, this would be true throughout Australia except perhaps in such very sheltered waters as occur inside the Great Barrier Reef along the north-east coast.

Without being too speculative, we can argue that, if craft with similar capabilities to those just described were developed in Sunda-land and Wallacea in Late Pleistocene times, then islands separated by less than 10 km would have been open to intentional voyaging. Looked at in this way, a number of Wallacean islands would indeed have been open to human settlement, although this would not have been true of all of them, nor of Sahul itself. Table 3.2 shows that 40% of the islands likely to have been encountered by humans in their moves through Wallacea were less than 10 km from another island, and this tabulation overlooks many islets.

One factor in the process of human spread into Wallacea is the fluctuation in Pleistocene sea levels. Lowered sea levels would have increased the number of accessible islands quite considerably. Figure 3.6 shows estimated changes in sea level over the last 150,000 years, revealing clearly that present sea levels are the highest known throughout prehistory. Within Wallacea, we can assume that some tectonic alteration of land altitudes also occurred

(Chappell and Veeh 1978), but detailed work is necessary to demonstrate the exact situation during the Pleistocene. Tectonic activity could have assisted human migration as much as hindered it.

In theory, archaeological evidence should enable us to determine the rate of human spread through Wallacea and give some idea of cultural use of the sea. But evidence from this area is still very limited, and generally of poor quality. In Sulawesi, simple stone artefacts, said to be like those from supposedly early deposits in Java, have been found on the surfaces of terraces, along with bones of now-extinct animals (I. Glover and E. Glover 1970). Some flakes are also stratified within the terrace sediments, but it is not completely clear whether they are of human manufacture, while the date of faunal extinction also has not been determined radiometrically (Hooijer 1970).

In Flores a total of 74 andesite flakes, pebble tools and bifaces have been found in the same beds as *Stegodon* (elephantid) fossils, while in Timor some large flake scrapers have been collected from the surfaces of gullies eroded in gravels of Pleistocene age. Within these gravels *Stegodon* has also been found (Bartstra 1977). None of these occurrences have been directly dated, nor is the geological record very precise, although it must be said that the artefacts from Timor are unlike any recovered from stratified sites radiometrically dated to within the last 15,000 years (I. Glover 1971).

TABLE 3.2
Distances in kilometres between Wallacean islands in routes from Sunda to Sahul at times of −150 m sea level

Distance between islands	Number
0–10	19
11–20	8
21–30	3
31–40	3
41–50	2
>50	9

Source: Birdsell (1977: Table 1).

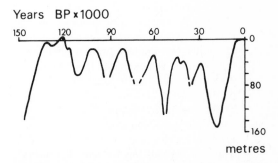

FIGURE 3.6. Sea level changes during the last 150,000 years. Source: Chappell (1976:14). Courtesy: Australian Institute of Aboriginal Studies, Canberra, Australia.

Several interpretations of these finds are possible. *Stegodon* has been found with both the Trinil and the Ngandong faunas in Java, and is presumed to have swum to the various Wallacean islands. Once there, it seems likely that dwarfing evolution occurred (the most recent forms are only 1.5 m high), as was the case on small islands elsewhere (e.g. Sicily). The time required for such evolutionary changes to occur is not known, but it need not be very long. On the other hand, it is quite possible that *Stegodon* may have survived on the isolated islands of Timor and Flores for several hundred thousand years. This is relevant to our interpretation of the artefacts. If the association is with the smaller form, then the artefacts may be much more recent. We do not know when and why *Stegodon* became extinct on these islands, but it could have been as recent as 50,000 years ago. Until some more precise associations are known, the dating of the earliest humans in Wallacea will remain unclear. Obviously, the date there must be earlier than in Sahul, but how much earlier is unknown.

The human settlement of Wallacea, and its ultimate conclusion, Sahul, involves the following aspects:

1. Even if all voyages were made at times of lowest sea level, some trips well in excess of 10 km would have been required. This implies that some settlements were almost certainly accidental.
2. Given the number of islands to be settled, the process would have been a long one. A scenario that pictures groups of 25–100 people moving rapidly from island to island seems very unlikely, given all that we know of other human cultural developments at this time. Acceptance of a long chronology of settlement implies human familiarity with the sea well back into the Pleistocene.
3. To reach Sahul by the route requiring the least number of long voyages, through Timor, would have required at least one sea trip of around 90 km, even with the low sea level of 53,000 years ago (Birdsell 1977). This implies that the settlement was both accidental and unlikely to have been much supplemented by later voyages.

Initial Settlement of Sahul

In this section we discuss some general problems relating to the initial settlement of Sahul and the viability of initial populations. Since sea-crossings are irrelevant if adventurers die without continuing descendants, some measure of the probabilities of successful colonization must be made.

One way of examining the problem is to look at ecological theory surrounding invasions of new habitats such as islands (e.g. Cody and Diamond 1975; Diamond 1977; R. H. MacArthur 1972). The theories suggest that founding populations are most likely to succeed when per capita rates of net increase are high (especially when due to lower than usual death rates), when competitors or predators are few and when the species is pre-adapted to short-lived, scattered patches of suitable habitat in its original homeland. In general, observations on animals such as ants and birds have demonstrated the validity of this theoretical modelling and have stressed the importance of r-selection* in providing a viable population (Horn 1975). R. H. MacArthur and Wilson (1967:69) point out that in real life few populations can be expected to grow without internal controls until they reach K (the population equilibrium for a particular environment) and then abruptly change their reproductive strategy. Controls on the growth of real populations are both gradual and complex, even among animals with more simple cultures than humans, and it is notable that most ecologists have not attempted to apply their models to human populations, among which cultural constraints must play a considerable role (but see Diamond 1977). Thus, although there is some evidence to suggest that fertility may increase in any recognized "frontier" situation, the causes of this are both obscure and apparently variable (e.g. Easterlin 1976). In terms of ecological theory, humans may shift slightly towards increasing

---

* r-selection favours rapid development of organisms, a high innate capacity for increase, early reproduction and small body size; K-selection favours slower development, greater competitive ability, delayed reproduction and larger body size (see Colinvaux 1980; Krebs 1978:579–80).

their population growth rate in appropriate situations, but there are no indications that this can be regularly expected or that the shift is very great. In fact, it seems to be more likely that growth curves will vary with the fitness advantages of different reproductive strategies under different environmental circumstances, especially very specific local ones concerned with overall group mobility and women's work-load. It seems unlikely then that growth rates of founding populations will automatically be high.

A more precise guide to the chances of a human founding population successfully establishing itself lies in computer-generated simulations, into which certain constraints may be built. N. McArthur *et al.* (1976) have carried out a series of simulations of the survival chances of small human populations, which are simply a special application of more general stochastic models (see Krebs 1978:199–204). Although concerned primarily with Polynesian settlement, their model is certainly applicable in general to the early stages of Sahul settlement. In transferring the model to this area, it would be wise to assume that it errs, if at all, on the optimistic side, particularly in relation to assumptions concerning birth and death rates.

For their simulations, McArthur *et al.* constructed a "Pacific" life-table with high risks of death in infancy and early childhood and low risks thereafter until about 50 years of age. Whether this can be appropriately transferred *in toto* to a hunter-gatherer population is unclear given the disputes about the demographic structures of these (e.g. Howell 1976) and the probability that particular circumstances are likely to exert strong local effects (e.g. Blurton Jones and Sibly 1978). But perhaps McArthur's table will serve as a first approximation.

The marriage practices proposed by McArthur *et al.* for their fictitious populations are simple — males marry at 18 years, females at 14, the oldest available male monogamously marries the youngest female, and there is no incest, divorce or adultery. The first three, at least, maximize the chances of reproduction, and this is reinforced by the absence of any inhibition on births, such as infanticide.

Our most obvious area of difficulty arises in equating the "Pacific" fertility schedule with the probable early situation in Sahul. It is generally agreed that some kinds of birth-spacing mechanisms exist among nomadic hunter-gatherer populations, although the genetic and cultural aspects of these are still much debated (Cowlishaw 1979:309–52; Hayden 1972; Howell 1976; Schrire and Steiger 1974). The occurrence of such mechanisms can significantly reduce the number of potential descendants. If this was the case in Sahul, then we need to envisage a larger founding population or lower death rates than McArthur *et al.* proposed to maintain the same chances of success.

McArthur's actual simulations focused on initial groups of three, five and seven unrelated married couples without children but several years into their reproductive periods. Her results show that larger and younger groups have much greater chances of continuing viability, but incest prohibitions make little difference. One crucial factor in the continuing survival of her groups was the sexual balance between offspring, though this was the case primarily because a rule of monogamy was imposed. Another important factor concerned assumed birth and death rates. If both were either high or low and produced an intrinsic growth rate of 0.5% per year, most populations failed to become viable even when enlarged to consist of ten founding couples. Only if growth rates were 1% a year or greater (the "Pacific" model assumes 1.78% p.a.) was viability likely (see also Black 1978).

Further research by McArthur, still largely unpublished (but see N. McArthur 1976), has suggested that one major restrictive factor is the rule of monogamy. When that rule is removed, a group consisting of no more than three people, a man and two women at the start of their reproductive careers, have a three-in-four chance of surviving and populating a continent. The implication of this study is that a founder population can be derived successfully from the voyagers in a single small water-craft.

Simulations are strictly mechanical and refer only to probabilities. They reveal that, while the size of the original group is important, in the short term at least the rules by which they live are even more so. It is in modelling these rules that we must draw more on our knowledge of human societies than on general ecological theory (at least for the present), with lower chances of an accurate result.

Another approach to the study of early Sahul settlement is to look at ethnographic records of the viability of very small human founder populations (Birdsell 1957). We have no long-term examples of these and only a few short-term examples, but they provide some interesting data. The best-known situation is undoubtedly Pitcairn Island, where the *Bounty* mutineers sought refuge in 1790 (Shapiro 1968). The original settlement consisted of fifteen men (English and Polynesian) and twelve or thirteen women (all Polynesian). One woman had a baby girl. Murders and other deaths reduced the group to one (English) man and eight or nine women by 1808, but by then there were twenty-five or twenty-six children (see also G. Kennedy 1978:242–63). By 1825 the total population was sixty-six, and by 1839, 106 people. Only a tiny proportion of this increase can be accounted for by immigration. It is significant that the mutineers and their women were reasonably well equipped with both Western tools (including the *Bounty*) and Polynesian knowledge, that much of the work in establishing the settlement was done by people who were not there to reap the rewards of it, and that there were few or no physical or cultural restraints on mating in the early period, so that this group was perhaps singularly likely to survive.

Two other historically recorded communities are reported by Birdsell (1957) as having similar growth rates. These are the Tristan da Cunhans and the Furneaux Islanders. However, in the former case the group was added to by immigration (see also Roberts 1979), while in the latter the records appear to require careful interpretation, and rapid growth is a *post facto* explanation rather than being fully recorded at the time. Finally, Birdsell quotes an 1893 report of the discovery of an Australian Aboriginal man who, with two women, had hidden in the mallee scrub of Victoria for about 30 years, during which time his family had grown to number about twenty-five. It seems certain that this group was living by hunting and gathering, but whether it was indeed as isolated and fecund as the original report suggests cannot now be determined. Birdsell summarizes these cases to suggest that "the intrinsic rate of increase in human populations at simple economic levels ... approximates a doubling in numbers with the passage of each generation" (1957:52). Finding counter-examples is not easy since many are, by definition, now extinct. There are, for instance, many archaeological records of the unsuccessful settlement of Pacific islands, and it must be assumed that demographic failure was a prime cause in these cases (Bellwood 1978:352). On Pitcairn itself, stone platforms and statues, pig bones, fish hooks and adzes attest to a prehistoric population, deceased by 1790. Settlements are also known from Henderson, Palmerston, Suwarrow, Washington, Malden and Fanning Islands. Few of these remains are consistent with those of small canoe-loads of male Robinson Crusoes, and while we cannot prove that demographic instability was the cause of depopulation, the fact that all are isolated islands that could not serve as supply islands for a larger group nearby lends some weight to this argument. Isolation would also suggest that renewal by intentional immigration subsequent to first settlement was unlikely. Finally, we reiterate that current theories and data do not seem to support "intrinsic" rates of population growth. Therefore, we are not convinced that the ethnographic data Birdsell cites record even the most probable human response to a colonizing situation, although his recognition of such problems has been an important contribution to Sahul's prehistory.

Summing up the above, we suspect that a suitable picture of initial settlement consists of a large family — a man, two or three women and some male and female juveniles. This would best fit the chances both of continuing viable reproduction and of being a likely migratory group. There may never be any way of testing this, but it is important for prehistorians to make their models explicit so that the subsequent demographic, genetic, cultural and linguistic consequences can be considered, and the prehistoric data looked at in the light of these. Discussions of several problems later in this book depend to a considerable extent on the models of early settlement.

Once the original population was well

established and consisted, as we might expect after a thousand years, of between a few hundred and a couple of thousand individuals, another small group of people arriving in the same area is likely to have had little genetic or cultural impact, especially if their technology and economy were fairly similar. Chance may determine that, in the long term, new arrivals do have a genetic impact well out of proportion to their original numbers (cf. Gajdusek 1964; Roberts 1979), but we believe that tens of thousands of years later this will be undetectable within a much larger population. Another possible scenario envisages two (or even more) small groups landing in different parts of Sahul and establishing separate viable populations that would be expected to have different physical characteristics. For example, this might partly account for the considerable physical diversity now apparent between Australians and New Guineans. There is much more diversity between these groups than there is between Australian and Tasmanian Aborigines, although the latter pair of populations has been separated for longer than the former. In part, differences between Australians and New Guineans doubtless derive from long-term adaptation to the great environmental differences between the two areas, but separate initial populations that became well established before coming into contact within Sahul would certainly seem to be a possible contributing factor. The period between their becoming one population pool within Sahul and their subsequent separation by rising sea levels would not, in our view, be sufficient to mask the original differences totally (see also Howells 1973).

It must be stressed that we cannot expect to obtain many archaeological remains of these earliest settlements, for they are now under 100 m or more of tropical sea. No very early materials have yet been recovered from current coastal or inland northern Australia, or from New Guinea. Part of the reason for this may lie in the strongly coastal adaptation of the earliest settlers. However, before erecting this into a principle, two other factors must be considered. One is the extent to which we expect any sites to survive from the early period with its low population numbers; the other is the quantity of archaeological research. Prehistorians have concentrated on the coastal south-east of the continent, and long-term studies of the kind made by Bowler and others at Lake Mungo, or Gill, Gallus and others at Keilor have not occurred elsewhere. The absence of sites older than 30,000 years in the northern lowlands of Sahul may well turn out to be an artefact of our research.

Continental Occupation

Fifty thousand years ago, the first settlers came to a continent some 25% larger than its three constituent islands are today. Most of this increase came from the land that existed where the Arafura Sea now lies. The existence of that land itself would have affected the climate and environment of early settlements. We can give a general picture of the palaeo-climate by extrapolating from studies of the effects of a later low sea level (Nix and Kalma 1972; Webster and Streten 1978). Cyclones were probably reduced in number. Rainfall throughout the area, except along the coast, was reduced by possibly 50%, though seasonal fluctuations were maintained. The drainage of rivers from both New Guinea and Australia over the very flat Arafura Plain resulted in large swamps or lakes from time to time. Changing sea levels affected the littoral environments. Falling levels encouraged mud flats with mangroves near the sea and salty flats behind them; rising levels encouraged steeper beaches with periodically replenished lagoons behind the beach lines. The lagoons were good places for marine and littoral plants and animals to survive, and we suspect that human camps were better fed from these than from off-shore resources at times of falling seas. In neither case was the diversity and richness of resources as great as on the relatively stable shoreline of the last 6000 years (Chappell and Thom 1977).

Once initial settlement was accomplished, and a viable population established, we can assume that settlement spread throughout the country. By 20,000 years ago people were all around the coast and certainly on the fringes of the central desert (Balme 1980; Marun 1974; Maynard 1980), though whether they occupied the core is still unknown. By 10,000 years ago, people were established throughout all major environmental zones (Jones 1979) even if some small areas such as the tops of the south-eastern highlands (Flood 1980:279–80) and parts of the Victorian desert (Ross 1981) may not have been in regular use.

But how quickly and in what fashion do we envisage the continent being occupied? Answers to this question will reveal something of different researchers' approaches to human societies by the way their models emphasize the conservative or the adaptable facets of human life.

Over the years various answers to the question of continental settlement have been given. In the earlier part of this century, arrows were simply drawn from north to south across Australia. Subsequent and slightly more sophisticated proposals brought people around to Cape York and down the eastern highlands, thus avoiding the worst of the desert (e.g. Birdsell 1957; Mulvaney and Joyce 1965; Taylor 1950). More recent models have ranged from a rapid dispersal throughout the continent by big-game hunters in pursuit of their prey to the suggestion that all coastal areas and major, reasonably permanent river systems were utilized before there was anything more than the most marginal use of the drier parts of the country some 10,000–15,000 years ago (Bowdler 1977, 1979). We review here the "rapid growth" and "coastal colonization" models, since these have generated the greatest interest in recent years.

"RAPID GROWTH" MODELS

The two main examples of these are the "intrinsic growth" and the "big-game hunter" models.

In 1957, Birdsell argued that, if the population had doubled every twenty years from the time of first settlement, a period of 2000 years would have been all that was necessary for the population to reach the density it was in AD 1788. He suggested that this was a probable picture of

Australian prehistory, given the "intrinsic rate of increase" of human populations at this economic level. Birdsell's belief in the reality of rapid population growth has already been discussed, and it is not apparent to us that even a small, newly arrived population would automatically react in the way he proposes. In fact, we think that the only major area of change would be in who constituted acceptable mating partners. Arguments about birth spacing and numbers of children are usually phrased in terms of constraints on hunter-gatherer life, including the ability to feed and transport children, as well as in physiological terms (e.g. Blurton Jones and Sibly 1978). We can see little reason to expect great changes in these as people moved from tropical Wallacea to tropical Sahul. What is possible is that slightly more children survived to breeding age because of more readily available food resources. Since we are unconvinced that rapid population growth was automatic, we do not believe that Sahul, or Australia, was rapidly populated.

The "big-game hunter" model depends on exactly the same assumption about intrinsic population growth rates as Birdsell's but suggests a reason, the pursuit of game, for the rapid rate of spread across the continent. While the evidential basis of this model is discussed more fully in Section 4.3, we can point out here that there is no evidence that early settlers were big-game hunters when they arrived, nor are there any "kill sites" to demonstrate that they took up this subsistence strategy on arriving in Sahul. Indeed, demonstrating any interaction between humans and the largest game animals is still difficult.

THE "COASTAL COLONIZATION" MODEL

In 1977, Bowdler proposed that (1977:205):

Australia was colonised by people adapted to a coastal way of life; that initial colonising routes were around the coasts and thence up major river systems and that non-aquatic adaptations, such as desert and montane economies, came relatively late in the sequence.

This proposal was amplified, but not materially altered, in 1979, and we will discuss the published account here. The model rests on three main props. First, Bowdler argues (1977:221) that:

> if Australia was settled by people already adapted to coastal conditions, it seems most likely that their routes of diffusion would have been along the Pleistocene coastlines. Their previous mode of subsistence and technology would need little modification...

Second, she draws attention to the fact that (a) the earliest sites, notably around the Willandra Lakes, indicate a heavy dependence on riverine and littoral resources rather than on land mammals, and (b) the earliest sites away from major rivers or coasts were very sparsely used and this continued to be the case until major climatic changes around 15,000 years ago. Third, she notes that the hunting of big game seems to have been a relatively recent adaptation if we restrict ourselves to consideration of the evidence available. Despite some strengths, we believe that this model is unsatisfactory, and the props it rests on need further examination.

Our disagreement with Bowdler's first prop is primarily one of degree. We would agree that the earliest settlers are likely to have made use of environments most like those in their home area. But trying to envisage possible steps in economic adaptation as time passed and the population expanded, we are inclined to follow a suggestion made by Iain Davidson (pers. comm. 1978) that, while movement around coastal areas would certainly have been quicker, expansion would have proceeded on all fronts. First settlers may well have depended primarily on known marine and littoral resources, but they would have soon recognized and exploited those resources which gave a high return for effort expended. Among these are likely to have been land mammals. Cost-benefit criteria, along with the human exploratory urge and pressure from a growing population (however slow this was), would soon take some groups gradually away from total reliance on coastal resources. Figure 3.7 illustrates our view of this process. We think that inland adaptations may have occurred more quickly in the tropical rainforest, being a floral, if not faunal, environment more similar to those which the people had left, but it seems unlikely that people were excluded for tens of thousands

FIGURE 3.7. A sequential model for the settlement of Sahul. No time scale is implied.

of years from productive non-riverine environments through failure to learn how to extract a livelihood. In terms of environments, the major adaptation Sahul settlers probably had to make was not to Sahul *per se*, but to the dry, seasonal woodland ecosystems common to most of the Australian part and perhaps to much of the Arafura Plain (Nix and Kalma 1972). Indeed, the West Australian coast has always been practically desert, and we doubt that any people used to living on tropical coastal resources would have done well south of about the seventeenth parallel. We think it more likely that the eastern and southern parts of Sahul were first reached by people traversing the Arafura Plain rather than following the northern coasts of what is now New Guinea.

Concerning Bowdler's second prop, it is not true that all the earliest sites display a strong dependence on water-based resources. Among the sites older than 25,000 years, Devil's Lair in particular displays what Balme (1980:84) calls a "well-established land economy" from the time of earliest use. The presence of humans at 1600 m in the New Guinea highlands at this time argues for complete occupation of the tropical forest area and a degree of adaptation to cooler zones. Further, the fact that there is an archaeological record of human occupation of all areas of Sahul by 20,000 years ago suggests earlier occupation of them. This is because the earliest populations would have been small and may well have remained so for some time. Small populations usually leave so few remains that they are archaeologically invisible.

In this section we must also again point out that we have a skewed picture of sites within the drier regions due to changes in sea level. Not only do the earliest sites lie beneath metres of tropical or sub-tropical ocean, but coastal areas, particularly those that contrast with the inland in terms of rainfall, can be expected always to have supported more people. Thus the scarcity of older sites in what are now near-coastal areas but were, 50,000–10,000 years ago, scores or even hundreds of kilometres inland is probably as much an artefact of expectable human population densities as it is of a real lack of adaptation to those areas. In addition, there is some reason to believe that coastal or riverine sites are far more

visible than others, especially those where shellfish are abundant. To take a modern example, the number of sites on the south-eastern Australian coast exceeds those recovered up to 50 km inland by a factor of ten or more, primarily because of the quantity and visibility of shells (M. E. Sullivan 1976). However, ethnographic evidence suggests that neither the human numbers in each zone nor the relative intensity of use of each differed to this degree (e.g. Poiner 1976).

During the first 20,000 years or so of Sahul's prehistory, it might also be argued, as Lourandos (1980a) has done, that overall population densities were simply lower. Furthermore, we do not see any reason to believe that the population built up to its recent (maximum) density in any given area before another was populated — the presence of unpopulated country and the lure of more profitable resources ahead would probably mean that people would have moved before this time. The only barriers to this would have been learning how to exploit the resources of new areas and keeping a biologically and socially viable mating system organized.

Bowdler's third prop, that big-game hunting is a recent phenomenon, may indeed be true, though we do not think it has been shown. Even if it is, her argument simply refutes the big-game hunting model rather than supporting one of coastal colonization.

We have argued in this section both that a very rapid colonization of Sahul was unlikely and that, once established, early settlers probably colonized all available environments. People had reached south-eastern and south-western Australia, as well as the New Guinea highlands, by 30,000 years ago or earlier. The first of these areas is 2500 airline or 6500 coastline kilometres from the presumptive area of entry on the north-west coast. If the available radiocarbon dates are accurate indicators of the approximate earliest date of colonization of those areas, then we think the earliest human settlement of Sahul must be at least 10,000 years older. This allows time for a build-up in population, for adaptation to new environments, new plants and animals for food, weapons and shelter, and gives some margin to compensate for the fact that we almost certainly have not found the very first settlement in any area. The first settlements could well have been

20,000 years earlier. If they were, we have so far recovered only about two-thirds of the prehistory of Sahul.

THE AMERICAN COMPARISON

The original discovery and peopling of the American continent is the only situation in human history truly analogous to Sahul. All other examples of new settlements — Madagascar, New Zealand, Hawaii, Greenland — are of small areas with relatively uniform environments to which the first settlers were pre-adapted. The American situation is worth mentioning because it is the only comparable case. However, we will discuss it in some detail because the dominant models used in the two cases are so different. Researchers in each area may well benefit from comparing the two, as Hallam (1977) has cogently argued.

We are less concerned here with the dispute between land and sea (Fladmark 1979; Klein 1975) as the route of travel than we are with the subsequent spread of people throughout both hemispheres, although we do think that sea routes to North America may have been underrated.

At present, the oldest reasonably well-authenticated site in the Americas is at Old Crow, in the North-West Territories. This may be dated anywhere from 25,000 to 60,000 years in age (Morlan 1979). Since it occurs in an area that was ice-free during the Pleistocene but was separated by ice-sheets from the rest of the continent for most of that period, it is often seen as irrelevant to continental peopling. South of the ice-sheets the picture is far more confused, with some workers accepting no dates older than about 14,000 years (Klein 1975; Lynch 1974), others seeing merit in sites such as Meadowcroft, dated to around 18,000 years ago (Adovasio *et al.* 1978; cf. Dincauze 1981) and a third group accepting some sites as old as 30,000 years or more (MacNeish 1978). However, all groups appear to accept that sites in southernmost America are dated to at least 10,000 years ago. Given the Sahul controversies, we find it curious that there has been little discussion among proponents of the shorter chronologies about the rate of human spread. The

distance from central North America to southern Chile is at least 17,000 km in a direct line, and within that distance there is a complete range from sub-arctic to tropical environments containing a number of very different floras and faunas. How were these environments colonized?

One widely quoted model is that proposed by P. S. Martin (1973). A supporter of the short chronology, he explains the rapidity of human spread in terms of big-game hunters pursuing their prey to extinction throughout the continent, and shows that this would be consonant both with possible numbers of megafauna and possible human growth rates. Martin's model relies on two assumptions. First, if people arrived in the Americas as big-game hunters, they would continue with this adaptation until forced by the extinction of their prey to do otherwise (1973:972). Second, human populations can grow rapidly enough to fill up a continent within a thousand years.

The first belief rests on an assumption about human adaptation which is similar to Bowdler's. Put crudely, this is that people are traditionalists in their subsistence strategies and can be expected to maintain existing patterns until it is absolutely impossible for them to do so and they are forced by sheer absence of their preferred foods into new adaptations. Now it might be the case that, if the earliest humans in the Americas *were* big-game hunters (which is not certain), they would have maintained this subsistence strategy through the game-rich plains of the north. But it seems highly unlikely that they would have been able to press on in monomaniacal pursuit of these animals throughout the entire continent, including the arid areas of Mexico, the tropical forests of Central and northern South America, or even the more open, high Andes. Would tradition have been sufficient to keep a majority of the population moving forward scores of kilometres a year? This is a necessary part of the model. Lynch (1974:371) claims that the fish-tailed and fluted points found throughout South America (except the Brazilian rainforests) are "unequivocable" evidence of a hunting-oriented adaptation which he equates with the North American Paleo-Indian one. This adaptation, he says, provides the oldest set of well-dated sites throughout the continent. At least within South America no geographic pattern can be discerned among the earliest dates and, until Meadowcroft or some similarly early site is accepted, this statement can be applied to the whole American continent. Martin's second assumption relies both on Deevey (1960), who sees a growth rate of 1.5% p.a. as "pre-historic man's best effort", and even more on Birdsell (1957), whose proposals of 3.4% p.a. growth-rates have already been discussed, and which in our view are very unlikely to be correct.

Inherent in Martin's model is the idea that the presence of big game made the environments which humans exploited so similar that no other adaptive factors need be considered. This is fallacious. Early colonizers of the Americas were not explorers equipped with everything but their meat protein, sealed off from the rest of the world like a pod of astronauts. They had to identify and locate other foods, find plants, rock and other resources suitable for making and mending all of their equipment, using only what local environments provided. They had to be born, live and die in the social environments of human communities. To learn to live in the range of American environments was no mean feat, but it was one that took time. Time, we believe is the critical lacuna in Martin's model. And the implication of our argument is that people have been in the Americas for at least 20,000 years.

The bottom lines to this discussion are the archaeological data detailing human colonization of the American and Sahulian worlds. We suspect, however, that some aspects of the discussion will not be solved by them, partly because of their incompleteness and partly because the acceptance and strength of data are conditioned by our ideas of what they ought to be. For example, some American researchers set very rigorous standards for the acceptance of sites dated more than 10,000 years old. Others are more inclined to point out that there are many indications of earlier settlement, even though no single one is perfect. The situation is not currently as polarized in Australia, though it occurs to some extent (Mulvaney 1975:146). Disputes of this kind are resolved as much by the strength of competing models as they are by the archaeological data.

3.3   25,000–10,000 Years Ago

We can be confident that most of the continent was occupied by 25,000 years ago, perhaps excluding only the central desert and upper elevations of the Great Dividing Range. Radiocarbon dated sites of that age are known from all parts of the continent except these two areas. Sites are too few in any area to tell us anything of population densities, or much about the range of environmental adaptations, but we can obtain glimpses of human behaviour in different environmental zones.

During the period 25,000–10,000 years ago, major climatic changes occurred. Sea level reached its lowest point (-130 to -160 m) some 17,000 years ago, and lowered sea levels were associated with a drop in mean temperature of $5°C$ and considerable ice-sheet formation in the south-eastern highlands (Bowler *et al.* 1976). This did not result in more water flowing down the south-eastern river systems, but less, with the result that the Willandra Lakes started to suffer fluctuating levels from 26,000 years ago and apart from minor episodes became more saline and eventually dry (Table 3.1). Decreasing effective rainfall from around 26,000 years ago is documented from a number of lake-level, sediment and pollen studies in the south-eastern quarter of the continent. A similar pattern may be assumed for south-western Australia but has not yet been demonstrated (Merrilees 1979).

At the opposite end of Sahul, in the highlands, recorded climatic changes refer primarily to temperature, which declined by about $5°C$ at the maximum. This was sufficient to allow glaciers to form on the highest peaks, to create a large area of alpine grassland below them, and to move the forest zone to below 2200 m. If changes in rainfall did occur, they were not of sufficient magnitude to significantly alter the overall pattern.

The lowland picture is much less clear. The Arafura Plain lying between present-day Australia and New Guinea was extremely flat, and while Torres Strait was never cut by water throughout this period, fluctuations in sea level from -50 to -120 m varied the plain's extent considerably. This, in turn, would have affected the rainfall. The north-west monsoon's effect today is restricted for the most part to a narrow coastal strip, and there is no reason to expect otherwise in the past. Thus areas which now receive that rainfall probably failed to do so throughout this time, so that present northern Australia and southern New Guinea would have been rather drier than they are now. Some direct evidence for this comes from studies of sand dunes and undersea nodular calcrete (Bowler *et al.* 1976:368). It is also likely that a large brackish or salt water lake would have formed within the Gulf of Carpentaria since this was a lower part of the plain.

The environmental changes throughout the central area seem to have been towards greater dryness with a consequent extension of both desert and semi-desert areas, but other effects are not known. The situation along the east coast is also not clear. As most rain comes from the Pacific and the continental shelf is narrow along this coast, regimes similar to present climatic regimes would be expectable. Even if an absolute decline in rainfall occurred, this was probably too small to have had any marked effect anywhere in this area.

The overall effect of climatic change on human populations is relatively easy to predict in general terms but very hard to demonstrate. We may start with the observation that population densities in modern Aboriginal Australia, as in other hunter-gatherer situations, are related to density and distribution of resources and are limited by critical resources. Throughout desert and semi-desert areas, the critical resource is availability of water, and any changes will have immediate repercussions on populations. The drying of the Willandra Lakes, for example, would certainly have affected the duration of human use and, in the long term, would have resulted in fewer people living in that area. For other areas, limiting factors are not so clear. Extremes of temperature seem never to have been important, except in the immediate neighbourhood of glaciers. Heavy population densities in the nineteenth century occurred especially in areas combining high rainfall with rich coastal resources (the northern, and parts of the eastern and southern, coasts, especially the estuaries), along with a few "adequately" watered inland

areas such as the eastern part of the south coast and Tasmania. However, the degree to which coastal faunas, especially shellfish, could keep pace with changing sea levels is unknown (cf. Chappell and Thom 1977), and probably fewer people were able to make a living in coastal areas at those times. Such changes as these are almost impossible to assess, since all coastal sites from this period are now under water, and even if they were not, determining population levels from archaeological data of the kind found in Sahul is exceptionally difficult.

However, it seems to be the case generally that the number of sites used, and the intensity of their use as measured by stone artefacts, increased throughout this period. How much this relates directly to preservation factors is difficult to determine, but it is inherently plausible that site destruction should vary directly with time. It is not easy to quantify any statement concerning site numbers because of definitional problems relating to open sites, and it may be premature to do so since total numbers are so small (Hallam 1977).

It would be surprising if some changes in human use of environments did not occur as the environments themselves changed. For example, at times of rapidly falling or rising sea levels one human response would be to move with the coast, but another, viable at times of falling sea, would be to stay in the same place and emphasize different aspects of existing resource usage. What is chosen will depend on what is available, preferred and economic to acquire and process. In the absence of almost any subsistence evidence from this period a picture is hard to draw.

Another factor to be considered is the overall intensity of human occupation in Sahul. We believe that by 30,000–25,000 years ago, it must have been of the same order of magnitude as it was in the ethnographic present. We can infer this because sites have been found throughout Australia. If the population was only one-tenth of what it was to become, we doubt that so many traces would have been found so readily. The exact numbers are rather less clear. Population estimates for Aboriginal Australia at the time of White contact have ranged from as low as

100,000 to more than one million, but most have concentrated in the 200,000–400,000 range. In 1930 A. R. Brown arrived at 300,000 people and although it may be time for a complete re-study of the problem we have accepted this figure. The Tasmanian population is put at about 4000 people (Jones 1974). The tropical north of Sahul is more difficult to assess, for present high population densities are related to intensive agriculture. The large Arafura Plain, the probably shortened coastline and the very different environments around 19,000–15,000 years ago must also be taken into account. Our guess is that overall density in the tropics was somewhat higher than in Australia as a whole, since in the latter the very large area of low-density desert populations would have strongly affected the total. How much denser the tropical population was is uncertain. If we assume that on average the density was twice that of Australia, then about 75,000–100,000 people are involved, of whom perhaps two-thirds lived in the area of modern New Guinea. For Sahul as a whole then, we think a population of 400,000 is a likely estimate, with densities liable to considerable fluctuation in specific areas (see also L. Smith 1976:93–121).

Sites

We turn now to a description of some of the sites which provide evidence dating from this period, and to some consideration of the implications of that evidence. We will not attempt to describe all sites, but have selected from different areas those having a range of data, resulting from a specialized use, or important for some other reason.

Kosipe (AER) lies in the tropical highlands some 2000 m above sea level (J. P. White *et al.* 1970a). The site consisted of a scatter of stone tools and pieces of carbon on a hillside which slopes down gently into a swamp several square kilometres in area. The artefacts and carbon were stratified within a series of distinctive volcanic ashes that were ejected from Mt. Lamington some 140 km to the south-east. Dates back to 24,000 years ago have been obtained both from carbon at the site and by correlation of ashes with a series closer to the volcano (Figures 3.8, 3.9). The

artefacts found comprise eleven flaked, flat, lenticular-sectioned tools, about the same size as axeheads, with side-notches or stems apparently for hafting. (Fig. 3.10a, c). Six oval or lenticular-sectioned flaked tools of about the same size and overall shape, but without notches, were found with them, as were a few flakes. Most of the tools are made of phyllite, a rather soft, coarse-grained metamorphic rock, but three are basalt and one indurated shale. The scattered occurrence of the tools suggests that they represent items lost or stored but not recovered over a considerable period of time, while the fact that carbon occurred as lumps within a soil horizon rather than in hearths confirms that a campsite was not excavated. It is likely that people were in the area to exploit the stands of pandanus trees growing in Kosipe swamp. If this is so, their use of the area may have been seasonal rather than permanent, for around 20,000 years ago the climate in that region was considerably colder than at present, and pandanus is a seasonally fruiting tree.

Other sites in the tropical highlands are later in time, but still date from this colder period. NFX consisted of a scatter of postholes and 135 small flaked stone artefacts spread over about 225 m² of hillside (V. Watson and Cole 1977). The postholes, 3–5 cm in diameter and 6–8 cm deep, were found in 7 × 3 m oval patterns suggestive of house outlines. Mineralized charcoal from the

FIGURE 3.8. Kosipe: part of the excavation. Most artefacts came from the lower part of the lower dark soil horizon. Scale in 20 cm.

bottom of one hole gave a date of 18,050 ± 750 (RL-370), with younger dates of 10,000–14,000 years coming from other samples. Most of the tools consist of chunks of rock weighing less than 20 g and have chipped edges. About 900 flakes and waste pieces suggest that flaking did not occur commonly in the excavated area, or that the debris had been tidied away.

Yuku (MAH) rock-shelter is on the northern side of Mount Hagen, at about 1300 m above sea level. Although excavated in 1959, no full description of the strata or material has been published (S. Bulmer 1966, 1975, 1979a; S. Bulmer and R. Bulmer 1964). A sample of bone 2 m down in the 3.6 m deposit was dated on collagen to

12,100 ± 350 years (GX-3112B), and the levels below this probably go back at least another 5000 years. These lower levels contained waisted tools similar to those at Kosipe and small retouched tools like those at NFX. About two-thirds of the animal remains recently described by Menzies (S. Bulmer 1979a) are of cuscus (a phalanger) and another 20% are macropod. Bats, rats, reptiles and other marsupials make up the remainder. Pig was common in levels dated to less than 4500 years. It was claimed that two undoubted pig cranial specimens came from a level older than 9780 ± 150 years (ANU-358, on charcoal).

At Nombe (NCA), another rock-shelter, excavations by Mountain have shown the presence of

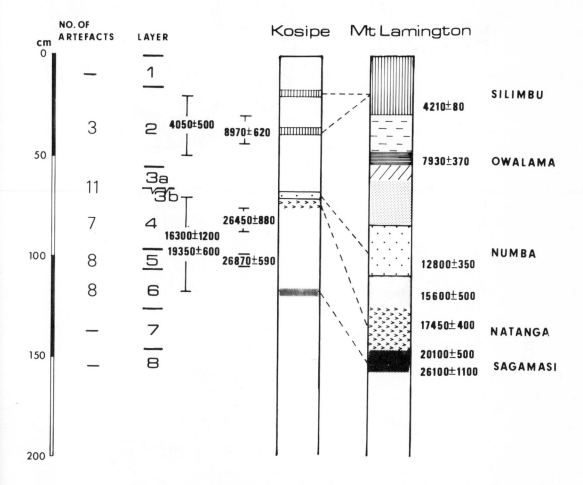

FIGURE 3.9. Kosipe: stratigraphy, radiocarbon dates, artefact numbers and volcanic ash correlation with Mt Lamington. Most artefacts in layer 3b were flakes. Source: J. P. White *et al.* (1970a:156).

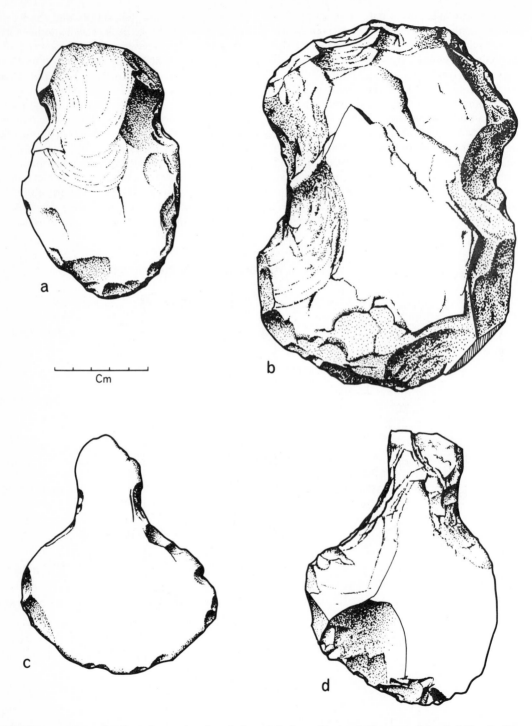

FIGURE 3.10. Waisted (a, b) and tanged (c, d) tools from Sahul. a, c: Kosipe; b; Kangaroo Island; d: Nombe, New Guinea. Drawing: Win Mumford.

now-extinct herbivores which presumably date to the Late Pleistocene period (since they have not been found in sites younger than 12,000 years). They were associated with waisted blades (Fig. 3.10d) and flaked stone tools (Mountain 1979, 1981 and pers. comm.).

It is clear that the tropical highlands were extensively utilized by people who were hunting and collecting food there during the period of maximum cold, 20,000–15,000 years ago. There is no reason to believe that population numbers changed much during that period, and we suspect that full use of all highland environments was being made by 30,000 years ago or even earlier.

A complete contrast faces us with regard to the tropical lowlands, where, despite considerable searching by at least ten workers along present New Guinea coasts, no archaeological evidence older than 4000 years has been found. The reason for this is quite unclear, though the answer may lie in a combination of low populations and poor site preservation. However, if the palaeoenvironmental interpretations are correct (J. Hope and G. Hope 1976:38), much of what is now coastal rainforest was broadleaf open forest some 20,000–14,000 years ago. In similar, or rather drier and more open conditions on the other side of the Arafura Plain, in what is now northern Australia, many sites with large numbers of artefacts have been found. We find it inconceivable that lowland areas of New Guinea were not occupied at the same time, even if the occupation was sparse. In tropical northern Australia, the greatest concentration of sites has been found in western Arnhem Land, for this is where most research has been carried out and where conditions, in the form of stable rock-shelters, are favourable to preservation. Sites have also been found in open situations such as on lagoon edges, but these have not been dated.

The best-described series of sites occurs near Oenpelli Mission (C. White 1967, 1971). The local environment may be divided into two main zones, a low-lying plain, across which tidal rivers meander and which is mostly swampy in the wet season (November–April), and a sandstone plateau lying south of, and some 100–300 m above, the plain. The plateau has thinner soils and more scrubby vegetation than the plain but produces more abundant plant and animal resources in the

wet season. Sites dated to 25,000–15,000 years ago have so far been found only in the plain (see also Kamminga and Allen 1973) where scattered carbon and occasional hearth concentrations have provided dating material. Because of the acidic sandy soil, only stone artefacts have survived. These include a range of flaked tools not dissimilar to those from Lake Mungo or the New Guinea sites, and at least twenty ground-edge tools of volcanic and metamorphic stone. Some of these have a groove across both faces, and they resemble in all respects tools hafted by Aborigines as hatchets in the recent past (Fig. 3.11).

Miriwun shelter, on the Ord River about 100 km inland from the present coast, is in an area of open savannah with a low, monsoonal rainfall (Dortch 1977) (Fig. 3.12). Although less than one metre deep, the base of the deposit was dated to 17,980 $\pm$ 1170 years (ANU-1008), at which time the coastline must have been several hundred kilometres from the site. Two features stand out in the material recovered. One is that the range of animal bone and eggshell from the lowest levels differs little from that found above (Dortch 1977:111). On this basis Dortch implied that, even if the area was somewhat drier than it is now, this would have been insufficient to cause major faunal changes. This is consistent with the site's semi-desert position. The other feature concerns the tools. Although most are of the generalized kind found at Lake Mungo, there are also a few (2?) flakes which are worn in a manner characteristic of those hafted in gum on a shaft and used for adzing (Gould *et al.* 1971; Hayden 1979a). In the recent past these adzes were in more common use in dry than in wet areas, and it is likely they were an invention in the desert or drier areas. The Miriwun evidence is paralleled in Devil's Lair, further south.

The Miriwun data suggest that, since environmental changes have not been major for 20,000 years, human response will have been slight. This was not the case in Arnhem Land, where a rise in sea level brought littoral resources to the Oenpelli region some 7000 years ago, as in many other areas of Australia.

No other material dating to this period has been found in the west, apart from in the southwest corner at Devil's Lair. There is a wide range of artefacts resulting from human use of this

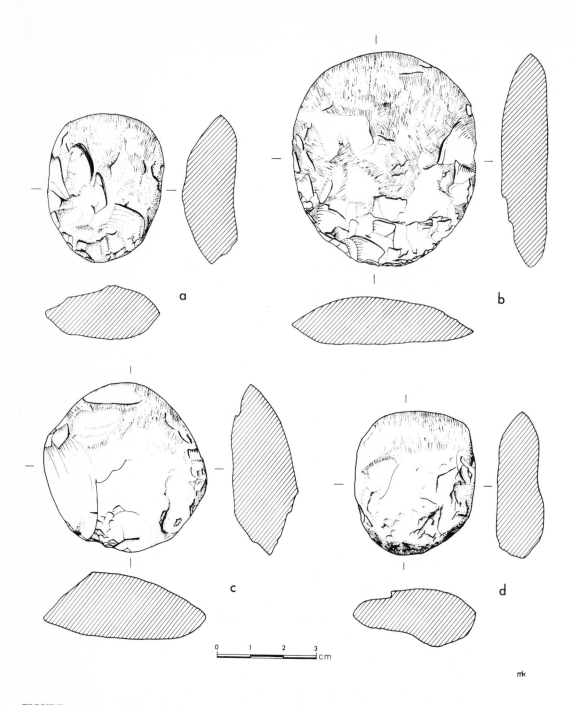

FIGURE 3.11. Ground stone hatchet heads from northern Australia. a, b: surface collections near Oenpelli (a, unregistered; b, Australian Museum E35816); c: Late Pleistocene from Cannon Hill site, near Oenpelli (C. White 1967; Australian Museum, E63247); d: early Recent from Tyimede II site near Oenpelli (C. White 1967; Australian Museum, E63247).

cave, including bone points, and beads made on lengths of macropod long bones (Dortch 1979a) (Figs 3.13, 3.14), stone tools flaked from quartz, chert and limestone and possible examples of casual engravings on stone plaques (Dortch 1976). Among the stone tools are examples of a bipolar technique. One quartz flake dating to around 25,000 years ago is covered with flecks of organic material that may be plant gum, and the exposed edge is flaked in a way very reminiscent of recent adzes. Throughout the period down to 12,000 years ago, the chert used at Devil's Lair is of a distinctive kind that derives from quarries which were apparently covered by rising sea levels 6000–4500 years ago (J. E. Glover 1979). Open sites with similar raw materials and technology are known to date from at least 18,000 years ago (Ferguson 1980, 1981).

An unusual example of site use is found in Koonalda Cave on the flat, treeless, limestone plain facing the Southern Ocean (Wright 1971a). The cave is a dissolution cavity which has broken through the ground surface (Fig. 3.15). About 150 m inside, excavations revealed a series of hearths, with some flakes and many broken pieces of flint. The hearths were dated to between 15,000 and 23,000 years ago. Broken flint nodules in the limestone of the cave walls, and the broken pieces, indicated that people were mining flint from the passage and minimally shaping it in the near darkness.

The other special use of Koonalda can be seen in the art which has been found further along the passage away from the light. An area with very soft chalky limestone walls has been scratched with fingers and sticks into wavy patterns, one

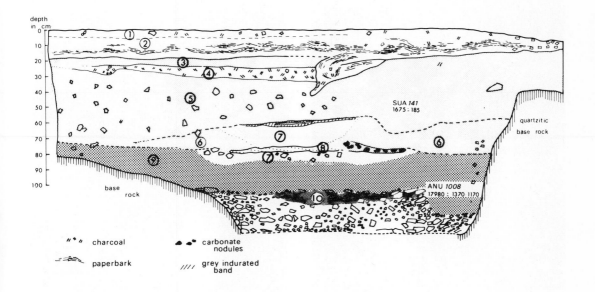

FIGURE 3.12. Section through Miriwun rock-shelter, north-west Australia.
1. Disturbed silt.
2. Light-brown silty earth with leaves and bark.
3. Grey-brown silty earth.
4. Hearth and ash.
5, 6. Light-brown silty earth.
7. Light silty earth.
8. Sandy lens.
9. Dark-brown silty earth.
10. Dark-brown silty earth mixed with rust-orange sand.
Source: Dortch (1977:114). Courtesy: Australian Institute of Aboriginal Studies, Canberra, Australia.

grid and one set of concentric circles. They are the oldest art forms in Australia. The argument that this art is dated to around 20,000 years ago rests on three facts: all radiocarbon dates are from this period; there is no evidence of subsequent use of the cave; and a small fragment of engraved limestone from the walls was found in the deposit.

Claims have also been made (Sharpe and Sharpe 1976) that a number of the boulders in the entrance passage are scratched or grooved by humans rather than natural agencies and that these boulders are linked by a series of paths of ceremonial import. Most researchers regard both sets of features as the result of natural causes, but tests are difficult.

Brief mention should also be made of cave site N145, on the same plain (H. Martin 1973; Marun 1974). Data from this site have not been well described or published, but there is evidence of human occupation back to 20,200 ± 1000 (ANU-1042). This consists of a few artefacts and animal remains characteristic of open plains like those found to the north of the site today. At the lowest sea level, 17,000 years ago, the site was 160 km from the sea and seems to have been unused.

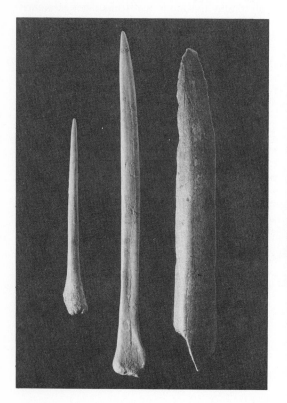

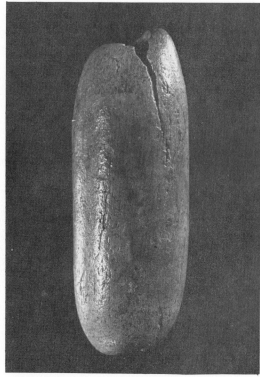

FIGURE 3.13. Bone points from Devil's Lair, WA. Age, Late Pleistocene; length of centre specimen, 149 mm. Courtesy: C. E. Dortch and Western Australian Museum.

FIGURE 3.14. Bead made from macropod fibula, Devil's Lair, WA. Age, about 12,000 years; length, about 21 mm. Courtesy: C. E. Dortch and Western Australian Museum.

On Kangaroo Island and the immediately adjacent mainland, large numbers of distinctive core tools have been known since the 1930s as the Kartan industry. The most recent, thorough study by Lampert (1977, 1979a, 1979b, 1981) delineates pebble tools flaked on one side, a horse-hoof series ranging from high-domed cores (Fig. 3.3) to flatter, more discoidal *karta*, steep edge scrapers and waisted tools made on slabs of quartzite of which the two main faces are natural fracture planes (Fig. 3.10b). The combination of types makes a distinctive local industrial tradition. Despite very careful collection and excavation, no dated stratified sites containing this material have been located, nor have the surface or sub-surface tool scatters ever contained more than a handful of flakes. All stratified sites in the same area have been dated to less than 16,000 years and most to less than 11,000 years ago. They contained a suite of small scrapers, adzes and flakes made from a range of raw materials quite different to the Kartan industry. The distribution of the large industry is predominantly around lagoons, streams and swamps: tools are absent from post-Pleistocene dune-fields and tools are not concentrated along the present shoreline.

Lampert's interpretation of the Kartan industry is that it dates from the period roughly 40,000–20,000 years ago, when Kangaroo Island was a higher part of the Pleistocene coastal shelf, lying between the sea and the major river valley formed by the mouth of the Murray. By analogy with modern tool uses (e.g. Hayden 1979a), he suggests that the tools were used for chopping and other heavy woodworking tasks, being casually made from local materials in the course of brief foraging trips away from the more regularly inhabited estuary and shoreline. While this is a more likely scenario than one involving different tribes making large and small industries or one claiming that the tools were used in different seasons, it still does not really account for either the profusion of heavy tools at favoured campsite locations or the relative absence of flakes. It seems likely that the ethnographic analogy is here leading us astray, and the great Kartan mystery remains unsolved.

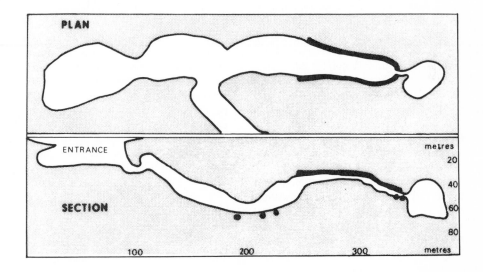

FIGURE 3.15. Koonalda Cave, SA, plan and section. The heavy line marks area of engravings; small circles mark area of flint mining and working. Source: Wright (1971a). Courtesy: Australian Institute of Aboriginal Studies, Canberra, Australia.

The cold Tasmanian peninsula was also occupied during this period, as sites on both sides of present-day Bass Strait demonstrate. On the Tasmanian side, the recovery of a few flakes from Beginner's Luck Cave (Site P) in sediments washed in from the entrance and consolidated, along with carbon and burned and cut bones, in a breccia shows that humans were able to use areas very shortly after the glaciers melted. Carbon from the breccia dates to 20,650 $\pm$ 1790 (GaK-7081), and this date is paralleled by an aspartic acid racemization date (P. Murray *et al.* 1980). The burned animal bone consists mostly of modern forms. Faunal and pollen studies show that the area was much more open than it became in post-glacial times (after about 10,000 years), and it seems likely that it was more frequently used then than later.

A longer-term indication of the nature of human habitation on the peninsula comes from the lower levels of Cave Bay Cave on what is now Hunter Island, off north-west Tasmania (Bowdler 1974, 1975, 1977, 1979). Several thick hearths dated to between 20,000 and 23,000 years ago (ANU-1498 22,750 $\pm$ 420 and other dates) indicate human use of the cave on Hunter Hill. The hearths contained food-bone remains entirely from land animals (wallaby, bandicoot and tiger cat) and a few stone artefacts, and are presumed to result from short-term camps. Apart from a brief visit around 15,400 $\pm$ 330 (ANU-1613), the cave was used only by scavengers and owls until about 7000 years ago, at least on the evidence of the three small trenches excavated so far.

On the other side of Bass Strait, coastal sites and those on the seaward side of the mountains have generally displayed a limited use in this period. Sites such as Clogg's Cave (Flood 1974, 1980), Burrill Lake (Lampert 1971a), Bass Point (Bowdler 1970, 1976), Noola (Tindale 1961, I. Johnson 1979) and King's Table and other sites in the Blue Mountains behind Sydney (Stockton and Holland 1974) have all contained much less material, both artefactual and ecofactual, than is true of levels dating to the last few thousand years. The reasons for this can only be guessed at, and may include lower population densities, less use of caves and shelters or less use of stone tools.

A similar situation is common to other highland areas of eastern Australia (Beaton 1977; Bowdler 1981; McBryde 1974, 1976, 1977; Morwood 1979, 1981). Use of Kenniff Cave, at the headwaters of the Darling River, dates from about 18,000 years ago, but artefacts were low in number (Mulvaney and Joyce 1965).

Aside from Clogg's Cave, levels dating to the Late Pleistocene in eastern highlands sites have produced only stone tools and carbon. This is because of their location in sandstone shelters or other acidic soil conditions which destroy bone and other organic remains. Even recently used sites have contained little of this material unless preserved within a shell midden. In this situation, it is difficult to say much about the economies of the area: we assume they were based on hunting and plant collecting. For the Carnarvon area, Beaton (1977, 1982) argued that the recent staple plant food *Cycas*, which requires considerable processing, was not used at this earlier time, but his argument is inferential rather than direct. Other economies are simply unknown. At Clogg's Cave, several sources including birds, animals and humans contributed to the faunal assemblage, and it has not yet been possible to distinguish the humanly contributed material from the rest (Flood 1980). Bones aged between 17,720 $\pm$ 840 (ANU-1044) and 13,690 $\pm$ 350 (ANU-1182) include a range of phalangers and macropods, marsupial mice, koalas, wombats and bandicoots. The fact that many bones of smaller animals were found along the cave walls suggests that they were probably from owl pellets. Flood remarks that the absence of freshwater mussel shell, if real, probably indicates winter use of the cave when the river water would have been too cold for collecting.

Technology and Subsistence

The two aspects of Late Pleistocene Sahul about which the archaeological material is most informative are technology and subsistence patterns, with the former being much better known. Technological data consist primarily of stone artefacts and some indications of bone working. None of the extensive range of wooden and other plant materials presumed to have been in use have been recovered from sites older than 10,000 years.

Throughout Sahul, the flaked stone tools older than about 5000 years exhibit a very restricted morphological range. Although there is some regional and temporal variation, the similarities are so marked that all examples can be treated as part of the "core-tool and scraper tradition", as it is most commonly known. Though this is not an accurate functional designation, it does draw attention to the two more common forms. Descriptions of this material have been primarily at the site level, with some beginnings of inter-site comparisons (Flood 1980; Lampert 1979a; Lorblanchet and Jones 1979). A Sahul-wide perspective is therefore impressionistic, but it may be useful in delineating major features and identifying some problems. We look first at definitions and occurrence of forms; then we outline regional variations.

CORES

The most widely recognized form of these are "horse-hoofs", so-called because of their shape when placed with the flat striking platform down (Fig. 3.3). It has been common in Australian archaeological literature to depict them in this way and to believe that the obtuse overhanging edge is the result of use or resharpening (e.g. Bowler *et al.* 1970:49, Mulvaney 1975:172). This is not always or even usually the cause. Many of these artefacts seem to be explicable as single platform cores from which flakes continued to be struck until flaking was no longer possible without rejuvenation of the striking platform, which was not undertaken. Careful inspection of the so-called "working edges" of these tools reveals that many result from multiple hammer blows and consist of a series of small notches, with step-flaking below them, rather than being a continuously flaked edge. Kamminga (1978) has attempted, but failed, to find definite traces of use-wear on a number of horse-hoofs. On the other hand, the widespread distribution of these tools in the landscape and their common occurrence without associated flaking floors

does suggest that some, at least, might have been used for pounding or chopping before they were discarded. But these cores may have been stored at particular locations for use during recurrent occupation rather than being carried about. Similar practices are known in relation to other artefacts such as grindstones in more recent times.

Another problem with thinking of them as chopping tools is to understand why they were not used in recent times. All ethnographic evidence relating to chopping tools (Gould 1980; Hayden 1979a) reports these as large, chunky, hand-held pieces having a sharp, if steeply angled edge which is used unretouched. There is no evidence that they were formally shaped in any way. And finally, the working-out of a pyramidal core and the failure to rejuvenate it seems to be in line with other aspects of stone technology both of this period and more recent times, with all strictly "functional" stone-working procedures being casual and not involving sophisticated flaking techniques. We therefore believe that "horse-hoofs" should be seen primarily as worked-out cores, evidence of a particular pattern of flaking raw materials such as silcrete, rather than as tools in their own right. If this is the case, we suggest that, although clearly worked-out pieces may be distinguished as a "type" (and have been particularly collected from surface sites), they are likely to form but one end of a continuum of core morphology in sites where flaking regularly occurred. We might also expect more "worked-out" cores in areas where stone was less freely available, such as in the Willandra Lakes region. Some support for this comes from Kangaroo Island (Lampert 1979a) and from the Murchison River (WA) (Byrne 1980).

There is some regional variation in distribution of "classic" horse-hoofs. Industries from the tropical north had only rare examples (S. Bulmer 1966; C. White 1967; J. P. White 1967a), and in New Guinea multiple platform cores were a preferred alternative. Similarly, horse-hoofs are rare in Western Australia and along the southeastern coast and highlands. They seem most common in dry and semi-desert areas, ranging from Kangaroo Hill (Island), through the inland south-east and as far west as the central desert

(Gould 1977a) though their date in the last is younger than 10,000 years. Whether a full survey would show a tight correlation of occurrence with a particular range of environments is unclear. At present no strong associations with particular sources of raw material or functions can be shown.

SCRAPERS

The term "scraper" is used to refer to a very large group of flakes and some cores which have unifacial step-flaking or invasive flaking along one or more edges, but which are rarely otherwise shaped into regular morphological patterns. It is generally believed that the edge flaking was intentional and happened either when an edge was shaped into a form suitable for a particular task or when an edge blunted by use was resharpened. It is apparent that some patterning of edge forms can be observed in some areas, though whether either or both of the above factors were the cause in any one case is not known.

The use of the term "scraper" is usually said not to imply a particular function but to be purely a formal term. It seems certain that these tools were not used only for cleaning skins, since scrapers have been found throughout Sahul, are the commonest class in nearly all sites, and the forms continue everywhere until recent times when we know that skin scraping was restricted to parts of south-eastern Australia. On the other hand, many researchers think that these tools were most likely used for various kinds of woodworking, including planing, scraping and cutting (Bowler *et al.* 1970; Jones 1971a; Mulvaney 1975:172, 174–80). Modern experiments and observations (e.g. Gould 1977b; Hayden 1977a, 1979a; J. P. White and Thomas 1972) show that these are the most common activities for which stone tools are used, as well as demonstrating that resharpening can sometimes result in a "scraper-like" edge. However, this is not always the case (e.g. J. P. White 1968a), and in areas of the New Guinea highlands, edges bearing this kind of retouch do not seem to be the result of either use or resharpening, nor are they now considered suitable for any task at all (Strathern 1969).

On the basis of studies of use-wear, Kamminga (1978) has suggested that many of the smaller flake scrapers, dating from the terminal Pleistocene onwards, were used for adzing soft and medium density woods. He also strongly supports the idea that scrapers with concave notches in them were used on rounded items such as spear shafts and tips. Further functional classes have not been determined.

There are two major approaches to the description and analysis of these artefacts. Early approaches (McCarthy *et al.* 1946) stressed the formal varieties that could be delineated. Such classes as end and side scrapers, concave and nosed scrapers were identified by focusing on particular attributes. A continuation of the formal morphological approach occurs in attempts to see rather fewer, broader classes of tools such as flat, steep-edged and concave scrapers (e.g. Flood 1980; Jones 1971a). These forms have some reality, and changes through time can be observed both in their attributes and in their representation in sites (Lorblanchet and Jones 1979). Jones' analysis of a very small sample of tools from a north-west Tasmanian site was able to demonstrate, for instance, that overall size within one intuitively defined class decreased over the last 8000 years, implying more efficient use of raw material (1977a:194), and he also showed that two other classes exhibited complementary occurrences over time.

The meaning of changes of this kind has been harder to interpret. At times more economical use of raw material can be inferred, but in many cases neither this nor obvious functional change is apparent, and explanations in terms of "style" or "fashion" are briefly referred to.

The other approach to these tools began with Mulvaney in 1965 (Mulvaney and Joyce 1965) and has been continued by Lampert (1971a), J. P. White (1967b, 1969) and others. This is to treat as one class all tools which do not have a clear set of morphological characteristics and to observe attributes of the retouched and altered edges and of the tools as a whole. Correlation between attributes has sometimes resulted in the implication that a formally defined class is present, but the functional or temporal aspects of such a discovery have not been explored. By comparison with tools used in recent times in a variety of environments, we might suspect that the relative absence of formal patterning is a real one, with the implication being that analyses recognizing this are likely to be more informative than those which assume that clear morphological patterns exist.

Although the basic "core-tool and scraper" tradition was common throughout Sahul, there were a number of variants within the Late Pleistocene. The most likely explanations for regional variation are the different resources used in broadly different environments, combined with similarities arising from human interaction networks. So far it has not been possible to tie down such ideas more precisely.

EDGE-GROUND TOOLS

The most striking regional variation is the occurrence of edge-ground stone tools in the north of Australia (Fig. 3.11). This tradition is known best from sites in Arnhem Land near Oenpelli (C. White 1967), the only other example being a series of flakes of igneous/metamorphic rock, each with a ground surface, found throughout 2 m of deposit lying below a level dated to 6870 $\pm$ 150 (I-1735) at Laura (Cape York) (Wright 1971b:139). One of the lowest flakes has two intersecting ground surfaces and, given the reasonable assumption of a steady rate of site formation, dates to around 14,000 years ago.

On the other side of the Arafura Plain, grinding has only been found on tools and flakes less than 10,000 years old.* The tools are similar to those hafted as axes and adzes in the recent past, as well as to some waisted or stemmed blades like those found at Kosipe. Examples of the former occurred at basal levels of Kafiavana (NBZ) shelter (J. P. White 1972), dated by three consistent radiocarbon dates to around 10,000 years ago, but similar tools have not been found in other sites of the same age. One ground, waisted blade was found at Yuku in a level dated to perhaps 10,000 years ago (S. Bulmer 1977a:57), but most are younger than this (1977a:43).

Axe-like tools, ground either all over or along one end, are about as old on the other side of

Wallacea. They are best documented in Japan, where they are up to 30,000 years old (Ikawa-Smith 1979; Oda and Kealy 1973). The tools there are fully ground and without waists, stems or side grooves. Other edge-ground tools may have occurred in Kalimantan (Golson 1974:543–44) and on the Indo-Chinese peninsula (Hayden 1977b), but in neither case are the dating or stratigraphic credentials impeccable.

The occurrence of grinding at such an early date in the tropical western Pacific has caused some surprise to prehistorians conditioned to think, on the basis of the European evidence, that "Neolithic" tools were a clearly post-Pleistocene phenomenon restricted to field-making farmers. An alternative view, propounded by Hayden (1977b), suggests, in essence, that grinding is the western Pacific equivalent of the European and African traditions of highly economic stone flaking and that all were simply developments along the path of technological efficiency which is characteristic of human history. This is a convenient view which puts our data into a perspective, but it is hardly explanatory. Hayden suggests that grinding occurred because of a lack of large quantities of stone suitable for flaking. However this is not the case in a number of Asian areas. What is true is that a ground-stone technology is often more economical in terms of transport and curation than a flaked one, in which new tools must frequently be made, and its origins may well lie in considerations such as these.

It is more of a puzzle why ground stone tools should have been restricted to the tropical north of Sahul until the Holocene. F. P. Dickson (pers. comm. 1977) has suggested that ground stone tools were used for particular tropical tasks such as canoe building, but as the oldest specimens are found inland, this seems unlikely. In recent times ground tools were hafted as hatchets and used for similar tasks throughout Australia, especially chopping holes in trees to collect honey and possums (phalangers) (cf. McBryde 1977:233–37). At least while many larger animals were still available (see 4.3), it is possible that these resources were of much less importance. This might have been the case until Holocene times, though it seems unlikely. Nevertheless, a resource-oriented explanation seems most reasonable at present.

---

* At the ANZAAS Congress in May 1982, M. J. Mountain announced the discovery of an edge-ground axe-like tool dated to about 26,000 years ago, from the Nombe site.

There is also the matter of hafting to be considered. We have noted already that most of the tools found in Arnhem Land are similar in size and form to those hafted as hatchets in recent times. Throughout Australia in recent times hatchet handles were short, light and flexible, designed for the tool to be used one-handed. The universal method of hafting was to bend a flexible piece of vine, cane or wood around the head, tie it and fix the head with slightly flexible resin (Dickson 1980). This technique is very different to any found in New Guinea, where no less than four hafting traditions are known, none of which is similar to the Australian one (Crosby 1973, 1977). Ground stone heads in New Guinea were hafted at a variety of angles to the handle, ranging from parallel with it to a plane at right angles to it, and in some cases it was possible to alter this angle depending on the task being performed. No consistent morphological differences between heads hafted at various angles has been observed, and it is for this reason that the term "axe-adze" has been generally adopted for these tools. From observation of them in use it is clear that the hafting allows them to be used two-handed like a modern steel axe, although for chopping a shorter and lighter swing is used. However, the heads are not usually too heavy nor are the handles too long for the implements to be used one-handed, as a hatchet is used (see J. P. White 1977a for examples). It should also be pointed out that the New Guinea axe-adze heads are generally longer in relation to their width than the Australian hatchet heads, while grooves, stems or waists to assist hafting are almost unknown, whereas they occur on small numbers of Australian hatchet heads.

The extent to which the modern contrasts in hafting and use can be projected into the past is difficult to assess. Throughout Sahul, prehistoric ground stone heads are formally similar to those found in the same regions today. We cannot easily compare uses, since the subsistence patterns and range of tasks in the two sets of societies are so dissimilar, as are the environments within which they operate. Although resin for hafting would be more difficult to obtain in New Guinea than in Australia (and conversely for the vines used for lashing), it seems unlikely that this is sufficient explanation for the differences. Thus there are really two puzzles to be approached — differences within tropical Sahul and restriction of the grinding technology to that area until recent times. Neither can be solved at present.

WAISTED BLADES

A possible further complication arises from the occurrence of waisted blades. These tools, as we have seen, were found at Kosipe, and flaked examples also occurred at the rock-shelter sites of Yuku and Kiowa at rather later dates. Much thinner examples, with tangs and not waists, have been found at several locations in the New Guinea highlands (J. Allen 1970; S. Bulmer 1977a; Christensen 1975a) (Fig. 3.16), but these have been dated, if at all, to within the last few thousand years. Waisted blades like the Kosipe examples are also known from Australia, most notably from Kangaroo Island (Fig. 3.10b) (Lampert 1975), while S. Bulmer (1977a) and Golson (1974) report similar waisted implements from various parts of the Pacific and eastern Asia. Aside from the formally similar characteristic of waisting, these tools are not very alike. For example, several hundred collected from New Britain are made of flint and chert and exhibit a much wider range of form and size than those from the New Guinea highlands (S. Bulmer 1977a; J. P. White in press). But the mainland Sahul examples are similar to each other in form, size and raw materials. Whether their functions were also similar is unknown. The New Guinea examples have been interpreted as primarily agricultural implements, for cutting grass, hoeing and digging rather than for woodworking (S. Bulmer 1977a). However, without stronger evidence, we are unwilling to extend this interpretation either to the Kosipe artefacts or to the Australian examples.

Other similarities across Sahul are still unexplored. There is the formal stylistic similarity between flaked stone tools, but this forms no more than a general pattern. Given the different environments, we would expect any artefacts directly concerned with subsistence to exhibit regional differences.

Within the Australian region, we can draw attention primarily to variations within the south-eastern quarter of the continent. In south-eastern South Australia and along areas of the east coast (Lampert 1979a; Matthews 1966) there was a frequent use of large flat pebbles, flaked wholly or partially over one surface. They may have served as both tools and cores. Along the southern coast they were complemented by bifacially flaked flint cores which formally resemble Acheulean hand-axes. It seems that these technologies relate primarily to the existence of appropriate raw materials, and if these artefacts were used as tools, then they were probably used for heavy-duty chopping and pounding. For many years comparisons have been made between these tools and similarly flaked pebbles from South-East Asia. In fact the term "sumatralith" was coined by Tindale (1937) to draw attention to this similarity. Some years

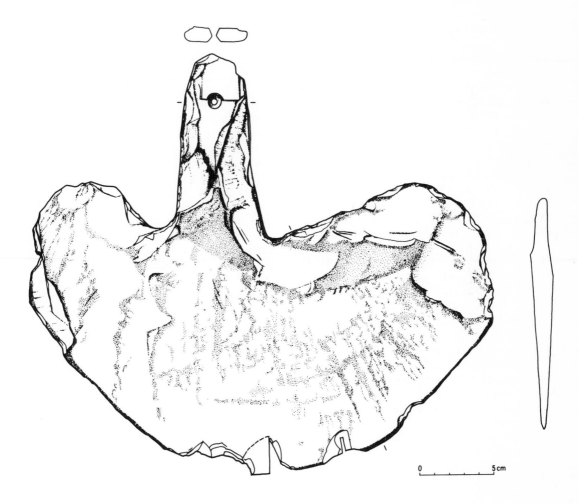

FIGURE 3.16. Tanged blade from the central New Guinea highlands. Drawing by Win Mumford. Source: Christensen (1975a).

ago Matthews was able to demonstrate metrical similarities between collections from the two areas, but as he pointed out, this may tell us no more than that similarly shaped raw materials were being flaked by a similarly simple technique.

OTHER TOOLS

Rather more interesting is the occurrence in south-eastern coastal and highland Australian sites of small numbers of flake implements with very finely serrated edges caused by pressing small flakes out of the edge at intervals of about 2 mm. At Burrill Lake, three of these implements were found in a level dated to 20,830 ± 810 (ANU-137) and two were somewhat higher in the deposit. Other examples come from Bass Point (Bowdler 1970) and Curracurrang (Megaw 1968), as well as from more recent contexts such as Capertee (McCarthy 1964). At Burrill, three of the implements had two edges notched, but this feature has not been recorded at other sites. Often called saws (e.g. McCarthy *et al.* 1946:27), Kamminga (pers. comm. 1974) points out that the lack of offsetting of the points would have made them of little use for this kind of work, at least on wood, though they may have been used on skins. However, no traces of wear have been seen on the specimens inspected.

We have already referred to the few adze flakes which occurred in the semi-desert sites of Miriwun, Devil's Lair and Quininup Brook in Western Australia. Gould (1977a) claims to have recovered similar tools from the lowest levels of Puntutjarpa in the central western desert. His report specifies only one example of an adze slug, or worked-out tool (Gould 1977a: Fig. 87.8), which would be dubious evidence on its own, but R. Jones, who has inspected the material, confirms the presence of other adze flakes in these early levels (pers. comm. 1979). Assessment of the material on the basis of the published data is complicated by the fact that Gould interprets as adzes all tools which would usually be called scrapers, but he provides a formal rather than a functional definition for them. However, an even greater problem is the age of the Puntutjarpa specimens since there are several anomalies in the radiocarbon dates, and it is not clear whether

the adzes are from the same levels as the oldest dates. It is not unlikely that flakes were hafted in resin and used as chisel-adzes well back into the Pleistocene in the western parts of Australia. What needs to be explained is why they remained restricted to these areas until some 5000 years ago, given that after this date they were in common use throughout most of eastern Australia. As adzes were used for woodworking and not directly for subsistence activities, we may need to seek a socioeconomic explanation for their spread.

In this discussion of regional variations, we have been restricted almost entirely to stone tools, for these make up by far the largest part of our evidence. We know from a few sites such as Devil's Lair and Lake Mungo that bone tools of various kinds and bone beads were made, and we may expect regional variation in these also, but this is not yet determinable. In the material discussed so far, however, there has been no direct reflection of the major environmental changes that occurred during this period.

Any discussion of subsistence patterns and their changes before 10,000 years ago is currently crippled by a lack of evidence. From only a few sites do we have animal remains, while no plant remains have been recovered. We argue elsewhere (4.3) that before 20,000 years ago people may well have depended to a greater extent on hunted animals than was the case more recently, but evidence of subsistence strategies along the coasts, where a good proportion of the population probably lived, is non-existent.

In this situation one useful procedure will be to examine the evidence we have for changes in subsistence and see what explanation might account for them. Probably the best documented change in actual resources exploited is in the Darling River basin. In several sites around Lakes Tandou and Mulurulu, grinding slabs made of sandstone first occurred about 14,000 years ago and continued in use until the nineteenth century (H. Allen 1974:311). There is little doubt that these tools were always used for seed grinding, especially of *Panicum* and *Portulacca*, which grow on the riverine plains in summer, and especially well after floods. The oldest grinding slabs have been dated to the time when the lakes finally dried up and a range of animals became extinct in the area and other resources became scarce. One such resource may have been *Typha* (bulrush) roots, which grow in swampy areas and are still an important part of the local summer diet. The lakes and swamps of Pleistocene Australia may easily have grown large stands of these as well as other plants which died out as water levels fell. Thus it is probable that the first use of grindstones marks a wider change, with the decline in animals, fish and perhaps some plant resources that required little processing pushing people into using foods which required a greater effort to prepare for human use.

Grindstones have also been found in Arnhem Land sites dated to 18,000 years ago and were used at Miriwun and Quininup in Western Australia at some time in the Pleistocene. Although the data are patchy, this distribution is congruent with the area over which large grindstones occurred in the recent past, consisting of a wide band of semi-arid country in the west, east and north of Australia bordering the central desert core (Tindale 1977b). Smaller grindstones have been found in other dry areas. The important part of this distribution is its climatic relation, for grindstones seem to have been used rarely or not at all in areas of moderate to high rainfall, where roots rather than seeds formed the important staple vegetables (cf. Golson 1971).

In our view, the invention of seed processing is of local origin (cf. Tindale 1977a), but when and where the technology was developed is a more open question. Some researchers have assumed it was a necessary part of the first human movements out of the wet tropics into drier areas. As Golson says (1971:205):

> the absence from central Australia of a whole series of food-providing tropical genera forced upon settlers of the area not only the exploitation of alternative sources of supply but a greater reliance on seed foods.

This statement is true, however, only if we envisage the drier regions being settled by people with a subsistence base and population density comparable to that of modern times. Patchier distribution of people and a concentration on animals and roots may well have provided the basis for initial penetration of, and early settlement in, the area, with seed grinding being invented then but only utilized to any extent in the stressful conditions after 20,000 years ago. The effort required in the collection and processing of seeds would have made this resource unattractive before then (O'Connell and Hawkes 1981a).

We should note here that grindstones must be distinguished from mortars, which, with pestles, occurred in a number of wetter parts of Sahul. Although perhaps at times used for processing such foods as nuts and roots, they were also used for other tasks, including ochre grinding. Little research has been carried out on the complementary distributions of mortars and grindstones, which were used in different ways and for different purposes.

Any attempt to move beyond the technology and subsistence of Pleistocene Australians and, as Mulvaney puts it (1979), "reflesh the Pleistocene" is difficult, for the data are limited. Restricting a survey to material older than 10,000 years allows the following:

1. Clear evidence of a range of burial practices from simple to compound at Lake Mungo, and probably at Kow Swamp (4.1).
2. The widespread use of red ochre pigments, found not only in the Mungo III burial but also at many other sites, points certainly to the practice of decoration on bodies, walls or artefacts and to the possibility of ceremonial systems.
3. The beads cut from long bones, along with enigmatic grooved and punched plaques from Devil's Lair (Dortch 1976), show that decorative and perhaps ceremonial traditions in the Pleistocene were different from those of the present day.
4. The finger tracings and abraded grooves in Koonalda, along with the pecked representations of human and kangaroo tracks sealed in by archaeological deposits dated to some 13,000 years ago at Laura (Cape York) (Rosenfeld 1975; Rosenfeld *et al.* 1981), also suggest that very different artistic traditions existed in Pleistocene times.

Maynard (1979), following R. Edwards, has argued that Panaramitee-style engravings, consisting of macropod and bird tracks, circles, crescents, dots and footprints, can be dated at least to the terminal Pleistocene and are found throughout central and eastern Australia. If confirmed, this will again suggest that not only are the motifs different but the cultural patterning behind the engravings was very different to anything known from the recent past. So far, no studies of stone materials or other resources allow us to infer the kinds of trade and exchange networks that are so well documented in the recent past (Mulvaney 1976). Did these in fact exist?

To briefly sum up this section, perhaps the most striking characteristic of Late Pleistocene Sahul is the degree of similarity in many aspects of the preserved record over very large areas. Any regional variations certainly seem to be much less profound than those which developed later. Can we argue, as Isaac (1972) has done for earlier Pleistocene times, that this was a function of lower population densities and a lower rate of interaction among human groups? Or did similarities in initial technologies and subsistence strategies persist throughout Sahul, giving visible historical continuity and less rapid rates of change? Problems such as these lie behind attempts to understand the prehistory of Pleistocene Sahul. We can already see that this was very different to what we might expect from a study of Holocene ethnography, but the processes which led from one to the other are only beginning to be glimpsed.

In this chapter we discuss three problems that do not fit easily into the chronological framework, partly because they have been treated as separate problems in the past and have thus generated their own literature, and partly because they involve certain assumptions and theoretical approaches which need some explanation.

The first problem concerns the physical anthropology of Sahul's population and in particular the question of whether there was more than a single founding group. We review the major attempts to demonstrate that there was more than one "migration" to Sahul and conclude that neither the evidence from modern populations nor from the fossils supports such an idea. In fact, there are strong reasons for believing that the people of Sahul derived from a single population.

The second problem concerns the largest single group of archaeological remains, flaked stone tools, and what these can tell us. We argue that traditional typological approaches, which have served well in other parts of the world, are irrelevant and largely uninformative in Sahul. A broader perspective on the problem is needed, one concerned with sampling, spatial patterning, geology and use-wear, as well as formal classification.

Chapter 4

Intermission: Three Problems

In section 4.3 we discuss current knowledge and approaches to the problem of why several genera and species of animals became extinct during the late Pleistocene. Unicausal explanations such as climatic change, stress, increased firing of the landscape or "overkill", all of which have been suggested, can be shown to be inadequate when applied to the whole of Sahul. Different explanations may turn out to be appropriate in different regions, though we do

not doubt that the spears of men were everywhere used on these animals and were often crucial to their demise as a species.

4.1   1, 2, 3, ..., n Groups of Settlers?

In earlier chapters we have assumed that Sahul was originally settled by one small group of people, the founder population. It is possible

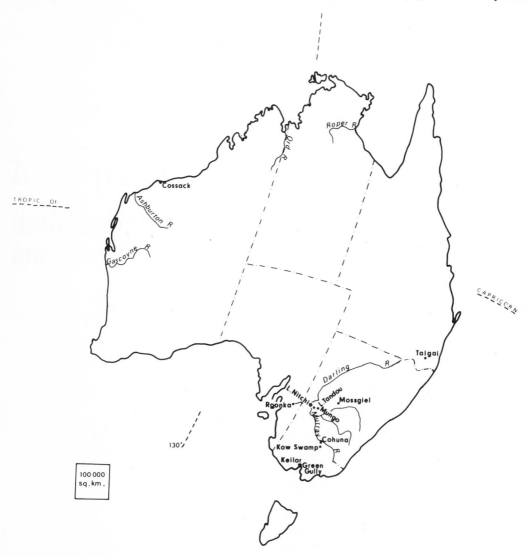

FIGURE 4.1. Sites with human skeletal material discussed in this section.

that the areas of Australia and New Guinea had different small founder populations, although at present there does not appear to be any firm evidence for this. It is also possible that any founder population was increased by other small groups, but these would not be visible in the fossil record, and probably not in the genetic record either.

For many years physical anthropologists have been concerned with the origins and relationships of the Sahul population, especially its Australian part. As Kirk and Thorne state (1976:1), "Two general classes of theory have been proposed, one that modern Aboriginals are descendants from a single introduction of people at some time in the past, the other that two or more waves of immigrants arrived at different periods." Note, in particular, that the theories of multiple origin involve large numbers of people — even a small "wave" would need to equal at least ten per cent of the number of people already existing on the beach where it arrives. We will return to this point later.

We start this account with a general review of the two basic approaches currently used in discussing the history of human evolution and migration. One is based on diachronic data; the other on synchronic. The first is the study of fossil data, the chance remnants of human skeletons that can be recovered, put into context and dated. This material is especially useful for answering broad, general questions about human evolution, for testing arguments about changes in skeletal features and, in particular, for looking at long-term changes in the human body. But trying to use this material in small-scale or short-term studies of human morphology raises problems. The greatest of these is the obtaining of a sample of reasonable size, adequately dated. The processes by which skeletal material comes to us result in small, haphazard and often fragmentary samples. Care must be taken to ensure that the questions asked are not too fine-grained for the data provided.

The synchronic approach utilizes sets of data from current populations. Data selected for discussions of human history must be thought by the researcher to encapsulate or record the series of evolutionary events which a particular population has experienced. In order for this approach to be acceptable, the features being examined must have been subject neither to selection nor to random drift. At the very least, it must be assumed that those influences can be detected and allowed for, leaving an historical explanation of genetic relationship to be sought for the remaining variation. Two broad classes of data have usually been used in these studies — anthropometric and biochemical.

Anthropometry has been used widely as a research tool in Australia for many years, although there is an increasing challenge to its practitioners to demonstrate how much variability between and within their samples can be accounted for in heritable and how much in environmental terms. For example, Cavalli-Sforza and Bodmer (1971:704) state:

> All anthropometric traits are usually [sic] genetically complex and also subject to strong environmental influences ... Stature and most other anthropometric traits are difficult to use for phylogenetic analysis because of the unknown short-term effects on them of environmental changes. In addition, they are influenced by an unknown number of genes ...

Birdsell, whose own research in Australia has been based largely on anthropometry, has basically agreed with this view (1975:475–89). He draws attention to the fact that some characteristics of the human body can, in populations, often be related to the environment, instancing among other examples an inverse correlation between body shape and mean temperature and the fact that small stature and light weight are characteristic of many tropical rainforest populations. D. Hughes (1968) draws attention to a wide range of studies, both of humans and of animals, to demonstrate great plasticity in many of the traits normally observed in anthropometric studies and relates this plasticity to environmental features ranging from diet to climate. (For an Australian example, see T. Brown 1976.) Further, the heritability of any particular physical trait is not trait-specific, but population-specific and time-specific, which makes it difficult to use any one trait in tracing comparative evolutionary histories. The advantage of anthropometric traits is that they allow direct comparisons to be made between modern and ancient skeletal material: the difficulty lies in interpreting the similarities and differences observed.

The other data base which has been used consists of biochemical traits, which have a simpler Mendelian base. These characters include blood group antigens, serum protein groups and red cells, and serum enzyme groups. These individual characters, gene markers, are now being widely used to examine affinities between populations and sometimes to reconstruct their historical relationships (e.g. Kirk and Thorne 1976). Cavalli-Sforza and Bodmer (1971) argue that characters for which a simple Mendelian base has been ascertained are likely to be more historically informative than more complex traits (see also Kirk 1971; for a contrary view see Giles 1976). A review of current studies within Sahul, however, suggests that results are inconsistent and historical indications given by various gene markers are contradictory (e.g. Curtain *et al.* 1976; Howells 1973: Ch.4; R. T. Simmons 1976). It appears that the contributions of polyphyletic descent of particular alleles and the operation of selection factors, including drift, in determining present patterns of occurrence have not yet been clearly determined. As Crawford (1973:29) points out, "Observable gene frequencies in human populations are the product of all the forces of evolution, acting not one at a time but simultaneously." Unlike anthropometric studies, genetic-marker studies are difficult or often impossible to undertake on archaeological materials, so that although the historical picture given by them may be accurate, unless the conclusions arrived at concerning prehistory can be independently validated by other kinds of data, they cannot be given high credibility.

We turn now to particular theories concerning the origin of Sahul's populations. We stress initially that, although New Guinea, Australia and Tasmania were one continent throughout the early period of human occupancy, and we must think of its inhabitants as a single population, many studies have been restricted to one or other of the recent land masses and have not dealt with the whole area. But any conclusion must take account of the palaeo-environment, and the fact of one continent.

The most influential, in the sense of widely quoted, theory of Sahul population origins is that of Birdsell (1949, 1967, 1975, 1977). Birdsell's "trihybrid" theory (1977:114) sees three "types of populations contributing to the modern populations ... an initial wave of Oceanic Negritos ... a second kind called Murrayan [who] rolled back the original inhabitants in Australia proper ... [and] a third wave of peoples called Carpentarians from their positions around the gulf of that name". All three waves reached Australia during the last glaciation, two of them before about 25,000 years ago (1977:160–61). The first arrivals are said to have formed the basis of the present populations of New Guinea, Tasmania and some small areas of the Queensland rainforest, while the second occupied most of eastern and southern Australia.

The data on which this model is based were collected during 1938–39 in the course of field work ranging from Cape York to South Australia. Birdsell claims (1967:101) data collected in 1953–54 in the northern part of Western Australia "reinforce the conclusions", but those data have not been published. The original data consist of 14 measurements (4 body, 4 head, 6 facial) taken on a sample of 578 adult male Aborigines. From this group, Birdsell then selected 95 people from 12 tribes inhabiting rainforest areas near Cairns, 44 described as "most of the last surviving Aborigines" from south-eastern Australia, and 107 from around the Gulf of Carpentaria. The remaining 332 "racially intermediate" men were not further considered. The basis on which the samples were selected has never been clearly stated, but we suspect that it was based on appearance at least as much as on the genealogical records. For the total sample of 246 people, Birdsell calculated 15 indices (3 body, 5 head, 7 face) from the measurements taken, and it is these 29 traits which characterize his groups. We will not investigate Birdsell's statistical operations, but we do wish to draw attention to the fact that (a) his original measurements include such characters as stature, weight, head length and nasal height, any of which may be highly plastic in particular environments (cf. D. Hughes 1968); (b) the indices used are dependent on these same measurements; and (c) the use of such indices in multivariate analyses does give rise to many problems (Corruccini 1978). Another difficulty with the theory is the concept of population replacement. As Birdsell himself says (1977:164), "the problem [is] getting them ashore in sufficient numbers to replace earlier populations." We agree, and consider that this problem, the inadequate numerical basis of the theory, and the other problems mentioned are sufficient to remove the trihybrid theory from further consideration (see also L. Smith 1976:103–17).

The monogenetic origin of Sahul's population as a whole has not been strongly argued, although it is implied by a number of workers (e.g. Howells 1973:48). For Australian Aborigines, the strongest espousal is by Abbie (e.g. 1968, 1976). His data are similar to Birdsell's, namely 38 measurements on 205 "still mostly nomadic" males at six locations (three on the north coast, one on the south coast and two in the central desert). Like Birdsell, Abbie measured stature, weight, various parts of the trunk, the limbs and head, and also derived indices from these, but unlike Birdsell, he found no significant tribal or regional differences in his data. For the same reasons, his conclusions are not much stronger than Birdsell's.

Investigators of biochemical attributes have been more reluctant to propound clear theories of origin on the basis of their data, and we will not summarize their findings here (see Kirk 1976). Many recent workers are aware of the difficulty of drawing historical conclusions from these data and are prepared to do so only in very cautious terms. For example, Parsons and White (1976:227) point out that it is difficult if not impossible to confirm either of the hypotheses we have discussed above. They continue:

A semantic problem is the issue of the amount of divergence between two human populations that constitute a race. The term race is unfortunately arbitrary, since there are no biological isolating mechanisms between human populations, as characterise different species. The multiplicity of racial classifications in the literature is therefore not surprising. It could be said that populations differing by a certain arbitrary amount measured in terms of standardised genetic distances represent distinct races. But even the calculation of genetic distances themselves is arbitrary, depending on the

loci and/or the anthropometric measures used. Therefore even if heterogeneity exists between different Aboriginal groups it does not, in itself, without historical evidence of separate waves of migration of different races from outside Australia, argue for either of the above hypotheses.

After reviewing the evidence from a range of traits, the authors conclude (p. 242):

it would seem that part of the dilemma of the origin of the Australians concerns genetic changes after arrival in Australia due both to selection (at the macroenvironmental level) and genetic drift including founder effects at the microenvironmental level. Furthermore, we have no information as to the population sizes at the time of settlement, which if small could lead to further founder effects. Compared with most populations, it is difficult to avoid the conclusion that microenvironmental variation may be of considerable significance in the evolution of the Australian Aboriginal both during and after their arrival in Australia.

If studies on modern populations have been of little help, they were, until recently, the only data base available. Before 1970, so few dated prehistoric skeletal remains were known from Sahul that no attempt to use them for anything more than the most general studies was possible. Even now, the number of specimens older than 6000 years is considerably less than 100, while the number on which any data have been published and which are thus able to form the basis of any discussion is about twenty, of which twelve are from one site (Kow Swamp) and are penecontemporary (Table 4.1; Fig. 4.1).

Well before the Kow Swamp material was described, the fact that some prehistoric skulls were massive and rugged was recognized (e.g. Macintosh 1965:58). While there was some suggestion that archaic characteristics ("the mark of ancient Java") could be observed, Macintosh concluded that "differences between these relics and skulls of the present-day are not great". We reiterate that only about six skulls were the basis for this discussion (and for many others) and that, although they all came from south-eastern Australia, in neither time nor space could they be considered a population.

The Kow Swamp burials contained the whole

or fragmentary remains of at least forty individuals. They were excavated between 1969 and 1971 (Thorne and Macumber 1972) from a sand dune bordering an extinct lake in the southern part of the Murray drainage system. Five published radiocarbon dates on bone apatite and associated charcoal originally suggested that all the burials could be contemporaneous (c. 9500 bp) or were spread over a two thousand year period (8500–10,500 bp). However, Thorne later claimed (1976:96) that additional determinations showed that the burials ranged from 9300 to 13,000 years in age. The remains of fifteen adults were originally considered complete enough for detailed description (Thorne and Macumber 1972:316), but that analysis used ten specimens and a later one used nine (Thorne and Wilson 1977: note that this account says KS4 is female and KS5 male, while Thorne and Macumber, 1972, said the reverse. The twelve specimens used by Thorne in 1976 (p.105) include subadults.

Two major analyses of this material have been published (Thorne 1976, Thorne and Wilson 1977). These are based on 58 measurements of the crania and mandibles (1976: 46 cranial, 12 mandibular; 1977: 47 cranial, 11 mandibular), and the 1976 analysis also includes 10 cranial indices. The maximum number of measurements taken on any one individual was 49, the minimum 5, the mean 19; nearly one-half of the possible measurements were fronto-facial. These measurements are compared with the same set taken on museum material (1976: 170 adults; 1977: 167 adults), nearly all of which comes from within 100 km of Kow Swamp and which is assumed to be less than about 2000 years old (Thorne 1976:96). Both univariate (1976) and multivariate (1977) comparisons demonstrated, as indeed visual inspection had already shown, that a majority of the Kow Swamp specimens have significantly more rugged mandibles and faces, and more pronounced brow ridges and receding foreheads, than recent Aborigines from the same area. These features are also said to occur on the cranium from Cohuna on which similar measurements were taken. It should be noted that one of the nine Kow Swamp individuals (KS5) showed no significant differences from the museum collection, while all

TABLE 4.1
Human skeletal remains older than 6000 years

Site	No. of individuals	Date bp	Reference
Lake Mungo	2	I: 24,500–26,500	Bowler *et al.* (1970)
		III: 28,000–30,000	Bowler and Thorne (1976)
Talgai	1	14,000–16,000	Macintosh and Larnach (1976)
		12,000–18,000	Mulvaney (1975)
Lake Nitchie South	1	*c.* 15,300	Macintosh and Larnach (1976)
Keilor	1	*c.* 13,000	Macintosh and Larnach (1976)
Lake Tandou	1	*c.* 12,500	H. Allen (1972)
Kow Swamp	>40	9000–11,000[a]	Thorne and Macumber (1972)
		9000–13,000	Thorne and Wilson (1977)
Cohuna	1	Late Pleistocene	Macumber and Thorne (1975)
Mossgeil	1	>4800 }	Macintosh and Larnach (1976)
		?11,000 }	
Lake Nitchie	1	5000–6000	Mulvaney (1975)
		6620–7020	Macintosh (1971)
Green Gully	1	6460 ± 190 (NZ-676)	Mulvaney (1975)
Roonka	>1	?*c.* 6000	Pretty (1977)

[a] Published dates include two on bone collagen and three on apatite from skeletons, four on charcoal surrounding burials and three on freshwater shell associated with burials. The two dates accepted as indicating the range are 9300 ± 220 (ANU-619B) on apatite and 13000 ± 280 (ANU-1236) on shell.

measurements on the facial area of another (KS14) lay within the museum ranges.

Comparative analysis of the crania from Keilor, Lake Mungo I, Mossgeil and Lake Nitchie show that these also differ significantly from the modern sample. For Keilor, Lake Nitchie and Mossgeil the main difference is one of overall size, with frontal and facial features contributing, particularly in the case of the last. For Lake Mungo I, however, it is the small size, and measurements at the back and base of the cranium which are important. Different analyses of these crania emphasize different phenomena. When only frontal and facial observations are considered, two clear groups of skulls can be seen; in multivariate analyses in which these observations are included, it is Lake Mungo I alone that is highly distinctive.

We turn now to the interpretation of these results. Since the first announcement of the Kow Swamp discovery (1971), Thorne has maintained that two groups of fossil crania exist and that these are primarily distinguishable by frontal, facial and mandibular differences. He has argued that these two groups of crania represent two prehistoric populations. The rationale for this argument has not been fully published, but it includes the following reasons: (a) a majority of the fossil crania lie metrically, in terms of fronto-facial observations, outside the range of the modern sample; (b) extremes outside both ends of the current range are represented (Thorne 1977: Fig 1); and (c) it is unlikely that so many specimens would have been drawn haphazardly only from both ends of a single range (see also Thorne 1980). These populations are epitomized by the Lake Mungo I skeleton and the Kow Swamp group. Thorne has further argued (1977:196) that the differences between the two forms are so great that it is most unlikely that random or adaptive morphological trends would have been sufficient to derive a Kow Swamp type morphology from a Lake Mungo one in the short time available, and he has called Kow Swamp "an isolated and remnant population" (Thorne and Macumber 1972:319).

It is important to point out that, although the analyses show that in the fossil group as a whole cranial size was significantly greater than in more modern specimens from the same area, there have been no suggestions either that there are any significant differences in the post-cranial skeletons or that the form of the posterior and basal portions of the cranium are different from those of modern Aborigines. The formal differences in terms of shape are all concentrated around the face. Although a series of measurements of this difference can be made, it must also be clear that we are not dealing with a number of independent traits, each of which is a variable in its own right, but with a complex of interrelated morphological traits. For example, a very large mandible cannot normally occur without a large palate. It is therefore possible that the more our attention is focused on this region and the more measurements are taken on it, the greater the *overall* distinction of Late Pleistocene people will appear to be. It is also likely that the formal characteristics that appear different are in fact inter-related and linked to a common cause.

It has been suggested frequently, both in the scientific and popular literature (e.g. Deiley 1979; Jones 1979; Thorne 1971:89), that the occurrence of two populations in late Pleistocene Australia means that two groups of migrants with different skeletal morphologies originally settled the country. We do not agree: present data are insufficient to claim the existence of two groups. In particular, the number of specimens actually described is very small. For instance, if we consider the two specimens from Lake Mungo to represent a population covering 10,000 years and assume, very conservatively, an average population for the Murray–Darling drainage area of 20,000 people, with an average lifespan of 25 years, then the two fossil individuals described form 0.00025% of the total population. As Thorne said originally, "It must be admitted that the Mungo individual is slim evidence on which to define a population anatomically" (1971:88), and the discovery of Lake Mungo III (Bowler and Thorne 1976) improves the situation only marginally.

Another aspect of the sample size concerns the way it has been drawn. There is no reason to believe, for instance, that a random sample of the population has been brought to our attention. Using the same life-span as above, and assuming an average population of 100 people over a 4000 year period at Kow Swamp, we have a sample of about 0.25%. Certainly this is better than in most prehistoric situations (cf. Behrensmeyer 1975:38), but it is hardly adequate. In addition, particularly with small populations, there is no reason to believe that the full range of possible facial morphologies were evenly distributed in time and space. The current haphazard sampling may well be giving us a distorted picture. Certainly, if this is the case, we would expect more overlap in morphologies to become evident as more skeletons are examined.

A major argument for the existence of two populations in late Pleistocene south-eastern Australia is the difficulty of deriving the Kow Swamp facial morphology from the Lake Mungo one. Whether genetic drift and environmental adaptation could account for the shift from one to the other is a problem. Certainly, if all the people in south-eastern Australia 25,000–30,000 years ago were similar to Lake Mungo I, it would seem to be difficult genetically to derive a population with the frontal and facial characters of KS1 and KS5 from it. But this assumes the existence of two populations characterized in this way, and this is not the situation. Wolpoff (1980:330), who has recently examined the material, argues in the same vein. We conclude that, if two fossil human groups cannot be shown to exist, then we cannot argue that two groups of people, with very different facial morphologies, formed the original settlers of Australia.

If separate migrations are not likely, we must look for other explanations of the curious fronto-facial forms in some late Pleistocene Australian people. At least three arguments have been or can be proposed.

1. Pathology. No sign of this is present in the bones, and we agree with Thorne (1976:109) that this case will need to be made more precisely to be considered further.

2. Artificial cranial deformation. This has been suggested by Brothwell (1975) for Cohuna and KS5 and, by implication, for the rest of the Kow Swamp group. A cultural explanation like this would certainly remove many of the problems discussed above. However, we would expect artificial deformation to influence the entire cranium. This is the case among the Arawe of New Britain (Blackwood and Danby 1955) and other head-binding groups. By contrast, parietal

measurements and angles of the Cohuna and Kow Swamp skulls fall close to modern Australian Aboriginal norms. Stringer (1978:40) demonstrates that it is only the frontal of Cohuna that is aberrant. Also, the very large palates, mandibles and teeth cannot be accounted for by this explanation.

3. Environmental adaptation and drift. This is easy to believe but difficult to demonstrate, and only Wright (1976) has attempted it. The following argument is based on his. If it could be shown that generally speaking the late Pleistocene was a time of stress of a kind which would make it particularly adaptive to possess large teeth and jaws, then we could be part way towards an explanation. Thorne (1976:110) has argued that there is little evidence of environmental change in the area in terms of aquatic and terrestrial fauna, though he also said that fluctuations in the Willandra Lakes and similar systems in western New South Wales, culminating in their drying up some 14,000 years ago "undoubtedly placed considerable stress on human populations". We have already argued elsewhere (3.3) that this stress is manifested in the development of grass-seed grinding some 18,000–14,000 years ago and will suggest it is also manifested in the decline and demise of the megafauna (4.3). It seems likely that this is precisely the kind of stress that Wright's argument needs. However, there is no way of measuring "stress" of this kind other than by the results. The argument further requires that we have an adequate population sample before and during the period of stress. Since we do not, we cannot yet measure the change. Finally, although it is not completely necessary to the model, we would anticipate that, as the number of skeletal specimens older than 25,000 years increases, more of them will be rugged in the frontal and facial areas. In other words, it is likely that the physical differences between the Mungo and Kow Swamp populations were less than the current samples suggest. If this is so, then the degree *and* rapidity of change, which now appear too great to be believed, will be reduced.

Two other related matters need to be discussed. First, discussions of the fronto-facial morphology common at Kow Swamp frequently refer to it in terms of the "persistence" of Middle Pleistocene period cranial traits, as if skeletal attributes could somehow exist as an entity, encapsulated in a body (and part of a head) which continues to evolve towards the modern human form. This is not feasible. When a particular aspect of the body takes on or remains in a certain form, there must be good evolutionary reasons for it, usually related to the environment in some way, although the phenotypic expression of genotypic potential can be very variable. Thus the argument that the particular facial form of many Kow Swamp individuals indicates direct descent from *Homo erectus* must assume that the environmental conditions within Australia (and those that existed in whatever isolated nook of South-East Asia from which this line is supposed to have come) were such as to favour the continuation of heavy jaws and sloping foreheads. Further, we must also assume that these environmental pressures were dramatically eased in south-eastern Australia during the post-Pleistocene (say after 8000 $\pm$ 1000 years ago) so that faces rapidly altered towards their modern form. No exploration of the causes of this supposed change has been made. In the two-population model it is assumed that the Kow Swamp morphology was simply "bred out" or "swamped" by the more modern form, an explanation which in itself makes various assumptions about both the adaptedness of the Kow Swamp morphology and the relative size of populations with Mungo-like and Kow Swamp-like faces. These assumptions need to be made explicit, and justified, before proceeding further with this model.

The second problem arises from the cultural and social assumptions which must be made if a two-population model is to be satisfied. In its extreme form, the current model requires that two groups of people, looking like Mungo I and KS5 respectively, coexisted within a small and environmentally similar area without any natural barriers to peoples' movements for at least 20,000 years, and that they did so with little genetic interchange. This seems unlikely, not to say implausible.

It is true we can point only to the record of individual movement and genetic interchange among modern hunter-gatherers and traditional agriculturalists but, apart from those isolated on islands (e.g. Easter Island, Tasmania, New Zealand, Andamans), that record is always one of considerable contact. This is true even in areas of major relief, desert or other features which might be expected to pose barriers to communication (e.g. the New Guinea highlands). The Murray-Darling drainage poses no barriers of this kind. Nor is it likely that social barriers would have been maintained over this time. Even if we envisage that people looking like KS5 were the original residents of the Murray–Darling and the more "modern" people were newcomers, the idea of rigid barriers between two groups who lived not in geographically separate areas but intermingled strikes us as absurd. Whatever the social rules, the "Romeo and Juliet syndrome", albeit expressed in different idiom, is recorded in all human societies. Thus, in relation to the late Pleistocene skeletal material, we do not think that the existence of two populations with different fronto-facial morphologies has yet been demonstrated, and the proposal that this could have been possible gives rise to conflicts with general models of genetic change, environmental adaptation and social behaviour. There is little support in the fossil record for the idea that two major population groups entered Australia.

A different basis for a two-population model is the suggestion that Tasmanians were of a different origin to the rest of Australia's Aborigines. Originally deriving from the external appearance of Tasmanians, notably their shorter stature and tightly curled hair, some differentiation was confirmed by the study of skeletal material, especially in the nineteenth century (Kirk and Thorne 1976), although the degree of differentiation has always been a matter of interpretation. More recent studies of museum skeletal material carefully selected for authenticity (Giles 1976; Macintosh and Barker 1965) suggest that, although Tasmanians differed from Australians, their greatest similarities were with populations from south-eastern Australia, and their differences from some Australians were no greater than differences among Australians. Properly excavated and dated skeletal material is so scanty we hesitate to draw on it, but at least it does not contradict this assessment in any way (A. G. Wallace and Doran 1976).

In New Guinea, modern populations appear so different from those in Australia that it is often assumed that the two derive from different sources. This has seldom been argued in detail. Birdsell (1977) relates New Guineans and Tasmanians to the same source; Howells (1973, 1976) and Giles (1976) avoid the question.

We start by recognizing that no human fossil material of Pleistocene age is known from New Guinea. One fragmentary cranium from Aitape may be as old as 5000 years, but this is uncertain (Fenner 1941; Hossfeld 1965); all other material is less than 3000 years old (Freedman 1972; Pietrusewsky 1973). This is unfortunate, for the determination of relationships within the Sahul region needs archaeological as well as biological evidence (Howells 1976:142).

Modern biochemical and anthropometric data now seem to put New Guineans and Australians closer to each other than either are to any other group. Suggestions that New Guineans are more closely related to Africans seem to have no basis (Guiglielmino-Matessi *et al.* 1979; Howells 1973: 45–46), although the occurrence of such serum proteins as TFD_1 and $Ge^{Aborigine}$ among all three groups has suggested to Kirk (1971:331) that they may have an ancestral population in common.

Using measurements of modern crania, both Howells' (1976) and Giles' (1976) multivariate statistics led them to conclude that, while the Sahul populations are distinctive on a world basis, within the group New Guineans are distinct from Australians and, somewhat surprisingly, the former are more similar to Tasmanians. A similar distinction between the two main groups is evident in the biochemical evidence (Kirk 1976:341; no data are now available from Tasmania). Thus there appears to be a common Sahul sub-stratum, with subsequent divergent evolution, especially perhaps after the creation of Torres Strait.

The rate of micro-evolution appears to have been much greater in New Guinea than in Australia. Considerable differences in the incidence of genetic markers are found among closely adjacent groups (Kirk 1976; Terrell and Fagan 1975: 7–10, with refs). Since there appears to be no correlation of these differences with languages, language groups or other cultural phenomena, it is tempting to account for most or all of the variation by the operation of selection and drift working on small populations. However, why there should have been more variation in New Guinea than in Australia is unclear. Howells (1973:78) refers to greater warfare and isolation of communities, but this is difficult to substantiate even in the twentieth century, as can be seen by comparing the studies of Friedlaender (1975) in Bougainville, or Giles *et al.* (1970) in the Markham Valley with those of N. White in Arnhem Land (1976). Differences in variability do appear to be part of a common pattern (Friedlaender 1975:5).

Neither anthropometric nor biochemical evidence requires us to derive the Australian and New Guinean populations from two sources or two migrations or to consider that they evolved in total independence. It must be stressed again that both areas have been inhabited for at least 40,000 years and that they have very different environments. Despite climatic changes, the overall environmental contrasts of humid/dry and rainforest/woodland have persisted and, despite some genetic interchange, we can probably assume a high degree of local evolution and adaptation among the population. Environmental adaptations over some 1600 human generations may well explain many of the differences in stature, weight and other external variables (cf. Roberts 1978). As possible instances of this, we draw attention first to the relationship that Guiglielmino-Matessi *et al.* (1979) demonstrate between discriminant functions based on cranial measurements and climate. In terms of rainfall and vegetation structure (though not of course in temperature) Tasmania and New Guinea are perhaps more similar to each other than either is to Australia, and we wonder whether the similarity in cranial form seen by Howells, Giles and other workers can be explained in terms of adaptation to similar environments, as well as perhaps by some random drift. Certainly any direct link seems uncalled for at this time. Second, note that Birdsell's description (1975:525–26) of his major groups within Australia refers particularly to characters such as body size and weight, which correlate closely with temperature (Bergmann's rule). Some of the variability he has observed, if confirmed, may well be explained in those terms.

In concluding this section, we reiterate that none of the data presently available from Sahul require its population to be derived from more than one source, and local differentiation appears to be an adequate explanation for all variations that have been demonstrated, either in modern or prehistoric populations.

4.2 Flaked Stone Tools

The fact that Palaeolithic studies were first developed in Europe has been both a blessing and a curse to archaeologists. It has been a blessing (a) because the large numbers of well-preserved sites allowed researchers to destroy many sites while continuing to develop field techniques; (b) because human antiquity could be demonstrated through association with a sequence of extinct fauna; and (c) because one very large class of cultural remains, flaked stone tools, could be sorted into a series of types each with distinct morphological patterning, and it could be shown that these types occurred in such a consistent sequence that artefacts could be used as chronological indicators (Daniel 1975: 99–108, 122–139). The curse has been the assumption that the same antiquity and cultural patterning existed in all parts of the world, and that the purposes for which classifications of tools are required remained constant. In this section we propose to discuss briefly aspects of the European background and then to look at present and potential approaches to the Sahul artefacts.

For at least 150 years, until the development of radiometric dating, the overriding problem in organizing prehistoric material was its ordering in time. Time, not in terms of years but in terms of sequence, was the first requirement, for without time no arguments about the relatedness of events, or their causes, could be developed. Thus, within prehistory, the every-day importance of typology lay in its ability to temporally order material within, and especially between, sites. Given this need, it is not surprising that the recognizable formal patterns to which many artefacts were made were seized on and became the subject of elaborated and detailed study. Many such studies persist to the present day.

It must be pointed out that many classifications of stone tools, and hence their use in chronological ordering, were based on small samples of the total corpus of material. "Typical" forms were selected and the rest were ignored. Indeed, often only a small percentage of the artefacts was collected during excavation, as a visit to the spoil-heaps of many sites makes very plain. Finer and more careful excavations are revealing that the chronologies worked out before 1950 were correct, but only in rather gross terms.

The European sequences of flaked stone tools served a second function. They showed that there was a continual (though not continuous) rise in the number of tool types. In broad terms, this demonstrated the development of human technological proficiency through time, thus justifying the theoretical stages of human progress outlined by such anthropologists as Morgan and Tylor. More particularly, the rising number of tool types was assumed to be related to the increasing variety of tasks humans were carrying out, since a one-to-one correlation between tool form and tool function was assumed. Functional names (point, burin, scraper, etc.) were given to formal classes without any other justification being considered necessary.

That an increasing number of tool types demonstrates man's increasing cultural ability is still widely believed (e.g. Bodmer and Cavalli-Sforza 1976; J. G. D. Clark 1970; M. Harris 1971; Isaac 1972). The converse is usually also assumed to be true, so that areas in which an increase in the number and variety of flaked stone tool forms did not occur are seen as backward and marginal to human progress (see J. P. White 1977b). Sahul is one such area.

Since Europeans began to colonize Sahul in the eighteenth century it is not surprising to find that a European approach to prehistory, including prehistoric artefacts, has been the basis of most research. Mulvaney (1977) has documented how systematics based on the identification of formal tool types was the normal procedure through the nineteenth and early twentieth centuries. But, in contrast to Europe, neither a clear sequence of associations with extinct animals nor a sequence of artefact types could be readily demonstrated (see also Horton 1979a, 1981a). Classification of tool types thus appears to have been undertaken without any particular aim in view. As was the case in Europe, formal patterning was the basis of ordering, with names being sometimes functional (e.g. "chipped-back surgical knives") and sometimes descriptive (e.g. "spread-eagles"). Some challenge to these ideas came from those who saw Aborigines making and using stone tools. Observers such as Bates (Wright 1977) and Aiston (Horne and Aiston 1924) noted that many of the tools were *ad hoc*, consisting of the casual and immediate use of appropriately edged pieces of stone, and that formal patterning was far from common. But how these observations could be of use in the study of prehistory was not clear.

Excavations in Australia in the early twentieth century demonstrated the strength of European models. Tindale at Devon Downs (Hale and Tindale 1930) and McCarthy at Lapstone Creek (1948) both identified a small series of formally patterned stone and bone tools (e.g. *pirri*, *muduk*, *elouera*, Bondi point), and Tindale, in particular, insisted for many years (e.g. 1968) that the ordering at one site would be typical of that found throughout the country.

The earliest archaeological recognition of the difficulties with a formal typological approach is found in Mulvaney's report on Kenniff Cave (Mulvaney and Joyce 1965). Having previously bewailed the absence of carefully shaped stone tools in other sites (Mulvaney 1960, 1962b), at Kenniff he analysed the largest and least consistently patterned group of retouched artefacts, usually called "scrapers", in terms of variation in size and amount of retouch. Rather than seeking formal groups within this very broad class, which comprised some 80% of the total implements, his description emphasized the lack of sharp distinctions and the wide range of variation in tool forms. This approach has been pursued by Lampert (1971a) and to some extent by Jones (1971a) and Flood (1980). However, despite the recognition that formally distinct tools are uncommon, that types grade into one another and that one piece of stone may be used in several different ways, it is still general practice to divide tools up into formal classes. A

recent study by Lorblanchet and Jones (1979), for example, recognizes steep-edged, notched, concave, nosed and flat side-scrapers (*racloirs*) along with end-scrapers (*grattoirs*) and core-planes. The problems recognized by Mulvaney have thus been de-emphasized, and the failure to identify other than purely descriptive goals remains.

There is no doubt that within the Australian part of Sahul some intentionally formal shapes have been made, notably within the last 5000 years (5.2). These include points and backed tools, which unquestionably serve as chronological markers and are amenable to formal analysis (I. Glover 1969; Pearce 1977). Although no temporal trends are apparent as yet, some spatial variation has been observed (e.g. Morwood 1981). The occurrence of such tools has probably encouraged the idea that the detection of formal patterning is possible and potentially useful in other Australian assemblages.

The situation in the New Guinean part of Sahul has raised greater difficulties for formal analysts. Throughout the highlands and in most lowland areas, flaked stone tools with retouched edges do not appear to have been made to any formal patterns (for a specialized exception see J. Allen 1972). What is more, all recent demonstrations by highlanders consistently show unretouched edges are used as tools and the steeply retouched artefacts found in all archaeological deposits are rejected as inappropriate for any tasks (Strathern 1969; J. P. White 1967b, 1968a; B. Craig, pers. comm., 1967; R. Rappaport, pers. comm., 1967). Notwithstanding this lack of exact fit between ethnographic and archaeological evidence, J. P. White (1967b, 1969) has been led to argue not only that Mulvaney's approach is essentially correct, but that it should be taken considerably further, to the point which (a) denies that formal shape is a suitable criterion for any flaked tools in most sites and (b) affirms that analysis can proceed by looking at altered edges (whether this is due to retouch or use) and the changing occurrence of these edges through time. This approach, although using different categories, is still one of looking at the seriation of formal changes, as V. Watson's use of a similar set of observations makes explicit (V. Watson and Cole 1977).

In our view, most of the current studies of

stone tools are unsatisfactory, largely because they are still working within a framework designed to answer questions of temporal order. We have not yet accommodated the radiocarbon revolution. To do so, we need to reconsider Brew's wise words about classification (1949:46):

> ... classificatory systems are merely tools, tools of analysis, manufactured and employed by students, just as shovels, trowels and whisk brooms are ...
>
> The classifications are personal to the student and his problem and are conditioned by the nature of the information he seeks to extract.

In line with Brew's words, it is worth considering some approaches to stone artefacts and technology which seem to offer more promise than formal classifications. These approaches are promising because they are attempts to ask and answer questions about stone artefacts other than strictly chronological ones. Each requires a different classification of the stone material being studied.

Perhaps the most obvious problem is to decide which stones, of all those present in an assemblage, have been used, and if possible for what purpose. Within Sahul, it is very clear on the basis of the ethnographic evidence (cited above; see also Gould 1977b, 1980; Hayden 1979a) that formally patterned tools, or even stones with any major macroscopic traces of wear on them, form only part of the total range of tools used. Answers to any questions about such things as the range of tasks represented in prehistoric sites and their relative importance, or the relative economy in use of raw materials, must depend on identification of the full complement of tools. To this end, rigorous sampling and examination of the full range of specimens in assemblages will be necessary.

Once collected properly, the most promising analytical method seems to be the study of microscopic use-wear. This is now developing rapidly (Hayden 1979b; Keeley 1980). Other approaches, such as analysis of organic residues, may also be useful. Among Australian tools, attention has been concentrated on general experiments (Kamminga 1978, 1979) and on a few clearly defined kinds of use-wear (Bronstein 1977; T. A. Brown 1978; Gould et al. 1971; Jones 1971a; Kamminga 1977, 1979). It can now be said

with some certainty that adzes and adze slugs, as identified by their wear patterns, were used primarily on hardwood, that use-polished *elouera* from both the south-eastern and northern coasts were used on softwood or bark, and that reniform slate scrapers from South Australia were used to clean skins. The next stage, the somewhat laborious study of *all* stone artefacts from one or a series of sites in order to look at the total pattern of use-wear, and the analysis of this, has yet to be undertaken. No studies of comparable sophistication have been made in New Guinea, although there have been some initial attempts to look at the patterns of use-wear.

The second approach involves a study of raw materials used for stone artefacts and their distribution in space and time. Several papers have drawn attention to the distribution of stone materials in the archaeological record (e.g. Branagan and Megaw 1969; Byrne 1980; J. E. Glover 1979; P. J. Hughes et al. 1973; Jones 1971a; Sutherland 1972), and there are also some ethnographic studies to be considered (Thomson 1949). However, few analyses go beyond simple distributions. Jones (1971a) has shown that, over a period of 8000 years in north-west Tasmania, the distance from which raw material was drawn increased significantly. Lampert (1981) notes that in several areas the appearance of one class of formal implement correlates with increased use of stone from more distant sources. Among the Alyawara of Central Australia, O'Connell (1977) has shown not only that the representation of rock types in sites varies directly with distance from sources, but also that the occurrence of certain classes of tools is correlated with this, since particular rock types are preferred for them. In another Central Australian study, Gould (1978a, 1978b, 1980) argues that within the last century stone resources have been used not only because of the mechanical efficiency of the stone for certain tasks but because they had sacred associations. The result is that low-grade stone was used more frequently than might be expected. On the basis of this evidence, he suggests that, in one area of the central desert, the fact that a high proportion of backed blades were made in "exotic" stones leads us to believe not only in their symbolic associations, but also in their distribution through an expanded network of inter-linked lineages or some similar social network. Although this study has some weaknesses, among them a failure to consider sampling design or site formation processes, it is an interesting attempt to go beyond simple distributional data.

In the New Guinea area, the distribution of obsidian from the three known sources has attracted most attention. Along the south coast of Papua its occurrence in the first millennium AD and subsequent disappearance have been related to changing patterns of exchange relationships and especially the development of regional trade systems (J. Allen 1977a, 1980; Irwin 1977). Elsewhere, on the north coast and in the highlands, only its distribution has been noted.

A third approach concerns the technology of tool manufacture. The presence of only a few complex tool forms (notably Kimberley points) will mean that this study will be limited in its scope. However, understanding flaking processes can be important if we are trying to follow the logic behind the selection of raw material and quarry use, as well as when looking at technical knowledge in its own right. It will also be worth investigating whether apparent differences in tool morphology were intentional or the result of carrying through one flaking process to a greater degree than formerly. For example, Kamminga (1978:265–69) has shown that all tools classed as "burins" in Australia are likely to have been the chance result of flaking processes. Studies of manufacturing processes have been rare. Elkin (1948) and Akerman (1978, 1979) have described Kimberley point manufacture and Dickson (1975) has replicated backed points, but intensive studies of local technological processes have not been undertaken. The recent discovery that stone may have been heated before flaking (Akerman 1979) also opens up areas for investigation. In New Guinea, J. P. White (1968b) has shown that continued bipolar flaking produces a remnant core indistinguishable from artefacts identified as tools in Australia and other parts of the world. In many prehistoric situations these were clearly waste pieces, but in some they were used as tools subsequent to their creation. Each case will now require investigation. The fact that this technique is an economical method of producing thin, flat flakes, and by using it cores can be reduced to 1 cm^2, has been seen as the reason for its frequent use on "exotic" obsidian in Melanesia.

A fourth approach to stone artefacts is the study of long-term trends. Lorblanchet and Jones (1979) have drawn attention to the fact that over the last 25,000 years in several parts of temperate Australia there has been a change in some parameters of the non-formalized tools. The changes include decreases in the average weight of tools and flakes and in the angle of the striking platform, and increases in the range of tool sizes and in the length of edge retouched or used per gram of stone used. They attribute these technologically related changes to a gradually increasing efficiency in the use of stone. Although the numbers involved are small (800 tools drawn from seven sites) this is worth further investigation. It may be that this trend, the appearance of the "small-tool tradition" (5.2) and the increasing use of exotic stone were all related, though how they could have been requires further investigation.

Studies of the kind outlined above all show there is a need to study *all* the stone artefacts in a site or area, and to consider them as part of a functioning technology and economy. They suggest that classification and type listings of formally shaped tools are an inadequate study of what is often the largest part of our evidence. Mulvaney (1977:267) has suggested that formal typologies may be of value in the study of "cultural preference". However, while they may be of value in alerting us to the fact that more than utilitarian considerations were involved, studies involving technology, raw materials, variations in tool use and long-term trends are more likely to give us insights into prehistoric societies (cf. Isaac 1977).

A related matter appropriate for discussion here is the studies that have been made among present-day Australians and New Guineans of the procurement, manufacture, use and discard of stone artefacts. Such studies aim to provide data for, or actually derive models for use in, the interpretation of the archaeological record. The extent to which the present is like the past, and which generalizations derived from the present can be applied to the past, is the subject of a vigorous and widespread debate. Here we will simply indicate the nature of some of the studies which we believe may assist us to understand prehistory.

Initially it must be pointed out that there have been no long-term studies of groups of people wholly dependent on stone tools. A few, such as those by Gould in the Western Desert, have been among people for whom stone tools were an every-day reality, but the majority are based on "memory culture".

Studies of prehistoric procurement have already been mentioned: they concentrate on varieties of raw materials used and the distances over which these were transported. Studies of modern procurement are limited. Thomson's account (1949) of the use of Nillipidji quarry in northern Australia is among the most immediate, while Modjeska (J. P. White *et al.* 1977) also gives a good account of how stone is actually procured. Gould (1977b, 1980:123–26) and Hayden (1979a) outline the acquisition of quarried and non-quarried rocks.

The manufacture of stone tools has been given considerable attention both recently by Gould (1971) and Hayden (1979a) in Australia and by J. P. White (1968b; White and Thomas 1972; White *et al.* 1977) in New Guinea, and in earlier times in Australia by Elkin (1948), Horne and Aiston (1924), Roth (1904), Thomson (1949, 1964) and Tindale (1965). As a result of these studies we know a good deal about the manufacture of adzes, Kimberley points and simple flaked tools, but not much about many other artefacts. Some replicative studies now in progress will be helpful.

Studies of the uses of tools have been among the most helpful to prehistorians. One universal observation is the rarity of retouched tools. It is also notable that *ad hoc* resharpening frequently looks like intentional shaping and that unretouched flakes and chunks were commonly used. Hayden (1977a) describes the rarity of unretouched tools as the "biggest surprise" of his research but also points out that it is characteristic of all studies made in Sahul. The implications for the analysis of prehistoric assemblages are obvious (see also Hiscock 1980).

A second lesson we have learned from all ethnographic accounts is the extent to which flaked stone tools represent woodworking. Hayden (1977a:183) can cite only three rather specialized references to the processing of vegetable food in Australia, and sago pounders are the only comparable use in New Guinea (Rhoads 1980; J. P. White 1967b). In both areas flakes are used for scarifying and haircutting, while in Australia they are also used for circumcision and sub-incision. The degree to which flaked stone tools were used on other kinds of meat is unclear. In the New Guinea highlands, they do not appear to have been used at all, while Robinson (12 May 1832, Plomley 1966:517) suggests that Tasmanian natives used flakes or implements to "dissect their game", but it is not clear whether he actually observed this. In Australia, all observations on game butchering refer to unmodified flakes, with either these or other tools being used for skin-working in the south-east. It is notable that, to date, studies of use-wear confirm the dominant role of woodworking in producing heavily retouched tools, and further testing of this generalization can be expected.

A third lesson we have learned is that, by and large, the users of stone tools are male. This seems to be generally true throughout the world (e.g. see Gallagher 1972; MacCalman and Grobbelaar 1965; Miller 1979), though there are exceptions everywhere (e.g. Hayden 1977a). The probability that most prehistoric tools were used by males seems high, but although this principle may be used by prehistorians to interpret aspects of their data, its chances of being tested in the archaeological record seem low.

Attempts to determine the number of tools used per capita and the locations of their use and discard have been made, but all are limited by reliance on memory culture. However, since these are the best data we are likely to get (other than in relation to specialist technologies: see Gallagher 1972) we must work with them. Working in desert areas Gould (1977b, 1978b) and Hayden (1977a) have both arrived at estimates of the number of tools used per capita (Table 4.2). It is interesting to note that Hayden's estimate is four times as great as Gould's in relation to *ad hoc* unretouched flakes. J. P. White and Modjeska

(1978a) have estimated that in one area of the New Guinea highlands more than 150 flaked tools (in this case unretouched flakes) were used within a year by some individuals, who concentrated their wealth-producing activities on craft production, but other individuals would use few or even none. By contrast, estimates of use by Aborigines tend to assume that only small variations occurred between families and individuals (see also Luedtke 1979).

Locations of discard and, in particular, the long-term effects of these, have proved difficult to determine. Recent studies within the central desert show most tools are distributed at casual, task-specific locations, with only a few occurring at campsites (Gould 1978b says 0.5%). Of tools at campsites, a higher proportion is made of quarried stone and consists of curated tools than in the population as a whole.* In New Guinea, we think most tools would be deposited around individual men's houses, with some at the communal men's house and in the gardens. Over long periods we expect the degree of residence movement and the re-location of house sites to mask both individual and locational variability.

---

* A "curated" technology is one "in which a tool once produced or purchased is carefully curated and transported to and from locations in direct relationship to the anticipated performance of different activities" (L. R. Binford 1973:242). Such tools have a long use-life and a lower representation in archaeological sites than tools which are made, used and thrown away after use (see also L. R. Binford 1977; Schiffer 1976).

In no area have excavations, even of recently used sites, shown a high correlation between ethnographically known and archaeologically recovered data. Hayden (1979a: Chs 9, 10) illustrates this superbly. His account should be a starting point for any further discussion of flaked stone tools and what can be learned from them.

4.3 Megafauna: Dying and Dwarfing

One major change that occurred within Sahul during the Late Pleistocene was the extinction of a number of large marsupials and a reduction in the size of others. Whether and, if so, to what extent, humans were involved in these extinctions has been widely discussed. The problem is a complex one, which is unlikely to be solved using archaeological data alone.

First, there are some general problems which must be considered before discussing the evidence from the Late Pleistocene and the models which have been proposed. For a start, we need to know whether the most recent set of extinctions differed qualitatively or quantitatively from those earlier in the Pleistocene. Calaby (1976) points out that extinctions of large browsing diprotodontids and macropods occurred earlier in the Pleistocene and thus the most recent extinctions might have been the last examples of a long-continued process. Next, we need to know the full range of animals which became extinct. Were birds or reptiles involved as well as mammals?

TABLE 4.2
Numbers of stone tools estimated to be used per capita for various woodworking tasks in the Australian desert

Tasks per year	Stone tools used				
	Chopping tools		Adzes	Hand-held flakes	Adzes and hand-held flakes
	Hayden	Gould	Hayden	Hayden	Gould
1 Spear thrower	5	1	14	1	0.5
3 Adzing/throwing sticks	6	2	—	3	1
25 Spears	12	17	50	25	9
Resharpening spears	N/a	—	N/a	N/a	9
1 Bowl	5	—	—	—	1
4 Digging sticks	12	2	4	—	—

Sources: Gould (1977b); Hayden (1977a).
N/a = not available.

The importance of this question is shown by analogy with the North American situation, where Grayson's (1977) demonstration that many species of birds became extinct in the Late Pleistocene raised problems for the models of extinction favoured at that time. Within Sahul, we know that some birds did become extinct during the Late Pleistocene, but the exact dates of extinctions and thus their correlation with mammalian extinctions are unknown (J. Hope, pers. comm., 1980). Further, were all extinctions of the largest animals or only of the larger species within each genus? The latter appears to be the case within Sahul, and any explanation must take this into account.

Within Sahul, it has often been assumed that the extinction of the megafauna was a unitary phenomenon requiring a single explanation. For this to be true it needs to be shown that all extinctions were approximately contemporaneous throughout the continent. This has not been shown yet, and we could argue that the evidence suggests that extinctions occurred much earlier in the south-western part of the continent than elsewhere. If this was so, extinctions there may have occurred for different reasons.

We turn now to the evidence for Late Pleistocene extinctions. The extinct animals include two genera of kangaroos and one species (*Sthenurus, Procoptodon; Protemnodon* sp.), the family Diprotodontidae, several species of wombat (*Phascolonus* spp., *Vombatus* spp.), at least one large flightless bird (*Genyornis*) and a predator or scavenger (*Thylacoleo*) (Fig 4.2). Animals which have evolved into smaller forms

FIGURE 4.2. Reconstructions of some extinct Australian megafauna. a: *Procoptodon* sp.; b: *Zaglossus* sp.; c: *Vombatus* sp.; d: *Thylacoleo carnifex*; e: *Sthenurus occidentalis*; f: *Zygomaturus trilobus*. Scale: human, 180 cm tall. Sources: P. F. Murray (1978); Merrilees (1979). Courtesy: Royal Society of Western Australia and P. F. Murray.

during the last 30,000 years include koalas (*Phascolarctos*), wombats (*Phascolomys*), dasyurids (*Sarcophilus laniarius*) and three varieties of macropods (Wells 1978). One predator (*Thylacinus*) and a scavenger (*Sarcophilus*) are excluded from this account since they became extinct much later, and probably for different reasons (Horton 1980:91).

The remains of quite large numbers of many of these animals have been found in both cave (e.g. Archer *et al.* 1980; Gorter 1977; Merrilees 1968) and open sites (Marshall 1973; Tedford 1967). However, palaeontological identification has nearly always been the primary aim of researchers, and precise dating of sites or extinctions has rarely been undertaken. Thus, although there are many "Late Pleistocene" sites, whether they are 20,000 or 100,000 years old is usually not known.

Until recently, clear temporal overlap between extinct animals and prehistoric humans had not been demonstrated, and a clear association between the two is still elusive. In 1968, when the evidence was reviewed by two scholars (Jones 1968; Merrilees 1968), the best evidence for such an association appeared to be at Lake Menindee and at Keilor.

Lake Menindee lies some 250 km north-west of Lake Mungo, and it too is bordered on the eastern side by a wind-and-water-lain crescent-shaped dune (lunette). In the northern end of the lunette, specimens of twelve extinct species were recovered from a horizon said to produce radiocarbon dates of between 16,000 and 25,000 years. Some flaked stone tools were also reported to have come from the same horizon, while one macropod mandible was said to be charred by fire. However, inconsistencies between the various reports, the wide range of dates and the lack of a clearly defined geomorphological sequence in the lunette means that this evidence should not be taken as conclusive.

At Keilor, remains of five extinct and four dwarfed species have been found in the D Clay, along with humanly struck stone flakes and some carbon. In all cases, only isolated bones rather than whole or part animals have been found, and none of the specimens were burnt or associated with a campsite. Thus the conditions of association appear to derive from the nature of

site formation rather than from any original relationship.

Within the last few years, several sites containing extinct fauna have been more precisely dated. The best example is from the swamp deposit at Lancefield, Victoria (Gillespie *et al.* 1978). The stratigraphy of this site consisted of a bone bed some 2000 m^2 in area, resting on green clay and sealed in by about 70 cm of prehistoric black clay. Below the bone bed at one point, and cut into the clay, was a small channel containing gravelly clay, bone fragments and charcoal. The charcoal has been dated to 25,200 ± 800 (SUA-685) and 26,600 ± 650 (SUA-538); bone apatite from the bone bed has given a minimum age of 19,800 ± 450 (GX-4118A). The animals present included *Macropus titan* (90%) and three other species of extinct kangaroo, *Diprotodon* sp., *Genyornis* sp. and emu. The bones themselves displayed no direct effects of human action (cutting, charring, etc.) and only two quartzite artefacts were found in the areas excavated. This suggests that human responsibility for the bone accumulation is far from clear, and indeed the excavators have not agreed among themselves on the cause of it, though Horton and Wright (1981) suggest that debris from *Thylacoleo* feeding is a likely cause. This site clearly documents the existence of a range of extinct animals well into the period of human occupation.

Confirmatory evidence of this dating has now been found in several sites in southern Australia, although the nature of the interaction between fauna and humans is nowhere clearly delineated, as the following examples demonstrate.

At the Willandra Lakes, McIntyre and Hope (1978) found eight fragments of *Procoptodon* jaws or teeth, all in blow-outs but all in situations where they were closely and not directly associated with similarly eroded artefactual material. Most of the material probably came from the Mungo unit and was originally deposited between 45,000 and 20,000 years ago.

On Kangaroo Island, three molar fragments of an extinct kangaroo *Sthenurus* cf. *gilli* were found in and around an occupation level (III) in Seton rock-shelter (J. Hope *et al.* 1977). The fragmentation of the bone in levels II–IV at this site was such that it seems likely that the scavenger *Sarcophilus* was the cause of accumulation. However, the excavators suggest that in the specific case of *Sthenurus* the bones may have been carried into the shelter by humans and subsequently gnawed by *Sarcophilus*. No case is made for this special pleading. It seems unlikely that the *Sthenurus* bones have been re-worked from an older deposit, as has been the case in other sites (e.g. Milham and Thompson 1976). Level III is dated on charcoal to 16,110 ± 100 (ANU-1221), so that *Sthenurus* is unlikely to be much older than this.

Sthenurus sp., along with other extinct Pleistocene genera (*Diprotodon*, *Zygomaturus* and *Protemnodon*) were reported by J. Hope *et al.* (1977) at the Rocky River site, also on Kangaroo Island. A recent small excavation by the same authors suggests that the bones of different animals were separately piled up at the edge of a swamp in marly peats, and they say that a preliminary radiocarbon date of 19,000 years has been obtained from the organic sediments. There was no direct evidence of human activity, but the sorting and piling of bones was certainly suggestive of it.

At Clogg's Cave, in Victoria, a *Sthenurus orientalis* mandible was found in a level just below a radiocarbon date of 22,980 ± 2000 (ANU-1220) (Flood 1980:260). No human artefacts were found in this layer, and the bones found appear to be the result of carnivore or scavenger action. The date is consistent with that from Lancefield.

In the central Tasmanian highlands, Beginner's Luck Cave produced a single bone probably from *Macropus titan* in a level (sub-unit B) which also contained many stone flakes and food bones. A date on charcoal from this level is 20,650 ± 1790 (GaK-7081) and a similar aspartic acid racemization date has been obtained on bone material from the same level (P. F. Murray *et al.* 1980). Both *Macropus titan* and *Sthenurus occidentalis* remains have been found in cave colluvium in nearby Titan's Shelter. This material is probably younger than 20,000 years, but no human remains or effects on the bone have been shown (Goede and Murray 1979).

In the south-west of Australia, many bones from Mammoth Cave display marks of crushing and impact, standardized breakage patterns, charring and, in one case, an apparently artificial notch (Archer *et al.* 1980). Among these bones are specimens from *Sthenurus* sp. and *Zygomaturus*. Archer and his colleagues believe that human activity was the most likely cause of many of these effects; they discount natural actions such as stream flow as the original cause of the accumulation. No other signs of human occupation have been recorded from the cave, most of which was excavated in 1909–15. The deposits contained some charcoal, but its age is beyond the range of routine radiocarbon dating (older than 37,000 years).

A similar age for two extinct species of *Sthenurus*, as well as *Vombatus hacketti*, *Protemnodon* and *Zygomaturus* seems to be indicated for Devil's Lair, also in south-west Australia (Balme *et al.* 1978). Specimens of these animals mostly occurred in layers 30–39, which have a pooled mean radiocarbon date of 33,150 ± 840, but at least eight of the twelve specimens were judged to be re-worked from older deposits. A few artefacts were found below level 30 (Balme 1980; Dortch 1979b), but these may also have been re-worked or washed into the cave and thus fortuitously associated with the extinct fauna. The excavators concluded that the coexistence of man with extinct animals was not proven by the Devil's Lair deposit. It is worth noting here that levels above 30 contained large numbers of animal bones (e.g. the minimum number of larger mammals was 320 for layers 21–29) many of which, on the evidence of charring, seem to have occurred in the site as a result of human activity. These bones are all of extant animals.

Extinctions were not restricted to the southern part of the continent. Extinct giant species are known from several locations in the New Guinea highlands (Plane 1972; P. W. Williams *et al.* 1972), as well as in northern Australia. In only one case was there an apparent association with human activity. At Nombe shelter *Protemnodon* remains were found in the basal layers, which also contained human artefacts (Mountain 1979). The excavator remarks that the direct association between the bones and artefacts is still being tested. A probable date for the deposit is 10,000–15,000 years old.

To summarize the situation, it now seems clear that a number of species, and sometimes considerable numbers, of now extinct animals coexisted with humans in some parts of Sahul down to at least 20,000 years ago. However, at present we have no clear evidence of whether they were hunted or eaten on any large scale, though occasional use of them seems reasonably well demonstrated.

Before discussing the various possible extinction mechanisms, we draw attention to a potential variation in archaeological visibility which may be affecting interpretations of this problem. It is possible that the size of animals affected their transportation after killing. When Aborigines encountered beached whales in the eighteenth and nineteenth centuries, rather than butchering the animal and removing it to the campsite, people moved to the animal and ate it *in situ*. If this was also the practice with the largest land animals in the Pleistocene, we would not expect to find many large animal bones in archaeological campsites, or many indications of human activity in association with deposits of animal bones. Bowdler (1977), the strongest opponent of the idea that Aborigines hunted megafauna, draws attention to the fact that most Pleistocene sites contain neither megafauna nor many bones of animals larger than wallabies. While for some sites this may be attributed to their location, it is unlikely to be the case everywhere, for example at the Willandra Lakes sites. We suggest that, just as in more recent times we have a skewed archaeological sample, with few kangaroo-cooking sites being located compared to shell midden accumulations, so during the Pleistocene the larger game-using sites were sufficiently differentiated behaviourally not to become part of the normal campsite record. Thus, part of the reason for the absence of large-game sites may be that we have not yet located them.

The reasons why the Australian megafauna became extinct have been debated for 130 years (Horton 1980). The two most favoured causes have been humans and climatic change, acting either directly or indirectly in each case. Those who have favoured the first cause have seen humans preying on animals or firing their habitats. Those who have favoured the second cause have suggested that the direct effects of catastrophe or climatic fluctuations that exceeded a species' tolerance can be blamed;

alternatively, they see the indirect effects of vegetation change and "competitive exclusion" as primary causes.

Other possible causes, such as new diseases, have not been seriously canvassed in Australia. Our view on this problem has fluctuated over the years, and while we still find it difficult not to believe humans had a hand in the extinctions, it seems to us that Schrire (1980:10) may well be right when she says that "there may well be no single unifying principle [sic: mechanism?] underlying Pleistocene extinctions, and the matter needs to be seen in terms of its details, contradictions and complexities". We cannot, at this point in Australian prehistory, examine the matter in great detail: we do not have data of the richness available in North America or even southern Africa (Klein 1980). But we can examine and evaluate some of the explanations which have been given.

Human predation as the single cause of the extinctions in Sahul has not been seriously promoted within Australia during this century, though it was suggested by N. Tindale (Horton 1980). The two strongest recent adherents to a human cause (Jones 1968, 1973; Merrilees 1968) have favoured a combination of hunting and habitat alteration due to fire and have emphasized the latter. It is perhaps worth stressing that, although "Pleistocene overkill" is commonly mentioned, and even seen as the primary cause in some of the more popular literature, none of the researchers into the problem have developed a model as crudely unicausal as that of P. Martin for North America (1978, 1973; Mosimann and Martin 1975). Even Jones' original model only says that man's arrival was "the decisive factor" (1968:205), and in no case has human predation been identified as a cause as precisely as Klein (1980) has been able to do for some animals in the Cape zone of southern Africa.

Even if intensive hunting was not the sole cause of extinction, we can still outline the probable nature of the human–megafauna interaction and model its implications. These certainly include the possibility of considerable human assistance in the extinction of some species. We begin with the presumption that hunter-gatherers were, for the most part if not always, economically efficient foragers. Their food-selection strategies, including choice of animal prey, can be explained in cost-benefit terms. These terms are specifically those defined by models derived from optimal foraging theory (Hawkes *et al.*, in press; O'Connell and Hawkes 1981a, 1981b; Winterhalder 1981). Among other things, the models imply that whether a species of prey is taken when encountered depends on its rank relative to other prey in a cost-benefit analysis, and on the abundance of higher-ranked prey in the area. Without explaining the details, we can say that the higher a particular species ranks, the more likely it is to be taken. We note that this implies that Sahul hunter-gatherers would have been "generalists" and their prey selection strategy opportunistic within a range of high-ranked species. There is no evidence that any Sahul populations became "specialists" dependent on some species whatever their cost.

A priori, large animals seem to us likely to have been ranked higher than smaller game and plant foods. This is supported by a limited range of data from modern Ache and Alyawara hunter-gatherers (refs above). We assume that at least some large Pleistocene animals would have been ranked very high relative to other available foods. This seems likely in view of their size, unfamiliarity with human predators, and the fact that they could have been killed with simple and easily made (i.e. low-cost) spears. These animals should have been taken whenever encountered.

A useful analogy here is the relationship between Aborigines and European cattle in the nineteenth century. In many parts of Australia, Aboriginal hunting techniques were easily adapted to kill these animals, which looked and acted very differently to any other prey (J. P. White and O'Connell 1979). We have noted, but not yet explored, two interesting aspects of this analogy. One is that in arid parts of Australia cattle were added to Aboriginal diets immediately they became available, in spite of the large penalties (whipping, shooting) connected with taking them. This suggests that they ranked very high in cost-benefit terms. The other is that, in the much richer Arnhem Land environment, European-introduced buffalo (*Bubalis bubalis*) were usually avoided by Aborigines unless guns and wheeled vehicles were available, since they were so large, fast and fierce; that is, the cost was too

high. Such, indeed, may have been the case with some Pleistocene megafauna, but it seems unlikely to have been true of all of them. We are thus strongly of the opinion that Aborigines preyed on megafauna when they were available.

Our final proposition is that "generalist" hunters can cause extinctions, especially among animals which rank high in calorific return for their search, killing and cooking time. This can be so because such prey will usually be taken if encountered no matter how rare they may be. If death-rates from predation and other causes exceed a species' birth-rate, then that species will become extinct.

The other human impact on the megafauna could have been through firing, though it is difficult to determine the long-term effect of this either on the vegetation or directly on animals whose mode of existence is unknown. There can be little doubt that humans have used fire extensively, probably from soon after their arrival in Sahul (Hallam 1975; Jones 1968). But it is also true that many elements of the distinctive Australian flora are adapted to fire, and some need periodic fires to keep them in existence. Fairly frequent fires must therefore have been a normal feature of the environment throughout the Pleistocene, and their incidence may have increased as the widespread mid-Tertiary rain-forests were slowly replaced by woodlands and grasslands (Calaby 1976; and see various papers in A. M. Gill *et al.* 1981). The megafauna cannot have been unused to fire, although human firing of the landscape may have been of a different kind and had different effects to natural fires. Throughout Australia today and in some parts of New Guinea people burn off small and large tracts of country either seasonally or whenever they are able. The immediate effects of this are to remove dense undergrowth, signal their presence, make prey and harmful snakes visible and allow fresh growth (and thus better hunting) when the rains come. These humanly induced fires are nearly always on a relatively small scale, and their usual effect is to recycle nutrients back into the soil and, over time, to create a much more patchy array of habitats, which probably helps increase the numbers of some animals, the range of plant foods and the diversity of local faunal communities (Latz and Griffin 1978).

It could be argued that those species which became extinct were the ones which were deleteriously affected by the changed firing pattern, but to make the case it would be necessary to have a much greater knowledge of food habits and mating and breeding patterns of extinct animals than we are likely to acquire.

The long-term effect of human firing appears to have been considerable, at least within Australia. The best measure of this is the rapid changes that occurred in many parts of Australia when Aborigines and the pressure of their firing were removed in the nineteenth century. Over large areas of Tasmania and in south-eastern and south-western Australia the savannah grasslands which delighted the earliest Europeans were replaced by dense scrub within a few decades (Hallam 1975; Jones 1968, 1969, 1975). Other studies (Story 1969, 1976) suggest that the tropical north of Australia would have many more stands of tropical rainforest but for Aboriginal firing (see also Jones 1975), while the role of fire in creating and maintaining grasslands seems well documented in parts of New Guinea (Brookfield with Hart 1971:51–53). But it is at least arguable that firing by the Aborigines did little more than reinforce the trend towards grassland already present in pre-human times, and if this is so then the consequences for animals should have been only minor.

Assessment of both the short-term and long-term effects of fire depends to a degree on the subsistence regimes of extinct animals. In southern Africa extinctions occurred almost exclusively among grazing animals, and although environmental change pressured animal populations, it seems to have been too light to have endangered their survival. In Sahul the situation is less clear, since almost nothing is known of the diets of the extinct animals. On the basis of dentition, Wells (1978) claims that three of the four sub-families of Diprotodontidae were browsers, but *Palorchestes* was a grazer; P. F. Murray (1978) says all were browsers. One diprotodon, recovered with stomach contents intact, had eaten its final meals of bluebush and saltbush. But was this its typical diet? (Schrire 1980). Among the macropods, *Procoptodon* has been called both a browser (Wells 1978) and a grazer (Sanson 1978), and there are similar disagree-

ments concerning *Sthenurus* and *Protemnodon*. Taking another line of evidence, it might be argued that *Macropus titan* and *Procoptodon* were probably grazers since their remains are the most common in the almost treeless areas around Lancefield (Ladd 1976) and the Willandra Lakes respectively. An incidence of seven per cent of *Protemnodon anak* at Lancefield may suggest that this too was a grazer (Gillespie *et al.* 1978), while the very low numbers of several other species might suggest they were browsers, though only on the unlikely assumption that recruitment into the swamp was not selective.

We can summarize the effects of human firing by saying that, while it may have interfered with breeding or lifestyles in some areas, it seems unlikely to have been the sole cause of extinction throughout Sahul.

The other major presumed cause of extinction is climatic. The effects of climatic change are seen either in terms of catastrophe or as altering the range of climatic variability. There is no doubt that during the Late Pleistocene the climate changed throughout Sahul, but climatic changes of similar magnitude had been experienced earlier in the Pleistocene, and as far as we know without such drastic effects on fauna. The survival of megafauna through the Pleistocene supposes a certain adaptability to environmental change. Thus, with this class of explanations in particular, we need to move away from Sahul-wide considerations and focus more on different environmental zones and the climatic changes that occurred within them (cf. Klein 1980). For south-eastern Australia, Horton (1980) has drawn attention to the period of extreme aridity evidenced at Lake Mungo and other sites 18,000–15,000 years ago, and he suggests that a series of major droughts would have forced large animals to congregate around sources of free water, eventually dying of starvation or thirst as they ate out the landscape. His view is clearly catastrophist (p. 95):

> A series of droughts in an area could cause the deaths of vast numbers of megafauna. The few survivors could not have repopulated quickly because of reproductive problems ... Similarly, immigration from areas untouched by drought would have been too slow to be effective before those areas in turn were hit by drought.

Although this view is difficult to test — "such droughts need not show up on the pollen record because they can be of short duration" — it does not seem an unlikely model for inland south-eastern Australia. What is much less certain is its applicability to the south-west or the tropical north.

Similar problems also affect Main's (1978) sophisticated analysis of the physiological requirements of large macropods, which he suggests may have been similar in all the large extinct animals. Main's interpretation of dietary and water needs suggests that it was the increasing amplitude of short-term climatic fluctuations, together with a long-term arid trend, which were the principal components in the Late Pleistocene extinctions (p. 181):

> ... once the environment changed from a steady or even declining state to an oscillatory one with respect to drought and temperature, biological factors other than large body size began to operate. The result was that extinctions became commonplace for all species that were large and lacked the variability in size or age to maturity to exploit the new competitive ecology ...

There are two particular strengths in Main's model. It is the only one that satisfactorily explains the late Pleistocene dwarfing and current sexual dimorphism of some forms, as well as the extinction of others. By contrast, a humanly caused dwarfing involves a rather improbable Darwinian-style explanation which suggests that larger animals make easier targets and are thus hit more often. (If they were being selected because they produced higher yields of protein per kill (W. E. Edwards 1967), the model becomes less improbable.) The other strong point is that we can assume that climatic changes other than aridity would have had the same effect on animals in other environments. Further, it should be noted that human predation on megafauna is not precluded, and this may have caused the "hastening of extinction of already doomed species" that Calaby (1976:27) has suggested.

Of the indirect effects of climatic change, vegetation change has already been discussed, and competitive exclusion may be briefly dismissed as simply being an animal-centric view of changes in climatic equability (Witter 1978).

In summary, we doubt that "the cause" of late Pleistocene extinctions in Sahul can be established in any absolute sense. We can certainly reject the view that these extinctions were like those of the moas in New Zealand or dodos in Mauritius. We can also reject a model similar to Martin's for the Americas. Klein's model of African hunters mismanaging resources by hunting a diminishing population to levels below which it could not recover seems more likely, but it can only be tested when larger samples are available. Whether the causes of population shrinkage were disastrous droughts, more perturbed climates or something else remains unclear. The causes may have varied in different parts of the country.

Finally, we point out that there are two reasons why prehistorians are interested in extinctions. One is to assess the impact which early Sahul people had upon their environment, and thus on our views of hunter-gatherers. If the extinction of some Pleistocene species was wholly or even partly the result of human action, then we cannot so easily think of these people as careful environmental managers with a very long-term perspective. Rather, like other humans, they may have been only working for short-term gains, without considering the long-term effects. The second reason for interest is to see what effect the disappearance of these resources had on human populations in different parts of Sahul. This question will only develop as details of the extinction process become clearer, but one hint which has already been noted is that extinctions and the earliest seed-grinders occurred about the same time (O'Connell and Hawkes 1981a). We do not anticipate that the question will be easy to answer — though we may be able to learn from the debate over a more recent resource loss in Tasmania (5.4) — but it is a question which bears strongly on the extent of change in Sahul prehistory.

Chapter 5

Australia: The Last 10,000 Years

5.1 Introduction

The date at which this chapter begins is arbitrarily chosen, for unlike the situation in some other parts of the world (e.g. northern Europe) there is no one period of drastic climatic change which ends the Pleistocene and begins the Recent period. Consequently, there is no moment when a sudden and widespread change is forced upon human existence throughout Australia.

In this introduction we discuss three topics. First, we briefly outline the evidence for environmental change and its impacts on human life. Next, we point out to what extent the evidence is sufficient for us to investigate prehistory from regional and local perspectives, and we discuss some of the problems which this poses. Finally, we introduce the major themes of the chapter and set them into a broader context.

Environmental Change

The most obvious change during the Recent period was the post-glacial rise in sea level. This created three major islands and a host of minor ones, thus destroying the geographic unity of Sahul. Significant times were at 12,000 bp when

Australia and Tasmania were sundered, at 8000 bp when the isthmus between New Guinea and Australia was finally breached and at 6000 bp when present-day sea levels were first reached. The rise in sea level drowned large areas of country and would have directly affected many people (Blainey 1975; Jones 1977b). But this rise was just one expression of broader climatic changes which affected even larger areas over a longer period.

About 16,000 years ago sea level started to rise from its lowest point (-160 m), and by 14,000 years ago much of the Arafura plain, the southern Bight and the Bassian plain were flooded

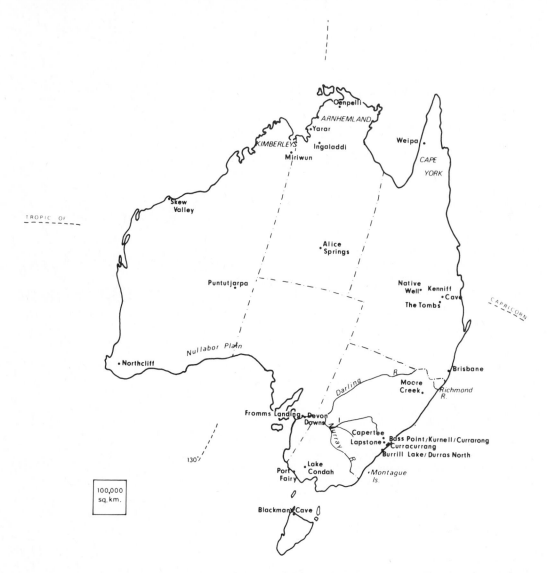

FIGURE 5.1. Locations of sites referred to in sections 5.2 and 5.3. The following sites are all within a 50 km radius of Oenpelli: Cannon Hill I, Leichhardt, Lindner, Malangangerr, Nawamoyn, Ngarradj Warde Djobkeng, Tyimede I, Tyimede II.

(Chappell 1976). By this time many inland lakes in south-eastern Australia were completely dry (Bowler *et al.* 1976). In the south-eastern highlands, reduction in the snow and ice cover began by at least 13,000 years ago, though major vegetation changes occurred rather later. Similar changes occurred in Tasmania, but rather later, as is expectable from its more southerly location (Bowler *et al.* 1976; Macphail 1979).

Along with the increasing warmth, rainfall became slightly greater in some areas. For example, by 11,000 bp it increased around Australia's northern coasts. Bowler *et al.* (1976) draw on pollen and geomorphic evidence to conclude that by 10,000–5000 bp the "humid southern fringe" of the continent was relatively wetter than it had been in the preceding 10,000 years. They suggest that wetness reached a peak about 7500–5000 years ago. However, evidence from some areas suggests that the wettest time may have been rather earlier (e.g. Ross 1981).

These climatic changes must have affected human life, but the data are inadequate to document what happened. This is because of both a lack of concentrated research and the inadequacy of the archaeological evidence. Almost no data are available on the prehistoric plants used at various times, and fauna has not been shown to be a sensitive enough marker to be related directly to these climatic variations. Thus, while for inland areas we may suspect that economic changes occurred, and that these changes were not synchronous in all areas, we cannot show this.

One region where the effects of environmental changes can be seen is along the coasts. About 8000 years ago the sea came close enough to its present level to allow shell middens to accumulate and be preserved along extant shorelines. Such middens have been excavated in Arnhem Land (C. White 1971), south-eastern Australia (P. J. Hughes and Djohadze 1980) and Tasmania (Jones 1971a) and probably occur elsewhere. An even earlier date of 9320 ± 160 (SUA-484) has been claimed for the base of a midden on the north coast of New South Wales (Connah 1976), but the charcoal that was dated may in fact derive from the beach ridge on which the midden rests and the date has not been duplicated (J. Coleman 1978:52–53).

It is important to recognize that coastal environments the same as today's were not always formed as soon as the sea reached its present level. For example, along the south-east Australian coast the lagoons and their sandy barrier systems, as well as the extensive rock platforms, needed time and stable sea levels to form. Today, many shellfish live in these environments. When these littoral environments were smaller, shellfish numbers would have been significantly less than they are today. Thus, 6000 years ago the importance of shellfish to humans is likely to have been less than it later became. Similar kinds of environmental change are known elsewhere (e.g. Chappell 1982; Luebbers 1978). By contrast, the steep rocky coasts of north-west Tasmania differ little today from their appearance 8000 years ago (Jones 1971a), so that there has been little difference in the range and quantity of shellfish available. Overall, we stress that the same environmental change may have had different implications for human life in different places (see also Callaghan 1980).

It is also important to remember that the stabilization of sea level has allowed the evidence of coastal exploitation to survive. The fact that all coastal middens are less than 8000 years old is not because prehistoric economies changed drastically then, but because the evidence has not been wiped out by the rising sea.

Regional Patterns

Both the quantity and range of archaeological evidence from the last 10,000 years is much greater than from earlier periods, and much of it comes from very recent times. This means that in writing of this period there is an increasing possibility of investigating regional and local events and adaptations. Before doing so, however, we need to consider the concept of regionality in prehistoric data and explore the relationship between sets of archaeological data and social and other groupings in recent Aboriginal societies. This must be done because the youngest archaeological materials overlap the rich ethnographic record of the eighteenth and nineteenth centuries and can be interpreted with its aid. It is very tempting to extend such interpretations well back into the past. But to what extent is this valid? We will concentrate on the relationship between Aboriginally-defined groups and sets of similar archaeological materials.

Aboriginal societies of the recent past were certainly sufficiently similar for us to identify features common to all of them. It is also relatively easy to define bands and other very small-scale groups which were basic to everyday life. But any attempt to identify intermediate-sized groups has proved very difficult, whether we use social or material traits. For example, patriclans or languages did not have simple, clearly defined boundaries. Attempts to correlate various cultural features, such as languages, art styles, artefact forms, legends, or social and ritual practices have not led to any coherent, recognizable clusters. This situation is true in other parts of the world also (e.g. Lee 1980), including parts of New Guinea. Where recognizable cultural groups do exist among low-density populations, the stylistic aspects of things (fringes on costumes, etc.) are often used as boundary markers (Hodder 1978). One of the more notable features of Australian life, even in areas of semi-sedentism, was the lack of material things and the enormous elaboration of social and spiritual life. We suggest that among Aboriginal groups these intellectual structures, along with language variations, which were carefully noticed by the speakers, replaced the stylistic variability in material goods which was developed in other contexts such as the European Upper Palaeolithic or the North American Archaic (cf. Conkey 1978).

A similar problem occurs in studying human–environment interactions. We can generalize about Australia-wide behaviours, but we have difficulties with smaller-scale patterns. At the continental level there was, in the recent past, a strong relationship between population density and primary productivity. (Birdsell in 1953 showed that tribal area and rainfall were reasonable measures of these, though this relationship was weaker where water was not the critical resource it was in arid areas.) A regular pattern in economic life was also apparent, with population aggregation at times of maximum resource availability and dispersal in poorer times. The spatial and temporal amplitudes of these movements, and the numbers of people involved, varied according to local environments. Thus detailed knowledge of local environments should allow us to infer the general pattern of human life and interpret archaeological sites in these terms (e.g. H. Allen 1972; McBryde 1974: Ch.9; Poiner 1976; C. White and Peterson 1969). However considerable inter-site variation is likely to be found, since we know that modern Aboriginal groups primarily exploit local environments. For example, Meehan's (1977a) study of shellfish-gathering by Anbara people makes it clear that the immediately local environment provides most of the food. We can thus predict that a site will only document a small part of the total environment over which a single group ranged. Therefore, unless we have data from a large number of sites, the relationship between the data and the seasonally varying subsistence activities predicted on environmental knowledge will usually be an inferential one.

Can any groups of people larger than the creators of single sites but smaller than Australia as a whole be defined in the recent past? Peterson (1976) has bravely suggested that Kroeber-style "culture areas" can be based on the major drainages (Fig. 5.2). However, using our current general knowledge of linguistic and cultural differences (1976:65) he requires seventeen culture areas compared to the twelve drainages usually distinguished in Australia. He predicts that, if the culture areas have some reality, interaction and inter-marriage across their borders should be less intensive than within them. This has not yet been demonstrated, and there are some counter-examples. For example, in the highlands of south-central Queensland three culture areas (north-east, Riverina and Lake Eyre) join, yet in terms of language, rock-art style and ethnographic communication networks, the highlands form a well-defined area in their own right (Beaton 1977; Donovan 1976; Morwood 1979, 1981). If clearly defined regions are so difficult to define using the relatively rich ethnographic data, we should be cautious about the meaning of regional similarities in the archaeological data.

We now know that particular kinds of

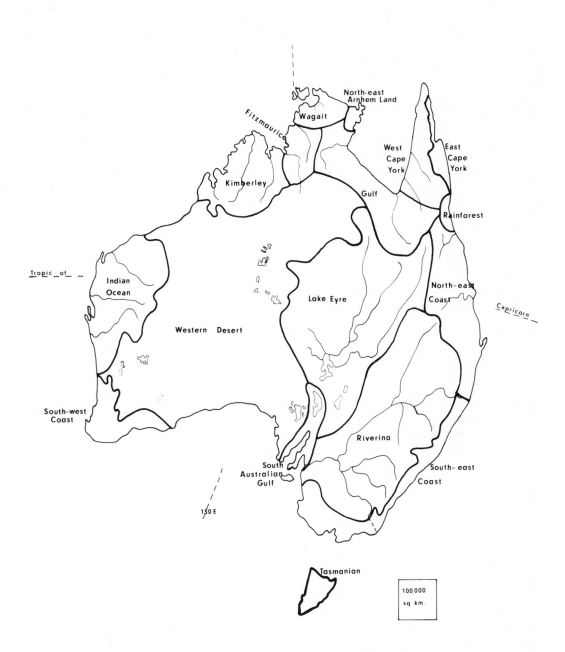

FIGURE 5.2. Cultural areas of Aboriginal Australia, according to N. Peterson. Natural drainage basins are not marked on this map. Source: Peterson (1976:66). Courtesy: Australian Institute of Aboriginal Studies, Canberra, Australia.

stylistically and technologically similar archaeological data are found over larger areas than occupied by any clearly definable Aboriginal group. This is best demonstrated by rock paintings. Even though only a few art styles have been well-defined and their boundaries charted, many are known at a broad conceptual level. Correlations between these boundaries and those of Peterson's culture areas or environmentally defined areas cannot be seen. For example, the paintings of Cape York are not easily divisible into an Eastern and Western group as the cultures are (Peterson 1976:66), while those of Peterson's Riverina area do not form an entity. To take a different artefact class, the distribution of greenstone hatchet heads in Victoria is clearly non-random (McBryde 1978b), and the eastern boundary of their occurrence coincides with an important nineteenth century Aboriginal political one. But that boundary has not been recognized in other aspects of material culture, including those from the nineteenth century.

It has also not been shown that different classes of archaeological data display coincidental boundaries; in fact there are clear indications that they do not. Nor do these boundaries usually coincide with any known linguistic, social or political ones. Nevertheless, even if we do not know precisely how the patterns observable in the archaeological data were formed, or how they relate to past human societies, their existence is demonstrable and it is they, not the ethnographic groupings, which must be used to organize our prehistories.

Change in Prehistory

In the body of this chapter we will deal with changes in technology (5.2) and subsistence (5.3). Here we introduce the major themes, some ancillary material and some of the broader implications.

Throughout the Pleistocene and into Recent times the basic stone tool-kit remained much the same. Additions — ground stone hatchets, adzes, grindstones — did occur, but in restricted areas or on a small scale. However, 5000–4000 years ago a range of small, well-made, flaked stone tools was suddenly added to tool-kits throughout most of Australia, in numbers sufficient to make these kits distinctive and allow them to be used as a chronological marker. (The evidence is outlined in 5.2.) The large-scale appearance of these small tools raises a number of problems. Was their inspiration local or external? Why were they adopted over such a large area, so quickly and in such large numbers? What were they used for? How did their adoption relate to other changes in behaviour at that time? In some places the new tools were made from different raw materials to other tools, and these raw materials had sometimes been transported considerable distances. However, this was not always the case. What pattern can be detected in this usage, and how may it be explained? To these and other questions no very detailed answer can be given since insufficient work has been done. At present a stylistic explanation rather than one clearly related to subsistence or new tasks seems to fit the data best, but we may find different explanations appropriate in different parts of the country. We note here that, although we argue for the sudden development and spread of the new technology, there are some hints that all the constituents of the new technology were in use during earlier millennia.

In 5.3 we describe subsistence patterns in different parts of Australia. We outline some of the regional models which have been proposed and provide some data from excavations. Although we have had to be selective, we have tried to give a fair cross-section of the material.

Within the Recent period, subsistence patterns differed throughout Australia, and many of them changed over time to accommodate environmental changes and probably population growth and other developments. The archaeological evidence attests to a great variety of locally specialized practices, some based on a considerable degree of environmental manipulation (e.g. Lourandos 1980a). However a full picture of any economy is rare, and even the period over which patterns known in the nineteenth century developed has always proved hard to determine. In cases where some evidence is available, such as the Coorong (SA) (Luebbers 1978) and the south-eastern coast, important changes seem to have occurred within the last 2000 years.

Readers of this section will find that it consists

of a series of accounts. There is no over-arching theme beyond the development of diversity, no general framework through which we interpret data from different areas. The reason is that we have been unable to see an Australia-wide theme. We considered, for instance, assessing the extent to which known economies were "agricultural" or looking at the changing contributions of men and women to the food quest (cf. Modjeska 1977; Hamilton 1980), but could not see that these were profitable strategies. We also considered writing a series of regional prehistories, but the data are adequate for only one or two areas. Therefore this section discusses a series of local economies. These display the diversity which was possible in Australia and which Aboriginal people developed.

Finally, in this chapter we discuss Tasmania (5.4). Neither the new stone technology nor any other of the new Australian developments (discussed below) reached Tasmania. Its separate status in this regard would alone be enough to merit separate treatment, but Tasmania is also important for other reasons. For many years it has been seen as the home of people whose physical and cultural origin differed from other Australians, but we now know this is not true. Recent discussions have focused on the significance of isolation in Tasmanian cultural evolution. Were the island's inhabitants slowly becoming culturally depauperate or were they simply evolving along cultural lines which differed from those of Australia? Our view is that the singularity of Tasmania has been overstressed. We agree with Horton (1979b) that the differences between Tasmania and Australia were no greater than inter-Australian differences.

We turn now to a broader consideration of change in Australian prehistory, since sections 5.2 and 5.3 are restricted to stone technology and subsistence. Changes of many kinds occurred, but here we will refer only to examples of treatment of the dead, to art and to changes possibly associated with the major change in stone technology.

1. Changing methods of treatment of dead people is evident from burials spanning 7000 years at Roonka (SA). This cemetery, excavated by Pretty (1977), does not of course exhibit all known Australian practices (see Meehan 1971),

but it is the only one with a long, dated sequence.

Roonka Flat is an alluvial and aeolian fossil river bank on the lower Murray River. People have lived on this bank for at least 18,000 years, and during the last 7000 years at least eighty-two people were buried there. The twelve burials older than 4000 years were strikingly different to anything known more recently. Some were in shaft tombs, with the body being placed vertically. In a few cases the bones were subsequently rearranged, and most were accompanied by grave goods of some kind. These included animal mandibles with drilled ramuses, drilled shells, bone pins and human infants.

The seventy later burials exhibited a variety of features, but all consisted of extended or contracted burials in pits. No vertical inhumations were found. Several graves were accompanied by elaborate trappings. In Grave 108 an adult male was accompanied by a small child. On the man's head was a chaplet of matched pairs of wallaby incisors, while his body seems to have been wrapped in a cloak made of animal skins with the paws left on and fringed with a band of bird feathers on partial limbs. In other graves, food offerings or stone tools constituted the major grave goods. It is clear that only mature adults were buried in this way — old and juvenile people were not present. One interesting find was a rib cage pierced by a point made of mammal long bone, good evidence of violent death and one use of bone tools.

As well as changes in burial patterns, there were also what the excavator interprets as "status" graves. Whatever the "status" involved, similar practices are not known in the ethnographic record, nor is some of the animal bone and tooth jewellery. The changes at Roonka occurred independently of subsistence variation, but probably not of technological change.

2. There have been many attempts to define relative dating sequences of paintings and engravings on cave and shelter walls. These have usually relied on superimposition analyses and studies of weathering. A recent study in the Carnarvon Ranges (Qld.) shows that three combinations of techniques and colours were spatially differentiated, and from a study of super-impositions these could be ordered in a sequence (Morwood 1980).

Morwood's basic data consists of 16,347 design elements grouped into ninety-two types and recorded in eighty-three sites on the Warrego and Barcoo Rivers. Using a principal components analysis, he found that colour usage and techniques each occurred in two main groups. Among the colours, pink and white occurred together as did red, purple, orange, yellow and brown. Among techniques, pecking occurred separately from stencilling, painting, abrading and imprinting. When the two kinds of data were combined a three-stage sequence appeared. This was: (a) pecked and pecked-and-abraded designs; (b) stencilled, painted and drawn designs in a variety of colours other than white; and (c) a predominance of white.

It has not so far been possible to directly date any part of this sequence. Morwood notes that pecked engravings occur early in other Australian sequences. Maynard (1979) suggests that designs made by this technique, and which occur Australia-wide, are old, and may sometimes be Pleistocene in date. Taking a different approach, Morwood (1981) plotted the occurrence of pigment fragments in excavations at several of the painted sites, but the relative frequencies were quite different from the frequencies of colours represented in the art. Further, most colours were found throughout most of the sequence, so that no chronology of use was indicated by the archaeological deposits.

Morwood's study (1980) is one example of demonstrable changes in the art of an area. Other areas, such as Arnhem Land, Cape York and western New South Wales, will certainly be shown to have their own sequences of artistic change. Interesting questions for the future are the extent to which a common sequence runs through Australian art, the timing of changes and their correlation with other archaeological events.

3. Within the last few years it has become apparent that many aspects of Australian life may have changed at about the same time, some 4000–5000 years ago. We have already mentioned the changes at Roonka cemetery, the only excavated set of burials from this time. Morwood (1979) would like to associate the introduction of paintings in various colours with the new stone technology. Certainly, human use of many shelters with paintings only begins at this time (see also Beaton 1977). Other changes may have included:

(a) The arrival of the dingo in Australia (Milham and Thompson 1976; K. Gollan, pers. comm., 1980). The only published claim for the dingo being older than 5000 years is from excavations at Mt. Burr (SA). However, Mulvaney (1978) reports that the stratigraphic integrity of the site is very doubtful and the specimens may well have come from more recent levels. The dingo is certainly an introduction, but its source and mode of arrival in Australia remains a mystery. Its adoption by Aboriginal societies had major effects on hunting methods and on social and spiritual life in some parts of the country (Hamilton 1972; Hayden 1975a; Jones 1972; I. M. White 1972).

(b) The introduction of macrozamia (*Cycas*) processing from outside Australia (Beaton 1977). The complex technology used in Australia for producing edible starch from this highly poisonous plant is the same as that found in other parts of the world, and Beaton (1982) argues that this cannot have been a local invention. In the Carnarvon Ranges macrozamia kernels have been found in deposits dating back to 4300 years ago, but not earlier.

(c) A tenfold or greater increase in archaeological remains in the highlands of eastern Australia (Bowdler 1981). Drawing on the work of Beaton (1977), McBryde (1974, 1976), Stockton (1970), I. Johnson (1979), Flood (1976, 1980) and others, Bowdler points out that many sites and some regions seem to be used for the first time, while in others the quantity of debris (almost exclusively flaked stone) increased very greatly. She suggests that at this time significant new food resources began to be used and it was these which allowed the highlands to be occupied. Some of these resources, such as yams, required little processing and became staple foods in these areas; others, including macrozamia and seasonally available items such as bogong moths and bunya nuts (H. Sullivan 1977), became "ritual" foods used at ceremonies or large gatherings. Bowdler is cautious about identifying the driving force behind these changes. Following Jones (1977a), she suggests that large-scale religious changes, including big ceremonies held at high altitudes, may have been responsible. This fascinating and provocative proposal is difficult to test, directly or indirectly, though one approach would be to refine the dating of sites, especially ceremonial sites.

(d) A change in the nature of "hearths" around the Willandra Lakes (P. Clark and Barbetti 1982). Late Pleistocene and early Holocene "hearths" were made with lumps of indurated sandy sediment or clay or carbonate nodules. By contrast, all the fifteen "hearths" made of lumps of termite nest have been dated by radiocarbon to less than 4500 years old. Further, Clark and Barbetti's palaeomagnetic analyses show that termite nest lumps were not moved after initial heating, whereas in one 7500-year-old "hearth" which they tested most of the carbonate nodules had been moved after the "hearth" was used. They cautiously suggest that a different cooking method may be shown by their analyses.

Another series of suggested changes in Recent prehistory concerns population densities. For example, P. J. Hughes and Lampert (in press; see also Lampert and Hughes 1974; P. J. Hughes and Sullivan 1981) believe that there was a "marked increase in population in coastal regions of south-eastern Australia during the last 5000 years". They base this on the numbers of sites with archaeological deposit, increases in humanly caused sedimentation and the "intensity of site use" as measured by artefact and stone tool numbers (but see Hassan 1981; Hiscock 1981). We note that these changes did not occur suddenly: they progressively increased with time, although they began about the time that the new stone technology appeared.

Similar increases in population have been suggested for the Victorian Mallee (Ross 1981) and south-western Victoria (Lourandos 1980a). In both cases the recognizable changes occurred within the last 2000 years.

The mechanisms which might lie behind population increases have been discussed by Lampert and Hughes (1974) and Lourandos

(1980a). The former suggest that "as a general rule hunter-gatherer population size is adjusted to the capacity of subsistence resources" and that as coastal resources increased in quantity during the Recent period, so populations would have risen. They also argue that barbed fishing spears and shell fish-hooks came into use during this period and these would have increased the range of resources taken by Aborigines. Lourandos suggests that population growth may sometimes be an independent variable, but argues that this is sustained or promoted by changes in energy-harnessing techniques such as those used in south-western Victoria to increase the supply of eels. Changes in energy harnessing were encouraged by environmental changes and by political competition between local groups. Lourandos' argument gives us good reasons to believe that population density changed during Australian prehistory.

The whole field clearly needs further research on two levels. One is the general problem of population change and its relation with other aspects of society; the other is the particular problem of inferring information about populations from archaeological data.

5.2 Stone Technologies

We have shown in Chapter 3 that flaked stone industries of the Australian Pleistocene basically form a single technological tradition. Despite such local variations as the pebble-tool industries of Kangaroo Island and the adjacent mainland, and the small-flake industries of the same area (Lampert 1979a), there were great similarities throughout Australia, similarities stemming at least in part from the simplicity of this tradition with its lack of a wide range of formally shaped artefacts (4.2).

Two main changes in stone technology are currently believed to have occurred during the last 10,000 years. The first is the spread of two artefact types, ground stone hatchets and flaked stone adzes, through all and most of the continent respectively. The second is the addition of a number of new forms to the technological repertoire. There is some evidence suggesting that these two changes occurred at about the same time in southern Australia.

Backed Blades and Points

The fact that changes had occurred in the Australian flaked-stone technology was first recognized fifty years ago when Hale and Tindale (1930) excavated Devon Downs rock-shelter on the lower Murray River and found stratified variability in stone and bone artefacts. Further recognition of the nature and geographical extent of these changes by McCarthy (1948, 1964) and Mulvaney (1966b, 1969; Mulvaney and Joyce 1965) led R. Gould to propose the term "Australian small-tool tradition" for the new forms, and this has been widely adopted. However, although this tradition is recognized as consisting of a number of new forms, most of which display formally identifiable patterns, there are still a number of problems concerning the definition of these, the dating of both their commencement and disappearance, and the description of their economic and sociological importance.

According to Mulvaney (1975:210), the small-tool tradition is defined by the development of blade-tool production (sometimes from prismatic cores), along with some pressure and delicate percussion flaking primarily to make a variety of points and backed microlithic blades. Rather more broadly, I. Johnson (1979) sees the difference between this and the earlier technologies as consisting of a general reduction in artefact size, more controlled flaking with careful core preparation, the greater use of fine-grained raw materials, often imported from some distance, and the introduction of new, more formally, and perhaps functionally, specialized tool types. These features occurred differentially throughout Australia, and the first two have not been studied or documented in detail. The new tool forms are as follows.

BACKED BLADES

These are thin blades or flakes, usually triangular in cross-section, mostly 1–5 cm long, with abrupt, blunting retouch along part or all of one side. Within this general group a variety of forms has been recognized by different workers (e.g. T. D. Campbell and Noone 1943; I. Glover 1969; McCarthy *et al.* 1946; Mulvaney and Joyce 1965), including Bondi points, Woakwine points and geometric microliths of various shapes (Figs 5.3, 5.4). However, the specific characteristics of each group have seldom been clearly defined. Even the extent of regional differences is not clear (Croll 1980; I. Glover 1967; Pearce 1973; Wieneke and White 1973).

ELOUERA

These tools might well be described as large and crudely made backed blades, shaped like the segment of an orange (Fig 5.5). They are usually 3–8 cm long, with the mean length being nearer the lower end of the range. The chord of the segment is unretouched, and this thin edge is often use-polished. The definition of the tool has not been precise: McCarthy *et al.* (1946:28) refer to scraper-trimming on the thick edge, and Mulvaney (1975:231–33) and Kamminga (1978) say it carries blunting retouch. The presence of use-polish on the chord has sometimes been used as a defining characteristic.

POINTS

These are made on flakes, often triangular in cross-section, usually leaf-shaped in form, with width being about one-third the length. Mean length is about 4 cm with a range of 2.5–7 cm. Both unifacial and bifacial forms occur, and within each group secondary trimming and shaping ranges from fully covering the surface to occurring on one margin only. Among unifacial points, a distinction has been drawn between *pirri* points (Fig 5.6) and *lelira* "blades" (Fig 5.7) (length/breadth ratio, > 2 : 1) on the basis of the function of the latter in the nineteenth century (McCarthy *et al.* 1946:32) and on the relative lengths, *lelira* being defined as longer than 6 cm (Flood 1970:47). The distinction seems arbitrary in many assemblages. Technologically, small trigonal points can often be described as Levallois points (Dortch 1977; Dortch and Bordes 1977). The *lelira* blades are not usually retouched.

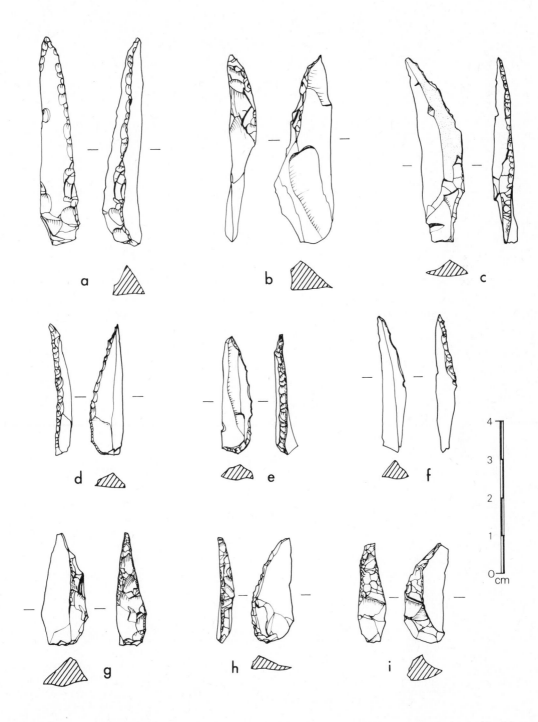

FIGURE 5.3. Backed blades. a–f: unprovenanced; g–i: Murramurrang, NSW coast. From Australian Museum and University of Sydney collections.

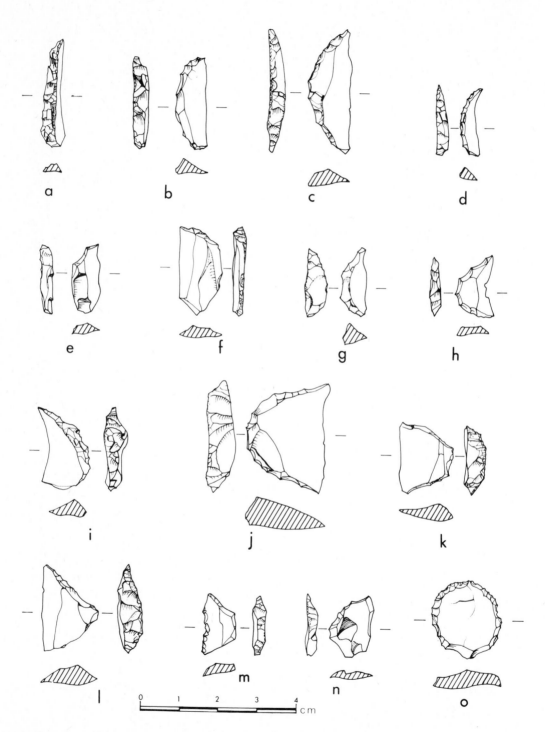

FIGURE 5.4. Backed artefacts. a, b, d–j, o: unprovenanced; c: Baldina Creek, SA; k–n: Victoria. From Australian Museum and University of Sydney collections.

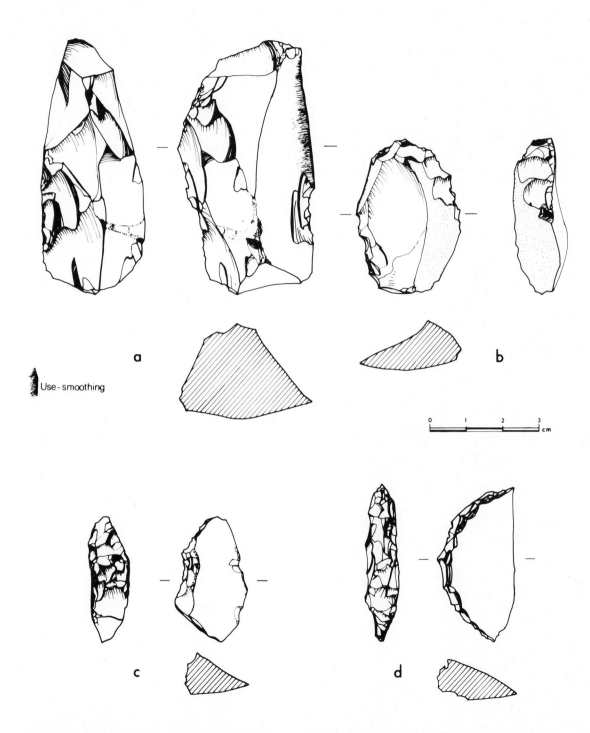

Use-smoothing

FIGURE 5.5. *Elouera.* a: Tirrikiba, NSW; b: Lake Illawarra, south coast NSW (Australian Museum, E39037); c: Murramurrang, south coast NSW; d: Deep Creek, near Sydney (courtesy V. Attenbrow).

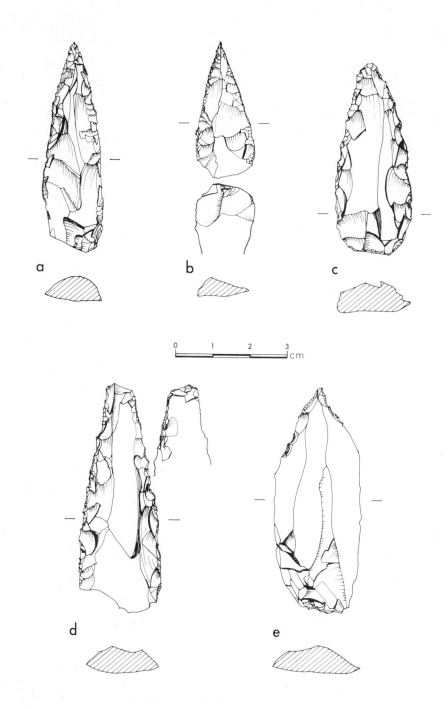

FIGURE 5.6. Unifacial points *(pirri).* a: Lake Eyre district, Central Australia (Australian Museum, E36173); b, c: North Bosworth Dam, SA (Australian Museum, E70700); c, d: unprovenanced (University of Sydney).

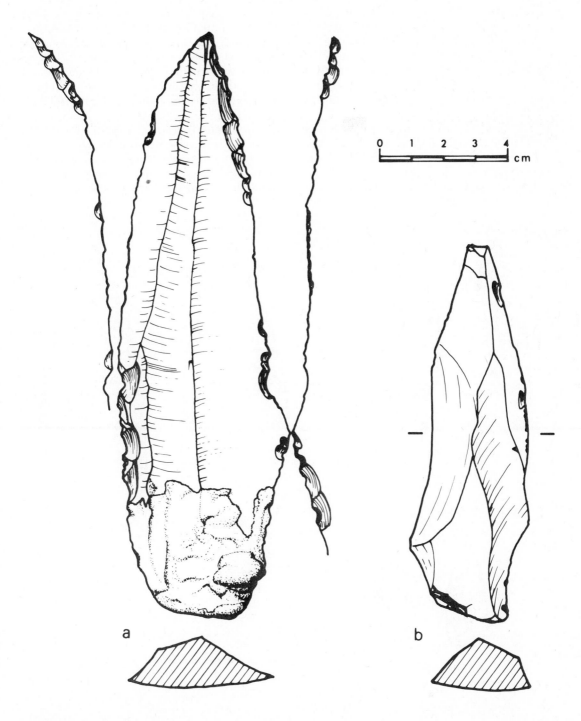

FIGURE 5.7. Unifacial points *(lelira)*. Dorsal surface and ventral edges are shown. a: Central Australia; b: unprovenanced. (University of Sydney).

Among bifacial points it is usual to distinguish plain-edge (Figs 5.8, 5.9a) from serrated-edge (Fig 5.9b) or Kimberley points, but this difference is in fact most apparent in points made of porcelain, glass (Fig 5.10) or chalcedony (e.g. McCarthy *et al.* 1946), and thus may be mostly post-contact in date. Stone Kimberley points, like other bifacial points, are 2–10 cm long, with surface flaking by percussion or pressure. Kimberley points made of fine-grained materials may be up to 20 cm long, less than 1 cm thick and exhibit very fine flaking on both surfaces.

The distributions of the various tool forms are not coincident. Backed blades occur in some numbers in the southern half of Australia, into the central arid zone (about 24°S) and along the east coast as far north as Brisbane (27°S). Some finds have recently been reported from around the southern end of Cape York (18°S), but the numbers and geographical extent of the tool form in this area need further definition (Hiscock and Hughes 1980). They are absent from Cape York itself and from sites in Arnhem Land. Dortch (1977:117) has reported backed points from sites in the Kimberleys, well into the tropical monsoon zone, but these are rather different from the more

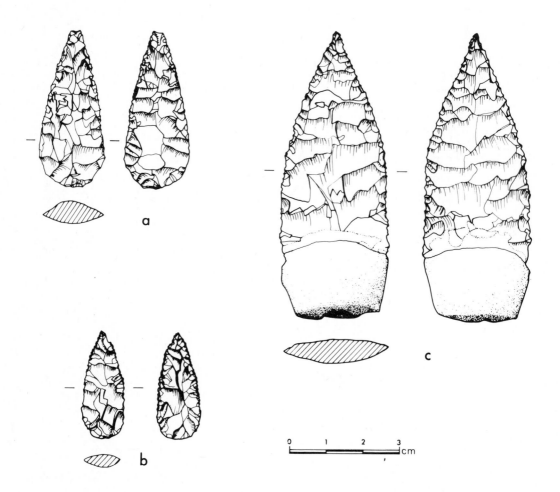

FIGURE 5.8. Plain-edge bifacial points, all unprovenanced. (University of Sydney).

southerly forms of backed blades. Differences include size and the fact that the backing is semi-abrupt, often denticulate and made by direct percussion. J. P. White has inspected some of the specimens and is not convinced that these tools are backed blades; they are probably varieties of abruptly trimmed points (Fig 5.11).

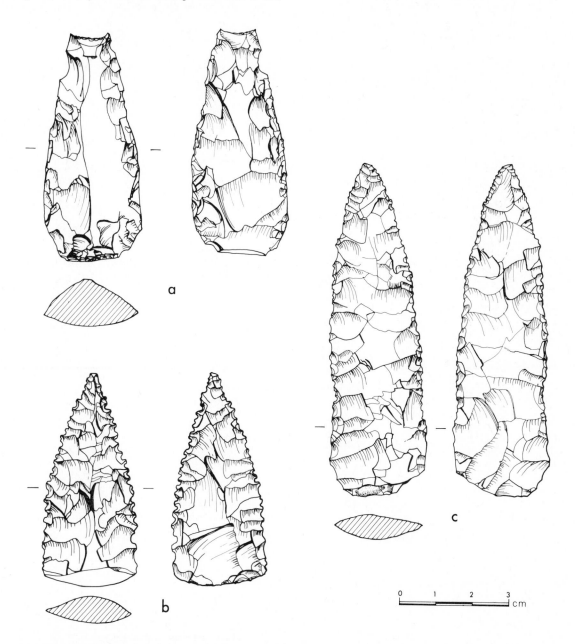

FIGURE 5.9. Bifacial points. a: re-worked at tip, unprovenanced (University of Sydney); b: Serrated edge, north-western Australia, glass (Australian Museum, E20546); c: unprovenanced (University of Sydney).

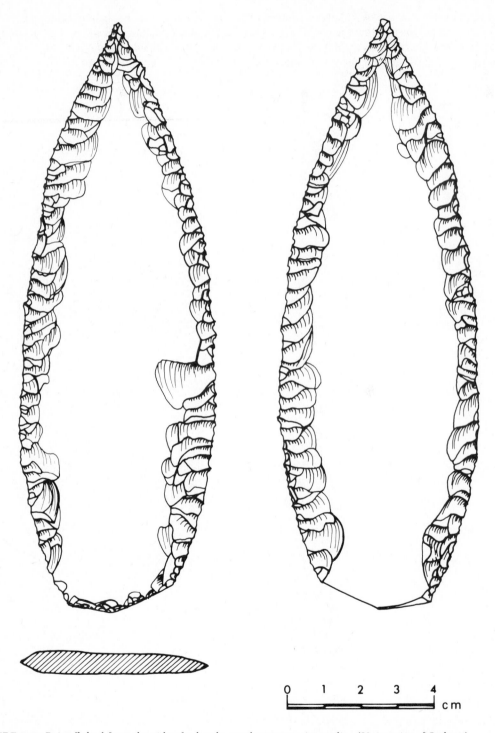

FIGURE 5.10. Point flaked from the side of a bottle, north-western Australia. (University of Sydney).

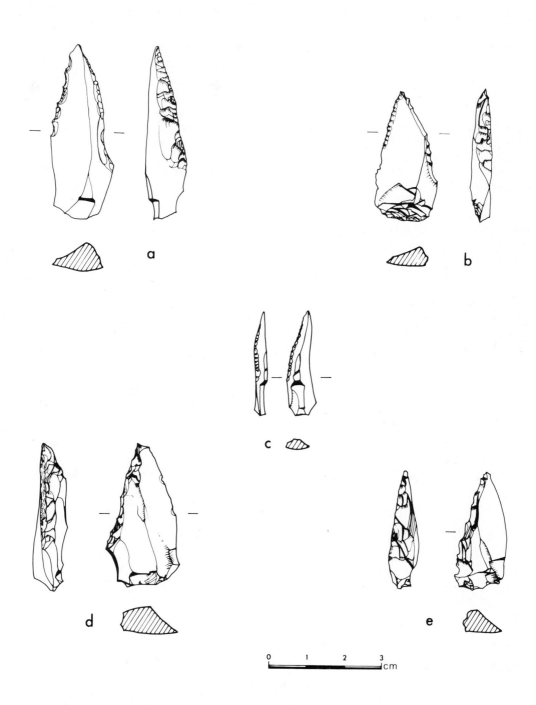

FIGURE 5.11. Backed points from Miriwun site, Kimberleys, WA. Reference nos: a: B20; b: B2914; c: B937; d: B392; e: B2012. Courtesy: C. E. Dortch.

The distribution of *elouera* has been less well described. They have been reported from most parts of Australia but usually in very small numbers. The only areas where large samples have been found are along the central coast and nearby highlands of New South Wales and in the Oenpelli region of Arnhem Land. A few may occur in northern NSW. In the Oenpelli region they have been recognized primarily by the presence of use-polish along a straight edge (Fig 5.12), and formally shaped *eloueras* are in a minority (Kamminga 1978:301; McCarthy and Setzler 1960:278–82; C. White 1967:235). *Eloueras* on the NSW east coast conform to the formal definition and were probably hafted on a straight handle to be used for scraping and adzing light wood and bark (Kamminga 1978:280–88). Elsewhere, it is doubtful that they are distinguishable from other scrapers (cf. I. Glover 1967; Stockton 1971). Within New South Wales they occur only in association with backed blade industries, and although McCarthy (1948) argued that they continued to be made subsequently to backed blades, this has not been substantiated by later excavations.

Points display a very different distribution to backed blades or *elouera*. Generally, unifacial examples occur in a broad band across the central third of Australia, although the precise boundaries have not been established. Points are found throughout the tropical north (except Cape York), in western Queensland and the Queensland highlands, around Alice Springs, and throughout South Australia and western New South Wales. They are rare on the Nullarbor Plain. We are unaware of the occurrence of points between the intermediate longitudes, 18°S and 24°S, but it seems likely that they will be found there. Bifacial points have a distribution restricted essentially to the tropical north (i.e. north of the arid zone), effectively the Kimberleys and Arnhem Land. Occasional butt trimming, technically bifacial, occurs among unifacial points further south. Kimberley points, as the name implies, are found mostly within that region, but apparently they were traded over a much wider area to the south and east (Kamminga 1978), stretching to about central Australia and western Queensland.

The distributions outlined above suggest that the new technology was not a "package", and that the new artefact forms were not all parts of a

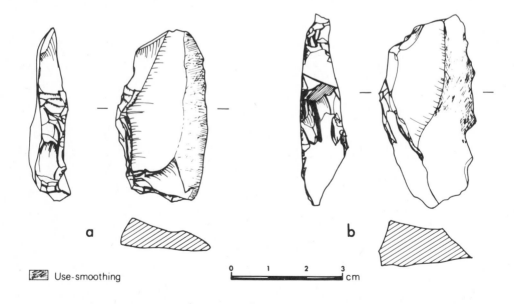

a   b

☒ Use-smoothing   0   1   2   3 cm

FIGURE 5.12. *"Elouera"* from Cannon Hill I, near Oenpelli. (Australian Museum, E63247).

single composite tool. But to move from these negative statements to positive ones is difficult. We start with the dating.

Since the early 1960s, radiocarbon dates for the start of the small-tool tradition have suggested both that its elements appeared at about the same time and that their spread across the continent occurred in less than a millennium (Mulvaney 1975:213–15). On the other hand, the dates have also suggested that the appearance of these new forms was erratic within any region. For example, backed blades are claimed from Burrill Lake at 5320 ± 150 (ANU-535) but from Curracurrang, less than 200 km north along the same coast, from only 2865 ± 57 (GaK-688). Several years ago, Stockton (1977) drew attention to the fact that several of the earliest dates in New South Wales came from sites with loose sandy deposits and low sedimentation rates and suggested, on the basis of experimental evidence, that treadage and scuffage* might have been responsible for the downward movement of some artefacts. In a comprehensive survey of the evidence, I. Johnson (1979) has strongly supported this. He suggests that, if the introduction was rapid and widespread, we would find a large number of dates for backed implements falling at, or younger than, their "true" date of introduction, with a scatter of dates older than this arising from humanly and naturally caused downward movements of materials, primarily but not exclusively in sandy deposits. Johnson shows (1979:Fig 54) that this pattern indeed occurs. He has also carefully reviewed the available data on the seven sites with dates older than 5000 years and concludes that all are ambiguous. Six of these sites are in the coastal region of New South Wales, the other, Puntutjarpa, is in the Central Desert (Gould 1977a). P. J. Hughes and Djohadze (1980:26) have disagreed with Johnson's interpretation as it applies to the Currarong 1 site. They note that the deposit had a high degree of stratigraphic integrity, it had four backed blades in levels dated to 4800–7000 years ago, and there

was no large reservoir of material in the level above, which contained only seven backed blades. They therefore claim that this site provides strong evidence for thinking that backed blades could be 5000 years old, or more.

In dating the start of the new technology, Johnson suggests that we should expect that every large assemblage of artefacts dated later than the "true" date of the introduction of the new forms should contain them. While this might be challengeable given variability in site use, it does seem generally a useful principle. Johnson thus shows that backed blades probably occurred about 3500 years ago in the coastal regions of New South Wales, and between 4000 and 4500 years ago in the central Queensland highlands and along the Murray River. In the first case he relies particularly on data from Capertee 3 (McCarthy 1964, Johnson's own re-excavations), Curracurrang (Megaw 1965) and Bass Point (Bowdler 1970, 1976). For the second he uses data from Kenniff Cave (Mulvaney and Joyce 1965), Native Well I (Morwood 1979, 1981) and Fromm's Landing (Mulvaney 1960, 1975:290). Tindale's data (1968:634) from Devon Downs also support this. There are fewer dates for backed implements in other parts of the continent. For the Central Desert, Gould (1977a:63, 104) argued that backed blades occurred at Puntutjarpa more than 4000 years ago, but the inconsistencies among radiocarbon dates and the stratigraphic problems evident in the report prevent us from relying on it (see also I. Johnson 1979:131–34). At Northcliffe, in south-west Australia, backed blades lay not far above a date of 6780 ± 120 (SUA-379) and well below one of 3080 ± 75 (ANU-1131) (Dortch 1975), but the fact that the site was in a sandy deposit leads us to be cautious. Although the excavator argued strongly that all material was *in situ*, the vertical scattering of waste fragments makes us think this unlikely, and a date of about 4000–4500 years old is more probable (Table 5.1). Further north, backed blades from Skew Valley (near Dampier) may be as old as 3700 ± 90 (ANU-1834), but we await a fuller stratigraphic report (see Lorblanchet and Jones 1979). Kimberley-type backed blades, associated with points, were dated only at Miriwun site, to 2980 ± 95 (SUA-142) (Dortch 1977).

---

* We think these terms were first used in print by Stockton (1973) though we suspect they were coined rather earlier. Treadage refers to the vertical action of feet pressing objects downwards, scuffage to the action of feet forcing objects laterally and upwards (see also Matthews 1965).

The earliest occurrence of points has not been well dated. Along the lower Murray River, in central Queensland and in the Kimberleys they have been claimed as contemporary, or nearly so, with backed blades (e.g. Mulvaney and Joyce 1965:188). We return to this problem later. For points alone, there are very few sites published. At Yarar, 300 km north-east of Miriwun, a large point assemblage was dated to 3350 ± 90 (V-72). Although this date seems reasonable, it is inconsistent with a much younger date for the same horizon (Flood 1970:30). At Ingaladdi less than 200 km inland from Yarar, points did not occur in a level dated 4920 ± 100 (ANU-58) but were found in numbers only 23 cm above, dated to 2890 ± 73 (ANU-57). In western Arnhem Land, excavations in three sites were said to give a consistent date for the earliest point industries of about 6500 years ago (C. White 1971), and subsequent excavations were said to have confirmed this (Kamminga and Allen 1973:108). However, as this is much older than dates from other areas, some discussion is warranted.

The original data came from four sites excavated by C. White in 1964–65 (C. White 1967). At Malangangerr, about one metre of shell midden overlay much earlier sands containing only stone artefacts and disseminated carbon. A 10 cm transition zone was distinguished between the two main levels, and neither this nor the lower level contained points. A date of 5980 ± 140 (GaK-627) was obtained from 85–90 cm below the surface, from "charcoal from the base of the midden, lying on a large slab of rock" (1967:136), the implication being that contamination by older charcoal was unlikely. Seventeen whole and broken points were excavated, fifteen of them from the upper half of the shell midden, well above the dated charcoal. The location of the two within the lower half of the midden has not been published, but one occurred in loose dirt at the back of the shelter and the other was found towards the top of this level (C. Schrire, pers. comm., 1980). Neither was directly associated with the radiocarbon date.

At Nawamoyn site a similar stratigraphy

TABLE 5.1

Distribution of excavated material from Northcliffe

Radiocarbon dates	Depth (cm)	Geometric microliths (No.)	Other flakes and blades (No.)	Chips (Min. No.)
3080 ± 75 (ANU-1131)	46–51	—	2	—
	51–53	—	10	6
	53–57	1	43	47
	57–59	2	50	57
	59–60	—	63	110
	60–62	—	83	50
	62–64	2	55	50
	64–66	—	94	50
	66–70	8	165	250
	70–72	5	114	250
	72–74	2	107	250
	74–78	1	127	250
	78–82	3	39	100
	82–85	1	15	20
6780 ± 120 (SUA-379)	85–90	—	2	20
	90–96	—	6	2
	96–98	—	5	9
	98–103	—	7	1
	103–120	—	5	4

Source: Dortch (1975).

occurred, and a date from "a charcoal sample from the bottom of level Ib" (1967:200), the base of the midden, was 7110 ± 130 (ANU-53). Apparently the sample consisted of a scatter of carbon fragments (see also C. White 1971: Fig 12.2), and the possibility of carbon of various ages having been included seems to be higher than at Malangangerr. Only four points were excavated, two from the upper and two from the lower midden (1967:239). Their exact location in relation to the date is not available.

At Tyimede II, away from the river, there was no shell midden. Two major concentrations of artefacts and waste flakes occurred within the 140 cm of sandy deposit. Carbon dates were obtained from diffuse scatters of carbon. ANU-50 "dates the earliest levels of the point-scraper industry" to 4770 ± 150 years (1967:388). The date came from the lower part of level Ib, which contained nearly 100 points and fragments. In level II, a zone of lower artefact concentration, only three point fragments were found, and intrusion from above seems likely. Level III, in which no points were found, was dated to 6650 ± 500 (ANU-18). An immediately adjacent site, Tyimede I, gave inconsistent dates of 10,790 ± 200 (GaK-632) and 3820 ± 100 (ANU-52) from samples one metre apart in the same level.

In 1972–73, Kamminga and Allen excavated test pits, usually one metre square, in several sites in the same area. Four of these sites are relevant to the dating problem, though evidence from such small samples must be treated with more caution than that obtained from the larger ones discussed above.

In Ngarradj Warde Djobkeng ("the cockatoo cut it") rock-shelter, a stratigraphy similar to that at Nawamoyn was excavated. Thirty-three (of 37) points were found within a heavy shell midden dated on charcoal at its base to 3450 ± 125 (SUA-164). (Note that there are minor differences between the dates given by Kamminga and Allen, 1973, and those reported by the Sydney laboratory, Gillespie and Temple, 1976. We use the latter.) Four points were found below the midden in sandy deposits with preserved bone. One point lay 10–15 cm below charcoal dated to 3990 ± 195 (SUA-225) (see also H. Allen 1977). Allen has subsequently excavated extensively at this site, but has not yet reported his results.

The deposit at Leichhardt site, away from the river, contained almost no organic remains except carbon. A charcoal date of 5045 ± 125 (SUA-244) was obtained from near the base of the one metre of deposit. This date underlay the earliest points by at least 20 cm, although the excavators claimed (on the basis of one scraper) that the "late phase" tools were found throughout (Kamminga and Allen 1973:88).

At the Lindner site, with a similar absence of organic remains but a considerably deeper and older deposit, the earliest points were dated to 3070 ± 85 (SUA-235), at a depth of 40–45 cm. All the points were made of granular quartzite, and the excavators drew attention to the fact this material comprised 65–75% of the total raw material in all levels above 70–80 cm, but fell to 10% or less below this. They suggested that this change may have marked the introduction of "late phase" industries. On the basis of a date of 13,195 ± 175 (SUA-236) from 125–130 cm, and assuming constant sedimentation rates, this would place the transition at about 6000–6500 years ago.

From these data we can conclude two things. First, point industries are clearly younger than 5650–7650 years (ANU-18 taken to two standard deviations). This is supported by a probable pre-point date of 8690 ± 125 (SUA-165) from Ngarradj Warde Djobkeng. Second, 4470–5070 (ANU-50 at 2 s.d.) from Tyimede II seems a reasonably firm date for the presence of points. Dates earlier than ANU-50 from Nawamoyn, Malangangerr and the Leichhardt site are not clearly associated with points, although limited support for an earlier date can be inferred from a change in raw materials at Lindner site. We thus conclude that, while points in western Arnhem Land may be earlier than those from other areas, we are entitled to ask for further proof of their presence before 5000 years ago.

We return now to the relationship between points and backed blades. The main area in which these two types coincide are in western Queensland and New South Wales, and throughout South Australia. Relevant excavations have occurred in the Queensland highlands and lower Murray River. At Kenniff Cave, seven *pirri* and eight rather dubious unifacial points occurred in the level just below a date of 4130 ± 90 (GaK-523) but above levels dated between 4400 and 5600 (GaK-524, -525, NPL-66; Mulvaney and Joyce 1965:169). Backed blades, other than a few questionable *elouera*, were found 15–23 cm higher in the deposit and were associated with a date of 3830 ± 90 (NPL-65). At The Tombs near Kenniff Cave, a few of both kinds of implements were found in the same level, dated to 3600 ± 93 (NPL-31), with one point being found 7.5 cm beneath this. Recent excavations by Morwood (1979, 1981) in the same area have dated the earliest backed blades and associated points at Native Well I site to 4320 ± 90 (ANU-2003).

At the other end of the Murray–Darling River system are the sites of Devon Downs and Fromm's Landing. Devon Downs (Hale and Tindale 1930) was not originally reported to contain backed blades. The excavator subsequently referred to microliths and Bondi points (Tindale 1968:627), but we are not convinced that we would accept them as such. However, Devon Downs did contain 37 *pirri* points spread over three levels (totalling 80–100 cm). A date from somewhere in the middle of these is reported as 4250 ± 180 (Lamont laboratory, possibly L-217G; see Mulvaney 1975:290; Tindale 1968:634) and one from the level immediately below them was 5180 ± 100 (GaK-1024). At Fromm's Landing, Shelter 2, only 15 km downstream from Devon Downs, Mulvaney (1960) obtained both *pirri* points and backed blades, though both in small numbers. The three earliest examples of each were found in level 10, which was dated on freshwater shells to 4850 ± 100 (NZ-364), and was well below a charcoal date of 4055 ± 85 (P-311). While a shell date might be questioned, there seems to be reasonable agreement between these dates and those from Devon Downs. Fromm's Landing, Shelter 6 (Mulvaney *et al.* 1964), produced no points and only two backed blades, so even though nearly 4 m of deposit was accumulated, mainly during the third and fourth millennia before present, this site does not throw much light on the problem. The available data thus suggest to us that the first occurrences of backed blades and points were not contemporary in some areas, although the number of sites and specimens is too small to make a very definite statement. However, the continued association of the two through to relatively recent times is not

well documented, and at least in some places points may have been short-term phenomena (Morwood 1981).

We can summarize the data on dating by saying (a) points do not appear to be older than the fifth millennium before present, although there is a tentative suggestion that they were older in Arnhem Land; and (b) roughly the same date is true for the appearance of backed blades, with the earliest examples perhaps occurring in south-central Queensland. In each case, a very rapid spread across the continent seems irrefutable.

Apart from their small size and consistent patterning, are there other features common to this new technology which will identify it as a "tradition"? The production of both backed blades and points certainly required finer control over the flaking process than with earlier tools, but whether core-preparation techniques changed throughout Australia is not known. I. Johnson (1979) and others before him (Gould 1977a, 1978b; Lampert 1979a, 1981) have argued that backed blades were more frequently made of high quality, "exotic" raw materials than other tools were. These raw materials were often transported considerable distances. The best documented examples are from the coast and coastal highlands of New South Wales. P. J. Hughes *et al.* (1973) note that in three sites on the south coast the use of silcrete increased by a significant amount in levels containing backed blades and other small tools. This material was used almost exclusively for these tools at two sites, one of which, Kurnell, is about 150 km from the nearest probable source (see also Etheridge and Whitelegge 1907). Transport of siliceous rocks for similar purposes over more than 100 km is also documented for the north coast (McBryde 1974:374-79). In the Blue Mountains west of Sydney, I. Johnson (1979:38, 98, Fig. 5, Table 4) has shown that the raw materials used changed in levels containing backed blades, but he was unable to locate the sources of these materials. Gould (1977a:124–25, 1978a) found that the amount of "exotic" raw materials carried more than 40 km tripled in levels of Puntutjarpa which contained backed blades and reported that about one-third of these tools were made in these materials. But he also noted that a higher proportion of adzes than before were made in "exotic" stone; thus, in this instance, the connection between new stone sources and new technology is not completely clear. Elsewhere, changes in the raw material used have been noted, but long-distance transport has not been involved (McBryde 1977:243; Morwood 1979; Sanders 1975).

Whether a similar situation existed for the point industries is not known. In the best studied series of sites, in Arnhem Land, Kamminga and Allen (1973) noted that, in the various sites where both old and new artefact types were found, the fine red quartzite of lower levels was replaced in the upper levels by grey granular quartzite, favoured for making points. Differences in the flaking properties of the two materials are not mentioned, nor is their relative availability. Among C. White's sites, regular change was found only at Tyimede II, where the point levels contained twice as much quartzite as the basal level, with a corresponding decrease in quartz and igneous/metamorphic rock (1967:392–93). If any raw material could be described as "exotic" at this site it is the last-named, which was used to make hatchet-heads. At Yarar, the quartzite for point manufacture came from the closest outcrop, 14 km distant (Flood 1970:34). We conclude that the use of "exotic" raw materials differed among backed blade and point makers, as well as between the two groups, but that regional patterning of these differences has not yet been shown.

In originally proposing the term "tradition" for these small tools Gould (1969:234–35) suggested that it should include not only those forms discussed above but "all small stone tools in Australia (that is, tools thought to be small enough to have required hafting)". Thus small end-scrapers, adzes and micro-adzes would also be included. He further suggested that all these small tools "may belong to a common historical tradition" (1969:235). However, as adzes and micro-adzes are, at least in the central and western areas of Australia, likely to be 8000–10,000 years old, to incorporate them into a single "tradition" would require acceptance of Mulvaney's now-rejected idea of hafting as a distinguishing characteristic, unless there is some other way a "common historical tradition"

can be defined. One way would be to identify a common origin for the various forms.

It should already be apparent that finding a common source will not be easy. Nonetheless, for many years it has been believed that not only would this be possible, but that such a source must lie outside Australia (e.g. Allchin 1966: 171–73; I. Glover 1967; McCarthy 1977:254–56; Mulvaney 1975:211; J. P. White 1971). Tools similar to backed blades and *elouera* have been found in India and Sri Lanka (Allchin 1966; Birmingham 1969), and others, such as points and backed blades, in the Macassar area of Sulawesi (I. Glover 1976, 1978; Mulvaney and Soejono 1970) (Fig. 5.13). As we interpret Glover's reports, backed blades (which should really be called backed flakes, since a blade core technique is not present) can probably be dated to between 5000 and 6000 years old, while small hollow-based "Maros points" with serrated edges appear to be no older than about 4000 years. The points, especially, are not very like any known in Australia. Nor have similar tools been found in Timor or New Guinea.

We believe that any argument supporting an external source for backed blades and points must meet three conditions. First, formally and technically similar tools must be shown to be older in some area outside Australia; second, there must be some area within Australia where all tool types occur at an earlier date than anywhere else; third, some plausible link between the two occurrences must be established. To date, however, no external source has been located. The second condition applies if a single internal origin of the new tools is claimed.

It is more interesting to consider what an "earliest assemblage" might be expected to look like. If we were dealing with an imported technology, we would expect the earliest Australian occurrences to be of developed forms. But if a local development is proposed the problem becomes more complex. Would we expect the earliest examples to be crude in form and technically unrefined, as Pearce (1974, 1975) suggests? If "blade" production is envisaged, should there be evidence of its development? Dickson (1975), following G. Isaac, argues that this is unlikely. At least so far as backed blades are concerned, he points out that they are "one of the most elementary devices that can be made by secondary working" (1975:46), and suggests that "thresholds" may occur in stone technology. This could also be true of the more complex points. Therefore, unless we can find sites which have many clearly differentiated sets of short-term human activities covering the appropriate period — something which has been impossible to find in any prehistoric situation — the discovery of any innovation processes is improbable. A very early assemblage might not be distinguishable either technologically or, given the limits of

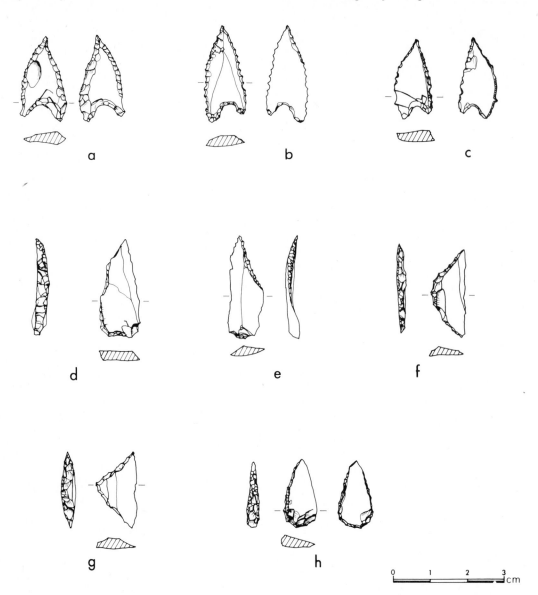

FIGURE 5.13. Backed blades and points from Ulu Leang I site, Maros, Sulawesi. Reference nos: a: 488; b: 500; c: 503; d: 137; e: 439; f: 025; g: 472; h: 475. Courtesy: D. J. Mulvaney.

radiocarbon dating, temporally, from any other.

The function of these new tools is another consideration and one highly relevant to their appearance, adoption and persistence. The discovery of some backed blades with resin or gum stains on the thick, backed edge indicates they had some kind of haft or handle. On the other hand, the absence of either macroscopic or microscopic use-wear on most specimens suggests that they were not regularly used as knives or gravers. It is usually assumed that they are spear points and barbs, one modern analogue being the many small quartz flakes on "death spears" (Kamminga 1978; Lampert 1971a). Relevant here, too, is the extraordinary number of these tools found in some locations and the fact that very few seem to be broken. For example, Dickson (1975) collected 7000 from 2–3 km^2 of sand-dunes near Sydney over a few years, and many others have collected smaller numbers from the same site. Mulvaney (1975:225) quotes 20,000 collected from a small area west of Lake Torrens in arid South Australia. These collections imply original deposition rates of at least 2–5 per year, and if we assume that only a fraction of those discarded have been recovered, a discard rate of 10 or even 50 a year is not unlikely. Other locations as thickly strewn are also known, mostly in south-eastern Australia, from the coast to the arid zone. It is not easy to explain such concentrations as being the result of tools being broken and replaced or as examples of chance loss. Part of the answer may well lie in the lasting qualities of the gum or resin used in hafting: when it became brittle, the tool would have been scrapped (cf. Sheridan 1979). Another explanation might lie in the use of some of these tools in ceremonial activities: perhaps each tool was used for only one ceremony and then discarded. This might also explain their intense concentration in some areas (cf. Hallam 1981).

The relatively smaller number of points that have been found, even in sites where they were most common, may indicate that this tool had more everyday uses. This is strongly supported by the numbers of broken specimens, tips and butts at some sites. For example, of more than 5000 specimens at Yarar, only 25% were whole (Flood 1970:34) and at Tyimede II, only 21 whole points compared to 71 butts, 55 tips, 40 shaft

fragments and two unfinished specimens were recorded (C. White 1967:397–421). Some breakage may have resulted from manufacturer's error, but the contrast with backed blades is too great for this to have been the sole cause. Similar analyses of points have not been made further south (cf. Stockton 1971) where the absolute number recovered in any excavation has been much lower.

The functions of points have been debated extensively, since there are ethnographic records of them being hafted and used for engraving in South Australia, while bifacial specimens from the northern tropics were gum-hafted as spear points. In a recent study of use-wear on nearly 300 whole and broken bifacial and unifacial points, mostly from archaeological sites in the Northern Territory, Kamminga (1978:328–38) found only a handful with wear compatible with use as an engraving tool. We also know that the nineteenth-century South Australians who were engraving with these tools were recycling prehistoric implements. But it is possible that formally similar tools had different functions in different areas. It seems to us that points and backed blades probably served rather different purposes.

We can now look more broadly at the implications these new tools have for Australian prehistory. We have shown that both tool types appeared within the same millennium and that their appearance in different parts of the continent was so nearly contemporaneous that a point of origin cannot be located. We have argued that, although distinguishing an intrusive from an indigenous tradition may be difficult, the dating and distribution of the new tools strongly supports a local origin. In addition, the use of "exotic" materials, though frequent, was not universal. Thus a simple explanation for the appearance and persistence of these tools is not obvious.

Apart from Mulvaney's (1966b) explanation of the new technology in terms of the invention of hafting — an explanation which he has rightly rejected (1975:210) — four other interpretations of the evidence have been made.

1. Basing their arguments on the increased use of "exotic" raw materials, Gould (1978a) and

Lampert (1980) have suggested that the new tools, especially backed blades, signal an expansion of inter-group exchange and recognition of the sacred association of particular classes of raw material over wide areas. According to this view, tool use was to some extent subordinate to raw material type, though Lampert also believes that the new tools mark a more "sophisticated specialised technology". Why these changes should have occurred has not been discussed.

2. In a picturesque article, Jones (1977a) has contrasted the technology of Tasmania with that of Australia. He claims that the new tool forms, as well as adzes, burins, edge-ground hatchets and bone and shell tools, were highly task-specific and more efficient in food-procurement. This gave Australian societies not more food or a wider range of foods, but more leisure time. He argues that this leisure time was used in ritual and religious life and draws attention to the apparent absence of this among Tasmanians in the nineteenth century. Jones' proposition is difficult to test, and he has so far failed to show that any of the anticipated consequences of a more efficient technology, such as increased population densities or longer bouts of leisure time, did in fact occur in Australia (J. P. White 1977b; see Lourandos 1980a for a contrary view). D. Horton (1979b) has also argued that the contrast Jones makes between religious life in the two areas is much overdrawn.

3. Following an argument originally put forward by D. S. Davidson (1936), Palter (1977) has examined a number of preserved hand-thrown and woomera-thrown spears and found significant differences in terms of weight and point of balance. The latter group were lighter and made to more precise specifications. Luebbers (1978) has suggested that points and backed blades would have made better barbs and heads than simple flakes for woomera-thrown spears, and that the creation of the new stone tools may have been related to the adoption of the spear-thrower. While this is an interesting suggestion, it will not account for the extensive

production of microliths in areas of New South Wales and Queensland where the spear-thrower was unknown (unless we posit its disappearance within the last 1000 years).

4. The final explanation is also difficult to test directly. It derives from a suggestion by Peterson (1971), followed up by J. P. White (1977b; see also J. P. White and O'Connell 1979), that the new tools cannot be shown to have been necessary, at least not in a functional sense. This argument rejects as unsubstantiated the idea that these tools were more extractively efficient,[*] and draws attention to the fact that in the recent past effective heads and barbs were made of unretouched stone flakes and bone points. It suggests that similar heads and barbs may have existed in Australia before the advent of backed blades and points, and that the spread of these tools is perhaps best seen as a stylistic phenomenon analogous to Solutrean points in the French Palaeolithic or Clovis and Folsom points in northern America. The extraordinarily rapid spread of the new tools throughout Australia and their local variations in size, shape, raw materials and numbers are all compatible with this idea; so too is the fact that both major classes occurred over almost the entire range of Australian environments, though not throughout any major environmental zone (see, e.g., McBryde 1977). Some factor other than pure economy is necessary to explain this.

In evaluating these four explanations the subsequent history of the types is also relevant. Regarding points, it seems clear that in the southern parts of their range, such as on the lower Murray River, they went out of use quite quickly (Hale and Tindale 1930; Mulvaney 1960;

---

[*] Extractive and maintenance tasks and tools were originally distinguished by L. R. and S. R. Binford (1966). Maintenance tasks involve "activities related primarily to the nutritional and technological requirements of the group [of people]", while extractive tasks "related to the direct exploitation of environmental resources" (1966:291). Stone tools, they argued, were used for one or the other kind of task, either exclusively or nearly so (see also S. R. and L. R. Binford 1969).

Mulvaney *et al.* 1964), whereas in the central Queensland highlands they continued to be used for two or more millennia (Morwood 1981; Mulvaney and Joyce 1965). In Arnhem Land and the Kimberleys, varieties of unifacial, bifacial and Kimberley points are still made in the twentieth century — even if some of the last are for tourists!

The situation with backed blades is harder to assess. In coastal NSW and Victoria, sites younger than about 1000 years have rarely contained backed blades. Indeed, they have been so rare that for some years McCarthy's (1948) suggestion of another "culture period" between them and the present was widely accepted (e.g. Mulvaney 1969). This phase was originally called "Eloueran" after the characteristic implement in the upper levels of Lapstone Creek site, but it was subsequently described as "Adaptive" because of the wide variety of tools found throughout Australia in this period (Mulvaney 1969:106). On the south-east coast, quartz flakes produced by bipolar flaking, shell fish-hooks and bone tools all became common (Lampert 1966a, 1971a; Megaw 1974; Mulvaney 1962b). In the north, forms of long, massive points and blades came into use, although smaller bifacial and unifacial points continued to be made. However, there is evidence from at least one area (northern NSW) that backed blades continued to be made well into the last millennium both on the coastal plains and in the highlands (McBryde 1974:264), so that an "Adaptive Phase" is not evident there. We also note backed blades made of glass, from Perth, South Australia and Sydney (Dickson 1971; Hallam 1981; Tindale 1968), though backing on these could have been a re-invention to cope with extra-sharp edges of the new material.

These varying periods over which backed blades were made lend some support to the stylistic interpretation of their occurrence. If, as other arguments suggest, these tools allowed food to be obtained more efficiently, were related to wider inter-group religious and ritual exchange, or were necessary for spears thrown by spear-throwers, then we would expect the decline in the use of backed blades to be marked by reversals of these trends. Yet it is generally agreed that food-getting remained highly efficient, while spear-throwers and sacred raw materials continued to be important in recent

prehistory. An explanation of these aspects has not yet been offered. Mulvaney's (1969:91) suggestion that the "Adaptive Phase" was an "optimum adjustment to local conditions" has not been substantiated further, while the recent uses of such terms as "post-Bondaian" (Lampert 1971b) suggest that there is no single direction to the technological changes over the last 2000 years.

Hatchets and Adzes

Prior to the point and backed blade technologies, ground stone hatchets existed in the tropics, and adze flakes probably existed in south-western Australia. But it was in association with points and backed blades that both these artefact classes spread throughout Australia. Although there is variability in occurrence between areas, with adzes being rare in south-eastern and south-western coastal and well-forested regions, and hatchets being very rare or even absent in some parts of the south-west (Noone 1943:279; Ride 1958), the earliest examples in all areas occur with the new small tools. However, unlike backed blades and points, hatchets (Fig. 5.14) and adzes (Fig. 5.15) continued in use until the nineteenth century, and both had clearly defined functions.

Evidence of the spread of a ground stone technology into the southern parts of the continent is scanty. In the nineteenth century, hatchets were not used in Tasmania, and since none have been found there, their absence from south-eastern Australia before 8000 years ago seems assured. Examples from sites between that date and the arrival of backed blades are rare, but there are three instances when ground stone hatchets may have been present. The first is a rock-shelter at Curracurrang (code 1CU5) where Megaw, in a series of preliminary reports (1965, 1968, 1974), recorded a date of 7450 ± 180 (GaK-482) for basal sands that contained pebble and flake tools and some edge-notched flakes. These graded up into a highly organic, dark, sandy soil containing both backed blades and edge-ground hatchets dated to no more than 2500 years old (Megaw 1968:328). C. White (1971:153) suggests that, since hatchet heads were very rare in more

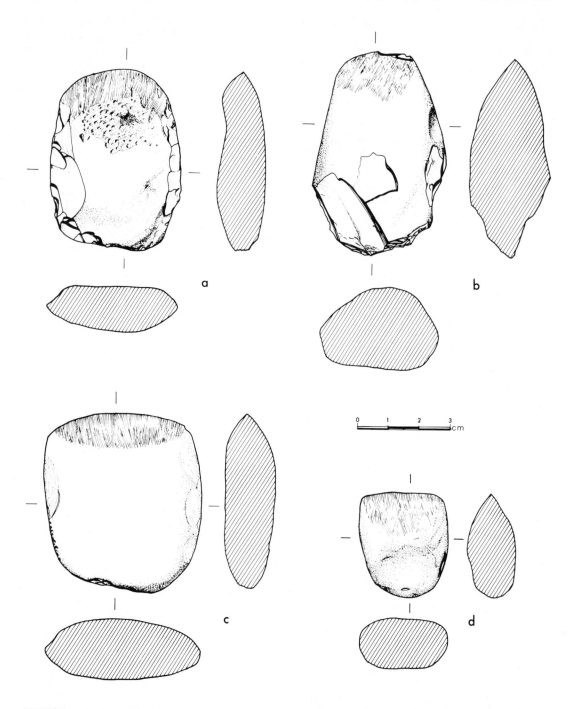

FIGURE 5.14. Ground hatchet heads from southern Australia. All surface collections. a: Penrith, west of Sydney, NSW; b: unprovenanced; c: Colo River, west of Sydney, NSW; d: Tambar Springs, north-central NSW. (University of Sydney collections).

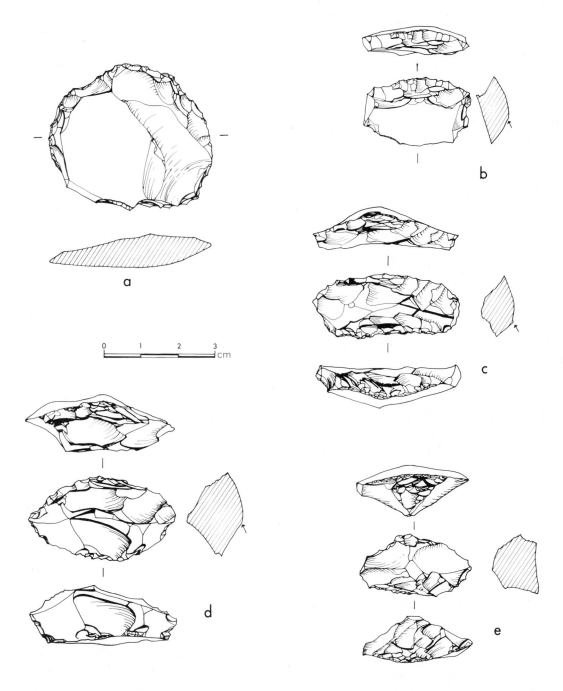

FIGURE 5.15. Adzes and adze slugs (worked-out adzes). a: adze, Pier Lake, north-west NSW; b–d; adze slugs, bulbs of percussion indicated by arrows, unprovenanced; e: adze slug with bulb removed, South Australia. a–d: University of Sydney; e: Australian Museum, E36022.

recent levels of the site, it could be that those at the interface of the dark soil and basal sands were *in situ* below the backed blade levels, with the few associated backed blades being derived from the very rich levels above.

The second case concerns four hatchet heads found up to 2 m below the present low-water level in estuarine blue clays at Shea's Creek just south of Sydney (Etheridge *et al.* 1896). The deductions made then suggested that the artefacts were deposited at a time when the ocean was some five feet (1.6 m) lower than at present, implying an age of perhaps 5000 years. But the nineteenth century analyses paid little attention to the possibility of changes within the local environment. More recent studies within Botany Bay (P. Roy, NSW Department of Mines, pers. comm.) have shown that sedimentation of Shea's Creek did not begin until sand barriers formed when the sea reached its present level about 6000 years ago. Although the tools (and some dugong bones) were found low down in the series of clay and peat sediments, the variability in the local rates of accumulation is such that although they could be 5000 years old, they could be younger.

Finally, Dickson (1977) reports recovering nine edge-ground tools at Potter Point, Kurnell Peninsula (NSW). The site was much eroded by sewer construction and four-wheel drive vehicles, and all material was from the surface. All the several hundred pieces of stone collected were larger than is usual on other late sites in the area and no small backed tools occurred among them. The raw material includes some igneous rocks from the Bass Point area 70 km south and indurated claystone from an unknown source, but there is almost none of the silcrete or silicified wood common in sites with backed blades. The nine edge-ground tools, some of which are broken or extensively worn, and which have heavy butt wear, were all made on long, slender claystone pebbles. Dickson considered them to be chisels rather than axes. Tools called chisels have been reported from various parts of Australia (McCarthy *et al.* 1946:53) (Fig. 5.16) but they have never been observed in use, nor have they been found in dated archaeological deposits. Dickson notes that no similar specimens have been found elsewhere on the Peninsula and that no hatchet heads (common elsewhere) have been found with

these chisels. While there is no direct date on this material, one coarsely flaked pebble chopper similar to those in the surface collection was found beneath the peat of an old inter-dunal swamp. The peat dates to 5620 ± 70 (ANU-402).

None of these three cases, nor even the three together, demonstrates the clear presence of hatchets or of edge-grinding as a tool production technique prior to the occurrence of small, backed tools, although they suggest it. Certainly, in sites and levels with backed blades, hatchets or ground chips from them frequently occur; that is, at this time, this tool form seems to have become more common. However, there are no models to explain either the association between the forms, or the mechanisms of spread. Does the spread into sub-tropical Australia of the hatchet made from igneous or metamorphic rock indicate a change in exchange relationships or food

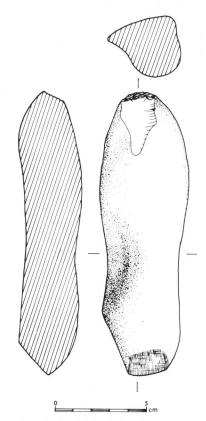

FIGURE 5.16. Edge-ground chisel. Tambar Springs, north-central NSW. University of Sydney.

procurement? Is the relationship with backed blades a firm one? These problems await further research.

Although a few hatchet heads and flakes from them have been found in stratified prehistoric sites, they are too few to show any changes in form over time. It is worth noting, though, that most of the 20,000-year-old hatchet heads from Arnhem Land are formally indistinguishable from modern examples. Studies to date have therefore treated them as a single class and asked non-seriational questions (e.g. Dickson 1978; McBryde 1978b, 1979).

Dickson (1972, 1976, 1978, 1980) has investigated the design, manufacture and use of hatchets experimentally as well as through collections. He suggests that, despite minor local variations, which may relate primarily to the raw materials available for the head, the essential features of Australian hatchets were invariant in space and probably in time (1978:246). He has been unable to locate any regional stylistic variables. One noticeable feature, the presence of hafting grooves on one or both faces, seems to occur erratically.

Experimentally, Dickson has been able to demonstrate that head weights ranging from 250 to 1600 g and handle lengths from 200 to 450 mm are dynamically equivalent, so that tools with larger heads (and shorter handles) are no more efficient than those with smaller heads and longer handles. Although Dickson stresses that the mean weight of 924 hatchet heads is 678 g, which is surprisingly close to the weight of modern steel hatchet heads (680 g), we notice his sample includes a great range in weights, with twenty-four weighing less than 200 g, while maximum weights are around 1400 g. The very small heads have been called toys or attributed to juvenile use, but there is little clear evidence that there was a lower size limit to those used by adults (cf. White and Modjeska 1978b for a New Guinea analogue). The smallest Australian hatchet head known to us weighs 43 g. The range of head weights found in collections suggests that re-sharpening of blunt or broken heads may have been quite frequent. Measurements on 153 hafted heads (Dickson 1987:Appendix 2) show that the full range of head weights occurs among them. These specimens convince us that the tools were

functionally acceptable, provided it can be assumed that they were not just made for collectors. The fact that many whole hatchet heads have been found by Whites suggests that simple loss, cache and formal discard have been important contributors to the archaeological record. This is supported by the fact that they are frequently found alone, without association with other artefacts.

Over the last decade, I. McBryde has directed two major studies on the distribution of stone hatchet heads from particular sources (Binns and McBryde 1972; McBryde 1978b, 1979). In northern New South Wales the lithologies of 517 ground-edge tools (the majority hatchets, with a few chisels) were determined. Most specimens were from surface collections. Ten lithological groups, some with several sub-groups, were identified, and many of these could be sourced to a relatively restricted area, though not to a particular quarry. The distribution of materials from these sources varies widely (Fig. 5.17). From some, especially Moore Creek in the highlands, stone (as lumps, blanks or heads) was transported up to 800 km west, and heads have been found along the tributaries of the Darling River; from others, notably those in the coastal plains of the Clarence and Richmond Rivers, stone was transported over more restricted areas. The various distributions are not discrete, but overlap considerably. Some of the smaller areas are leapfrogged by the larger, but whether there is a time difference between the use of any two sources is not known. Twenty-three examples (thirteen whole heads and ten flakes) from eleven sub-groups are known from stratified archaeological sites in the area (Binns and McBryde 1972:78–79) and in at least three cases the same sources as are recorded in the collections were being used more than 3000 years ago.

In a similar project in Victoria, 650 artefacts have been sourced to seven greenstone (hornfels) quarries. According to McBryde (1978b) two-thirds of the sample comes from two quarries. Some tools were found up to 700 km from these sources, with one-third of the sample occurring more than 300 km away (Fig. 5.18). By contrast, no artefacts from the other five quarries have been found more than 500 km from their source, and only 3% were moved more than 300 km.

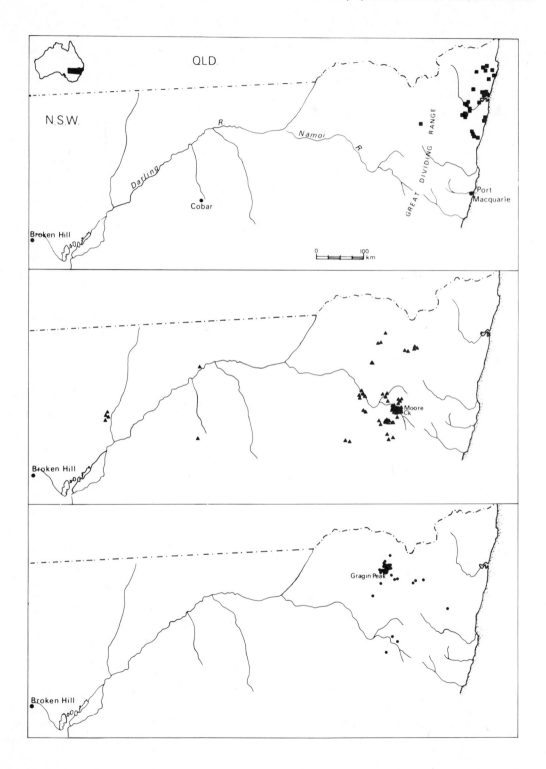

There are also notable variations in the direction of distribution. A majority of hatchets from most of the quarries were taken north and west; only the two smallest samples have limited and local distributions all around their quarries. Explanations of these variations in terms of the availability of stone resources or estimated population densities are hard to find. Fine basalts and dolerites are widespread in many areas in which greenstone heads are also found. On the other hand, the coastal plains of south-eastern Victoria maintained a high population at contact, yet almost no greenstone hatchet heads are known from the area. Interestingly, nineteenth century ethnographers distinguished two major hostile groupings within the Aboriginal tribes of central and eastern Victoria. The quarries all lay within the territory of one group and hatchet heads from them are almost completely absent from the territory of the other. The time depth involved cannot be determined, although if hatchets only occur in association with backed blades it is limited to 5000 years. If spread equally over that time span, McBryde's sample comprises one head for every 7.7 years from an area of about 125,000 km^2 inhabited by perhaps 25,000 people. Put another way, we have three hatchets for every generation of people. Clearly, much larger samples and some well-dated materials are needed before the tracing of nineteenth century political patterns into the past will get much further.

We mentioned earlier the evidence for the invention of hafted flaked adzes in the desert and semi-desert areas of western Australia. Their spread from this area has not been researched as a phenomenon in its own right, as these tools have been seen as part of the small-tool tradition (e.g. Gould 1969, 1973; Mulvaney 1975). There has also been no clear definition either of the varieties named *tula*, burren, Adelaide, and *merna-wadna* (McCarthy *et al.* 1946; Sheridan 1979), or of their formal distinction from flake scrapers, many of which were also hafted. There is a great deal of confusion in the literature between adzes and scrapers (Gould *et al.* 1971; Hayden and Kamminga 1973; Kamminga 1978:340–49), and while studies of use-wear are starting to resolve the problem in particular instances, it still exists.

As Mulvaney (1975:235) has pointed out, the *tula* adze is restricted to the drier areas of Australia, basically within the 500 mm isohyet. This tool was made on a thick flake and its two most important properties were a convex bulbar surface and semi-circular working edge (Fig. 5.15a). The first ensured that the tool could be hafted so that this face could strike the wood at a low angle without frequently breaking away from the resin, while the second ensured that there were no corners susceptible to fracturing. Both were important in terms of its primary use in adzing the very dense woods of the Australian desert flora (Sheridan 1979). Over time, successive blunting and resharpening of the edges produced a highly characteristic, steeply stepflaked edge, and if the tool was reversed in its haft, two such edges were produced and the characteristic *tula* "adze slug" formed (Fig. 5.15c). As Kamminga (1979:349) points out, at this stage these tools were not much use as adzes, though they continued to be good scrapers. However, at times, even the narrow end may have been pressed into use as an adze (O'Connell 1977).

Other forms of adze occur more widely, in Cape York (Wright 1971b:138) and the northern NSW highlands (McBryde 1977:Table 2) for example, as well as in the drier areas. They are absent from most of Victoria and the wetter, eastern parts of NSW. *Elouera*, with their probable function of adzing and scraping very soft wood or bark (Kamminga 1977) have been found in the latter area and may be seen as replacing adzes there. The use-polished flakes called *elouera* from western Arnhem Land (McCarthy and Setzler 1960) were probably used in the same way (Kamminga 1977). Elsewhere, it is possible that hafted flake scrapers were used rather than adzes, but this requires further study.

FIGURE 5.17. Distribution of stone hatchet heads from quarries in northern New South Wales. a: Coarse greywackes derived from local streams or coastal headlands (Group 1A); b: Metamorphosed Baldwin-type greywacke mostly derived from Moore Creek quarry (Group 2B); c: pyrometamorphosed boles, sourced to Gragin Peak (Group 6). Source: Binns and McBryde (1972). Courtesy: Australian Institute of Aboriginal Studies, Canberra, Australia.

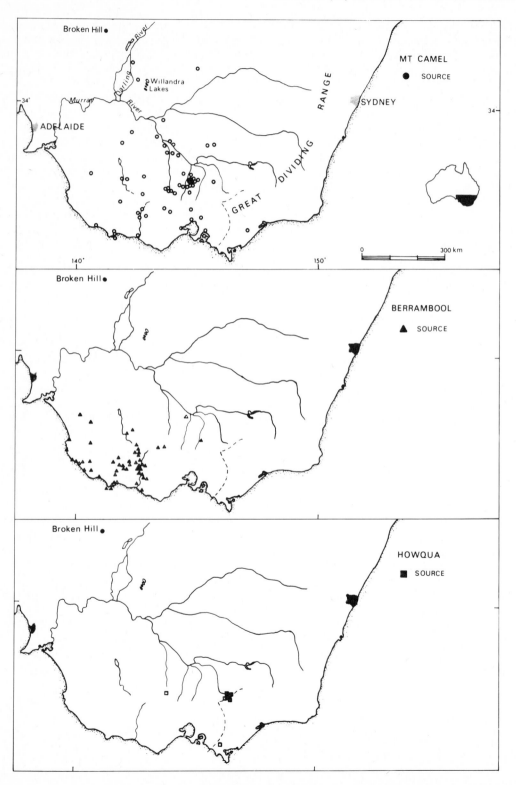

Finally, although in some areas clearly defined adze flakes occur only with small, backed tools or points (e.g. Mulvaney and Joyce 1965), too little stratigraphic archaeology has been carried out in the drier parts of Australia to demonstrate in which areas the spread of all these tools was concurrent.

We conclude this section on technology by stressing that, although new tool forms were developed in Australia five millennia ago, and spread widely throughout the continent, apparently primarily for stylistic and social reasons, other technological changes also occurred within the last 10,000 years.

5.3 Local Subsistence Patterns

During the eighteenth and nineteenth centuries, when they were first observed by Whites, Aboriginal subsistence patterns were extremely varied (2.2). Just how varied we are only now rediscovering, for many of them were destroyed very quickly and few accounts were written. But we can now recognize, for example, that Aboriginal life could be semi-sedentary, focused on reliable resources made more so by environmental manipulation, and with people living in regular villages of well-built, circular, one-roomed houses. Life could also be highly mobile, relying on resources whose occurrence in time and space was less predictable. These lifeways were the end-result of a long history, but their final form was developed particularly during the last few thousand years.

When we investigate the history of these subsistence patterns, especially through the medium of archaeology, the nature and extent of resource variability must be considered. Of critical importance is the fact that the lives of groups of people are focused on the resources of the domain within which they live, rather than on those of a broad region. This may sound trite, but a series of recent studies which have drawn on modern Aboriginal knowledge have particularly stressed the importance of local environments (D. Harris 1977; Meehan 1977a, 1977b; Peterson 1972; and for a classic early version of this see

Thomson 1939). For example, some of these studies demonstrate that, although the resources used along the tropical north coast are primarily determined by the highly seasonal rainfall, any one group of people ranging within that area will have a locally appropriate approach to this seasonal variation. People living near an estuary or beach may move to slightly higher ground at the beginning of the wet season, will camp in a relatively exposed area to avoid mosquitoes, and may hunt less but gather more shellfish. People living only a few kilometres inland, around dry-season lagoons, may move up into the hills, undertaking considerably more hunting, and gathering no shellfish at all (Jones 1981). Such locally appropriate decisions are, of course, not unknown in the archaeological literature, though perhaps they are more commonly encountered in terms of similarities in site choice by people specializing on a particular resource, whether it be salmon in western North American rivers or defensible off-shore islands in the case of Lapita potters. But it is worth stressing that among "hunter-gatherers" day-to-day decisions will depend almost entirely on specific local factors (cf. Lee 1980), and the data in archaeological sites may be expected to reflect this.

Another aspect of resource variability is the rapidity with which local situations may change. Such factors as storms, estuary silting, rock-platform erosion, rainfall variation and pond drying all affect plants and animals. For example, it is known that the quantity of many species of shellfish on a coast can vary enormously from year to year (Underwood 1979), and Meehan (1977b) has shown that this can result in an almost complete change in the range of shellfish gathered by one group of people from one year to the next. Many site-specific changes in the archaeological record may be attributable to such local variations.

The following accounts of subsistence economies are limited in at least two ways. The first derives from the archaeological sample. Even in the areas of most intensive research, the number of analysed sites is very small. For example, M. Sullivan (1976) reports that more than 200 shell middens exist along 150 km of coastline in

---

FIGURE 5.18. Distribution of hatchet heads from three greenstone quarries in Victoria: Mt. Camel, Berrambool and Howqua. Source: McBryde (1978b).

southern NSW, but within that area only two excavations have occurred, and only one of them has been published. Parallels could be drawn everywhere else in the country. The sampling of subsistence data within sites has also been very limited, and even the most comprehensive analyses are based on only one or a few column samples, especially when dealing with shellfish. Since we know that intra-site variability is often considerable, these analyses may not give us a full picture.

The second limitation is the population from which we can sample. In some places most sites have been destroyed. The mortar used to bind the sandstone blocks of many early Sydney houses was made with lime from the Aboriginal shell middens which lined the harbour's shores. Only two small, obscure sites survived to be reported on in the last twenty years (Bowdler 1971; Ross and Specht 1976). A similar picture is true of many coastal regions north of Sydney where sites have been destroyed by sand mining, road building and the construction of holiday homes. In one inlet south of Sydney, M. Sullivan (1981) found that only about 8% by volume of the shell midden present in 1890 remained by 1980. The extent of site destruction is often extremely difficult to estimate, but where it is extensive only a general outline of prehistoric subsistence can be determined.

We turn now to some examples of particular subsistence analyses. We outline first some general models based on environmental and ethno-historic data to which are linked any archaeological material that is available. It is notable that there is usually much less archaeological data than there are other kinds. We have chosen some of the most comprehensive studies, as they give some idea of the range of subsistence practices as well as of analytical methods. We then describe some particular analyses which are either site-specific or refer to small clusters of sites. They have been chosen to illustrate the range of available data and approaches to them.

General Models

Poiner's study (1976) concerns subsistence on the central and south coasts of New South Wales,

34°S–36°S. She makes predictions on the basis of the modern environment and then examines their fit with the archaeological data. The area is temperate with only a low degree of seasonal change so that neither temperature (critical in higher latitudes) nor rainfall (critical inland and in the tropical north) dominate. In this area, the range and abundance of food sources of all kinds is lowest in winter, the coldest and wettest period. The principal flush of plant growth occurs in spring (Oct.–Nov.), while certain fish and shellfish are more common and more readily gathered during summer (Dec.–Feb.). Variation in rainfall appears to be a minor factor only: droughts are always possible, but are not predictable and in any case will change the resource balance rather than having catastrophic impact. Poiner therefore predicts that seasonal economic strategies will not occur in an extreme form, that the greatest contrast will be seen between strategies for winter and other seasons, that group territories need not be very large and that crisis avoidance mechanisms such as extensive contact networks and flexible territorial uses need not be highly developed. She further predicts that winter, with the lowest number of available resources, none of which dominates the food quest, will be the time of greatest population dispersal and most frequent movement, with more people moving away from the coastal zones (Fig. 5.19, top).

Testing these propositions archaeologically raises some problems. For a start, as most resources are not present in one season and absent in another, but more or less common and accessible, there will be few direct indicators of seasonality in the record. Further, if winter groups were indeed smaller and more nomadic, then this, combined with the absence of highly visible shellfish away from the coast, will mean their sites will be much smaller, less visible and more likely to have been destroyed. Thus all parts of the model are not equally testable.

The archaeological evidence Poiner uses comes from eleven sites, three of which have been only briefly described by their excavators, and all of which have only small samples drawn from them. Only one is an inland site. Nonetheless, in terms of the range of resources found in them, she is able to separate the sites into those with generalized and those with restricted economies.

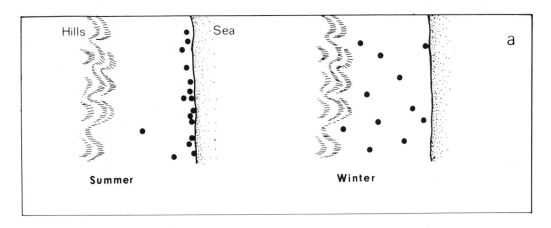

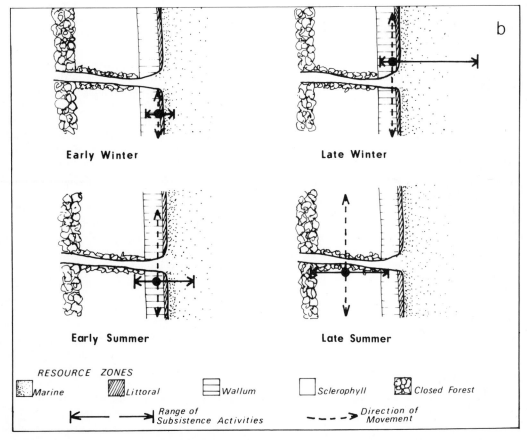

FIGURE 5.19. (a). Population aggregation and dispersal in south coast NSW. After Poiner (1976). (b). Subsistence patterns in four seasons on the coast near Brisbane, south coast Queensland. After Draper (1978).

The three sites with the most wide-ranging resource use are all coastal — Currarong (Lampert 1971a), Curracurrang (Megaw 1965), and Kurnell (unpublished) — and these also have the widest range of artefacts represented, with evidence of bone, stone and shell working. The range of food remains suggests that these sites were occupied in summer.

At least one highly specialized site was also occupied in summer. Durras North (Lampert 1966a) is a small cave on a beach just above high-tide level. Apart from shellfish, its major subsistence component was "mutton-bird" (a shearwater, *Puffinus tenuirostris*), a summer migrant. The considerable quantity of worked bone came mostly from other birds, all of which would have been readily available in summer. Several other sites in which the remains consisted only of fish, shellfish and mutton-birds exist on the coast (Lampert 1971b:125–26), and the exposed situation of some of them suggests a summer use was more likely. By contrast, a shelter on Bomaderry Creek, above the tidal estuary level, produced no fish, few shells, and a large number of mammal bones. Thus, while the archaeological evidence does not falsify the model built up from environmental data, in the absence of very clear seasonal indicators it does not demonstrate its validity. Poiner also drew on ethnographic evidence to test her propositions, but here too some difficulties arose because of conflicting reports.

A very different pattern of behaviour has been modelled by Draper (1978) for an area around Brisbane at about 27°30′ S. Nine hundred kilometres north of Poiner's area, the climate is rather more sub-tropical than temperate, with rainfall primarily occurring in summer. The coastal plains are low-lying and swampy, with some areas of sand-dunes. The main resources are schooling fish, shellfish, plant roots (especially fern root) and land mammals. The notable contrast with Poiner's model comes in the seasons of aggregation and dispersal. In this area, winter is the time when a range of fish school for spawning and are most easily caught. It is also the period when the sea mammal dugong (*Dugong dugon*) are most commonly in the region even though they are a rare resource. Some shellfish are available from surf beaches. As winter is the time when resources are most

available, this is when people can be expected to aggregate (Fig. 5.19, bottom). By contrast, summer should be a season of dispersal, and of movement away from the coast. Several reasons lie behind this. For one, the coasts are themselves more dangerous, being subject to floods and also to occasional cyclones. Mammals are in better condition too, although because of the rains and consequent vegetation growth, they are more widely scattered over the countryside. Finally, plant foods are available in the hinterland, and especially in late summer the prolific bunya nuts are available in the ranges 60–100 km inland. There are many reports of large aggregations of people meeting there for ceremonies and exchanges (H. Sullivan 1977). Draper has not so far demonstrated archaeologically that his model accurately represents the prehistoric situation, and he draws attention to the considerable variability from season to season, so that people's scheduling decisions will fluctuate around the general model given here. Some of the problems found by Poiner in her archaeological analyses are likely to recur.

Lilley's study (1978) is of the upper Brisbane River 40 km inland from Brisbane. The subsistence pattern he models is basically the same as Draper's, but he also shows how much the local environment conditions human use of it. The upper Brisbane River lies in a north–south trending valley. The valley floor is only about 30 m above sea level, but it is surrounded on three sides by 300–600 m hills, so that it is a clearly defined ecosystem. The two major resource zones are the riverine lowlands and the non-riverine lowlands and foothills. As is the case nearer the coast, winter is the drier season, and at this time food resources for people, animals and birds tend to be concentrated around the river. The technology Aborigines used for fishing — weirs, poison and spearing — is also more practicable at times of low river levels. A pattern of aggregation and dispersal similar to that found on the coast may therefore be predicted, but it will not be nearly so differentiated in terms of the resources drawn on. In the one excavation so far reported (Platypus Shelter, some 30 m from the river), Lilley found bones from a range of land animals, as well as platypus, tortoise and fish. Although only small numbers were involved, the presence of water-dwelling creatures implies a dry season use, or at least little use in the spring and summer breeding season. Like Poiner, Lilley says that he has difficulty in showing that the site was not occupied in other seasons, and can really only demonstrate that his model is not falsified by the evidence available.

The southern coast of the continent, on either side of the South Australian–Victorian border, has been the focus of two recent PhD studies which have attempted not only to describe the local economies but to show their changes through time and provide some explanation for these changes (Lourandos 1976, 1977, 1980a, 1980b; Luebbers 1978).

The area has one of the most reliable rainfalls and stable weather patterns in Australia. The narrow coastal plain, although cool, is a well-watered area, and one in which poor drainage has led to the formation of vast swamps. In the western part, rather greater lagoonal development led recent inhabitants to construct complex networks of mud and stone fish-traps, while further east one major subsistence focus was eels, caught in earthern channels and boulder-lined canals. In both areas, littoral resources formed a significant but not dominant part of the subsistence base.

As the title of his work, *Meals and Menus*, shows, Luebbers (1978) has tried to look at changes in subsistence economies, first by the analysis of single events (meals) from which he then constructs a temporally changing picture of menus. He starts by showing that during the last 5000 years the history of the massive tidal lagoons that stretch over about 120 km has varied from north to south. The northern lagoons, which originally supported a very rich estuarine environment, gradually deteriorated as the lagoon entrances were blocked by advancing beach ridges, and isolated unstable lakes formed. In the south the reverse was true, and rich, fresh-water lakes formed in recent times. Inland, the swamps varied less over time but have always varied in size with the seasons, being largest in spring.

During the nineteenth century, human subsistence patterns varied strongly with the seasons, with larger aggregations and more coastal exploitation in summer and more dispersed but perhaps more sedentary patterns in the cold winters. Several accounts refer to villages of warm, waterproof, well-built, one-roomed houses being used in winter.

Although he attempts to investigate various aspects of this pattern, Luebbers' most interesting analyses concern shellfish. He remarks (1978:96) that much of the prehistoric record still survives on the surface, and "small, discrete heaps of shellfish are a dominant depositional component of the coastal margin". If some pattern in visitation to sites could be established from these heaps, then the reconstruction of subsistence strategies would clearly become easier. To do this, Luebbers shows that some species of mollusc shells exhibit growth lines which, like tree rings, form a characteristic pattern related to a series of environmental events. In some small, discrete, prehistoric shell-heaps similarly sized shells exhibit similar patterns of growth lines. This is good evidence that the shells were collected at the same time, and clearly the technique has some promise for more wide-ranging analyses of shell middens.

It has proved difficult to determine the collection season from these patterns of growth, since studies on modern shellfish suggest that stress rather than season is a major growth-line determinant. Nevertheless, some data do support the idea that coastal resources were used in all seasons, especially during the last 2000 years or so. The use of coastal resources can be linked to changes in the inland swamps, which, although still large, were much smaller during the last 3000 years than they were between 8000 and 3000 years ago. After 3000 years ago freshwater habitats across the whole district changed as a result of climatic change, and the resources available from them decreased significantly. In this situation people turned more and more frequently to coastal regions and intensified their exploitation of the swamps. The former is seen not only in winter exploitation of the coasts but in the change in actual marine resources collected. The more recent collections included shellfish and crayfish from the sub-tidal zone, rather than being restricted to shellfish from the inter-tidal area. Intensification is seen in specialized equipment such as the extensive fish weirs and traps.

Lourandos' subsistence model, for an area some 200 km south-east of the area studied by Luebbers, is quite similar although without the detailed environmental chronology on which Luebbers bases his model. The most interesting aspect of the annual subsistence pattern is the extensive inland fisheries. Lakes and swamps within the inland plain, such as Lake Condah, had many lines of stones piled within their flood-plain beds and these served to hold fish and direct them into nets or basket traps. The most famous of these sites, at Toolondo (Lourandos 1976), lies 135 km inland at the headwaters of the south-flowing Glenelg River. There, a 2.5 × 1.0 m canal was dug for more than 2 km to connect two swamps in which eels lived. An elaborate series of shorter, dead-end canals leading off the main one appear to be traps. There are no eyewitness accounts of the operation of this system, but there are for others, such as Mt. William. They record the catching of large quantities of fish on which considerable gatherings feasted. Fish manage-ment in this area ranges from canals to a series of stone-lined clay and brush weirs and traps in the inland lakes and marshes. All were primarily concerned with the management of eels, which migrated in the early autumn. According to G. A. Robinson, who observed the Mt. William system in 1841 (Lourandos 1976:182), at least fifteen acres (6 ha) were covered with "ramified and extensive trenches" covering "thousands of yards". Their purpose appears to have been not simply to catch fish; it was also to ensure that all suitable marshy areas were stocked, and perhaps that all families or user groups had access to the resources. The period over which these traps were constructed, and the extent to which all were in use at any one time, is not known.

A recent detailed survey of the Lake Condah traps (Coutts *et al.* 1978) shows that there were four separate systems, each of which came into and went out of use according to different flood depths (Fig. 5.20). A maximum of eight traps were in use at any one time and between them the four systems could utilize water depths over a 3.5 m range. Construction methods included the dig-ging of channels through basalt as well as the building of walls and weirs. On higher ground, basalt blocks were used to build semi-circular shelters which may have been roofed. The Lake Condah systems have been constructed since the Late Pleistocene — within the last 12,000 years or so — for this is when volcanic lava flows blocked local drainages and created the swamp.

The eels which were caught in these and other fish-traps, such as at Lake Bolac, were a seasonally available resource. They were easiest to catch, most nutritious and more predictable in occurrence when migrating in early autumn (March–April). Lourandos argues that the pur-pose of the traps was not so much to increase the size of the catch as to increase its predictability. Since eels were highly profitable in terms of labour expenditure, increased reliability as a food source could allow both denser populations and the regular concentration of these for social and ceremonial gatherings. He also argues convincingly that the stabilization of resource occurrence ensured that certain groups had control over them, and thus over the location and timing of ceremonial activities that were advan-tageous to them. Whether the growth of these systems was originally related to climatic and environmental change, as Luebbers argues for further west, is not clear, but it seems quite likely.

Lourandos uses environmental and ethno-historic data to show that a range of other reliable coastal and inland resources existed in the area. Roots and tubers, especially the yam daisy (*Microseris scapigera*), formed a continuing staple. Coastal resources were mostly taken in summer, with shellfish forming a predictable resource, while seals and land animals were less reliable although highly productive when ob-tained. A picture of very high population density (up to one person/1.5 km^2) emerges, and there was considerable sedentism (Lourandos 1977). Early observers noted villages of 10–13 houses up to 3 m in diameter and "sufficiently strong for a man on horseback to ride over" (Kenyon, quoted in Lourandos 1976:128). These were in con-tinuous use for at least several months of each year and perhaps longer around major swamps, where resources could be relied on.

Along the coast, the subsistence pattern seems to have been one of semi-sedentary base camps, which were used particularly in spring and summer, and which were supplemented by short-term sites where a more restricted range of resources was used. Base camps have been identified at Seal Point (Lourandos 1980b: 221–300) and Armstrong Bay (Coutts 1981:73–74). At both sites a wide range of shellfish and other marine fauna have been found, along with land animals, especially

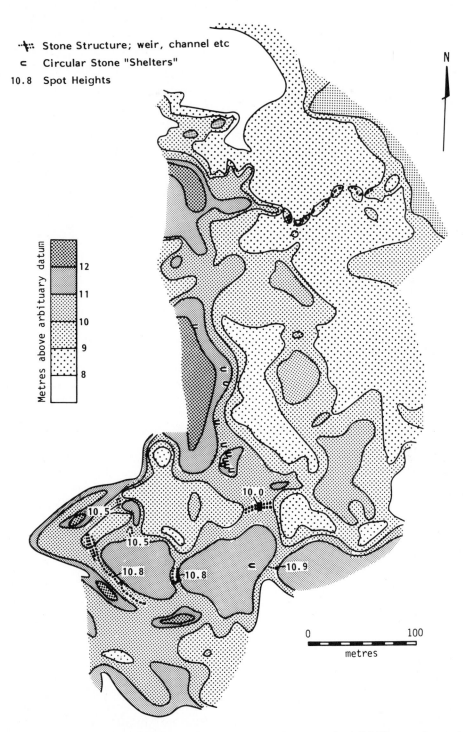

FIGURE 5.20. Part of the Lake Condah fish traps showing the exploitation of small differences in spot heights. The semi-circular, stone hut foundations may be post-contact in date. Source: Coutts *et al.* (1978).

possums (phalangerids). Both these sites have been dated to within the last 2500 years.

Small excavations of several temporary camps have been made. Four have been described by Coutts et al. (1976a) around the Port Fairy area of western Victoria. We mention them here to show how important local resources were. While only one site has been directly dated, all are probably more recent than the last eruption of the Tower Hill volcano, probably no more than 4000 years ago. How much environmental change was brought about by that eruption or by local drainage variation has not been studied. The sites will be described moving from east to west.

Belfast Lough (73213/037 in the Victoria Archaeological Survey site numbering scheme) is a shell midden in sand-dunes between a large back-dune lake and a sandy beach. Rock platforms are 2 km distant. As might be expected, the dominant shells (90% MNI of a sample of 838) were one sandy-shore species, Donacilla nitida. Among the sample were many very small specimens, along with a few sub-tidal sandy-shore species and some wave-rolled shell. This suggests that some form of dredging rather than individual collection of shellfish was employed. Another sandy-shore species, Plebidonax deltoides, was also present, but in very low numbers. This shellfish has a much higher meat to shell ratio than Donacilla, and its low representation in the sample suggested to the excavators that the local environment was not rich. There was no evidence in the sample of the exploitation of the nearby lake.

Reamur Rocks (73213/041) consists of some 60 m of shell midden, mostly about 20 cm thick, exposed by deflation in the edge of a sand-dune just above a sandy beach and a large area of tidal rock platform. The dominant shellfish was Subninella undulata from the lower tidal zone of the rock platform. This species has a high meat to shell ratio and since it did not occur in masses must have been hand collected. The excavators noted that no sandy-shore shellfish were found although beaches occur within 100 m of the site. Only a single fragment of bone, probably seal, was found, along with a quantity of cortex waste from flint.

The Craigs (73213/038) has been described as

having two cultural layers, although the only published section does not show this (Coutts and Witter 1977:47; Coutts et al. 1976a:Fig. 6). The midden, within a sand-dune, is on a cliffed headland above a large rock platform. At least 30 m of the midden is exposed by deflation. As at Reamur, the dominant shellfish was Subninella, with limpets, another rock-platform species with a high meat to shell ratio, as secondary. Heavily oxidized core waste showed that flint was being collected. Two radiocarbon dates of 780 ± 95 (SUA-775) and 2265 ± 100 (SUA-774) show that the site was used over the last 2500 years (Coutts 1978b:5).

Yambuk Heads (73213/036) is a small headland dune at the entrance to a lagoon mouth, where it emerges onto a rocky shore. The site excavated however, lies some 500 m inland, on top of a low cliff overlooking the beach-fringed estuarine lagoon. As with the other sites, it consists of thin layers of shell within a sand-dune. The dominant species was Plebidonax, a sandy-shore dweller, which occurred probably along the lagoon beaches (although the water is now sometimes brackish, which these animals dislike) and certainly on the sandy foreshore. The sample collected (n = 384) consisted mostly of mature individuals, which appears to indicate selection, even if dredging was the initial collecting method.

About 80 km west of this area, Lourandos (1976:189) excavated some undisturbed deposit in the Bridgewater Caves, limestone caverns overlooking large freshwater lakes 1.5 km from the coast. Both faunal and floral remains were recovered, but they have not yet been described. Most of the fauna was of medium to large land mammals — bandicoots, possums, wallabies, and so on. There was also a high number of retouched artefacts, cores and rejuvenation flakes, as opposed to primary flakes, suggesting that these caves were used as a temporary camp rather than as a long-term residence.

Away from the western coasts and stretching several hundred kilometres north to the Murray River and beyond, the most common archaeological site is an earthern mound (often called "blackfellows ovens" or mirryn-yongs). These range from 5 to 50 m in diameter and 0.5–1.5 m in height. As described by Coutts *et al.* (1976b, 1977, 1979), these mounds tend to cluster along major drainages, and they served a variety of uses, including camping and burial places. All appear to have been artificially made. Oven pits were dug into them: faunal and artefact remains occurred within them. Stone implements were usually made of locally available, coarse-grained materials, mainly quartz. There is little archaeological evidence that shelters were built on the mounds, and none of the early European descriptions mention this except in areas of very flat country where the mounds formed islands during floods. One account of shelters was given by William Beveridge (1889). He also described the creation of mounds in the swampy flood plain of the Murray in great detail. First a hole 2 × 0.5 m was dug, and fist-sized pieces of clay kept. A fire was lit in the pit and the clay balls were piled on top to heat them up. Then the hot clay was removed, the hole was lined with leaves and grass, filled with layers of food and hot clay balls, and, finally, it was covered with bark and earth. The clay refuse from this cooking process formed the base of the mound, which grew as more cooking, using fresh clay, was done in the same area. Beveridge's description has been recently confirmed, at least for smaller mounds, by a series of auger surveys (Coutts *et al.* 1979:15). Larger mounds, however, even if initially fortuitous, appear to have been deliberately added to in order to make living places.

We note in passing that cooking was done in pits elsewhere in south-eastern Australia (Bickford 1966:92), and the similarity to methods used in the New Guinea highlands at the other end of Sahul is quite striking.

Field surveys of mounds along both the Hopkins River in southern Victoria and at Nyah on the Murray River show that mounds tend to occur in clusters. Stratigraphic excavations of two mounds in the former area produced some bone and stone tools, burnt bone of mammals from the surrounding open woodland environment, egg-shell and freshwater molluscs. Hearths, and fireplaces made with rocks, were also common and probably contributed to the black colour of the mounds. Excavations in one large mound on the Murray produced some fish, crayfish, shellfish and land mammal remains, along with a very few artefacts. In all cases, the quantity of cultural material was very low compared to volume of earth.

Mirryn-yong mounds are difficult to interpret. It seems likely that they were campsites of some kind and that they were re-used over considerable periods. The earliest Europeans, with one exception, did not see them in use, and in many cases no clear topographic or local environmental reasons for their construction are now apparent. Some are only simple accumulations of debris, but others have been built up. The period over which they were made and used is unknown. But in southern Victoria they are so large that they argue for some effort, commensurate with more than occasional use.

The subsistence patterns of coastal inhabitants north of the Tropic of Capricorn have not been investigated archaeologically to the same extent as those of the south. Not unexpectedly in view of the current distribution of traditional Aboriginal knowledge, more effort has been made there to elucidate the functioning of extant or recently abandoned subsistence systems. These studies have suggested general similarities throughout the area — the dominance of the monsoon, the regular importance of estuarine swamps with their associated flora and fauna, the use of nets, weirs and spears in fishing and of spears in hunting, the seasonal use of fire in plant and animal management, and the importance of shellfish in the diet.

The subsistence pattern best linked with archaeological data is that of western Arnhem Land, around the former mission of Oenpelli (C. White 1967, 1971, C. White and Peterson 1969). Here the climate is tropical monsoonal with marked seasonality. About 90% of the rainfall (mean 1400 mm) falls between October and March. The area can be divided into two main habitats, the coastal plains and the sandstone plateau which rises 100–250 m behind them. When the rains come, large areas of the plains are flooded and humans and animals retreat to higher ground, being no longer able to reach many swamp plants, fish, shellfish and other resources. The higher ground at this time is better watered, and its animals and plants flourish. In the dry season the many swamps and lagoons become more accessible, and birds, fish and shellfish, along with water plants of many kinds, can be gathered. Five sites were excavated in 1964–65, three on the plains and two in the plateau. We discuss here only those levels dating from the last 6000 years, when the sea reached its present level. After this date we can assume that the climate has been comparable to that of the present, and direct material evidence of subsistence behaviour is found in some sites.

In the plains sites the chief component was shells, the majority of them from estuarine situations (Fig. 5.21). There were also fish, birds and tortoises, a few small mammals and, in one site, plant remains. In the two plateau sites (Tyimede I and II) acid ground-water had destroyed all organic remains apart from carbon. But it seems clear that shellfish were not taken to these sites in any quantity, for had they been their alkalinity would have been sufficient to preserve them, along with other organic remains, in their matrix. The plains environments were not exploited by plateau residents.

The environmental contrast is mirrored in the stone artefacts. In the upper levels of all sites, points were the most common type, but while

FIGURE 5.21. Excavation at Malangangerr site, near Oenpelli showing approximately 1m of shell midden lenses. Scale in 20 cm. Courtesy: C. Schrire.

several hundred whole and broken specimens, along with manufacturing evidence, were found in the plateau sites, a similar volume of deposit in the plains sites produced only a handful of points and very little evidence of manufacturing or repair. By contrast, there were many bone and shell tools in the plains sites. Stone points were almost certainly mounted as spear tips and used in hunting. so that their occurrence in the plateau sites, where hunting would have been a common wet-season occupation, is some confirmation of the model. The relative absence of hunting tools in the plains sites used in the dry season is also in accord with the predictions, though the contrast is rather more extreme than might be expected. We note that a greater use of stone tools might be expected in the plateau, since the sources of raw material were there.

More recent excavations (Kamminga and Allen 1973; H. Allen 1977) do not disconfirm the model either, although both they and re-analysis of the older data suggest that local conditions around the base of the plateau, where most plains sites are, have become more favourable to freshwater than brackish water shellfish during the last thousand years. Excavations at two other plains sites and one in a plateau valley also showed the technological contrasts between the two environments, although some minor variations, resulting perhaps from different uses of sites, were recorded.

The environmental and archaeological contrast may be interpreted in two main ways (C. White and Peterson 1969). One interpretation is that the plains and the plateau were occupied by people with distinctive technological traditions. People living on the plains would have made such perishable items as bone-tipped spears and baskets, and would have exchanged these for stone artefacts, especially points, with people in the hills. Of course, each group would have responded to the seasonal variations in its environment, the plains people by retreating to higher ground such as plateau outliers, and the plateau people by moving out over broader areas of country. Both groups may well have used rockshelters more in the wet season than in the dry. The other interpretation is that there was a general, though probably not universal, movement between plateau and plain in response to the seasons. There is some evidence for movement of this kind in the ethnographic record of the last 150 years; however, it is not conclusive. The best way of distinguishing between these interpretations would be to find some seasonal indicators among the archaeological food debris. These might occur in the relative proportions of adult and juvenile animals, in growth rings or other variation in some species of shellfish or crabs, or in some other source. It would be surprising if the marked seasonality of the environment were not reflected in some aspect of the biological data. But until this is investigated, an interpretation which apparently covers the last 6000 years relies solely on the ethnographic data.

Specific Subsistence Studies

We turn now from attempts at subsistence modelling to more specific studies undertaken in various parts of Australia. The first series of studies concerns coastal shell middens occurring from Sydney to 250 km south. This is the area covered by Poiner's model, and it is the one area where a series of midden studies has been carried out. They are available in either published or thesis form. The range, and some of the complications, in midden studies are thus expressed here better than elsewhere in Australia. One notable omission in these studies is the complete excavation or comparative sampling of different volumes within a midden, though given the amount of work involved this is hardly surprising.

The first sites we describe are at Currarong on the Beecroft Peninsula (Lampert 1971a, 1971b) (Fig. 5.22). The shelters occur on the northern edge of the rocky plateau which forms the peninsula. They are some 500 m from the sea, 9 m above it and about 100 m from an estuarine creek with extensive shellfish resources. The gully provides fresh water, some animals and firewood. Lampert excavated two north-facing shelters about 6 m apart. Sixteen square metres were removed from shelter 1, to a maximum depth of 1.5 m, and 4 m^2 from shelter 2 to a maximum depth of 1.2 m. Shelter 1 proved to contain shell midden at the back of the shelter and in the top

levels, with the rest of the deposit containing no organic materials. The matrix of shelter 2 contained shell throughout. Radiocarbon determinations showed that the shell in shelter 2 had accumulated over some 4000 years,* whereas all the shell in shelter 1 was recent. Such a difference between two immediately adjacent sites was surprising, but it was some years before the probable explanation was realized. An initial clue, given in the original report, was that many of the stone artefacts in the lowest, coarse, sandy levels of shelter 1 had smoothed edges as if waterworn. A second clue was that sandy levels just below the actual shell midden contained small quantities of rather decayed shell. Then, observations made during a rainstorm revealed that, owing to the configuration of the sandstone above shelter 1, a much greater volume of runoff water poured over the lip and down onto the outer part of the deposit than in shelter 2. This rainwater, running over sandstone, was slightly acidic, and over time had dissolved all but the most recent shell and other organic material. It is interesting that, although this must have caused considerable shrinkage in the volume of the deposit, stone artefacts (which were not dissolved) occurred in about the same concentration in both shelters. Slightly more were found in the lowest level of shelter 1, consistent with its being the most eroded level, but the large-scale differences which might be anticipated following the removal of 40–60% of the deposit (the percentage of shell in shelter 2 and upper shelter 1) were not found.

Consistent with their location, the shelters contained a wide range of faunal remains: mammals (16 species, with bandicoot being the most common), birds (15 species, mostly sea birds, with mutton-bird most common), reptiles, rock-crabs and fish (8 species). Among the mammals, seals and whales were probably

---

* Lampert's original date for the basal material was 3740 ± 100 (ANU-386). A recent re-excavation for the purpose of re-dating produced a consistent series of dates on shell, the oldest of which is 5540 ± 90 (SUA-224 corrected after Gillespie and Temple 1977) (P. J. Hughes and Djohadze 1980:6). On the assumption of a consistent rate of accumulation, a maximum date of 7000 years is likely. A similar extrapolation on the basis of constant sedimentation gives the same date for shelter 1.

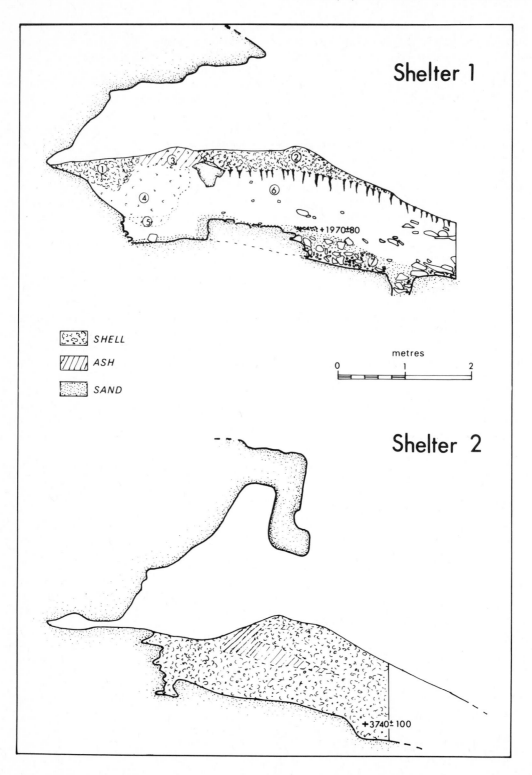

Shelter 1

SHELL
ASH
SAND

metres
0   1   2

+1970±80

Shelter 2

+3740±100

stranded animals. Fish came both from reefs (snapper, some wrasses) and estuaries (bream), and in recent times were probably mostly caught with hooks and spears respectively. Shellfish came from two environments, the shore (mostly inter-tidal rock platform and reef) and the estuary. The sampling of shellfish was only on a small scale (one 25 cm^2 column sample with check samples from other columns) and the results are given in terms of relative weights. However, in so far as they can be compared, the results from the two shelters are consistent.

Two changes over time are notable. While two estuarine species made up two-thirds or more of the shelter 2 deposit, there was a switch in relative importance from rock oysters to Hercules club whelk about half way up the deposit, some 1500 years ago. Lampert suggests that this change was caused by over-exploitation, but we think it as likely that small environmental changes within the estuary could have caused a change in the local occurrence of each species. The other change was the steadily increasing proportion of sea-shore shellfish, so that they formed about one-third of the shells at the top of both shelters. Why more shells were brought from further away is unclear. Possibly the change relates to changes in the seasonal use of the shelter, but there is not enough detail to determine this. It is also possible that these changes were caused by a combination of cost-benefit assessments and preference on the part of collectors, though we cannot apply a strictly calculated model. The considerable numbers of snapper and mutton-bird certainly point towards a summer use of the shelter, and the increasing proportion of sea-shore shellfish, which are best collected in that season, may confirm a slowly changing pattern of use. However, analysis of a larger sample is really required.

The artefacts people made, used and left in the shelters include some used directly for food-getting. Four fish-hooks and some partially made ones (blanks) were made on turban shell. The blanks and some tapering stone files with wear

consistent with their use on hooks show that these were made in the shelter. All were found in the upper levels of both shelters. The idea that they were an innovation of the last thousand years is strongly supported by evidence from Bass Point, discussed below.

Two major groups of bone points were found (Fig. 5.23). The larger comprised bipoints and unipoints of split bone ranging in length from 13 to 62 mm. Many have a general all-over gloss which is too diffuse to be the result of use. Several bipoints had median bands of resin or gum, which was also found at the base of some unipoints. It seems most likely that these were used as tips and barbs for multipronged fishing spears like those collected by Banks in 1770 (Megaw 1969). The other group were longer (42–126 mm) and stouter, made of unsplit bone (bird and macropod), and with a heavy concentration of polish at the tip. None had gum or other evidence of hafting, and they are most likely to have been used as awls or piercers on bark and perhaps skins.

Stone artefacts may also have been used in the food quest. The most important were small flakes and bipolar cores in quartz and other materials. Bipolar cores, often called "fabricators" in Australia (J. P. White 1968b), were common in the middle levels of shelter 1, and there quartz was the commonest stone. Lampert notes that a common spear type at the time of European contact had, near its tip, one or two rows of small unmodified flakes, usually of quartz. Although called a "death spear", its uses probably included mammal hunting, so that the occurrence and maintenance of similar artefacts at Currarong might well be expected.

Other stone artefacts are less clearly extractive in nature. Two hatchet heads (one broken) were probably used for such things as cutting holes in trees to get at honey or possums, but there is no direct evidence of this. Both tools were made of stone that came from 100–120 km further south along the coast. Twenty artefacts, most of them simple flakes, had abrasive smoothing along one

FIGURE 5.22. Sections through Currarong shelters 1 and 2. In Shelter 1, 1: loose shell, contents of most recent pit; 2: loose shell, recently disturbed; 3: compact grey ash with shell; 4: compact dark soil with shell; 5: compact fragmented shell with dark soil matrix; 6: compact, dark-brown, sandy soil. Source: Lampert (1971a).

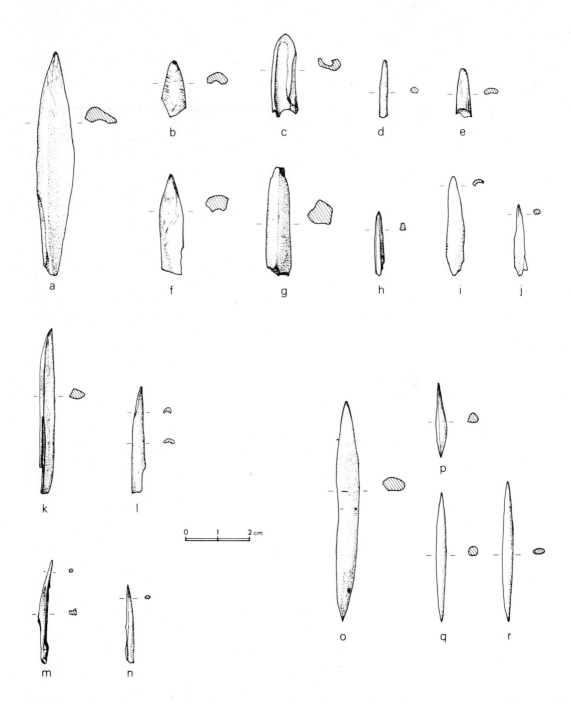

FIGURE 5.23. Bone bipoints and unipoints from east coast NSW. a, f, g, q, r: Kurnell, Botany Bay. south of Sydney; b–e, h–n, p: Bass Point, south coast; o: Curracurrang. Courtesy: R. J. Lampert and Australian Museum.

or two longitudinal margins, and many also had microscopic striations lying at 75°–85° to the margin. This kind of wear, along with some edge fracturing, is commonly found on tools classified as *elouera* along the central east coast both north and south of Sydney. Experimental attempts to replicate this use-wear by Kamminga (1979) suggest that these tools were more than likely adzes or chisels, hafted on to the end of a straight handle and used on very soft wood or bark in sandy environments. The restriction of this form of use-wear to a small part of the east coast has not so far been explained.

Thirty-five backed blades in various geometric and pointed forms were found in the lower levels of shelter 1 and eight examples were found throughout shelter 2. All were made on fine-grained quartzite and rhyolite, and lengths ranged 9–31 mm. None appeared to be broken, nor did any show traces of gum hafting, although this has been found in other sites. Their restriction to the earlier levels of shelter 1 is noticeable and consistent with a general pattern for the area, as is the later occurrence of bipolar cores and an increasing use of quartz. Lampert, among others, has argued that this suggests that many backed blades were points and barbs of spears, but there is no direct confirmation of this. One argument in favour of it is the occurrence of edge-fracturing on only 20–40% of backed blades from all sites.

Some 50 km north of Currarong, Bass Point pushes a rocky finger 3.5 km out into the ocean.

The midden, from which 7 m² was excavated by S. Bowdler (1970; 1976; see also P. J. Hughes and Djohadze 1980), covers an area of about 40 × 100 m on the upper part of the peninsula's north side. From it, one looks out over extensive rocky foreshores. The same stratigraphy was observed in each square (Table 5.2).

In terms of economic evidence, some interesting contrasts were observed between the Upper Midden and the Lower Midden. In the Upper Midden, mussel shell (*Mytilus edulis*) accounted for 50–80% of all shellfish, and eleven shell fish-hooks and blanks were found along with bone bipoints and unipoints like those from Currarong. Among the fish, snapper and rock cod were most common. In the Lower Midden, turban shells, tritons and other littoral sea shells formed well over half the total, many more leatherjackets and wrasses but fewer rock cod occurred, bone points were found but fish-hooks were not. Bowdler also says that there were more large fish in the Lower Midden than in the Upper, but in fact the difference between the proportions of vertebrae of different diameter, which is how this was assessed, is so small as to be statistically insignificant.

Bowdler argues that the changes in fish and shellfish types can be primarily accounted for in terms of technological changes. She relates the changes in fish types to the use of fish-hooks, an artefact dated here to within the last millennium (Upper Midden). Following observations made by the first White settlers, she suggests that women

TABLE 5.2

Bass Point stratigraphy

Level	Thickness (cm)	Contents	Date at base
Upper shell midden	c. 20	Mostly crushed mussel shell	570 ± 75 (ANU-534)
Lower shell midden	c. 20	More intact larger shells of non-mussel species	
Grey sand	c. 15	Very weathered shell and bone	2975 ± 145 (ANU-535)
White sand	c. 60	No organic remains except carbon	17,010 ± 650 (ANU-536)

Source: Bowdler (1970).

were the sole users of fish-hooks, and that once they started fishing this decreased their potential to gather the most economical shellfish (in terms of meat-to-shell ratio). These shellfish, which were more common in the Lower Midden, live lower in the littoral zone and the time available for their collection is much more restricted by tidal movements than is the case with mussels.

This ingenious proposition is clearly testable in several ways. For example, in similar open, sea-shore sites similar changes should be observed when fish-hooks are found. It should also be demonstrable that, in terms of food return per hour of labour, fish were more economical to gather than shellfish. Otherwise, why was the change made? One of Sydney's First Fleeters, Lieutenant Collins, said that part or all of women's catches was given to men, which raises the whole question, not pursued by Bowdler, of possible changes in male–female relationships. Then, too, variation in collection seasons might be examined. For example, Poiner (1976:191) claims that *Mytilus edulis* (which she calls *M. planulatus*) can be collected all year, but the most important of Bowdler's deeper water species, the turban shell (*Ninella torquata*) is only available in summer. In summer also, snapper tend to come nearer to shore and breed there, so perhaps more smaller ones can be caught. These two indicators at present suggest that summer use of the site continued throughout the last 3000 years — as Poiner's model would predict — but more detailed examination of the local environment and of seasonal indicators is obviously required. We take up problems of the origin and distribution of fish-hooks later.

Durras North is a small cave at the north end of a south-east facing beach some 100 km south of Currarong (Lampert 1966a) (Fig. 5.24). The highest tides today just lap at the front edge of the cave floor, which extends back about 30 m from the dripline. Large blocks of sandstone roof-fall and earlier fossicking limited the area of excavation to 4 m². Excavation was in units 30 × 30 × 5 cm, though with attention to visible stratigraphic variation. The deposit consisted of many lenses of ash, sand, charcoal and shell, and the total depth of about 1 m was divided into three units for analysis. A radiocarbon date on charcoal from near the bottom of the lowest level

was 480 ± 80 (GaK-873). As might be expected, shell fish-hooks were found, as were fish-hook files, though in the upper six spits only, which must date to the last 200–300 years. On the basis of one 30 × 30 cm column sample, Lampert showed that *Mytilus edulis* (mussel) formed about 35% of shellfish in the lowest level, increasing to over 50% at the top. Marine gastropods such as turbans and tritons were more common in the lower levels. There were also changes in the number and proportion of species of fish (all recovered material was analysed), but these changes do not follow the same pattern as at Bass Point (Table 5.3). No information on fish sizes is available. Among the fish, the presence of bream is noteworthy since this is often regarded as a fish most easily caught in winter (Poiner 1976:196). However, a winter attribution conflicts not only with the large quantities of snapper, but also with the strong evidence from bird remains that occupation was primarily in summer.

Lampert suggests that the changes seen in shellfish proportions may be because of variation in the availability of shellfish (Underwood 1979), which derives from both sampling variability and local topographic differences. While excavating, he observed an overnight storm wash away an area of sandy beach leaving an exposed rock platform. If maintained, this platform would host a different shellfish population.

It is clear that the Durras North evidence does not wholly support Bowdler's model, although the direction of change, in terms of shellfish

TABLE 5.3
Durras North fish

Level	Major	Minor (selected)
I	Snapper Bream	Wrasse Groper Blackfish
II	Snapper Wrasse	Bream Groper
III	Snapper Bream	Wrasse Groper Leatherjacket

Source: Lampert (1966a)

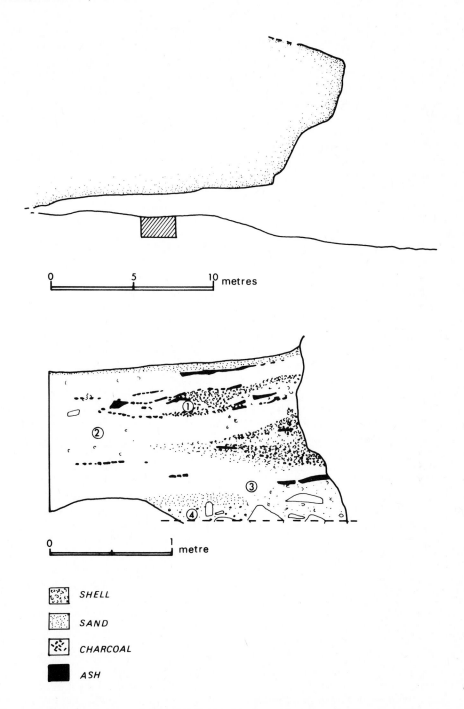

FIGURE 5.24. Durras North: section through shelter and excavated section. In the excavated section, 1: dark shelly lenses with ash and charcoal; 2: homogeneous, dark, soft soil and sand; 3: grey to brown, soft, loose sandy soil; 4: light sandy gravel with few pebbles. Source: Lampert (1966a).

collecting, is similar. At Durras North, there were fewer bone points in levels with fish-hooks (23.4/level) than there were in levels below them (36.8/level). If we accept the idea that bone points were tools used by men, this change suggests a greater use of the site by women in later times.

From the 4 m^2 excavated, 475 point-shaped pieces of bone were recovered, of which 218 showed definite signs of abrasive smoothing. Both groups showed the same means and ranges in length and about one-third of each was made from mutton-bird bone, so that it seems probable all were intended for use. Both single-ended and double-ended points were found, and since unipoints were not shorter than bipoints they were not simply broken ones: both were real classes. It is likely they were used as tips and barbs (simultaneously in the case of bipoints) on single or multipronged spears. A few of the Durras North bipoints had remains of resin around the middle, which confirms a hafting pattern of this kind. A few unipoints had resin at one end. Because one-third of the points were made of mutton-bird, this is a clear indicator of summer use, for these birds are migrants, arriving in a nearly exhausted condition from Siberia between October and January and often dying at sea to be washed up on the beach. All bones at Durras North were of adult birds, which confirms that this rather than the raiding of nests was the source. Nearly all bird bone in the deposit, other than points, was of mutton-bird, which implies that these birds were being brought whole onto the site and eaten there.

It is not clear why there were so many bone points in the Durras deposit. They were manufactured there, for there were large amounts of broken bone. Some had reached the end of their useful life and were discarded, although few were actually broken. It does not seem likely that many were made for future use elsewhere, for we would then expect them in caches if they were in the site at all. What we need to know in this situation is how frequently and under what conditions, spear points and barbs were replaced. Durras North was used over some 300–500 years, implying a rate of point replacement of 1–2 per year. This does not seem very many, so we can probably assume that the points were all discards, some perhaps at the time of

manufacture because their size or form was not quite right, some after use either because they were broken or their attachments had become non-functional. Lampert's experiments on fresh mutton-bird bone suggest that points were produced by battering longbones between an anvil and hammerstone, a method unlikely to give precise control over the size and shape of points produced, so that many of those with no further working may well have been manufacturing discards.

A series of sites excavated in the 1960s by Megaw and his collaborators (Megaw and Wright 1966; Megaw 1974) have the potential for displaying local variation in site use, although reports do little more than hint at this. For example, at Wattamolla Cove, 32 km south of Sydney, excavations were made in three shelters. The cove is a 400 × 100 m inlet in the cliffed coastline and the shelters are not far from the water. The first excavated (WT) proved to have only about 15 cm of shell midden. Two shell fish-hooks came from the shelter, but no analysis of the faunal material is reported. Similarly shallow deposits were found in rock ledge WB, where the sampling consisted of two bucketfuls of deposit (about 9000 cc) taken at six foot (1.81 m) intervals along the length of the deposit. This produced four shell fish-hooks (four others were picked up from the surface), the bones of ten fish, mostly snapper, and some three hundred shells, nearly all turbans and limpets available at mid-tide levels on local rock platforms. The presence of lead shot in one sample and the presence of fish-hooks suggest a fairly recent date.

Site WL is a shelter at least 15 × 4 m, of which at least one-third was removed. Three main levels are reported, an upper shelly midden with many fish bones and ash lenses, a dark sandy layer with no shell and a lower grey to yellow clay which derives primarily from the local sandstone. The maximum depth of deposit was about two feet (60 cm), and the lowest radiocarbon date was some 2000 years (1900 ± 115, ANU-178). Shell fish-hooks (8) were found in the top two levels only as were stone fish-hook files (4): these were dated to less than 1000 years (840 ± 160, ANU-177). Two bone points were found (both in the dark, shell-free layer), as were some 1000 stone artefacts (mostly flakes). Remains of at least one hundred fish occurred in the midden: most were snapper, with some groper and wrasse. Of the fourteen fish below the midden, five were leatherjackets, suggesting some similarity to Bass Point. The presence of shell in only the top layer meant that there was no opportunity to observe whether any change in shellfish collecting occurred over the last thousand years. The same kinds of shellfish from mid-tidal zones were found here as in other sites. Other animals included a few mutton-birds and no less than ten fur seals, some of them immature. These indicate both summer use of the site and organized hunting of marine animals, and are in striking contrast to the very few land animal remains found.

Only 2 km south of these sites, in another small cove, seven small shelters have been recorded along the sides of Curracurrang Creek valley. All are within 100 m of the creek and 500 m of its mouth. Small cuttings in several showed that most deposits were only a few centimetres deep and apparently recent. These shallow sites are generally similar to those at Wattamolla. One site (1CU), with a deep deposit, was extensively excavated and proved to have a complex stratigraphy with considerable prehistoric disturbance. It has never been fully analysed or published (Megaw 1966, 1968).

The best reported site (2CU) is a shelter covering at least 55 m² (600 ft²) of which about 10% (5.2 m²) was excavated. Extensive prehistoric and historic disturbance in the one metre depth of deposit is documented by the presence of a few small European artefacts in all cultural levels. As at other sites, the basic three-part stratigraphic sequence of shell midden, overlying a shell-free occupation horizon, overlying sand was found. The upper part of the middle layer was dated to 1930 ± 80 (GaK-898). No quantified faunal analyses were made, though E. Glover (1974:17) noted that in the upper midden 90% of the bone was fish, mostly groper, parrot fish and bream. All can be obtained in the cove. No fish-hooks or bone points were found, but two files were found in layer 3, the dark-brown, shell-free zone. This raises a problem in terms of their dating, since they are about twice as old as any other reliable evidence for fish-hooks. Questions about their exact location in the deposit and their

stratigraphic association with the radiocarbon date can be raised but not answered. Probably only the acquisition of similar results from other sites will finally solve the problem. It certainly seems unlikely, though not impossible, that hooks would be in use a thousand years earlier at 2CU than at Bass Point some 70 km to the south (Fig. 5.25).

The occurrence of fish-hooks over a broader area seems to relate directly to the nature of the coastal environment. Within NSW the northernmost example is at about 31°30′ S (Port Macquarie; McBryde 1974:11) and the southernmost is at about 36°50′ S (Thorpe 1932). Further north, fish traps, nets and unbarbed spears were all used at the time of European contact, and this almost certainly reflects a general change in the nature of the coast (fewer reefs and rock platforms) leading to changes in the dominant species. Fish-hooks are found further north again in Queensland, e.g. around 22°30′ S (Rowland 1980). While no midden analyses comparable with those south of Sydney have yet been produced for the north coast of NSW, J. Coleman (1978, 1980) has shown on the basis of small samples from three sites that there appears to be size selection among flathead and bream, suggesting the use of gill nets of fixed mesh size. Interestingly, the school fish, mullet and perch, which are several times referred to as a major resource in nineteenth century records, have not been recovered from archaeological sites so far. This may well be a result of recovery procedures since mullet, at least, have very small and soft bones.

Concerning the numbers and kinds of fish that appear at sites in central NSW, Urquhart (1978) noted that it was a property of commercial fishing in the region that the number of species caught was directly related to relative catch size — the more fish one caught, the more species were likely to be found. (Grayson, 1981, demonstrates that this proposition is of more general application.) Applying the principle to prehistoric materials will affect our assessment of the duration of occupations and intensity of fishing, though probably no sites so far described have been sampled or analysed adequately enough for this to be undertaken. Urquhart also noted that the number of species in the twelve sites she

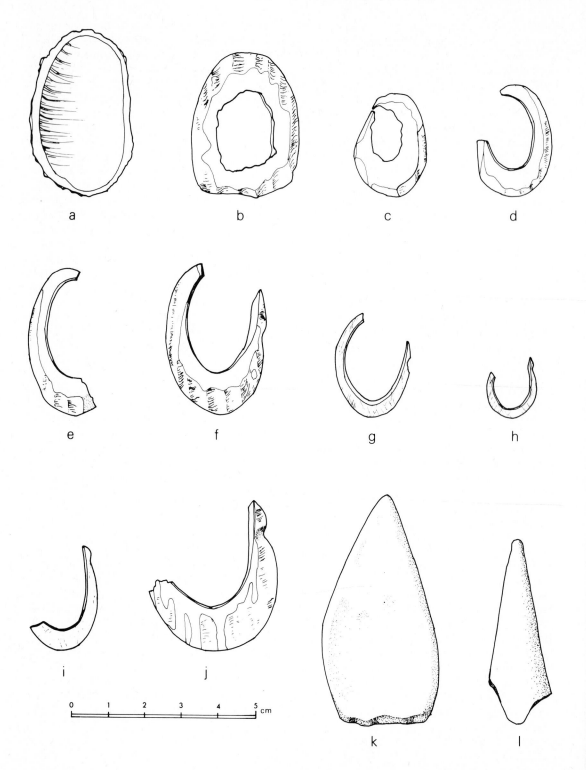

a   b   c   d

e   f   g   h

i   j   k   l

0   1   2   3   4   5 cm

investigated varied only between 13 and 20, and this has been true of other sites in similar locations. The one site which differed was a shelter facing onto a large estuarine lake. Although only 1.5 km from the sea, half the fish species (and nearly all the shellfish) came from the lake, implying that, although Urquhart's proposition may be true, it is so only when similar environments are being exploited, and when basically similar catching methods are employed.

A good example of the specialized use of resources occurred on Montagu Island, which lies 7 km off the southern coast and is 1.4 × 0.5 km in size. Formed of two igneous hummocks, it has a surficial covering of sand, the unconsolidated areas of which form rookeries for mutton-birds, which dig their burrows there. The breeding birds arrive about September, but the chicks are most easily and profitably taken from the burrows from December through to March. M. Sullivan's (1975) survey showed that stone artefacts were concentrated near rookeries, though she found no clearly defined campsites there. One was found at the other end of the island, where a shell midden (50 × 20 m) had been formed of species from the adjacent rocky shore. Other resources which may have been exploited included rookeries of other sea birds (penguins, terns) and of the fur seal. There is a permanent spring on the island, which would have allowed people to stay there for some time.

Although there is a chert-like rock and basalt on the island, most of the flaked stone collected by Sullivan (from twelve 20 m² samples) was of quartz and silcrete. Occasional pebbles of these are found on the beach today, but the quantities seem to be too small to have provided the raw materials. She suggests human transport of stone from the mainland.

There is no direct evidence of the duration of human occupation. The presence of backed blades shows that some of it occurred within the last 5000 years; and the predominance of quartz is similar to the situation on the mainland coast within the last thousand years. It seems likely that most use occurred then. However, 10,000 years ago the island was a rocky headland on the coast, like Bass Point, so its use may have begun then or even earlier. This can only be checked by excavations and direct dating.

We turn now to another area. Between 300 and 500 km north of Sydney, a series of large river estuaries, with ocean-shore sand-dunes and extensive back-dune swamps provide a rich estuarine environment. A series of studies by McBryde and her students (1978a) on the contact period economies of Aboriginal tribes shows they used estuarine resources extensively, though probably on a seasonal basis. Although the area is sub-tropical and receives its heaviest rains in summer (January–March), it also receives reasonable winter rains. These winter rains, combined with cooler temperatures, seem to have been the major determinant of human movement. These economies are more comparable to those found well south of this region than they are to those seen around Brisbane, only 250 km north. In general, movements seem to have been neither large-scale nor long-distance. This humid coastal zone, some 50 km wide, contained not only estuarine, but riverine and land resources which were exploited more in winter. There is evidence, particularly at some coastal locations, of semisedentary economies, with quite substantial houses being built (Belshaw 1978). Population density seems to have been high, with an overall aggregate ranging from one person/3 km² in the north to one person/8 km² in the south. Since this included the large areas of relatively unproductive forest, actual densities around the coastal swamps were probably much higher.

The fullest archaeological information comes from the Macleay and Richmond River estuaries. Some work on the Clarence River estuary has been carried out (McBryde 1974, 1976), but so far interpretations of results rather than site descriptions have been published.

The Clarence River estuary was rapidly built up during the last 10,000 years, and shell middens occur along the old, presumably Pleistocene, coastline some 15 km inland, as well as adjacent to present-day swamps and estuaries

---

FIGURE 5.25. Fish-hooks, blanks and files from east coast NSW. a–e: from shell-blank to fish-hook, a sequence from Kurnell, south of Sydney; f–j: fish-hooks from Kurnell site; k: fish-hook file of sandstone, Gymea Bay, near Sydney; l: fish-hook file of sandstone, Curracurrang site. Courtesy: R. J. Lampert and Australian Museum.

and among coastal sand-dunes. Several dates have been obtained on charcoal and shell samples from middens located on older coast-lines and river terraces. With one exception, all are less than 5000 years old (Campbell 1972; Connah 1976; Gillespie and Temple 1977). The exception comes from wood charcoal from the lowest level of a midden some 2.5 km in length at Stuart's Point, north of the Macleay River. This date is associated with cockle shells (*Anadara trapezia*) according to the excavator, but it is so much out of line with other dates from similar sites that further confirmation seems required.

The favoured environment of cockles is a shallow embayment rather than the tidal mud-flats which now surround the Stuart's Point site. These mudflats are now populated by mud oysters (*Crassostrea commercialis*), and a date on wood charcoal from just above the change from one species to the other at Stuart's Point is 3750 ± 280 (SUA-482). Other middens show a similar change although at varying dates dependent on their location. The Stuart's Point midden also contained a range of bone and stone artefacts and mammal and fish remains, but details have not yet been reported. Despite the destruction of many middens for road building and other uses in the nineteenth century (Statham 1892), and within the last few decades by sand miners, caravan parks and the like, there is still a major field of man–environment study in this area.

Some 200 km north, on the Richmond River estuary, Bailey (1975) carried out an elaborate analysis of samples from shell mounds up to 400 m long and 4 m high (see also Statham 1892). Dates obtained on wood charcoal show that the three large mounds in this area accumulated during the last 1700–2000 years, and, throughout, some 98% by weight of the shell came from oysters. Eighteen other species were represented sparsely, and there were very few mammal or fish bones. Bailey's interest in the middens was primarily to estimate the contribution shellfish had made to the diet of local people. Local ethno-historical records suggested that, along with oysters, fish (mostly mullet and "salmon" (perch), both schooling species) were the major animal protein source. Bailey only sampled one mound and only about 0.01% of its total volume, but he argued on the basis of extant sections that his sample was representative of all the mounds. He calculated from these samples to total mound volume, then through kilos of meat to kilo-calories per year represented by the mounds. He next compared this yield to that taken by modern commercial oyster farming (technically, still gathering in this area) in the same estuary and found that the two yields were roughly compar-able, at 17 tonnes live weight of oysters a year. Again using contact-period data, Bailey sug-gested that the population of the immediate area was 200–500 people, but even assuming that only 100 were exploiting oyster beds, he concluded that the 17 tonnes available would have supplied about 2% of the total annual food intake. This may seem a surprisingly low figure, and we think there are so many assumptions built into his calculations that his estimate may be in consider-able error. But the estimate would have to be in error by a factor of ten before oysters could be said to contribute significantly to the diet, and then they would constitute only 20%. Given that the oyster mounds are far and away the most dominant feature of the archaeological land-scape, Bailey's analyses are of some interest, even if of low reliability.

We might infer from this analysis that these mounds were used seasonally or on a short-term basis. At present it would not be legitimate to do this since the dietary contribution of oysters on a day-to-day basis is unknown. As Bailey points out, if oysters made up only 5% of the daily diet, then 100 people could have lived on the mounds for nearly five months every year for the last 2000 years. If oysters made up 20% of the daily diet — which seems rather more plausible — then the same population could have lived there for about a month every year. Without more precise means of estimating the duration of single occupations, these analyses can go little further, and research along the lines pioneered by Luebbers (1978) is an obvious next step.

In the tropical parts of Australia few exca-vations have been subsistence oriented. One of the more complete, though not yet fully reported, was carried out near Dampier (20°30′ S) on the coast of Western Australia (Lorblanchet and Jones 1979). The Skew Valley midden is located near a narrow band of mangrove swamp fringing the western side of rocky Dampier Island, itself separated from the mainland by a stretch of mud and mangrove. The midden (21 × 8 m) is near semi-permanent waterholes on the island and is surrounded by many engravings (Virili 1977). The area receives all its rainfall between November and March, so water is a critical resource for the rest of the year.

The excavation of 11 m² removed about 10% of the volume remaining after partial (one-third?) destruction by road building. Two main layers were distinguished, an upper (I), about 70 cm thick, in which the dominant shellfish was the bivalve *Anadara granosa*, and a lower (II), about 30 cm thick and rather smaller in extent, containing mostly *Terebralia palustris*. Two radiocarbon determinations on shell from level II gave dates of about 6000 years (ANU-1835, 1836) while six on level I shells ranged from 3700 ± 90 to 2320 ± 80 (ANU-1834, 1837–39, 1843, 1845). However, two dates on wood charcoal, apparently from the two levels, were 2180 ± 60 (ANU-1844) and 500 ± 70 (ANU-1833). The excavators prefer the older dates, alleging possible contamination of the wood.

Analyses of other subsistence data reported do not differentiate the two levels, nor do they quantify the shellfish component as against other economic data, which include fish, land mammals and large, mangrove-dwelling crabs. The fish numbers are dominated by wrasses, catfish and barramundi, all of which frequent the shallow water and can be taken by spears and traps. No hooks were found in the midden, nor have they been recorded elsewhere in Western Australia. Among land mammals only rock wallabies were important, and only two species have been recorded: the range of smaller land animals found in sites elsewhere does not occur here, leading the excavators to suggest that the site was both economically specialized and probably seasonally occupied.

It is notable that elsewhere in the tropical north the bivalve *Anadara* occurs primarily on mud banks exposed at low tide, while *Terebralia* lives in mangrove swamps. The change observed from one to the other at Skew Valley is likely to be the result of local environmental changes which increased the quantities of the more readily and pleasantly collected bivalves.

The midden at Skew Valley was also a site where stone artefacts were made. Changes occurred within this assemblage through time, but it is clear that these did not correlate with economic change.

Although they were not investigated, large shell heaps also occur around coastal areas at Dampier. Similar shell heaps have been seen at various spots on the north Australian coast, including Milingimbi in Arnhem Land and at Weipa on the west coast of Cape York. At Weipa, mounds up to 10 m high have been recorded, and Bailey (1977) estimated from an aerial survey that there are 500 distinct heaps around the four river estuaries which flow into nearby Albatross Bay. Features of those he mapped were: (a) the positioning of most along the inner margin of recent marine deposits (i.e. behind the current mangroves and swamps); and (b) their concentration at places where small streams through the mangroves provide canoe access to the river. Further, some 95% by weight of shellfish in the several mounds sampled was the cockle *Anadara granosa*. This is best eaten in the wet season, when walking to the muddy tidal flats is difficult but gathering by canoe is relatively easy. Not all mounds, however, are placed in relation to wet season access; some are found near freshwater swamp and forest resources, implying a dry season use.

Three interesting questions have been raised concerning the Weipa shell mounds. One concerns their formation, the others the accuracy of the dietary picture they provide and the duration of that subsistence pattern. For a start, all the shell accumulations are campsites. Not only do they contain archaeological materials but early Europeans saw them used as such, as they are even today on occasion. Bailey noted that, though some of the mounds are tall with steep sides, even the largest are not symmetrical cones but are irregular in shape with some easy routes to the top. Further, Bailey remarked that, of the 304 sites he examined closely, only a few were tall — 80% were less than 2 m thick. The largest mounds are the ones which attract our attention, but they are only one end of a continuous size range. Why should a few have grown so much larger? In other words, why were precisely these spots preferred by Aborigines? To this there is no ready answer. Bailey suggested that it was because of very local environmental variation; for example, catching a breeze. Peterson (1973), discussing similar though much lower mounds in Arnhem Land, suggested that once a mound had begun to build up it would be a favoured place to return to, being drier than the surrounding country, less heavily infested with mosquitoes, and so on. That is, local conditions again seem to be critical.

Concerning subsistence, Bailey noted that the tropical shell mounds can be interpreted no more precisely than those on the Richmond River. Only one of the mounds around Weipa has been dated, and that only in two small trenches, where the results suggested a duration of about 1000–1200 years (SUA-149, 1180 $\pm$ 80 at 5 cm from base; other dates in sequence). Assuming that all the Weipa mounds accumulated over the same period, Bailey estimated that they contain about 9 $\times$ 10^9 shellfish, providing about 27 tonnes of meat each year. If between 100 and 500 people lived in the area, this would mean shellfish provided 4–18% of their diet. This figure is remarkably close to that obtained by Meehan (1977a) who analysed the diet of modern shellfish collectors over most of one year. If one assumes as an alternative that the mounds give an accurate picture of the diet, it would be quite different, with 94% of the total food remains consisting of shellfish, and the remainder being of fish, crab and mammal. So far, plant food remains have not been recovered from these sites.

The Weipa mounds seem to have accumulated recently. Can we assume that the large *Anadara* beds only developed about 1000–1200 years ago? Other rivers north and south along the same coast have very similar environments, but are without the extensive mudflats of Albatross Bay. Along at least one of these rivers extensive mangroves harbour many *Batissa* cf. *violacea*, but these were apparently not collected in any quantity. Local environmental histories must be better understood before the question can be answered.

A clear indication of the possibilities of changes in local environments comes from Milingimbi Island, in Arnhem Land, which is surrounded by extensive tidal flats. Most of the shell mounds there have been dug away for road building, but an excavation in 1948 recorded an upper stratum of intact, loosely piled shells and

ash over lower levels of compact, fragmented shells and soil (McCarthy and Setzler 1960:Fig. 4). A date from the base of another mound of loose, whole shells was 1305 $\pm$ 80 (V-61) while samples collected from the compacted horizon at Macassar Well site dated to 2445 $\pm$ 80 (V-60). There is a passing reference to the fact that earlier levels contained more whelks and mangrove clams while cockles (*Anadara*) were more common above, but no quantification was attempted.

Another example of major change in the local environment has been observed by Meehan (1977a, 1977b) between 1972–73 and 1974 on the Blyth River in the same area. This has been mentioned already, but some detail is appropriate. A group of Anbara now live at or within a few kilometres of the river mouth, and the women collect up to 15 kg of shellfish on most days of the year. Although several environments are exploited, shallow, open-sea, sandy beds of *Tapes hiantina* (Diama) contributed nearly two-thirds of the total shellfish weight in 1972-73. Meehan draws attention to the fact that species collected on different days varied widely depending on whether the *Tapes* beds or other environments (mudflats, mangroves, rocky outcrops) were visited. During the wet season of 1972–73, some beds of mud-dwelling mussels were destroyed. More dramatically, the following very heavy wet season entirely wiped out all the *Tapes* beds which had been the basic shellfish resource the previous year. The Anbara wet-season diet of 1973–74 therefore consisted of fish, land mammals, birds and vegetables, the 20% of the gross weight of food formerly supplied by shellfish being almost entirely absent. It is noticeable that the Anbara were unworried by this change and expected the beds to recover eventually. B. Meehan (pers. comm. 1982) reports that they had done so by 1978. However, we note that a considerable, if short-term, change can be expected in the archaeological record, and it will be due entirely to local environmental variation.

This brief review of some coastal subsistence data raises several more general points. First, there is variation in the nature of shellfish accumulations between the tropics and the temperate zone. While there are enormous accumulations of shells in south-eastern Australia and Tasmania, they form lower, more extended mounds than is the case in some tropical locations. The reasons for this probably include an environmental factor. For one thing, while it is often pleasant to catch a breeze in the north, further south people may prefer to sit out of the wind. Then again, very restricted access routes to major shellfish beds do not appear to be a common feature of southern sites although mangrove beds do occur and this factor may need investigation.

The second point is the very wide range of dates for the start of a record of shellfish gathering in different areas. In Tasmania (Jones 1971a; Reber 1965) and western Arnhem Land (C. White 1967) dates of 7000–8000 years have been obtained. The same is implied for the south coast of NSW on the basis of depth/age curves recently obtained for Currarong 1 (P. J. Hughes and Djohadze 1980), and Hughes' analysis of the deposit (P. J. Hughes 1980). From middens in northern New South Wales (J. Coleman 1978; Connah 1976), and Skew Valley come dates of 3000–4000 years, while the Weipa mounds are very recent. Over the last 7000 years there also seems to be a great increase in the number and volume of middens. It might be argued that the recent, visually dramatic accumulations are evidence of increases in local populations or a shift in subsistence strategies. Although this seems to be true in south-western Victoria, elsewhere the data are not yet sufficient to support this. It seems more likely that attrition of earlier accumulations along with periodic re-location of favoured camping sites was enough to ensure the gradual decay and disappearance of many earlier sites. This seems to be so in the best studied area, along the southern NSW coast. There, as Lampert and Hughes point out (1974), we would expect few or no middens before the sea reached its present level some 6000 years ago: if any existed they would now be under water. We might expect that over time the absence of major sea-level change would allow the establishment of more extensive marine resources, and a consequent gradual increase in Aboriginal exploitation of these leading to their increased archaeological visibility. We prefer an explanation of this kind rather than one which suggests that shellfish eating itself is of fairly recent origin. After all, people were eating freshwater shellfish around Lake Mungo and similar sites more than 30,000 years ago.

A third feature for attention is the apparent absence of shell middens around the south-west coasts of Australia. At the time of European contact, Aboriginal people in this area did not eat shellfish, and no accumulations of shells like those elsewhere in Australia have been located. A few thin scatters of shells, some of them almost certainly prehistoric, have been found (Dortch, in press; P. J. Hughes et al. 1978; Morse 1981), but shell middens are not found in such places as King George Sound where Baudin collected a reasonable number of extremely big oysters in 1803 (Journal, 3 Ventô). Part of the explanation may be environmental, in that most of the coast does not carry large quantities of shellfish and other resources may be more profitably pursued. An original scheduling decision based on cost-benefit criteria could have been reinforced by social decisions, much as appears to have been the case with the more famous case of fish-eating in Tasmania (5.4). But at present it remains an intriguing problem.

5.4   Tasmania

For most of the last 50,000 years Tasmanian prehistory has been a small part of that of Sahul. The rugged, cold and often rainy peninsula thrusting out into the roaring forties was as far away from tropical Asia as any settlers could get.

Twenty thousand years ago some 5000 km^2 of Tasmania were covered with glacial ice, and larger areas were strongly affected by periglacial conditions (Bowler et al. 1976; MacPhail 1975, 1979). At that time and later, humans camped at Hunter Hill and in a few other shelter sites, and hunted animals throughout the open, cold, grassy plains and, to some extent, in forest habitats (Bowdler 1979; Goede and Murray 1977; Goede et al. 1978; Murray et al. 1980). We know relatively little about this Pleistocene occupation. If there was a coastal component, as Bowdler argues, the evidence has been covered by the rising post-glacial sea. The inland evidence is sparse — a few hearths, animal bones of modern species and a few stone flakes and retouched pieces. Some now-extinct herbivores may have lingered on till about 13,000 years ago but the extent of their utilization by humans is not known. The sites of this period all appear to be occasionally used, short-term camps.

About 12,000 years ago the rising sea cut through a last barrier and created Bass Strait. In doing so it isolated a small group of people in Tasmania. It may also have isolated even smaller groups on islands such as King (1100 km²) and Flinders (1900 km²), but if it did they did not survive for long (Jones 1977b; Orchiston and Glenie 1978). The Tasmanians, however, continued to live on their 65,000 km² island until dispossessed and largely exterminated by Europeans in the nineteenth century (Jones 1971a, 1971b; Ryan 1972; 1981; see also Appendix I). Separated from Australia by 250 km of stormy ocean, they show the potential of a small human population to survive and develop over thousands of years. The only comparable accounts of such isolation are by novelists and science-fiction writers (e.g. W. Golding, *Lord of the Flies*, 1954; B. W. Aldiss, *Starship*, 1969), and their vision is usually degenerationist. The major interpretation of Tasmanian prehistory has been similar. Jones,

in a series of papers (1971a, 1977a, 1977b, 1978) has argued not only that Tasmania was the "last refuge of a cultural system of immense antiquity and stability" but, more aggressively, that Tasmanian society was slowly becoming "depauperate", simplifying towards the point at which recognizably human behaviour and perhaps human life itself would cease to exist (Jones 1971:620):

> Perhaps the culture, remote for thousands of years from any outside stimulus, was becoming simplified and losing some of its "useful arts". Perhaps in the very long run ... 3000 people were not enough to support and maintain a culture even of a simplicity of that practised during Late Pleistocene Australia.

This view of modern Tasmanians is at one with earlier writers such as Lubbock (1865:354) and Sollas (1911:70), who saw modern savage life as exemplifying the conditions of Pleistocene life worldwide, and the Tasmanians as archetypes of that existence. Jones' view is also degenerationist in seeing the modern populations as descended from a more affluent, earlier situation (cf. Argyll

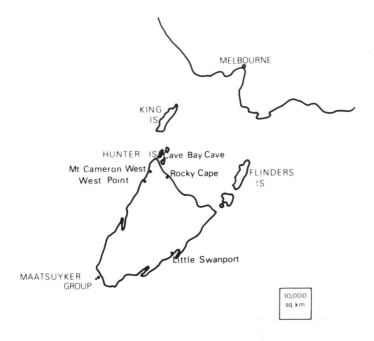

FIGURE 5.26. Tasmania, with location of sites discussed in this section.

1869:173; Diamond 1978). Such an account has been criticised for its political implications, and Jones' interpretation of the archaeological evidence itself has also been challenged (H. Allen 1979; Bowdler 1980; Horton 1979b; Lourandos 1977; Vanderwal 1978a). The challengers agree that the Tasmanian record is one of change but not that it is one of decline. It is impossible here to discuss this debate fully, as it draws on a very wide range of theory and evidence. We will concentrate on the most clearly delineated aspects, and on the form in which it is publically known. For other overviews and interpretations see Bowdler (in press) and Lourandos (1980b).

We start with the evidence from the largest excavation so far reported, that at the twin shelter sites of Rocky Cape North (RC North) and Rocky Cape South (RC South) on the north-west coast of the present island (Jones 1966, 1971a, 1978). In each of these sites, only a few score metres from the sea, some 3 m of shell midden, mixed with hearth remains, animal bones and plant fragments, had accumulated during the last 8000 years (Fig. 5.27). The excavation at each site was not very large: RC North, 3 m² (32 ft²) to a depth of about 3 m; RC South 6 m² (66 ft²) to 3.5 m deep. Only half the latter material has been analysed. The excavations comprised about 5%

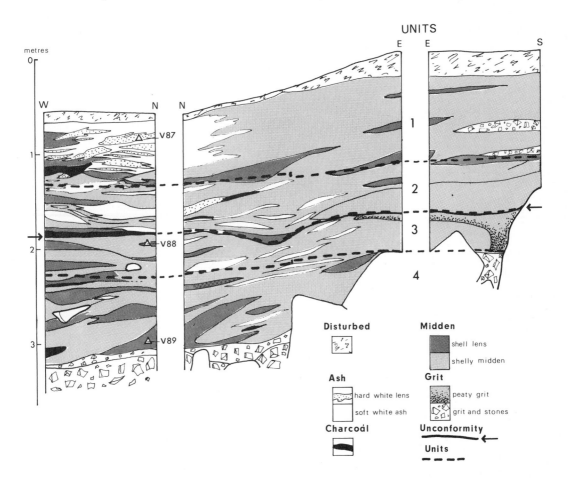

FIGURE 5.27. Rocky Cape North Cave: three sides of Pits A and B dug in 1965, with Units 1–4 superimposed. Source: Jones (1971a), Figs 9–10. Courtesy: R. Jones.

of the RC North deposit and an unknown proportion, but probably less than 10%, of RC South. The placement of excavations within the sites was based on convenience, but there is no reason to believe that the overall picture would alter with a larger sample. For analysis, the material was divided into broad units, each 60–100 cm thick, but it was originally excavated in levels 15–30 cm thick with attention paid to such features as erosional disconformities and shell lenses. The units were numbered con-secutively through both sites, and their radiocar-bon dates are set out in Table 5.4. (It should be noted that the upper levels of RC South had been removed during the last century.) Jones aligned only Unit 4 in RC North with Units 5 and 6 in RC South, on the basis of similarity in their contents, the key being the presence or absence of fish among the fauna. The differences in accumu-lation rates between Units 3 and 4 were probably the result of local deposition, for the faunal evidence is quite decisive.

TABLE 5.4
Rocky Cape analytical units and radiocarbon dates

Depth (m)	North	South	Depth (m)
0-	450 ± 104 (V-58)		
	I ———————		
1-			
	*2 ——————— ‾3450 ± 95 (V-88)‾ -		
	3		
2-	———————	3795 ± 100 (V-83) ———————	-0
	4 ——————— 5425 ± 135 (V-89)		
3-		5 ———————	-1
		5075 ± 250 (V-84) 6	-2
		6145 ± 200 (V-85) ———————	
	6445 ± 80 (V-51)	6745 ± 145 (V-97)	-3
		7465 ± 145 (V-86) 7	
		8120 ± 165 (GXO-266)	-4

Source: Jones (1971).
Note: All dates are on charcoal.
*Stratigraphic disconformity.

Jones' analysis concentrated on three main classes of materials — flaked stone, bone tools and faunal remains — and since it is the changes in these which provided the initial data on which the general interpretation has been based, we will briefly review this evidence.

1. The fauna found in both excavations included:

(a) Shellfish. Four rocky shoreline species were said to account for over 90% of the molluscs, although this was an impression derived during the excavation, and from the analysis of the floor of a chamber sealed off some 6500 years ago (Jones 1971a:189), rather than any analysis of excavated materials.

(b) Seal. Both fur seal and southern elephant seal were found throughout the deposit in approximately equal numbers.

(c) Land marsupials. The most important of these were wallabies and bandicoots, which occurred throughout. Possums, wombats and native cats (*Dasyurus*) also occurred.

(d) Birds. Nearly all identifiable birds were shags (*Phalocrocorax* sp., a waterbird), and the majority occurred in the upper levels.

(e) Fish. With extremely minor exceptions all were "parrot fish" (wrasses), a rocky-shore species. All except one bone occurred in Units 4–7.

Comparisons of fauna between the units can be undertaken in several ways. Jones (1971a, 1978) has presented the data in terms of number of bones, weight of bones, minimum number of individuals and meat weights contributed by various classes. Each method has clear disadvantages, ranging from variations in the number of bones per genus and butchering differences, to the uncertainties involved in the sampling and the string of calculations required to get meat weight (Grayson 1979). However, in so far as our discussion is primarily concerned with changing patterns of human behaviour, then clearly some figure such as meat weight is most appropriate. Table 5.5 therefore gives the minimum number of individuals in each unit, and Table 5.6 the meat weights. With all their faults these give some idea of the stability (particularly of seals) and change (especially in fish) over time that were found at Rocky Cape.

It must be stressed that fish disappeared very suddenly from the prehistoric record. As Jones

TABLE 5.5

Minimum numbers of animals at Rocky Cape

	Units						
	1	2	3	4	5	6	7
Land animals							
Macropods	6	2	4	2	3	3	5
Bandicoots	5	2	1	—	4	1	3
Other	3	—	1	—	1	4	5
Seals	4	1	4	5	1	5	5
Birds	8	2	3	1	2	3	1
Fish							
Wrasse	1	—	—	13	118	197	170
Other	—	—	—	1	1	2	—

Source: Jones (1971a: Table 134).
Note: These figures vary somewhat from those given by Jones (1978: Table 2.3). The cause of this difference is unknown.

TABLE 5.6

Meat weights (%) at Rocky Cape

	Units	
Animals	1–3	4–7
Wallaby	18	7
Other land animals	5	5
Seal	73	67
Bird	3	—
Fish	—	21
Total weight (kg)	600	1200

Source: Jones (1978: Table 2.5).
Note: If shellfish were included these percentages would be approximately halved.

dug down into RC North, between one thin excavation level and the next fish bones appeared in numbers far too great to be mere chance. There was some variation in absolute numbers of bones between different parts of the excavation, but the transition was abrupt in each pit (Table 5.7). This change is one of the key points in Jones' argument.

These tables do not include shellfish. Jones estimated (1971a:586) that they provided about as much meat as all other sources throughout the period of midden accumulation. They, along with seal, bird and fish, were so important that it is clear that the people living at Rocky Cape were almost entirely dependent on the sea for animal resources.

As Table 5.6 shows, when they stopped fishing, most of the replacement meat came from land animals. Jones claimed that at that time the

contribution of seal increased, but it can be seen that this was not significant. Bowdler (1979:Ch. 8) has reanalysed Jones' data in detail and notes that there may also have been a change in the kinds of shellfish collected, with large abalone and warrener shells being more common in Units 1–3. She suggests (1979:421 and Table 8.11) that the land animals and shellfish found in Units 1–3 give a much higher return per animal than the fish and small shellfish found in earlier levels.

2. Bone tools. A total of thirty-seven clearly shaped and ground bone tools were found at Rocky Cape. As Table 5.8 shows, nearly all came from the lower levels, forming there a significant proportion of the total marsupial (i.e. land animal) bone. Two broad classes of tools were recognized — unsplit macropod fibulas and unipoints with broad ends made on split fibulas — but no sequence of forms could be observed. It is noteworthy that there was a long-term decline in the numbers of points over the period 5500–3500 years ago and no evidence of a sudden cessation of their use. Generally these points were similar to those that were made on the Australian mainland, where they were used in making skin cloaks and bark canoes (Jones 1971a:521).

3. The 376 flaked and retouched stone tools were similar to those found throughout Tasmania, being a range of loosely formalized "scrapers", retouched around varying pro-

TABLE 5.7

Numbers of fish bones at Rocky Cape, by excavation levels

Shelter	Unit	Pit A (level)	No. of fish bones		Pit B (level)
North	3	9	0	0	8
		10	0	0	9
		11	0		
	4	12	1		
		13	22		
		14	40	0	10
		15	22	24	11
		16	34	29	12
		17	56		

		Pit B (level)			Pit C (level)
South	5	1	N/a	4	2
		2	73	19	3
		3	89	27	4
		4	292	28	5
		5	75	26	6

Source: Jones (1971: Tables 125–129).
Note: Finer correlation of levels is not possible from the data provided. The numbers given here vary significantly from those given by Jones (1971a: Table 135). N/a = not available.

TABLE 5.8

Ratio of bone tools to marsupial bone and stone tools at Rocky Cape

Unit	No.	Ratio to marsupial bone (1:n)	Ratio to stone tools (1:n)
1	—	—	—
2	—	—	—
3	1	65	20
4	1	68	11
5	4	30	15
6	18	5	2
7	12	15	3

Source: Jones (1971a: Table 121).

portions of their edges (Figs. 5.28, 5.29). This is the only tool form that has been found in Tasmania, and on the basis of nineteenth century data they were always held in the hand. Within the Rocky Cape assemblages several changes can be observed, encompassing both the retouched tools and the 5439 unretouched flakes. First, there are gross differences between the two sites, with the flakes from RC South having a mean weight only about two-thirds that of RC North (9.0 ± 3.0 g and 13.9 ± 6.4 g respectively). Jones suggests that this was because of a greater use of pebbles as raw material in the North Cave (60 m to the beach source compared to RC South's 120 m). These provided large and relatively heavy flakes (1971a:226). The situation is not, however, quite so simple, as it is RC North's two lower units (3 and 4) which provided the heavier flakes (17.7 ± 5.5 g vs 9.8 ± 4.6 g for Units 1 and 2) and showed a high percentage of pebble use (53% vs 19% for all other units). Given that there was no major change in site use, we suggest Jones' explanation may be appropriate for the lower levels, but lighter flakes in the upper levels may be more closely related to other changes there.

The second observable change is in the intensity with which stone was used. This is shown both in the ratio of the number of retouched pieces to the total number of artefacts (Table 5.9) and, Jones claims (1971a:306, 448), in the rise in the number of retouched edges per unit weight of stone used. Each of these observations suggests a more economical use of stone, which is compatible with the observed changes in raw material, at least within units 1–2.

Most artefacts at both sites were made from quartz, quartzite and argillite, materials readily obtainable from local beaches. A few were made from three varieties of chert, all of which were imported from locations 32–80 km east and west. The use of these materials increased with time, most notably in Unit 1 (Table 5.10). Imported stone was more heavily used than local, with 42% of all pieces being retouched compared to an overall mean of 7% (1971a:286). It is only the broad trend in raw material use which can be linked to changing intensity of use, and there is no exact correlation.

The third change within the flaked stone occurs in the forms of tools. Jones, following Balfour (1925) and others, was able to divide Tasmanian tools into five broad classes — round-edge scrapers; steep-edge scrapers; flat, straight-edge scrapers; notched scrapers; concave and nosed scrapers — and he showed changes in the occurrence of these over time. He suggested (1971a:447) that the last two groups were used for similar tasks and "simpler" notched scrapers were replaced by "more complex" concave and nosed scrapers which had more retouch per tool. The other main change Jones observed was a decline in large steep-edge scrapers, and this can also be seen as a more economical use of raw material. The numbers involved in Jones' analysis were extremely small (Table 5.9), and whether the statistically valid differences have real archaeological validity (cf. Wright 1974) must await further sampling.

TABLE 5.9
Number of retouched pieces and flakes at Rocky Cape

Unit	Total	Retouched pieces incl. cores	Flakes	Percent retouched
1	208	47	161	22.6
2	239	26	213	10.9
3	239	34	205	14.2
4	382	19	363	5.0
5	3062	132	2930	4.3
6	869	57	812	6.6
7	816	61	755	7.5
Total	5815	376	5439	6.5

Source: Jones (1971a: Tables 10–12).

TABLE 5.10
Exotic stone (%) at Rocky Cape

Unit	Exotic stone
1	36
2	5
3	10
4	3
5	1
6	—
7	⸴

Source: Jones (1971a: Tables 31,32).

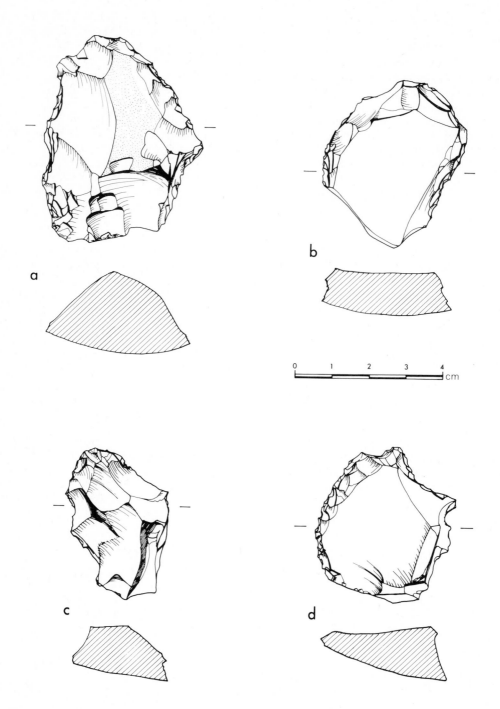

FIGURE 5.28. Tasmanian stone tools. a, b: Falmouth; c: Carlton; d: Norah Beach? Australian Museum, E33600, E39473, E40396, E53700, respectively.

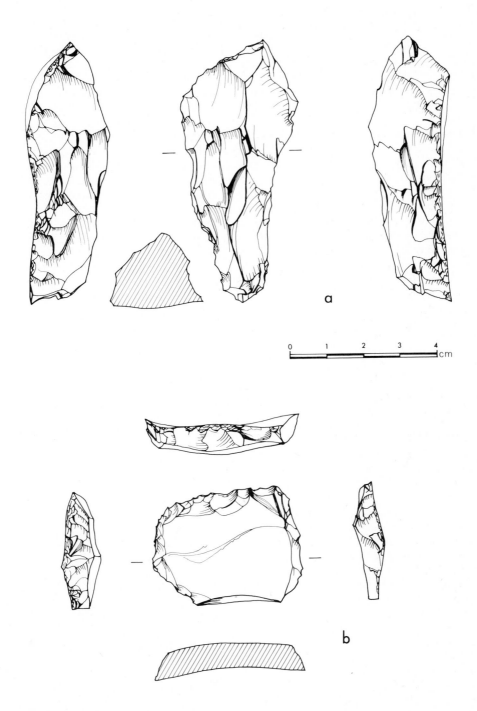

FIGURE 5.29. Tasmanian stone tools, viewed from various aspects. Both unlocated; Australian Museum, E15284 (a), E37845 (b).

If we now review the main data from Rocky Cape, we see that the changes are not all towards simplification and loss. The sudden cessation of fish eating is interesting, but did it mean a real constriction of the Tasmanian's ecological universe? Jones has used exactly the same data both to suggest that it did *not* vitally affect their livelihood (1971a:620) and to argue that it was an "economic maladaptation" which caused "significant deprivation" (1976:38; 1977b:343; 1978:45; see also the able review of this by Bowdler 1980). We will return to this argument.

Of the other changes, we think those in stone tools and raw material use show increasing finesse. Better raw materials from further away and greater economy in use seem to indicate human groups that were not only finding these resources but developing the mechanisms of their distribution. Perhaps it is no accident that the increase in land animals and in overland movement of materials occurred together. Both may have been related to the opening up of the environment through firing, which seems to have occurred in north-western Tasmania during the Holocene (Jones 1968; 1971a; 71–72; see also MacPhail 1980). It is now time to look at other Tasmanian data.

We start with the north-west. Another major shelter excavation is that at Cave Bay Cave on Hunter Island (Bowdler 1974, 1975, 1979). Although not fully published yet, it is clear that apart from its Pleistocene use, the cave was utilized around 7000 years ago (ANU-1552) when the sea reached its present level, and then again from about 2500 years ago (ANU-1362) until the present. Both these uses are marked by dense lenses of shellfish and hearths, the lower one also containing fish bones. Bowdler's explanation is that the lower midden marks the time when the sea reached approximately its present level but the present island was still a peninsula, while the upper midden marks the re-incorporation of the island, by then 6 km offshore, into the Tasmanian seasonal round. There is no other evidence of use of the island during the mid-Holocene, but in the last 2000 years several other sites on the island were in use (Bowdler 1979). All sites were probably used in summer when the weather would have been most favourable to sea travel in the frail bark-roll canoe-rafts. Small birds and rats, along with shellfish, were the main fauna at Cave Bay Cave with seal and mutton-bird being absent. Mutton-birds, in particular, occurred in quantity in open sites closer to the rookeries (Gaughwin 1978:Table 3.2). Faunal remains suggested that economically specialized summer uses were not the only ones possible on Hunter Island and that at this time Cave Bay Cave may have been a site for particular uses such as a refuge during storms.

Subsistence evidence similar to Rocky Cape is also known from Blackman's Cave and the open middens at West Point, all on the north-west coast. The former is another shelter by the sea, and the lowest levels, at least, contained fish bones and bone tools dated to 6050 ± 88 years (NSW-17). Reports of later levels are inconsistent (Jones 1966:5–6; 1971a:608–9).

At least two large shell middens were found at West Point. One is known only from a small trench with a basal date of 2600 ± 120 (GXO-420). Its contents appear to be similar to those of the other, into which a major excavation (65 m³) was made. This midden was built up on a seaside sand-dune between 2350 ± 150 (I-322) and 1330 ± 80 (V-66) years ago. Jones' excavations were all within one part of the midden, bracketed by the younger date and 1850 ± 80 (V-69). Within his excavations, shellfish provided about half the meat weight, the majority of this coming from abalone (E. Coleman 1966). Elephant seals, many of them young animals from a nearby breeding ground, provided most of the remainder, and only 6–10% came from a range of land animals. Given the numbers of very young seals, this site was probably used in summer, but use in other seasons also is a possibility. As with contemporary levels at Rocky Cape, neither fish nor bone tools were found.

A major activity at West Point was the manufacture, and presumably use, of stone tools. Over 30,000 artefacts were excavated, some 5% of them finished tools of the same types as in the upper levels of Rocky Cape. Within the analysed material there was a strong shift towards the use of a single type of high quality "spongolite" chert, probably quarried near the site, though the outcrop has not been located. This chert was found occasionally below Unit 1 of Rocky Cape North, but frequently within it. (Jones 1971a:Tables 31, 32).

In a preliminary report of a survey around

Nelson Bay some 20 km south of West Point, Ransom (1978) notes five different "types" of middens, based on their shape and size. He found that different kinds of raw materials occurred in different, thin, "linear" middens, while seal bones were common in very large dump middens like West Point. There is thus the promise of both activity (and seasonal?) segregation, and of temporal ordering of activities within a small area, but already a well diversified economic picture seems likely to be demonstrated.

Finally, although several sites with rock carvings are known in north-west Tasmania (Jones 1966:Fig. 1), only those made at Mount Cameron West have been dated (Fig. 5.30). The carvings were made between 2000 and 1000 years ago according to (unpublished) bracketing radiocarbon dates from deposits built up in front of them (Jones 1977b:345).

The sequence of economic and technological changes known from the north-west has not been duplicated elsewhere, but there are significant preliminary findings from the south-west and east coasts.

The south-west coast of Tasmania is wild, rugged and cold, and today is almost uninhabited. Vanderwal (1978a) has excavated at several sites around Louisa Bay, and also on Maatsuyker Island 13 km offshore. The oldest site (LR-1) was dated to 2970 ± 200 years (ANU-1771) and contained no fish bones, though one bone point was recovered. This and other mainland sites appear to have been used mostly in winter, with people relying on shellfish, land animals and some seals. Maatsuyker Island and other small associated islands were used in summer, when they had a high population of seals and birds and were also accessible in good weather. Recent lighthouse building and occupation has disturbed most Aboriginal remains on

FIGURE 5.30. Engraved slab at Mount Cameron West, Tasmania. The slab is about 1.5 × 2.3 m. Courtesy: P. F. Murray and Tasmanian Museum and Art Gallery.

Maatsuyker Island, and the oldest site has been dated to within the last 500 years. Vanderwal (1978a) and Horton (1979b), have argued on the basis of the subsistence data that there is a striking contrast between these late sites and earlier ones elsewhere. They suggest that the year-round exploitation of seals was probably energetically more efficient than fishing could have been. Vanderwal also suggests that this economy became possible with the local invention of the rolled-bark canoe-raft, so that both Maatsuyker and Hunter Island exploitations occurred as the result of this new invention.

The east coast is a much drier area than the north-west, and the historically described economy appears to have been much closer to that known from south-eastern Australia, with seasonally varying use of inland and coastal resources (Hiatt 1968; Lourandos 1970). Coastal resource use has been documented to at least 8700 ± 200 years (I-323, Reber 1965), but the only well reported site is at Little Swanport (Lourandos 1970, 1977). Initial use of this site, which is on the shores of a muddy estuary, first occurred 4490 ± 120 years ago (ANU-356), and its contents comprised mostly mud-oysters and mussels. Of 13 fish recovered, 12 came from the lowest analytical unit, older than about 3700 years. All were leatherjackets (*Aluteridae*), which live in the estuary today. An increase in land animals comparable to that found in other parts of the island was not shown here, but this was explained by the site being almost entirely the result of the specific activity of shellfishing. The very low numbers of stone tools confirmed this to some extent.

The other data which have been drawn on in the discussion of Tasmanian prehistory are primarily ethnographic. A contrast has been drawn between the wide range of tools and gadgets used in mainland Australia and their absence in Tasmania (Jones 1977a). In the former, spearthrowers, boomerangs, edge-ground and hafted hatchets, mounted adzes, multi-pronged and barbed fish-spears, fish-hooks, a variety of nets and traps, shields, sewn skin capes and bark canoes, and the presence of the dingo as companion and hunting aid have been recorded; in the latter no hafted tools, spear-throwers, composite tools, nets or examples of sewing have

been found, but simple, one-piece tools, single-skin cloaks, kelp buckets and shell necklaces occurred (Jones 1977a:197). Among these differences perhaps the most notable is the absence of boomerangs, that classic Australian tool, known from south-eastern mainland Australia some 10,000 years ago (Luebbers 1975). But while the technological contrast may be real, what are the implications? In some cases, the differences can be seen primarily as an environmental reaction. Boomerangs and spearthrowers, for instance, are not good hunting tools in closed forests (Horton 1979b). Other differences may result from isolation. Edge-ground hatchets do not appear to have been used much, if at all, south of the tropics more than 5000 years ago, and that they were not re-invented in Tasmania is hardly surprising. Can we say they were "essential" tools even in Australia? Simplicity in tool-kits does not automatically equate with simplicity in other aspects of existence, as the New Guinea highlands example should be sufficient to demonstrate (J. P. White 1977b).

Contrasts between Australia and Tasmania have also been drawn in terms of the richness of religious and ritual life, and in population densities. The widespread occurrence of great ritual occasions with the fulfilling of ritual and religious obligations dominates recent Australian Aboriginal life. But, apparently, "large scale religious events, such as are described for mainland society, were not part of Tasmanian cultural behaviour" (Jones 1977a:201). To make this claim is to rely almost entirely on the journals of one man, G. A. Robinson, a born-again Christian who in 1829–34 made a number of expeditions to all parts of Tasmania in order to round up the remaining Aborigines and remove them from their homelands to settlements under government control (Plomley 1966; Ryan 1981). Only Robinson, as far as we know, made more than casual and short-term observations on the Tasmanians, and many of his data are clearly of extreme value. But would he have observed Aboriginal religious life? By 1830 Tasmanian Aboriginal society was already at the point of annihilation (Ryan 1972). Many aspects of their economy had already been destroyed (e.g. Gaughwin 1978). No more than 300 "ageing remnants" (Jones 1971b:277) remained of the 4000 or so people estimated to have occupied the island forty years earlier (Jones 1974). Under these conditions ceremonies would surely have been held infrequently or not at all. Even if held, Robinson would not have appreciated them, as Horton (1979b) points out. Horton (1979b:32–33) also notes that a careful analysis of Robinson's journals reveals a number of occasions when rituals may have been carried out, although the entries are very brief. He concludes (and we must agree) that the supposed contrast in religious life has not been established either in the contact period or, more importantly, as a long-term phenomenon.

As far as population densities are concerned, the debate is less clear. "Density" is usually given as a simple number, such as people per square kilometre, but this ignores many variables (cf. Hayden 1975b). The estimation even of simple areal density for traditional (at contact) societies in Australia or Tasmania must be based on reconstruction, since no thorough investigations were made by the earliest explorers, and the earliest estimates were made at times when disease and deliberate extermination had affected all groups. Thus Tasmanian densities are largely reconstructed from Robinson's reports and by extrapolation from accounts of very short-term observations by earlier visitors (Jones 1971b:280). Data from the climatically most comparable area in Australia, the south-west coast of Victoria, is also based on the observations of Robinson, who became Chief Protector of Victorian Aborigines in 1839 and initiated census programmes in 1841. He started work in Victoria only seven years after first settlement of the area, and one might imagine his data would be a good deal more representative of the pre-contact situation than we have for Tasmania. Such may be the case, but we must be cautious. Lourandos (1977:203) points out that "inroads leading to the collapse of the Aboriginal society were already well developed by the autumn of 1841" and "all population estimates must be affected". Nonetheless, on the basis of a range of documentary sources and some archaeological evidence of house groupings, along with some shrewd estimation, Lourandos arrived at a figure of one person/3.6 km^2 for the area of 30,000 km^2, with densities of up to twice this in some coastal

areas. The lower figure is at least triple that estimated for Tasmania, which is one person/11.4–15 km^2 for the two-thirds of the island occupied at contact (Jones 1971a:A20). Similar differences exist if population is estimated on the basis of persons per kilometre of coastline (Jones 1974:326; Lourandos 1977:219), with the south-western Victorian groups scoring as high as any of the known tropical communities.

It is of course possible that population differences between the two areas were the result of European contact. Lourandos argues strongly that many of his data are highly reliable, being recorded so soon after contact, and that, if anything, pre-contact population densities would have been even greater. Jones' population estimates for Tasmania have been widely accepted, but they are probably much less reliable than the Victorian estimates. His figures are based on estimations of the number of people in an average band, while the number of bands were increased by at least 50% in order to include those believed to have been left out of the early records (Jones 1971a: A13–14). Many of those records were made two or more decades after European contact and thus may have been quite inaccurate. However, whether there is enough bias in the estimates to overcome the differences between the two areas may not be finally determinable. It seems to us unlikely.

If population differences are not discounted as merely apparent, what do they mean? Was there simply a difference in resource availability in the two areas? This seems unlikely. The Tasmanian environment is highly varied, with considerable numbers of streams and marshes containing eels and other freshwater fish. The coasts are convoluted and estuaries large and frequent, with a high density of reliable resources. A similar range of edible plants is found in both areas. Thus, although quantitative estimates are difficult to make, major variation between the two areas seems improbable and has, in fact, been discounted by all researchers.

Jones' view (1977a) is that both population densities and resources in each area were in fact equivalent, and he suggests that this supports the proposition that "population levels *were proportional to resources and not to technology*" (1977a:202, his italics), and that the technological

variation between Victoria and Tasmania resulted in ceremonial differences. We have questioned both parts of his suggestion. It must also
be noted that Jones' proposition is a simple
Malthusian one, and is not only untestable but
open to serious theoretical challenge (e.g. Brookfield 1972; Little and Morren 1976:22–23).

An alternative view has been propounded by
Lourandos (1980a, 1980b) whose Victorian data
are discussed above (5.3). Basically, he suggests
that population density is related to technological
complexity and that it was changes in energy-
harnessing techniques which so increased the
reliability of resources that higher population
densities could be supported in Victoria. His
argument points particularly towards the
management of large areas of wetlands which
produced regular supplies of high-quality protein. This provided a major basis for continuing
population growth. The push towards such
resource stability, he suggests, derived from
fluctuations in population numbers, an independent variable sufficient to spark off technological changes. Whether population changes
must be combined with climatic changes some
3000 years ago, as Luebbers (1978) data from a
nearby area strongly suggest, is something
Lourandos does not discount, although he pays
little attention to it. On this argument, then, the
contrast between the two areas seems to have
been caused by chance variation in local population densities combined with different organi-
zations of resource usage, which allowed these
variations to increase.

A third view, and one which still needs
investigation suggests that seasonal variation in
resources was more extreme in Tasmania, and
that for many Tasmanian resources, such as seals
and wallabies, stabilizing their occurrence would
have been much more difficult than in the case of
Victorian eels. Even in the case of plant foods, it is
not clear if management strategies as simple as
those effective in Victoria would have been
effective in Tasmania. It may well be the case that
the higher the latitude the greater the technological difficulties of resource control *throughout the*

year (cf. Hayden 1975b) and perhaps it was this,
coupled with some effects of isolation, which
brought about any differences in population
densities.

We are now in a position to make some
assessment of Jones' picture of Tasmanian
prehistory. In our view, it is seriously flawed. The
archaeological data from Rocky Cape and elsewhere suggest that during their 12,000 years of
isolation some Tasmanians modified their stone
technology in the direction of increasing both
efficiency and, whether for technical or social
reasons, use of exotic raw materials. There is
widespread evidence that, if some resources were
abandoned, new ones were brought into the
subsistence system, possibly with new technologies being developed to do this. At the actual
point when fish eating was abandoned, an
"intellectual decision" (Jones 1978:44) may well
have been involved. We say this because, if the
change occurred because of changing availability
of resources, we would expect it to have been less
sudden. But we think the change, when it came,
was of little effect. The ethnographic data on the
unimportance of religion in Tasmania, and the
differences in population densities and resource
management between Tasmania and Victoria are
an insufficient basis for an argument of cultural
"decline". Any differences which can be shown
seem to us quantitative rather than qualitative,
and it remains to be shown that the differences
between Australia and Tasmania were any
greater than those within the Australian continent. As Horton says "Bass Strait gives us our
ability to see uniqueness, rather than [giving] the
uniqueness itself" (1979b:34).

It might be thought that our interest in
Tasmanian prehistory is esoteric and that the
extinct way of life of a mere handful of humans is
of little general concern. But more than any other
discussion in Australian prehistory it has been
dramatised into an encapsulation of our view of
the whole of humanity. Do we believe Aldiss'
Starship (1969) or Stewarts' *Earth Abides* (1949)?
Jones believes the first: we prefer the other.

Chapter 6
New Guinea: The Last 10,000 Years

6.1 Introduction

The present island of New Guinea was created when the sea breached the Torres Strait barrier about 8000 years ago. But that breach was simply the final act in a separating process caused by the gradual flooding of the low-lying, swampy plain between New Guinea and Australia. Since a good part of that plain lies more than 50 m below present sea level (Fig. 2·2), it was flooded by about 11,000 bp, but the broad isthmus between Cape York and the Oriomo Plateau continued to provide a bridge between the tropical and subtropical parts of Sahul for another 3000 years. With the flooding of Torres Strait, climatic regimes very like those of today were established, but local landscape configurations, especially in places at about sea-level, may well have been rather different. For example, south-draining rivers from the New Guinea highlands have today built up vast deltaic flood plains, but these were certainly smaller then.

It is convenient to consider New Guinean prehistory of the last 10,000 years in two sections, one discussing the highlands, and the other the coast. These two regions can readily be distinguished environmentally, and human interactions with these environments must always have differed, resulting in distinctive archaeological remains. Research so far can also be divided

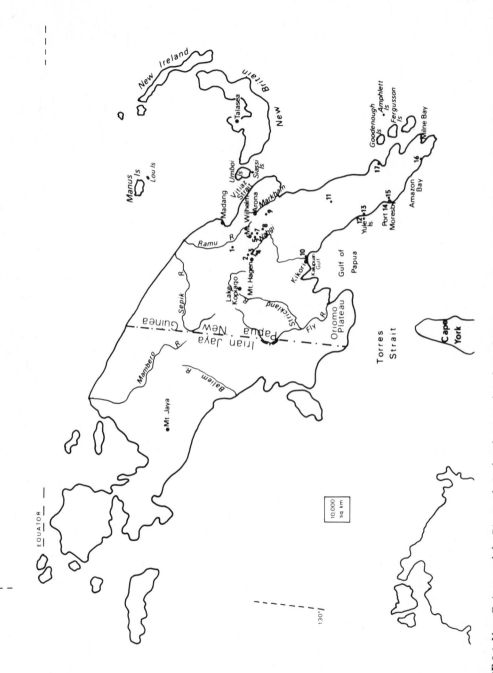

FIGURE 6.1. New Guinea and the Bismarck Archipelago. Archaeological sites are numbered. 1: Wañlek. 2: Yuku. 3: Kuk. Manton, Mugumamp Ridge. 4: Manim, Etpiti, Kamapuk, Tugeri. 5: Nombe. 6: Kiowa. 7: Kafetu. 8: Kafiavana. 9: NFB. Aibura. Batari. 10: Rupo. Kulupuari. 11: Kosipe. 12: Oposisi. Uro'urina. 13: Kukuba. 14: Eriama, Taurama. Ava Garau, Motupore. 15: Nebira 2, Nebira 4. 16: Mailu, Selai. 17: Wanigela.

neatly into that which has taken place above 1000 m and that in the lowlands, nearly all just above current sea level and close to the coast. For logistic reasons, research areas have been in regions of higher population densities, especially within the highlands. Surveys in areas of low population density have failed to reveal many sites (e.g. Egloff and Kaiku 1978; Lampert 1966b; J. P. White 1967a: 17–22; 1973). This is in striking contrast to the situation on many Melanesian islands, including some close to New Guinea (Clay 1974; J. Specht 1980; JPW pers. observation). On most islands there has been recent population decline and movement at the behest of colonial governments, but little of this has occurred in New Guinea itself, and it thus seems likely that present population distributions there are a good guide to those of recent prehistory.

At the time of writing, about forty archaeologists and other prehistorians have worked or are working in the field in New Guinea. Some have dug several sites, surveyed areas or researched particular problems over extended periods, while others have made short-term studies of small areas. No reports at all, or only very short ones, have been made on at least a quarter of these projects, while other reports are in thesis form. Amateur collecting of prehistoric artefacts by white people has focused almost entirely on highly finished stone objects (clubheads, mortars, pestles, figurines) which are not often found in sites with much habitation refuse, so that most of these have not so far been disturbed. Some have been destroyed by modern developments, including the Second World War.

In writing about New Guinea prehistory, we can discuss only research carried out in the eastern half of the island. The western half of the island, Irian Jaya, has been little explored archaeologically and very few researchers have worked there. The most spectacular discoveries to date are a series of eight or nine bronze(?), socketed axe-heads with widely flaring, semi-circular blades found near Lake Sentani, about 30 km inland on the north coast (Agogino 1980; Solheim 1979; Tichelman 1963). These blades are similar to some South-East Asian finds dating to the last two millennia BC, but they have not been dated or shown to be associated with other archaeological remains. Other finds along the

coast include recent burials, some ceramics and many rock paintings, but despite searching, no deep stratified sites have been found (Ellen and Glover 1974; Solheim 1979). At between 3000 and 4000 m altitude near Mount Jaya (formerly Carstensz), G. and J. Hope reported (1976; see also J. Hope and G. Hope 1976) a date of 5440 ± 130 (ANU-1015) from charcoal in a rock-shelter apparently used for overnight hunting and camping while travelling. They also reported more recent dates for other shelters in the same area, where it is too high for successful gardens. Flaked stone tools, animal bones, fragments of coastal shells and hearths were all noted, but they cannot be linked to a broader prehistoric picture. We suspect that parts of the Irian Jaya highlands will show a history of changing subsistence patterns similar to that discovered in Papua New Guinea, but this remains to be demonstrated.

The remainder of this chapter is thus restricted to Papua New Guinea, that part of the island lying east of 141°E, and will be divided into highlands (6·2) and coastal (6·3) sections.

The major focus of the highlands section is on agricultural history, elucidating the 10,000 years of development which have been traced so far. The most complete evidence comes from buried agricultural systems, but there are also data on the implements, crops and associated domestic animals. It is notable that there has been little consideration of the factors that led people into a horticultural subsistence pattern. Nor has there been discussion about why the growth of very high population densities in some areas has not been accompanied by the emergence of chiefdoms or other forms of stratified society. We will, however, discuss less well-studied aspects of highlands prehistory, including inter-regional variability, local and long-distance exchange, and the curious "mortar and pestle complex".

Lowlands prehistory, as currently known, dates back only 4000 years. Even in outline form, it is known from only one area, the south Papuan coast. Communities producing and exchanging ceramics appeared there some 2000 years ago, and the prehistory that can be written since that time is largely an account of ceramic change and the fluctuating fortunes of trading groups. Exchange systems of pottery, obsidian, sago and shell along the south coast eventually articulated with the Kula Ring, which may be of relatively recent origin. Hints of links with island Melanesia and lands to the west of New Guinea remain to be explored.

6.2   Highlands

In the preceding chapters we have used the term "highlands" as if it were easy to define this region, but this is not really so. As Brookfield (1964) has indicated, the "highlands", which have been regarded as an entity, display similarities in land-use patterns by a number of different human populations living at altitudes of 1200–2400 m. These high-density populations inhabit large inter-montane valleys (e.g. Wahgi, Baliem) and are now almost completely dependent on a single crop, sweet potato (Brookfield with Hart 1971: Fig. 3.1) (Fig. 6.2). All these dense populations occur within a region where rainfall varies very widely with local topography rather than conforming to a predictable region-wide pattern and where, in the inter-montane valleys at least, moderate temperatures, low

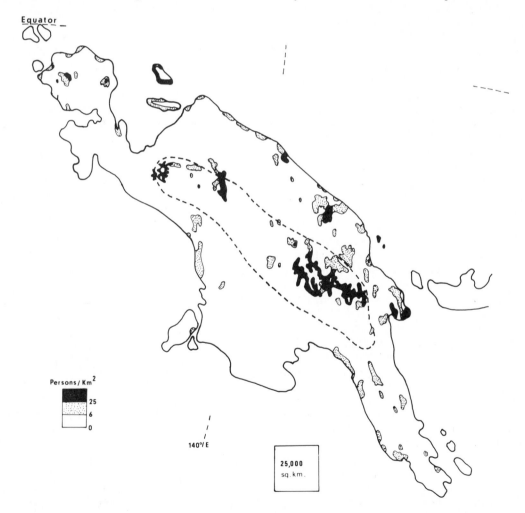

FIGURE 6.2. Population densities in New Guinea. The Highlands lie inside the dotted line. Source: Brookfield with Hart (1971, Figs 1.4 and 3.1).

midday humidity and absence of extreme cloud cover combine to produce very favourable climates for human life and subsistence. On the other hand, as Fig. 6.2 shows, there are some areas within the same altitudinal and climatic ranges which do not sustain high populations, notably from the Strickland River to the present border between Papua New Guinea and Irian Jaya. People in these areas are not so dependent on a single crop either, but the major determinants of this differentiation, which is also associated with important linguistic (Wurm 1964) and material culture differences, are unknown.

Within smaller areas, definitions can be more clear-cut, but still depend on both cultural and environmental features. Thus it is customary to speak of the "central highlands" as stretching from the Strickland River to the Markham–Ramu Rivers fall, since the people living in this area speak related languages and display basically similar economies, technologies and social systems (Paula Brown 1978; Read 1954; J. B. Watson 1964). However, although living at similar altitudes, they have to cope with rainfalls ranging from almost totally seasonal in the east to non-seasonal in the west. There are also great local variations in population density, as high as 80 people/km^2 in some major valleys and as low as 10 people/km^2 in more rugged country only 20 km distant. It is within the more densely populated parts of the "central highlands" that nearly all "highland" archaeology has been undertaken.

Environmental changes in this area have been documented through both geomorphological and vegetation evidence, though all of the former and some of the latter has come from altitudes above human settlement (Bowler *et al.* 1976:361–66; J. Hope and G. Hope 1976; Walker and Flenley 1979). Evidence of the retreat and disappearance of glaciers on the higher peaks 15,000–10,000 years ago is accompanied by pollen evidence of tree lines having risen to present levels by the later time. In the main valleys, limited evidence suggests that they were covered with closed forest until it was cleared by people (J. Hope and G. Hope 1976:37), but the exact boundaries and local nature of this forest may have changed as mean temperatures rose perhaps 5°–7°C to reach

present levels about 10,000 years ago. Pollen records from valley areas have not so far been published for periods earlier than about 6000 years ago. For the last 10,000 years there is some evidence of slight climatic change, but humanly caused alteration of the flora has been sufficient to make interpretation of all records difficult in areas below 2700 m. Evidence from Mount Wilhelm suggests that the three millennia of 8000–5000 years ago may have been a degree or two warmer than at present (Bowler *et al.* 1976).

Because of modern cultural similarities within the area, the small number of sites reported and some gross similarities between them, it has been customary to write of "highlands prehistory" as though a common pattern can be seen (S. Bulmer 1975; J. P. White 1972; J. P. White and Allen 1980). This has ignored the probability that the historical background to the very different local environments and modern population densities can be detected. There are hints that this is possible in the work of V. Watson (1979; V. Watson and Cole 1977), Swadling (1973) and Christensen (1975b), as well as in several synchronically based studies on humanly induced environmental change (e.g. Sorenson 1972, 1976; Sorenson and Kenmore 1974). Watson's analysis is of Cole's collection of unifacially flaked ("chipped") stone artefacts, surface-collected and excavated from twenty-three sites found along tracks and roads and in recently cleared gardens within an area of 3400 km^2 in the south-eastern end of the highlands. She found that the proportions of certain tool classes from sites in the south-western corner of the study area differed consistently from proportions found in the rest of the area, whatever the date of the sites involved (five sites were radiocarbon dated). Watson attributed functional differences to her classes of stone tools, but this has not been independently verified, and we are uncertain that the relatively minor differences between tool forms have a functional basis. In fact, consistent areal differences in the occurrence of stone tool classes suggest that local manufacturing traditions of the kind observed in tools made very recently in other parts of the highlands is a more likely interpretation (J. P. White and Dibble, in press; White and Thomas 1972; White *et al.* 1977). Watson assumes, also, that all collections with more than thirty tools are random and representative samples, and that a Brainerd–Robinson coefficient of similarity gives a temporal ordering to the assemblages. Given the sampling methods, we think the first assumption is dubious, but the second is confirmed to a limited extent by the radiocarbon dates. Watson does not discuss the relationship between areal differences in flaked stone tools and other classes of prehistoric data.

Swadling (1973), surveying the Arona valley on the northern border of Cole's study area, found several sites with flaked stone tools, axe-adzes and houses similar to those reported by Watson and Cole, but she also found small quantities of pottery at most of her sites. Oral evidence suggested that all sites were used within the last 200 years. Pottery was made in the recent past in a few villages to the east and north of the Arona valley (Coutts 1967; V. Watson 1955) and was also brought into the Arona valley from the lower Markham and Ramu valleys. Its frequent presence in the Arona valley sites contrasts with its occurrence in only seven of seventy-six sites recorded by Cole, while it is also noticeable that 97.5% of these sherds are from sites close to Swadling's study area (V. Watson and Cole 1977:Table 8). Variations in the artefacts found in different areas clearly suggest different histories, but the relationship between these variations and subsistence variations and population histories cannot be determined until artefacts — and thus surface sites — can be temporally ordered. For this, excavated and radiocarbon dated materials are required.

Sorenson's history of change, which discusses an area larger than Watson's, is derived entirely from an interpretation of environmental changes. Believing that agriculture based on taro (*Colocasia esculenta*) was restricted to valley systems lower than 1400 m, he suggests that only these areas were populated before about 300 years ago. Thus the conversion of higher altitude areas to grassland was a recent phenomenon, the result of clearance and of cultivation of sweet potato. Furthermore, he suggests that rapid population growth occurred at the same time.

One consequence of Sorenson's argument is that few, if any, sites older than about 300 years should be found above 1500 m altitude. This is not the situation (G. Hope and J. Hope 1976; J. P.

White *et al.* 1970a) although many older sites have been found below 1500 m. However, Sorenson's view is unlikely to be correct, for other reasons discussed below.

The best example of human use of progressively higher altitudes comes from four rock-shelters in the Manim valley, a small side valley off the main Wahgi River valley near Mt. Hagen (Christensen 1975b). The valley, some 10 km long and 3 km wide at the mouth, rises from 1680 m to nearly 3800 m at its head. Christensen excavated four shelters at different altitudes within the valley (Table 6.1).

TABLE 6.1
Manim Valley shelters

Shelter	Altitude (m)	Date (earliest)
Manim (MJY)	1770	9670 ± 220 (ANU-1375)
Kamapuk (MKK)	2050	4340 ± 100 (ANU-1325)
Etpiti (MJW)	2200	2170 ± 70 (ANU-1323)
Tugeri (MJX)	2450	2450 ± 70 (ANU-1321)

Source: Christensen (1975b)

As Christensen died in 1975, his material still awaits full analysis, but his preliminary report suggests that there were major changes in the uses to which Manim shelter was put, while the higher altitude shelters, as well as being more recently used, were only used as hunting and overnight camps (see also Aplin 1981). Christensen related the variations in stone tools at Manim to the development of agricultural systems in the lower part of the valley. He suggested that these systems were analogous with those found in the larger Wahgi valley a few kilometres distant, but neither the data nor the logic involved has yet been expounded.

S. Bulmer (1975) has suggested that a similar variation to the changing pattern of site use at Manim shelter occurred at the Yuku (MAH) rock-shelter at around 1300 m, but this pattern has not been seen in several sites excavated at similar altitudes further east (J. P. White 1972). In general, there has been insufficient intensive research within small areas to demonstrate the historical antecedents of current local variability;

this is why only general interpretations of "highlands prehistory" have been given.

As well as the open sites discussed above, three other major classes of prehistoric data can be used in discussing some aspects of highlands prehistory. These are (a) field and drainage systems resulting from agricultural activity; (b) rock-shelters, some of which have provided long sequences of technological and subsistence data; and (c) a few open-air residence sites. Other prehistoric evidence, mostly undated, includes a range of stone artefacts (especially axe-heads, mortars, pestles and club-heads) and rock art. Very little human skeletal material has been described (Freedman 1972). This section will focus on changing economic patterns, especially the development of intensive agriculture and the history of distribution of exotic materials, since these are most readily drawn from the available literature.

The evidence of prehistoric agricultural activity has now been investigated at several sites within the wetland and swamp areas of the Wahgi valley. Modern draining for plantations is rapidly destroying many other data of the same kind. The most comprehensive research project is at Kuk (MAB), some 7 km from the town of Mount Hagen, and a series of interim, largely interpretative, reports are available (Golson 1976, 1977a, 1977b; Golson and Hughes 1977, in press; Powell 1982). More limited research at Manton (MCS) (Golson *et al.* 1967; Lampert 1967) and Mugumamp Ridge (E. C. Harris and Hughes 1978) in the same valley has produced evidence consistent with the Kuk sequence. The research at Kuk involves (a) the mapping of prehistoric water-control channels which are visible in the walls of modern plantation drains, and the chronological ordering of these, largely by reference both to their superposition and the sequence of volcanic ashes from Mt. Hagen volcano found in their fill; and (b) the excavation of certain areas to reveal channel layouts, house plans and other features. No description of particular excavations, no plans, no maps other than of the main outlet drains, and only a few radiocarbon dates have so far been published from Kuk. Therefore the following discussion is drawn from Golson's interpretations. We outline first the actual archaeological data.

Within the wetlands, two main classes of features have been observed: (a) large channels, 2 × 1 m or more in cross-section, which run for distances of several hundred to 2000 m; and (b) smaller channels (*barets*), usually around 20–40 cm wide and deep, which form networks of different shapes at different periods. Figure 6.3 shows the large channels mapped by 1976 and the temporal phases to which they have been claimed to belong. It is noticeable that part of the purpose of all these channels was to transfer water from the southern catchment out to a natural drainage channel, thus by-passing its accumulation in the swamp. The artificial nature of these channels is clearly demonstrated both by their right-angled bends and by the way two cut across low natural rises.

The first phase of human activity so far discovered consists of one large channel and a complex of archaeological features — gutters, hollows, pits and stakeholes (Golson 1977a:613) — in close proximity to one part of it. No direct association between the channel and the other features has been seen, and Golson suggests that the major drain alone may have removed sufficient excess water to allow the wetlands to be utilized. But the exact use to which the complex of features was put is not clear. In one account (1977b) Golson suggests that many of them might be pig wallows, but the uncovering of 20–30 m² of them makes this unlikely, and an agricultural use seems more likely (1977a), although such an interpretation is derived almost entirely from the association of similar features with more clearly agricultural remains in Phase 2. Phase 1 appears to have been short-lived, and its end is marked by the deposition of a layer of grey clay derived by erosion from the southern catchment. The rate at which this clay was deposited was so much in excess of previous rates that the project's geomorphologist (P. J. Hughes) considers that clearance of a good part of the southern catchment must have been involved. Since some plant macrofossils suggest that the catchment was then forested (no pollen data are available), an agricultural purpose for such a clearance seems likely. Presumably it was associated with Phase 1 which has been dated to about 9000 years ago (Table 6.2).

At least four large channels have been dated to

Phase 2, but not all were in use at the same time. Associated stratigraphically with, but not directly connected to, these large channels are two different networks of *barets*, one like that described for Phase 1, the other a set of "islands" and "basins", each some one metre in diameter,

which appear to have provided areas of wet and dry ground (Fig. 6.4). A very similar system, situated on the edge of wetland and dated by volcanic ashes to about 5500 years ago, has been recorded at Mugumamp by E. C. Harris and Hughes (1978) (Fig. 6.5). The Mugumamp site shows that water control and not just drainage was involved, for the "basins" were designed to hold some water, while allowing any excess to flow away.

TABLE 6.2
Dates of drainage phases at Kuk

Phase	Years ago
1	c. 9000
2	6000–5500
3	4000–2500
4	2000–1200
5	400–250
6	250–100

Source: Golson (1977a).
Note: Phase 6 has not been clearly defined.

The major drains of Phase 2 at Kuk were all allowed to silt up some 5500 years ago, and there are no indications of human use of this area during the next 1500 years. No clear environmental changes, even at the local level, have been detected, and the abandonment of this area of the Kuk swamp may have been simply for particular historical reasons such as local, intergroup warfare.

Whereas the main channels of Phases 1 and 2 seem to have been designed to remove water from

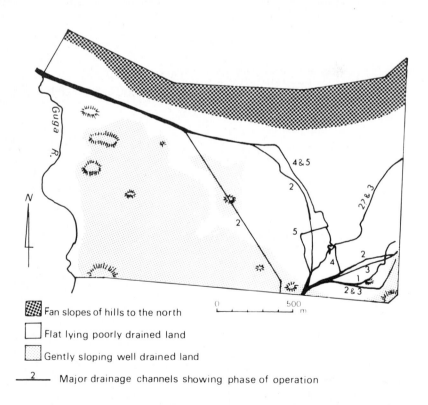

FIGURE 6.3. Part of Kuk Swamp showing main drains removing water from southern catchment. Phase numbers refer to Golson's divisions; see Table 6.2. Source: Golson (1977a).

FIGURE 6.4 Golson's excavation at Kuk, 1977. The basins and islands of Phase 2 visible in the triangular excavation have been cut across by a later ditch. Courtesy: J. Golson.

the swamp, from the beginning of Phase 3 *barets* are directly articulated with the major channels, obviously to remove water from agricultural areas. The *barets* are said to occur in a hierarchy of sizes, but the garden systems that they drained have not been described. Similar drainage systems have been found a few kilometres to the south, at Manton site. Some local pollen sequences start about 5000 years ago, and the start of Phase 3 at Kuk may have been contemporary with the lowest point in the occurrence of forest pollens, although Golson has said that the dates are not entirely consistent (1977a:620). Golson suggests that the start of Phase 3 in the wetlands may have been linked with an attempt to encourage forest regrowth in drier areas. While this implies a credible and creditable degree of environmental management, we suspect that the problem was probably only a local one.

At Kuk, though not demonstrably at Manton, Phase 3 ends with a change in the sediments deposited in the swamp, from clay to soil aggregates. This change has been interpreted by Golson as deriving from the start of soil preparation by tillage in the drier areas bordering the swamp, and the continuing use of this technique allowed the more intensive swamp agricultural systems to be abandoned. If this was the case, the innovation cannot have been very significant, for Phase 4 starts within a few hundred years. By then agriculture in the swamp required large tributary channels to the major drains, and the field *barets* had to be made 30–50 cm deep and spaced closely together in a grid pattern. Golson has argued that this elaborate system was required by increased swampiness of the area and that the elaboration of the drainage system implies larger areas were in coordinated

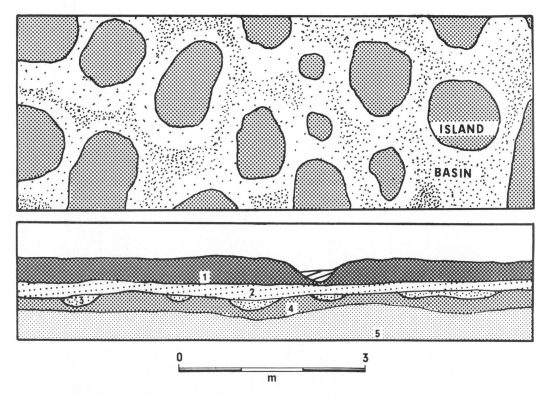

FIGURE 6.5. Plan (above) and section (below) through the "island and basin" system at Mugumamp Ridge. Layers numbered are: 1: Soft root-penetrated soil with strongly developed crumb structure; 2: Black compact soil with fine crumb structure; 3: Green, clayey, volcanic ash, infilling features; 4: Grey clay; 5: Basal white clay. Source: E. C. Harris and Hughes (1978).

use, although he does not support the latter point with other field data. Nor is it clear why abandonment of the Phase 4 system occurred. The latest *barets* of Phase 4 contained volcanic ash at the base of their fill, but it seems insufficient in quantity to have forced people to leave. In pollen diagrams from the area (Powell *et al.* 1975), it is apparent that this period saw a rise in *Casuarina* and *Trema* trees, which are today either deliberately planted or conserved. While the diagrams may indicate the development of these practices, which may, in turn, suggest there was a high degree of forest clearance, we do not think this would have had a major effect on wetland agriculture. At present we prefer to think of the cause as some local, possibly political, event, though no direct testing of this is possible. Further research on the extent to which wetlands were abandoned about 1200 years ago may provide some clues.

The most recent Phases, 5 and 6, are marked by the large extent of their major drains and the presence of small, flat-bottomed field *barets* within the overall grid network. The two Phases are apparently separated by the deposition of a distinctive volcanic ash, but the same major drainage channels continued in use. However, in Phase 6, from about 250 years ago, remains of houses are found in the swamp for the first time, charred fragments of sweet potato (*Ipomoea batatas*) are found, and the field *barets* are more closely spaced together. The latter two facts point to the cultivation of sweet potato, while the dating of the ash to around 250 years (exact radiocarbon dates have not been published) means that all this evidence is dated within the timespan normally postulated for the arrival of sweet potato in the western Pacific (Yen 1974; but see below). It is worth noting here that the shape and size of *barets*, as well as their patterning, are precisely the same as those found in garden systems constructed by many western highlands peoples during the twentieth century. A similar system is currently being employed by Kawelka people within the Kuk area (Gorecki, in prep.). It is this historical continuity which strongly reinforces the idea that all water-control systems back to 9000 years ago were intended to assist the cultivation of plants.

Within some of the channels described above, wooden and stone artefacts have been found. The oldest date published so far is 2300 ± 120 years (ANU-43) from a pointed wooden digging stick from Manton site (Golson *et al.* 1967). During the last twenty years, many wooden tools have been found in swampy parts of the Wahgi, so that we now have a good idea of the range of these. But there has been no attempt to see if chronological variation occurs in these artefacts or to relate them to the agricultural systems. Two main classes of wooden tools have been found — digging sticks of various lengths, which were apparently used for different purposes, and wooden tools with an expanded spatulate end, usually called paddle-shaped spades, up to 2 m long (Golson 1977c; Powell 1974). These spades have been found in a double-ended form also (Gorecki 1978). The stone tools consist of ground axe-adze heads, often whole and always unhafted. These tools are all similar to those that were being used for agricultural activities within the Wahgi valley and elsewhere in the highlands when Europeans first arrived in the 1920s and 1930s. Their presence within the drains (where digging tools are still stored overnight) certainly reinforces an interpretation of the prehistoric systems as agricultural in origin.

The occurrence of tools within the swamp may be explained through both caching and loss. Wooden tools were probably mostly cached (i.e. stored in drains to preserve the wood and not retrieved for a variety of reasons); whole axe-adze heads were probably mostly lost through falling out of their hafts during use and not being recovered (cf. J. P. White and Modjeska 1978b), while broken ones were presumably thrown away or lost. What is not so far explicable is why wooden tools have not been found in systems earlier than Phase 4. (We do not know whether this is true of stone axe-adze heads.) Golson and Hughes (1977) have suggested that a fluctuating water table leading to deterioration through repeated drying may have been responsible, but we think it is also likely that in the early phases, when Kuk was wetland rather than swamp, smaller *barets* would have provided less favourable storage conditions. The presence of major drains from Phase 1 onwards clearly requires that such tools were available, and indeed they are very simple tools likely to have an extended history.

There seems little reason to doubt that, during

the 9000 years of water-control technology at Kuk, it became more intensive, in the limited sense of requiring more labour to prepare an area of ground for cultivation and to maintain it. More recent drains and *barets* are longer, wider and deeper and more closely spaced than earlier ones, but whether this significantly increased the relative amount of labour required for a unit return cannot yet be shown. Further, while it is clear that one purpose of major drains, and of some *barets*, was to remove excess water, this cannot be always assumed. Some modern *baret*

systems do not articulate with any drain and appear to have been created entirely to provide deeper beds for crops (Fig. 6.6). Similar practices almost certainly occurred earlier. It is also clear that the very earliest systems of "islands" and "basins" would have re-distributed soil to the same effect and in about the same relative quantities as the latest systems, so that any suggestion of increasing sophistication of agricultural practices (presumably to increase crop yields) needs more support than it has so far received. Finally, it might be expected that, if

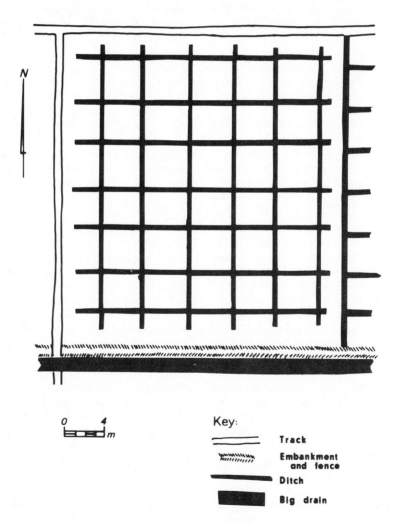

N

0   4
m

Key:

———— Track

vvvvvv Embankment
and fence

———— Ditch

▬▬▬ Big drain

FIGURE 6.6. Modern garden system at Kuk that does not articulate with a drain. Mapped and drawn by P. Gorecki.

changes in the agricultural systems at Kuk were designed to *increase* yields on a per area basis, then we might expect these changes to have occurred alternately with increased garden areas. However, if the history of wetland and swamp agriculture can be explained largely in terms of reactions to (humanly caused?) environmental change, we may question whether there was any need to increase yields. Behind this problem lurks the *deus ex machina* of population growth. We believe that population growth did occur in the highlands, but its direct linkage with changes in the agricultural system needs to be demonstrated and not assumed. It is also necessary to decide whether wetland and swamp are marginal environments, more difficult to manage than dry land and therefore only used as a last resort, as Golson suggests, or whether they are at least as easy to cultivate, and quite as fertile, as other environments, as Modjeska suggests (1977).

What crops were being grown during the last 9000 years in the Wahgi valley? This question presents a major puzzle, since no macrofossils or pollen evidence have been found. The argument must therefore proceed by retrodiction from the modern situation, and by an estimation of the possibilities for each Phase. Present-day subsistence gardens within more densely populated parts of the highlands, including the Wahgi valley, are either monocultural, growing sweet potato, or polycultural, growing a variety of root, fruit and vegetable crops such as taro, bananas, sugarcane and a variety of local greens. Families or individual people usually maintain both kinds of gardens, relying on the first for a very large proportion of their diet. It is generally believed (e.g. Yen 1974) that *Ipomoea batatas* arrived in the highlands sometime after its introduction by Europeans into Indonesia and the Philippines from western South America during the sixteenth century. That introduction is certainly historically documented. However, we believe there is still a possibility that this plant was introduced to New Guinea by other routes. Archaeological discoveries of agricultural soils, storage facilities and plant remains in New Zealand, and of plant remains in Hawaii, provide good evidence of the presence of sweet potato in Polynesia 600–1000 years ago (J. M. Davidson 1979:230; Kirch 1979:289, 1982; McCoy 1979:144;

Yen 1974). What is not clear is its range further west at that time. Early Spanish voyagers did not record it in the Melanesian islands, but they visited only a few of these and only briefly, so that they may not have observed it if it was only a minor crop. There is one very early Spanish reference, probably to sweet potatoes, in Micronesia (Brand 1971:357–58). Thus the arrival of this plant in the New Guinea highlands as much as 1200 years ago is not impossible and its arrival could have been related to the end of Phase 4 at Kuk. Golson (1977b) has tried to argue this position on the basis of the pollen evidence, but he recognizes that the present limitations of such evidence render that attempt futile. Nevertheless, the idea may well be right.

Whatever the date of its arrival, two features in particular must be noted about sweet potato. The first is that, compared with other root crops now grown in the highlands, it can be successfully cultivated at higher altitudes and matures more quickly there; the second is that in most circumstances equivalent land and labour inputs will give considerably greater returns than for other root crops. It is thus possible to argue that its arrival allowed an expansion of human settlement, perhaps less intensive agricultural practices and, in some areas at least, an expansion of pig herds. Other discussions of these effects have been wide-ranging and will not be explored here (see Brookfield and White 1968; Golson, in press; Morren 1977; J. B. Watson 1965a, 1965b, 1977).

Presumably, it was the highlanders' recognition of the clear advantages of sweet potato as a crop that led to its extensive, and probably rapid, incorporation into local agriculture. One obvious implication of this incorporation is that its cultivation and curation requirements were very similar to crops grown previously and it was able to be incorporated into the ongoing system without radical changes in either technology or labour organization. It has generally been believed that taro was the most likely prior crop (e.g. T. Bayliss-Smith, pers. comm., 1979; Brookfield with Hart 1971; Golson 1977a; Modjeska 1977). Taro is still grown throughout the region using the same non-seasonal planting and harvesting techniques as sweet potato, and it is the major crop in some areas of lower density populations away from the "central highlands" (e.g. the Telefomin area). Another possibility is that varieties of *Dioscorea* yam formed the earlier staple, especially in drier areas. These two crops, usually grown simultaneously, are also the main food sources in several lowland areas in which population densities are high and cultivation intensive (Brookfield with Hart 1971:98–106). In other words, they fit well into a variety of New Guinean environments.

It is widely accepted that both the major form of cultivated taro, *Colocasia esculenta*, and the main varieties of yams grown in New Guinea are of South-East Asian origin (Powell 1976:175; Yen and Wheeler 1968), the former in particular having wetlands as its favoured native habitat. If we assume that taro was grown at Kuk from 9000 years ago, then human transport of the plant to New Guinea must have occurred before this date. This would have been likely only if the plant was already a cultigen. There are at present no data from South-East Asia or Wallacea which demonstrate this transfer. It has long been argued, largely on the grounds of more intensive distribution within the Pacific and the supposed relative "simplicity" of cultivation methods, that root-crop agriculture must have preceded that of rice (Sauer 1952; J. E. Spencer 1963; Yen 1974) or at least developed simultaneously with it (Gorman 1974), but hard evidence has not been cited (cf. Spriggs 1982). Excavations at Spirit Cave (Thailand) and other caves in the region have produced plant remains, but not of root crops (Gorman 1971; Yen 1977). The earliest apparently agricultural sites in the area are village sites, where rice grains and rice straw have been identified in levels some 5000 years old (Bellwood 1978:161–65; Gorman and Charoenwongsa 1976). Gorman (1974) developed a scenario which relates the development of agriculture to environmental pressures on populations consequent upon sea-level rises 16,000–8000 years ago, and such pressures, indeed, seem quite likely. Whether the human response would have been the development of agricultural practices is less certain, but the model implies that people had enough knowledge to care for and transplant plants in the Late Pleistocene, which seems reasonable.

The belief that taro is a plant that originated in South-East Asia is central to this argument. Yen and Wheeler (1968), who reviewed the chromosome evidence, pointed out that India is now the region with greatest chromosomal variability and therefore this may have been the centre of origin. However, they also noted that one interpretation of the evidence from plant genetics is that greatest diversity in chromosome numbers is not an indicator of the original homeland, and that chromosome changes may aid a plant's colonization of new environments. We thus think that, although it is more likely that mainland Asia was the original homeland, this was not necessarily the case, and the evidence does not preclude the idea that taro was an indigenous part of New Guinea's flora. It is also worth noting that *Colocasia esculenta* is present in Arnhem Land (Anon 1981) and Cape York (Anon 1980:18; Golson 1971), though whether it is indigenous or feral is not known. Thus taro may have been a New Guinea cultigen (cf. Harlan 1971).

If we accept that taro was native to New Guinea, the earliest systems at Kuk would have been designed to cultivate only plants of local origin. If, as also seems likely, late Pleistocene highlanders were people used to making a living from the tropical forest, then the data from Kuk may simply be evidence of a different spatial organization to that of previous plant–people relationships. Many indigenous plants are still grown in highlands gardens, including the root *Pueraria lobata*, Australimusa section bananas, sugar cane (*Saccharum officinarum*), edible grass stems (*Saccharum edule* and *Setaria palmifolia*) and a variety of green vegetables (see Powell 1976:175 for further details). Thus the development of more organized agricultural systems at Kuk and elsewhere would have been the result of gradually developing expertise in plant exploitation. This probably began at lower altitudes in the Late Pleistocene, although there is no evidence of this (cf. Irwin 1980).

The other view, adopted by Golson (1977a:617) following Yen, is that the more clearly defined agricultural system of Phase 2 marks the introduction of taro and other South-East Asian crops. Only the recovery of crop-plant remains can test between these propositions, but we stress that the idea of taro as a local cultigen (a) is not in conflict with any of the present evidence, and (b) avoids the necessity of believing in a major transfer of plants and agricultural knowledge at a relatively early date, when population densities were presumably much lower than at present and the reasons for adopting a new crop on a large scale much less clear.

Apart from Kuk and its associated minor excavations, there are few other direct data on the development of agriculture in New Guinea. Preliminary analyses of the large quantity of *Pandanus* drupe fragments from Christensen's excavations (1975b) are said to show a gradual change from thick-walled (wild?) to thin-walled (curated?) varieties. This began about 9000 years ago. One interpretation of the present vegetation pattern in the eastern highlands is that it results from prolonged agricultural use. Much of this area is today covered with short grasses (e.g. *Themeda australis*). The climate is highly seasonal, with extended wet and dry periods (Brookfield and Hart 1966). It seems likely that forest patches used to cover a much wider area, but once cleared they failed to recolonize areas

subject to both (relative) drought and fire pressure (Brookfield with Hart 1971:52–53; Robbins 1963). Experimental evidence suggests that forest colonization in grassland disturbed by tillage is possible provided the seedlings are not destroyed by fire. However, extensive fires are regularly used for hunting in this area. The many prehistoric field systems visible on the hillsides show that much of the present grassland has been used for gardens (Fig. 6.7). The history of forest clearance should be visible in local pollen cores, but the stratigraphy of the main swamp in the area appears to be much disturbed (J. Powell, pers. comm.).

Two other classes of evidence suggest that quite different periods of time are involved. Much of the archaeological evidence suggests a long, gradually evolving human use of the area, while modern cultural, and some environmental, evidence suggests agriculture is a relatively recent phenomenon. The archaeological evidence of the two surveys (Swadling 1973; V. D. Watson and Cole 1977) has already been outlined. Here we

FIGURE 6.7. Prehistoric gardens visible on hillsides in the Eastern Highlands District near Aibura.

draw attention to the number of sites from different times. Watson and Cole suspect that fourteen sites are dated from 18,000 to 3000 years ago, and twenty-six sites are from the last 3000 years, with many from within the last few hundred. Most of Swadling's sites date to within the last 200 years, but she suggested that recent erosion had removed many earlier sites. The other archaeological evidence comes from a rock-shelter site, Aibura (NAE) (J. P. White 1972), where the mandibles of at least 500 animals were recovered from 14 m³. A radiocarbon date from the lowest level of the deposit is 3800 ± 110 (GaK-623) and from level 4 is 770 ± 110 (GaK-622). Table 6.3 sets out the distribution of animals by excavated level. The shelter is in a limestone outcrop, and bone preservation was good, so that the relatively small numbers of animals in lower levels are probably real. The most striking feature of this fauna is the steady decline in phalangerids and the rise in small rodents. The former are arboreal animals, while many of the latter live in grasslands. The pattern may derive from two factors which are difficult to separate — a change in the proportions of forest and grasslands, and a changing pattern of site use. The former is supported by the presence of more forest-dwelling macropods (*Dorcopsulus* sp., *Dendrolagus* sp.) in the lower levels. The latter is supported by an analogy. R. Bulmer (1976) has drawn attention to the variety of ways in which animal bone is treated among the Kalam and other highlands peoples, especially the different ritual status given to various species and the consequent variation in the disposal of their remains, including the preservation of some

mandibles in particular. There is no doubt that at Aibura more mandibles have been preserved than might be expected (Table 6.4), but the trend in their preservation runs contrary to the occurrence of cuscus, the most likely candidate for ritual cooking. It thus seems likely that to some extent the Aibura fauna documents the changing balance between forest and grasslands, with the grasslands which today surround the site having been steadily created during the last 1000 years or more.

Based on present-day evidence, J. Watson (1965a, 1965b, 1967) has provided a very different interpretation of the prehistory of this area. He has argued that the arrival of the sweet potato within the last 300 years caused radical changes, including the development of intensive agriculture and massive population growth. He has suggested that oral history, agricultural mythology and practices, and the "loose", open pattern of social structures all demonstrate that populations were much smaller and gardening of

TABLE 6.4

Aibura: Mandibles as percent of total identifiable bone

Level	Mandibles
1	6.4
2	24.5
3	25.6
4	20.2
5	16.0
6–11	12.7

Source: J. P. White (1972).

TABLE 6.3

Aibura fauna (%)

Level	Macropodids: mostly *Thylogale bruijni*	Phalangerids: mostly *Phalanger* spp. (cuscus)	Small rodents	Other	Number
1	2.7	5.4	91.9	—	37
2	28.6	7.1	51.8	12.5	56
3	33.0	26.9	35.2	5.0	182
4	23.8	45.9	16.4	13.9	122
5	20.5	47.4	19.2	12.8	78
6–11	11.1	66.7	14.8	7.4	27

Source: J. P. White (1972).

TABLE 6.5

Pig bone in Highlands archaeological sites

A. *Kafiavana*

Horizon	No. of fragments	Date[a]
I	58	
II	—	4690 ± 170 (ANU-42)
III	1	
IV	3	
V	—	
VI	—	
		9290 ± 140 (NZ-1026)
VII	—	>9500 (ANU-20)
		⩾10,730 ± 370 (ANU-41B)
VIII	—	

B. *Yuku*

Phase	No. of fragments	Date
H	58	
G	9	
F	—	
E	5	4570 ± 220 (GX-3111B)
D	1	
C	1	9700 ± 300 (GX-3113B) 9780 ± 150 (ANU-358) 12,100 ± 350 (GX-3112B)
B	—	
A	—	

C. *Kiowa*

Level	No. of cranial fragments	Date
1	—	
2	3	
3	?	4840 ± 140 (Y-1371)
4	?	
5	?	
6	?	6100 ± 160 (Y-1370)
7	—	
8	—	
9	—	
10	1	9300 ± 200 (Y-1367) 9920 ± 200 (Y-1368)
11	—	
12	—	10,350 ± 140 (Y-1366)

Sources: (A) J. P. White (1972); (B) and (C) S. Bulmer (1975, 1979a)

[a] NZ-1026 came from lower VI and upper VII; ANU-20 from lower VII; and ANU-41B from lower VII and upper VIII.

NZ-1026 and dates with B suffixes were on collagen or acid insoluble residues; others were on charcoal or wood carbon.

? = present, but number unknown.

much less importance until quite recently. A similar argument has been given some support by other researchers using similar evidence (e.g. Heider 1967; Sorenson 1972), but in our view the archaeological evidence is a more reliable guide to prehistoric events.

Another class of evidence that bears more generally upon highlands subsistence history is domestic animal remains, primarily pigs. Pigs (*Sus scrofa*) are definitely not native to New Guinea, and the presence of pig bone in archaeological deposits in the highlands at an early date has raised some interesting questions. Table 6.5 sets out the published data for the earliest presence of pig bone. It should be noted that all the sites are shelters and that definite evidence of pigs has not been found in any open sites.

Both at these sites and others (e.g. J. P. White 1972:17, 57), the number of pig bones was very low in all but recent levels (perhaps the last thousand years; see below), but some have been excavated from levels dating back to 6000 years. The very low number of specimens found in earlier levels, and their intermittent occurrence, has led to some doubts about whether these bones were really *in situ*. These doubts can only be resolved by data from other sites. However, the implications of the low numbers of early remains and of the more recent increases require some explication.

We must start with the possibility that pigs arrived in New Guinea adventitiously, having swum the water barriers of Wallacea. The great naturalist A. R. Wallace reported observations of pigs swimming "with great ease and swiftness" across the Strait of Malacca (1869, II:141; see also Fig. 6.8), and other examples are known (S. Bulmer 1975). But since the presence of pigs in Wallacea and Sahul has been recorded only in association with humanly caused deposits and not earlier, we think that they were transported to New Guinea by people. This could have happened to young wild pigs, in the same way as cuscus, cassowary and other wild animals are transported between islands today and were so in prehistoric times (Downie and White 1978:774; I. Glover 1971). Alternatively, the transported animals could have been tame (serving as pets and food) or domesticated. It must be remembered here that (a) there are no clear criteria for distinguishing between wild and domestic pigs; (b) only a handful of specimens have come from early sites; and (c) if the modern situation is any guide, any morphological distinction is unlikely to have occurred, since there would have been continuous mating between domestic (tame) and wild (feral) animals. On the whole, it seems most likely that pigs arrived in New Guinea tame, and with human assistance. Whichever way they arrived in New Guinea, it is, as A. R. Wallace realized, "somewhat curious that they have not found their way to Australia" (1869:I, 141). This fact has been used as the main objection to the acceptance of early dates for pig in New Guinea,

and two aspects of the problem must be considered.

First, it is almost universally the case in New Guinea today that human control over pigs is limited, so that not only do domestic animals inter-breed with feral ones, but frequently they become feral themselves. This was probably the case throughout prehistoric times. Secondly, if feral pigs were in New Guinea (highlands and lowlands) 10,000 years ago, the Torres Strait land passage would have been still open to them. Yet there is no evidence that pigs reached Australia before White settlement, less than 200 years ago. Moreover, within the last 200 years, feral pigs have colonized many environments successfully enough to have considerably affected indigenous flora and fauna (Anon 1977; Pullar 1953) and they now number about one million. We think it unlikely that there were strong environmental or

FIGURE 6.8. Pigs being hunted while swimming. Source unknown.

behavioural barriers to the spread of pigs into Australia 10,000 years ago. Perhaps the barrier potentially posed by many Aboriginal hunting bands in the Cape York area needs to be further considered, but either some mechanism must be found to explain the absence of pigs from Australia, or further archaeological evidence must be obtained from New Guinea.

Given the high ratio of pigs to humans (often reaching >1:1) in many parts of the highlands today, the increase in numbers of specimens in the upper levels of sites is not surprising. Whether this increase occurred everywhere subsequent to, and as a result of, the arrival of sweet potato in the highlands is not so clear. J. B. Watson (1977) has argued that the increase in pigs was related to the arrival of the sweet potato, and that dietary advantage and intergroup competition (the "Jones effect") led to the adoption of sweet potato as a major crop, which then allowed "substantial increases" in pig herds and the expansion of human settlement into higher altitudes. We have already noted that Christensen's preliminary results (1975b) suggest that expansion of the altitudinal range of highland settlement has been occurring over the last few thousand years. The archaeological evidence suggests expansion in pig numbers occurred recently, but precise dates are difficult to obtain. At Batari (NBY) rock-shelter, the increase occurred at and above 850 ± 53 years ago (ANU-39); at Aibura (NAE) it was "well above" 770 ± 100 (GaK-622); at Kafiavana (NBZ), it was noted halfway between 4690 ± 170 (ANU-42) and the surface (J. P. White 1972:16, 57, 92); at Yuku (MAH) (S. Bulmer 1979a) and at Nombe (NCA) (J. P. White 1972) the increase was in the top levels, which were not dated. At Kiowa (NAW) (S. Bulmer 1979a) only four cranial specimens were found. On these data, it would be difficult to argue that the increase has occurred entirely within the last 300 years, but if, as we suggested earlier, sweet potato has been in the region for about a thousand years, the temporal relationship would be better established. We note here that Morren (1977:311–13) has argued, similarly to Watson, that highlands economic history can best be seen as "the intensification and expansion of the pig chain" (i.e., a "Susian revolution"), but his model is developmental rather than being linked to a particular crop. Unlike Watson, he suggests that the revolution was a "very slow" one (1977:313), and we believe that this view accords best with the archaeological data.

We turn now from subsistence prehistory to other aspects: the extent and age of exchange networks, and some features of stone technology.

The oldest evidence for the movement of goods over considerable distances comes from four *Cypraea* sp. (cowrie) shells found in a cluster in Horizon VII at Kafiavana, and dated to around 10,000 years ago. The site is 90 km in a direct line from the nearest coast. Each shell has had the back ground down to make a hole in the same way as is done at present for threading. Fragments of four other marine and estuarine shell genera occurred above this, and others came from more recent levels at other sites (J. P. White 1972:18–19, 60; S. Bulmer 1966). As well as cowries, trochus, whelks, nerites, pearl oysters, cockles, olive and trumpet shells have been found, with the greatest variety being found in the most recent levels. Numbers are small in all cases, and variations between sites may well be due to chance.

At White contact, shells were highly valued by highland people, though preferences varied in different areas (I. Hughes 1978:311). Hughes' detailed study (1977) of the movement of these and other goods shows that down-the-line movement was most common. On the basis of interview evidence, he also suggests that the quantities of shells moved may have increased in the generations immediately before contact, possibly as a result of changes on the coast, but possibly also because of the above-mentioned economic changes in the highlands.

Other goods from lowland areas have been found in levels dated to the last 5000 years. A few flakes of obsidian have occurred in both shelter and open sites, at Kafiavana and further east (V. Watson and Cole 1977:199; J. P. White 1972:24). This volcanic glass is known to occur only at three locations in Papua New Guinea — Fergusson Island, New Britain (Talasea) and Manus (Lou and Pam Islands) (Key 1969; I. E. M. Smith *et al.* 1977) — and specimens from the first two have been found in the highlands (W. Ambrose, pers. comm.). Obsidian has been mined and traded from Talasea for at least 11,000 years (J. Specht 1980; J. P. White *et al.* 1978).

Pottery from eastern highlands sites has been dated to the last thousand years. Today, manufacture is restricted to a handful of villages on the extreme eastern fringe (Coutts 1967; V. Watson 1955), but pottery was also traded in from the Markham River valley, and probably the Madang coast 130 km to the north (Key 1972). Pottery from Madang and from the lower Sepik River is said to have occurred at the open site of Wañlek (JAO), at 1700 m altitude in the north-west highlands fringe (S. Bulmer 1977b). All sherds are said to be stylistically equivalent to wares made today, even though they come from levels 3000–5000 years old. This seems unlikely and further details of the stratigraphic attribution must be forthcoming. If confirmed, these ceramics would be the oldest in New Guinea.

Archaeologically, the only evidence for intra-highlands exchange has come from stone axe-adze heads which can be sourced to quarries. At present fourteen axe-stone quarries are known in the central highlands (Chappell 1966; I. Hughes 1977) and the stone from each can usually be identified. Several hundred axe-adzes, many of them undoubtedly prehistoric, have been sourced to these quarries (Chappell 1966; I. Hughes 1977; Lampert 1972; J. P. White 1977c; J. P. White and Modjeska 1978a), and their distribution shows that at a very general level there is a direct relationship between size and number of heads found and their distance from the quarry. But simple distance is not the key determinant, and many other factors, such as population density, political and social relationships, and the vagaries of loss and archaeological recovery, are also of critical importance (J. P. White and Modjeska 1978b). Only a few large-scale geographical patterns in the distribution of stone from these quarries have been seen, including a restriction to the area west of the Chimbu–Asaro divide, and the occasional movement of stone, probably as finished heads, as far as the north and south coasts. It should also be noted that, even within the central highlands, axe heads were made from a variety of stones found in local river gravels. These gravels provided the only source of stone in the eastern highlands. In the west, there is some evidence that many more

quarry sources existed than was believed a few years ago (Brennan 1979:5), and the documentation of exchange networks, let alone changes in them, will be very complex.

Almost no dated specimens have been sourced. Two ground chips from Kafetu quarry were found in the 5000-year-old level III at Kafiavana, 50 km distant (J. P. White 1972:95). In the Kiowa report, S. Bulmer (1975:36) refers to "trade polished axe/adzes up to 6000 years ago" but does not identify the source. The same is true for "polished axe/adzes of imported rock" at Yuku in layer 3A-B, about 4500 years old (1975:31). These are the only materials documenting dated prehistoric movement of stone.

If modern patterns are any guide, it is likely that exchange networks also included animals and plants and their products, as well as various valuables and manufactures (e.g., see Sillitoe 1978, 1979 for a quantified account of one society; I. Hughes 1977 for a more general account). But the origins and growth of the large-scale exchange systems seen in the twentieth century still elude us.

The New Guinea highlands have also produced sets of artefacts which have only occasionally been found in association with datable materials or in stratified prehistoric contexts. The most dramatic of these artefacts are the various stone mortars, pestles, figurines and club-heads found throughout the highlands and, indeed, most of New Guinea and the Bismarck Archipelago (see Newton 1979 for a comprehensive review). These artefacts are made in a variety of more or less elaborate forms (Fig. 6.9) and have been much sought after by White collectors. Readily recognizable as prehistoric artefacts, often extremely attractive to Whites, and not always of great interest to present inhabitants (but see R. Bulmer and S. Bulmer 1962), they have been removed from the country in very large numbers.

A few examples come from dated contexts. Some fragments of mortar from Wañlek (JAO) were in levels dated to 3000–5000 years ago (S. Bulmer 1977b). At NFB in the eastern highlands two probable mortar fragments were found in component 3, with three dates of 3000–3500 years (V. Watson and Cole 1977:28, 130). A fragment from Nombe (NCA) shelter (J. P. White 1972:134) may also be dated by current excavations there.

It has usually been suggested that all four kinds of objects form a "complex", being made by similar processes and with some similarites in design and materials (e.g. S. Bulmer and R. Bulmer 1964). Rows of bosses around the sides of mortars or the heads of figurines (Bellwood 1978:242) recall club-heads, while similar stylised human faces are found on mortars, pestles and figurines. Newton (1979) draws attention to the fact that club-heads have a somewhat different major area of distribution to the other three kinds of artefacts, being more common in the Papuan than in the New Guinean highlands. He suggests that the two groups should be regarded as distinctive traditions.

Stone club-heads were in use in parts of the island at White contact (e.g. Thompson 1892:175). Shapes varied widely from flat, sharp-edged

discs, through flat star shapes to some resembling a knobbed hand-grenade (Figs. 6.10, 6.11). Their manufacture has been well described in one area (Blackwood 1939). This consisted of pecking and grinding lumps of rock (source unspecified), a process which took some weeks.

Mortars, pestles and figurines have not been observed in modern use — or rather not in modern use of a kind which seems to be implied by their form. Suggestions about the "original" use of mortars and pestles include the grinding of grain (Barrau 1965) or ochre, and the cracking of seeds and nuts; mortars alone would have made excellent mirrors when filled with water (R. Bulmer 1964; Chappell 1964). However, in each case the activity is either totally outside the realm of expectable behaviour or one which we could expect to be continued today. Recent use of these objects seems always to have had a strong

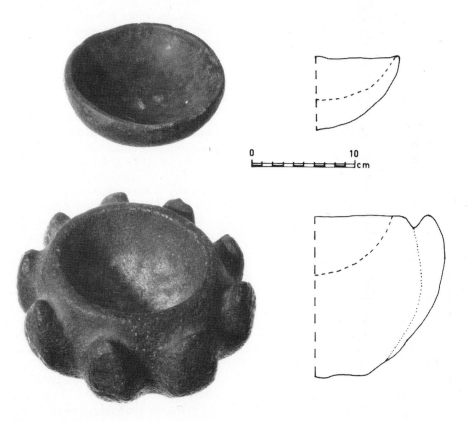

FIGURE 6.9. Mortars from the central highlands, New Guinea. (Private collection).

cm
0

10

FIGURE 6.10. Club-head, mounted for use, from the Papuan highlands, National Capital Province. Length of handle, 84 cm.

magical element. Modern highlanders seldom recognize them as humanly made, and in some areas (e.g. around Lake Kopiago in the western highlands) they are culturally associated with naturally shaped stones. Because many of them have been found in gardens, and because some informants say that garden magic is a large part of their use today, we think that many of these objects have come to be where they are through intentional caching and subsequent non-recovery. Magic may always have been the basic motivation behind their manufacture, and any "utilitarian" origin could be questioned. In considering their spread throughout the country, we do not need to envisage anything as complex as a "cult"; being stones of power accompanied by appropriate charms and spells would be enough.

The origin and age of these objects can also be considered. Their origin has usually been sought externally, either in terms of a "higher culture" intruding upon the present one (Riesenfeld 1950), or an "intrusive complex" (S. Bulmer and R. Bulmer 1964), resulting from Austronesian or Metal Age influences (Bellwood 1978), or the copying of pottery or bronze prototypes (Schmitz 1966). Newton (1979) argues against these ideas as undocumented speculation and draws attention to stylistic and ideological similarities between central highlands cultures and those of the Sepik Hills (where carvings are made in wood). He suggests that the highlands, where the majority of these objects occur, may have been the area of their invention. Although he does not explain why specific forms were adopted, his suggestion seems to have much merit.

Concerning age, the Wañlek and NFB data suggest that some of these objects are quite old; indeed all could be. Some antiquity is implied by the fact that most specimens have been found below 2000 m altitude. As S. and R. Bulmer pointed out in 1964, this supports the notion that they were made before the arrival of the sweet potato. Newton's stylistic comparison, however, might be taken to suggest a more recent age is likely, or that Sepik art styles have a considerable time-depth.

Paintings and engravings on rock faces and in shelters have been found throughout New Guinea and the islands (J. Specht 1979). Specht's review shows that a wide variety of techniques,

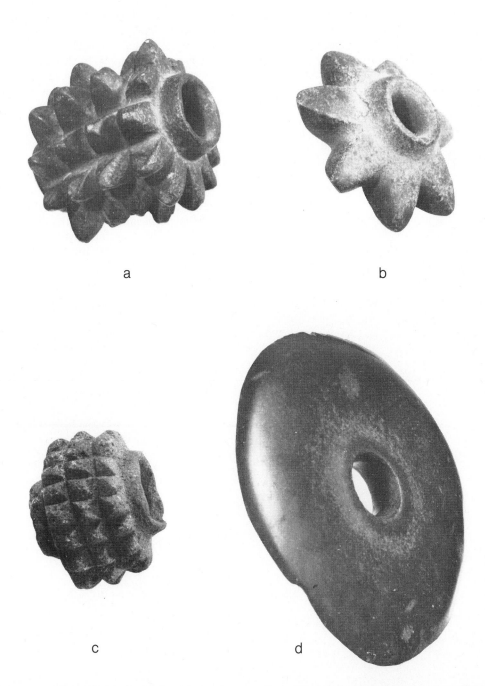

FIGURE 6.11. Club-heads from New Guinea. (a). 100 × 100 × 102 mm; hole tapers from 29 mm to 18 mm at centre. (b). 119 × 107 × 50 mm; hole, 28 mm tapering to 20 mm diameter at centre. (c). 86 × 77 × 72 mm; hole, 32 mm tapering to 24 mm diameter at centre. (d). 169 × 149 × 19 mm; hole, 25 mm diameter. (a). Private collection (Siane). (b). Australian Museum, E50129 (New Guinea). (c). E52014 (Trobriand Is). (d). E65621 (New Guinea).

motifs and styles have been found, some of them very widespread. Among the more interesting research opportunities is the chance to relate the material still being produced to its social context (Fig. 6.12). We can find modern sources for some art (e.g. banjos, aeroplanes, Fig. 6.13). In one site studied intensively by J. P. White (1967b), the designs formed part of a traditional corpus and were probably painted by adult men, but the "meaning" of each design varied widely, and seemed to depend on the individual artist. There was no suggestion that these paintings formed part of a larger ritual association of the kind very common in Australia.

More archaeologically oriented analyses of paintings have not yet been undertaken. If an analysis of formal and material similarities and areal variations were to be made, we predict that the patterns discovered would follow to some extent those visible in other aspects of material behaviour. For example, Bush (1976) has demonstrated that design elements carved on arrow linkshafts are related to linguistic differences. However, the possibility of temporal variations of the kind demonstrated in Australia (Maynard 1979; Morwood 1980) remains to be explored.

6.3   Lowlands and Coast

If it is difficult to describe "the highlands" as a single environmental entity, "the lowlands" are an impossibility, for the environments are so diverse. They range from the vast areas of flat,

FIGURE 6.12. An old man repaints part of the designs at Aibura cave, using white ash pressed on to the soot-blackened ceiling.

seasonally flooded and always wet swamplands with continuous heavy rainfalls, through classic "south seas" beaches backing onto bush-covered hills, to small areas of eucalypt, savannah grassland with totally seasonal rainfall (Paijmans 1976:23–105). Common factors include high temperatures with little seasonal variation, rainfall with some seasonal variation and a variety of subsistence systems which depend on root and tree crops. For the archaeologist, a notable feature of many lowlands populations, especially coastal dwellers, is that they now make pottery or acquire it by exchange. Where this was true in the past, prehistoric sites are highly visible.

Powell (1977:13) divides the peoples of the lowlands into three major groups, primarily on the basis of their use of vegetation. These groups are lowland swamp dwellers who rely heavily on sago; savannah and grassland shifting agriculturalists whose staple crops are yams and/or bananas; and tropical rainforest shifting agricul-

turalists whose staple crop is bananas but who also grow the other dry-land crops. The actual gardening practices in any location depend, of course, very much on local environmental conditions. Present population densities on the coast and lowlands are nowhere as high as those attained in the highlands. In a few areas there are up to 30 people/km^2, but over most of the lowlands, less than half this density is found (Fig. 6.2).

As in so much of Sahul, prehistoric research has been related, to some extent, to the distribution of resident archaeologists, and more is known about the area around Port Moresby than about other parts. Occasional collections of material (e.g. Etheridge 1908; T. A. Joyce 1912; Seligmann and Joyce 1907) and excavations (Pöch 1907a, 1907b) occurred from the turn of the century, but serious research began only about fifteen years ago, and in no area is a coherent picture available. There has been a series of excavations along the south Papuan coast, and

FIGURE 6.13. Modern New Guinean rock art.

isolated studies elsewhere. This account will concentrate on the former.

The most noticeable feature of accounts of coastal prehistory is their concentration upon pottery. Lowlands sites are nearly all open-air settlements — parts of villages or their garbage dumps — and the presence of quantities of pottery makes their discovery relatively easy. The variations in methods of manufacture, constituent materials, shapes, finishes and decorations have allowed local and short-term changes to be distinguished relatively easily, but long-term and long-distance relationships and trends have been more difficult to ascertain. Most interpretations of the prehistory have been overtly based on ceramic change, with the continuities that may have occurred in other materials being given less attention. It is therefore worthwhile to consider briefly the pottery-making situation as it is known from ethnographic records, since this will give us at least some general viewpoints with which to think about the past.

First, within any region in which pottery is made, pots are not usually made in all villages or by all people within a community. Those who do make pots usually trade many of them to other people, sometimes directly, as in the Motu *hiri* trade along the Papuan coast or in the Amphlett Islanders' trade with other south-east Papuans, and sometimes indirectly, as when pots made in villages on the Huon Peninsula are taken by Siassi Island middlemen across the Vitiaz Strait to Umboi Island and New Britain (for trade networks see Brookfield with Hart 1971:Ch. 13). The reason some communities make pottery and others do not seems to relate not to simple causes such as the availability of clay, but to complexes of factors including the need for other supplies such as food or stone, the local distribution of other traditional wealth-producing activities and technological knowledge, and perhaps also the need to provide "reasons" for maintaining contacts between otherwise similar communities.

However, we can recognize factors which cause variation in the areal distribution of pottery-making over time. These include such phenomena as the resettlement of a potting group through war, garden cycling or other causes, or the marrying of some women who do make pottery into a non-pottery-making group. Where

the oral history of coastal groups has been studied, it has shown that many groups of people have moved from place to place quite frequently (e.g. Oram 1977, 1981; Swadling *et al.* 1977). The consequences for the formation of, and variation between, archaeological sites are clear. Thus, when the 2000 years of prehistory of even such a small area as Yule Island (c. 20 km²) was investigated, at least two very different pottery industries were found, each of which has considerable internal variation and is accompanied by clear variations in other artefacts (Vanderwal 1973). To disentangle the causes of such variations and to see the continuities which do occur is no easy task.

Pre-ceramic Occupation

The oldest dated site in lowland mainland New Guinea is at Kukuba Cave (ADL), near Yule Island (Vanderwal 1973), a bat and tick infested shelter in a limestone hill about 2 km from the coast. In the larger entrance chamber, deposits which may have contained archaeological remains were removed for fertilizer early in this century, leaving only a smaller, poorly-lit inner cave undisturbed. Within this cave, Vanderwal excavated an area of about 12 m² to about 1.6 m depth. Two main cultural horizons were found under a thick level of guano. The upper horizon consisted of a thin scatter of broken pottery within an altered soil matrix; the lower consisted of scattered stone flakes and cores in a light brown soil flecked with phosphate (altered guano?). The two horizons were separated by sterile deposits. The highly acidic soil had allowed only inorganic artefacts and charcoal to survive. In the lower artefact-bearing level, Vanderwal noted that more flaked stone occurred near concentrations of charcoal, which were probably hearths. A sample from one of these gave a date of 3920 ± 90 years (ANU-395b). The 313 stone artefacts consisted almost entirely of flakes, 25% with some macroscopic use-wear along their edges. A few pieces had more clearly notched edges, or had been used as cores. The stone has been described as a low quality chert.

Somewhat similar sites, but with even less artefactual data, have been excavated by Rhoads in the Gulf District some 400 km to the west. The oldest date (ANU-2234, 2160 ± 180, at Rupo) is clearly older than the earliest pottery in the area (Rhoads 1980:185). The faunal remains have shown that riverine areas, alluvial plains and the margins between the plains and karst limestone hills were all exploited, while Rhoads also believes that extensive use was being made of natural and cultivated stands of sagopalm (Rhoads 1982). None of these lowland sites have yielded much data on the technology or economy of their inhabitants.

The presence of people on the Papuan coast 4000 years ago is not surprising, given the Pleistocene age of Kosipe (AER), which is only 75 km in a direct line from Kukuba. What is more surprising is that sites considerably older than this should not have been discovered. A month-long survey in the Sogeri region east of Port Moresby recorded many overhangs with paintings and engravings (J. P. White and C. White 1964), but in none of them was there any long-term build-up of material. A similar situation has been found on other coasts. Part of the cause, at least, is likely to be the very low visibility of remains other than pottery in areas with heavy primary or secondary vegetation and low population density. This is true even of very recent sites, as can be seen by comparing Rhoads' (1980) account of research in the low-lying swampy Gulf district with that of V. Watson and Cole (1977) in the highlands. Success in the highlands came primarily through surveying along tracks and roads and in newly cleared gardens, all features more common in more densely populated areas. Another part of the explanation probably lies in the rapid rate of landscape change in much of New Guinea, since landslips, erosion and rapid sedimentation militate against the long-term survival of many sites. In one area where some success might be expected, the rapidly rising coast of the northern Huon Peninsula, a comprehensive survey is only now being undertaken (L. Groube, pers. comm., 1981).

The Last 2000 Years

The prehistory of the Papuan coast has recently been summarized by J. Allen (1977a:391, 393–95),[*] as follows:

> The earliest known pottery using and producing communities appear on the south coast of Papua around 2000 years ago. . . . From Mailu in the southeast to the Papuan Gulf culturally related sites have been located with basal dates all within a century or so of each other. Culturally the people concerned are viewed as a back migration of Austronesian speakers presumably from somewhere in island Melanesia although an exact derivation is yet to be suggested. Significantly the earliest levels of these sites contain pottery similar and presumably generically related to Lapita. The best expression of this early manifestation is Vanderwal's Oposisi site on Yule Island, where the associated adze forms, *Trochus* shell bracelets and other artifacts strengthen the Lapita connection. Subsequent developments at this and other early sites imply a 'Melanisation' of these migrants during the first millenium AD. In many respects these people appear to be an example of 'human supertramps' rapidly occupying what seems on present evidence to have been an unoccupied economic niche in an under-populated region, . . . The economic data from these sites suggests an undifferentiated mixed gardening, hunting and fishing subsistence. While the main concentration is undoubtedly maritime, sites like Nebira 4 near Port Moresby demonstrate gradual adaptation to inland environments. At the same time long distance movement of raw materials is attested to by the presence of Fergusson Island obsidian in these sites, but apart from a suggestion of *Trochus* armshells as imports other possible long-distance trade commodities remain uncertain and indeed trade to any appreciable extent is not evident, although the parallel evolution of ceramic types over a thousand year period for sites as far apart as Nebira 4 and Oposisi argues for close intra-cultural ties, and emphasises an important addition to the technology of the region: efficient sailing vessels.
>
> This picture of gradual adaptation appears to be disrupted about 1000 AD with the termination of a number of long occupied sites. In the Port Moresby and Yule Island areas groups appear who cannot be derived from the coastal occupants of the previous 1000 years on archaeological evidence; ceramic styles alter radically and other artifactual changes occur. Site locations and settlement patterns become much more eco-specific, as does subsistence. The obsidian trade from Fergusson Island now passes no further west than the Aroma

---

[*] Note that references and notes have been omitted from this transcript.

coast. Such changes are exemplified by Motupore, a site some 15 km east of Port Moresby. First occupied some 750 years ago and probably abandoned somewhere before 1700 AD, this small offshore islet represents the typical extreme coastal location and economic orientation of people considered by me, on the basis of the evidence in the site, to be antecedents of the present day Motu. . . .
. . .

A remarkably similar picture has emerged in the Amazon Bay region some 300 km to the east of Port Moresby, where Irwin's connectivity analysis of prehistoric sites has demonstrated that during the first millennium AD the most connected site was on the mainland, despite the natural locational advantages of the offshore island of Mailu. About 800 years ago a ceramic, if not cultural, discontinuity occurred similar to that already described for the Port Moresby region, and from that time Mailu grew increasingly more important and centrally located in respect of other existing villages. By 1890, when it is known to have been the centre of a flourishing trading system, it was dominant in its location. . . .

The Mailu and Port Moresby evidence, together with that from the Yule Island area suggests that the last 1000 years of prehistory on the south Papuan coast is marked by the growth of localised and more specialised economies. Since such specialisation is basic to all of the Melanesian ethnographic maritime trading systems we can expect that in this region trading was escalated to the complex levels observed in the ethnography only within the last 500–800 years, that is beginning some time after we can observe a significant disruption in the archaeological record right along this coast. This more recent period I see as reflecting a significantly higher ordering of economic specialisation than can be observed during the first millennium AD, although trading patterns established then, particularly coast–inland contacts, would have laid a basis for the rapid acceleration suggested during the second millennium. . . .

Allen's scenario is, we stress, based on considerable local knowledge and experience. But in attempting to outline and review the evidence for it, a dearth of comprehensive excavation reports becomes apparent. Since most of the research has been carried out for postgraduate degrees, some accounts have been more concerned with exercises in problem solving than with reportage of basic data. For example, there is still disagreement over the

ceramic classification and terminology for the best known area around Port Moresby, with the terms used rarely being clearly defined. Even at this stage, comparability between reports is limited, while discerning the evidential basis for many generalizations is not easy.

The fact that oral histories in this region stretch back two centuries or more lends an additional dimension to research. These histories can be used to link some sites to specific groups of people and consequently certain pottery styles to them also. Where this connection is possible, it can be said with some confidence that a site was occupied by ancestors of present occupants. One example is the islet of Motupore (AAK) (J. Allen 1977c, 1978) where occupation dates back about 700 years. Beyond this, the situation is much less clear, particularly since there were major changes in ceramics and other artefacts, and probably a good deal of actual population movement at the clan, if not the village, scale (Oram 1977). However, it is often difficult to decide when present socio-linguistic groups cease to be visible in the archaeological records. In the Port Moresby area the dividing line appears to be thought of as the point where ceramic continuity, as measured by decoration, ceases, but that assumption still requires justification. Evidence from other parts of the world does not encourage us to believe that cultural, linguistic and technological continuity are always closely linked.

We start this review of the evidence with one of the better described early sites mentioned by Allen, that of Oposisi (ADI) on Yule Island, excavated by R. Vanderwal (1973, 1978b). Oposisi is a hilltop site on the eastern (landward) side of the island. From the slopes of the hill six trenches, comprising 50 m², were excavated. Trenches lower down the slopes produced greater depths of material, but even within these considerable variation in the visible stratigraphy was observed. Because of the apparent uncertainties in the stratigraphy, Vanderwal's analysis considered only the material from 18 m², most of which was 1.0–1.75 m in depth. Four main depositional units were encountered. The lowest layer of light grey soil was found over the whole hillslope and contained a considerable quantity of debris. It was capped by a thin layer of fine soil and crushed animal bone which was said to mark a period of abandonment, at least of this part of the site. Above this was a series of lenses of darker grey soils which often contained many marine shells, apparently the result of dumping rubbish from the hilltop. The surface layer was of partially redeposited material. This was identified by the occurrence of artefacts similar to those in all previous levels, but Vanderwal noted that it also contained some unique types of pottery, and he therefore believed that it must have derived partly from the last occupation at the site.

Radiocarbon determinations are available from the three lower levels. Three dates (ANU-425, 1890 $\pm$ 305; ANU-729, 1530 $\pm$160; ANU-728, 1600 $\pm$ 210) come from material which was clearly *in situ* in the lowest level. They are not significantly different from each other (Vanderwal 1973:48–49). One date (ANU-727, 1920 $\pm$ 180) is from the level immediately above the lowest and is not significantly different to ANU-728. The material dated may be older and derive from redeposited material, but probably the real age lies at the younger end of the range. If we assume, with Vanderwal, that all the dates are archaeologically acceptable, and combine them according to the procedures described by Long and Rippeteau (1974), an average date for the basal level of 1600 $\pm$ 120 (3 dates) or 1700 $\pm$ 100 (4 dates) is obtained. (Note that on Chauvenet's criterion ANU-425 and ANU-727 would both be deleted; if this were done the mean date of the other two would be 1560 $\pm$ 130 bp. However the number of determinations is too small to insist on this.) Our conclusion is that the initial occupation of Oposisi occurred 1500–1900 years ago, and not necessarily the two millennia generally ascribed to it (e.g. J. Allen 1977a:391; S. Bulmer 1978:276; Vanderwal 1978b:417).

For the middle grey level two similar dates (ANU-726, 940 $\pm$ 180; ANU-725, 1180 $\pm$ 200) were obtained. Vanderwal considers both dates referred to the upper part of the middle levels. The top layer was not dated, but was thought to be not much younger than the levels below.

As one of the earliest workers in the area, Vanderwal undertook an elaborate classification of the ceramics, including both discontinuous (decorative techniques and styles) and continuous (rim and body angles, mouth aperature)

variables (Vanderwal 1973:Chs 5, 6), which it is not necessary to describe here. However, it is worth noting that his analysis of decorative motifs and combinations is based on 1670 large sherds. As he summarizes it, (1978b:418) the lowest level contained 3 main forms — open bowls, and pots with large and small apertures. The bowls were often red-slipped, and were decorated with a groove around the rim and with impressions of the edges and sides of small shells on the body. A small-toothed stamp made of an altered shell edge was also used on a few pieces (1978b:418). Design motifs were squares, circles, arcs and columns. Powdered lime may have been occasionally applied to the decoration to highlight it, but Irwin thinks that encrusted lime on sherds may be of natural origin (G. Irwin, pers. comm., 1981). The other two forms had wide, flat rims, and their only decoration consisted of red paint applied sometimes to the rim and occasionally to the shoulder.

Above this, and coincident with the crushed bone level, Vanderwal saw a sharp break in the ceramic tradition. Although both narrow-mouthed and wide-mouthed jars, along with bowls, continued to be the main forms, the decoration consisted of burnishing to a black colour, and fine-line incision of sets of parallel lines, chevrons, arcs and zig-zags. As in the lowest level, lime may have sometimes been used to fill the incisions. Similar forms, and variants on the same decoration, are said to have continued until the uppermost level, which, despite being redeposited, did have some pottery with unique features. Especially notable was decoration etched into pots when leather-hard, and the widespread occurrence of red paint strips on the lip and body of some vessels.

The ceramic history at Oposisi is supplemented by a range of other artefacts (Vanderwal 1978b). At least eight classes were restricted to the lowest levels. *Clay discs* are moulded into an elliptical shape and perforated near the margin of one end before firing. The most likely explanation of them is that they were used as net sinkers. *Bone adzes* or *scrapers* are about 6 cm long and consist of longitudinally split longbones with one end ground from both sides to form an asymmetrically bevelled cutting edge. The edge is polished from use, and the body of the tool glossed as if hand-held. Scraping bark or other soft vegetable matter is thought to be the most likely use (compare the discussion of Australian *elouera*), although the possibility that they were used in sago processing must be considered, since this local crop produces a high gloss on implement surfaces (Rhoads 1980; J. P. White 1967b). *Tubular beads* made of human (5) or unidentified (3) sections of longbone are 80–140 mm long and have the ends ground smooth. Gloss on one facet of the ends suggests they were hung as a horizontal pendant, either singly or stacked in a vertical series. *Human cranial bone tablets* are square or rectangular in form, with rounded corners and edge lengths of 40–60 mm. All the edges are ground smooth and the surfaces are polished, or at least glossy from use. One example has an opposing pair of perforations, but the general absence of these suggests they were not suspended or sewn to another object, though they were in frequent use. *Pendants* — or at least perforated specimens — were made of teeth and bones. Turtle, crocodile and cassowary bones, four dogs' teeth and one pig's tusk were found. The cassowary bones have been cut and ground into a spatulate shape and may have been spatulae for powdered lime, which is today eaten with betel nut as a stimulant. *Gouges or gravers* made of wallaby incisors, some still set in their mandibles, others detached and apparently mounted differently, were probably used for woodworking.

Another important class of artefact is narrow *bracelets* made of *Trochus* shell. Four of these were found in the lowest level at Oposisi and one in the much later site of Uro'urina (ADG) on the other side of the island. Their importance lies in the fact that, both in the ethnographic and prehistoric records of the Papuan coast, bracelets were nearly always made from *Conus* shell, whereas *Trochus* bracelets were common in island Melanesia and north-east New Guinea.

Probably the most surprising class of artefacts at Oposisi, also found at one other undated site in the area, was a series of stone adzes, asymmetrically bevelled, rectangular to trapezoidal in cross-section and with a thickness nearly as great as their maximum width. There were also a few adzes of triangular cross-section. Both adze forms have been made on a basaltic tuff and are

quite unlike any other specimens from the Papuan coast. However, they are formally very similar to adzes found in Samoa and other Pacific Islands, although technologically the Oposisi adzes were mostly made on highly modified blades while Samoan adzes were core tools.

Allen's interpretation (given earlier) of the early part of the Papuan coastal sequence is based particularly on the material from Oposisi, especially the adzes, the unusual bone artefacts and the sudden appearance of highly decorated pottery. The last aspect in particular is not restricted to Oposisi.

What is said to be similar pottery has been found at several other sites along the coast to the east, including Nebira 4 (ACL) (J. Allen 1972), Nebira 2 (ACJ) and Taurama (AJA) (S. Bulmer 1978), and Mailu (Irwin 1977), and to the west at Kikori in the Gulf District (J. Allen 1972:121). The material which has been seen as most closely comparable to Oposisi pottery comes from Nebira 4, an accumulation of debris at the foot of a steep hill, 180 m high, in the Waigani Swamp plain about 15 km inland from Port Moresby. Here J. Allen (1972) dug a 1.8 × 0.9 m (6 × 3 ft) pit to a maximum depth of 2.6 m (8 ft 6 in), recovering nearly 50,000 sherds and 7500 pieces of flaked stone, as well as land and marine fauna and shellfish. Although the site is a hillwash and rubbish deposit, Allen suggested that nearly all the material was *in situ*, primarily because of (a) the clear sequential distribution of pottery types below a buried soil at about 30 cm below surface; (b) the presence of undisturbed burials; and (c) the presence in the lower levels of pottery styles which were not found on the hillslopes above. Allen's discussion concentrates on distinguishing *in situ* deposition from hillwash derivation and does not consider the likelihood of post-depositional reworking, primarily by human agency. That this probably occurred is suggested by the overlapping distribution of types of pottery decoration, which, on the Oposisi evidence, should have been segregated. Although the earliest (H) and most recent (A) styles are stratigraphically distinct, Table 6.6 shows that there is a wide vertical spread of nearly all styles.

The deposit accumulated over a considerable time-span. Two radiocarbon determinations on halves of a single sample from about 2 m depth

(Level 14) gave dates of 3340 ± 160 (GaK-2990) and 1760 ± 90 years ago (I-5796). Since there seemed to be no archaeological reason for this difference, and because of the similarities in pottery between this site and Oposisi, the younger date has been accepted. A date for level 6, about one metre in depth, was 880 ± 250 years ago (GaK-2667), the large standard deviation being because of the small sample.

Three kinds of vessel were distinguished on the basis of rim types — bowls, and narrow-mouthed and wide-mouthed globular pots. The most common surface finish was a red slip, sometimes burnished, and this was found throughout the deposit. Decoration included painting, burnishing, grooving, incision and stamping with shells. Some of the incised decoration may have been filled with lime. In the lower, but not only the lowest levels, eight sherds were found with intricate shell-impressed designs (style H) which are very similar to those from the lowest levels at Oposisi. Associated with them, and throughout the lower half of the pit, were sixty-one sherds with neat, finely incised patterns characterized by the presence of multiple lines or columns of arcs, often enclosed in rectangles (Style G). Lime infilling was common. Although the numbers were small, Allen saw a very close similarity between these sherds and those from the lower levels at Oposisi. The dates are also consistent. Allen (1972:105) noted that many more motifs made by intricate shell-stamped decoration were found in surface

TABLE 6.6

Ceramic decoration distribution at Nebira 4 (number of sherds)

	Style								
Levels	A	B	C	D	E	F	G	H	I
1–3	20	54	13	9	12	—	—	—	—
4–6	13	28	30	4	6	2	—	—	—
7–9	4	55	33	11	8	1	5	—	—
10–12	—	27	47	18	17	13	13	2	—
13–15	—	27	35	20	16	16	14	—	—
16–19	—	20	17	20	35	22	29	6	7

Source: J. Allen (1972: Table 4).

collections made on the other side of the hill. The presence of mica inclusions in the clay and of misfired sherds makes it likely that some or all of the pottery was made on site or nearby (J. Allen 1972:99).

The wide range of bone artefacts from basal levels at Oposisi is not paralleled at Nebira 4. At the latter, about 30 *Spondylus* and other shell beads were found, along with stone drill-points, awls and other flaked-stone artefacts. The stone industry is relatively sophisticated and unlike that found at Oposisi. However, two high-backed, trapezoidal adzes were found on the surface at Nebira.

Shell-impressed and incised pottery similar to that found at Oposisi has been found by Irwin at two sites nearly 300 km east of Port Moresby (Irwin 1977). An excavation on Mailu Island produced dates of 1900 ± 70 (ANU-1229) and, above it, 1690 ± 100 (ANU-1230); an excavation at Selai, a mainland coastal midden, produced dates of 1790 ± 70 (ANU-1316) and 1770 ± 70 (ANU-1317). Irwin examined several thousand decorated and plain sherds of "Early" pottery from these two sites (1977: Appendix A, Table 2), but we find it difficult to determine how many are very similar to those from the lowest levels of Oposisi.

Pottery in a similar decorative tradition to Oposisi has also been reported from several sites in the Port Moresby region by S. Bulmer (1971, 1978), the oldest occurrence being at Eriama (ACV) where it is said to be dated to 1930 ± 230 years ago (GaK-2670). This date came from charcoal from the deepest level in a small crevice at the back of a rock-shelter. It was not associated directly with any decorated pottery, but Bulmer argues (1978:253) that it is a credible date for the start of this tradition because elsewhere on the site she found one dentate-impressed body sherd similar to those found by Vanderwal in the lowest level at Oposisi. Similarly, at the site of Taurama (AJA) Bulmer used the presence of a pot rim form and dentate-impressed bowls to claim a similarity with the earliest levels of Oposisi (1978:311), and on that basis, and because of possible stratigraphic disturbance by crab burrows, she discounted the associated carbon date of 865 ± 140 years ago (I-6863). It should be noted that only twelve decorated sherds were found in the lowest layer at Taurama, and our examination of the figures (1978: Table 8.23) suggests that not all of these parallel the Oposisi material. This site has been severely disturbed by re-use over many years. and it is not clear whether Bulmer's excavations have revealed an unambiguous sequence.

By now, one of the difficulties in discussing this material should be apparent — that of sufficiently refining the data to allow a proper comparison. This is compounded by a nomenclature problem. The common occurrence of a red slip on pottery decorated with shell impressions in the Port Moresby area (S. Bulmer 1971), including some in the lower levels of Nebira 4 (J. Allen 1972), has given rise to the use of the term "Red Slip Tradition" for this early pottery. As Irwin (1977:98) points out, this term is very vague. More importantly, red-slipped pottery is associated with a wide range of other decorative techniques and, in the Yule Island area at least, has not been shown to be a continuously used decorative method (Vanderwal 1978b:426, n.2). Whereas at Nebira 4 a red slip, sometimes burnished, was the "most common surface finish... throughout the sequence" (J. Allen 1972:99), it did not occur on any pots at all in the level overlying the lowest at Oposisi (Vanderwal 1978b:426). Although there is undoubtedly some basis for Allen's (and others') claims that there was a similar development in south coast ceramics, the precise nature of this remains to be clarified. The situation is not helped by S. Bulmer's (1978:81) decision to use the presence of a red slip as the sole criterion for selecting pottery for inclusion in this "Tradition", thus leading to almost complete definitional circularity. A comparative review of the actual material excavated so far, and the acquisition of larger samples, are clearly needed.

One raw material which has occurred in most of the sites discussed so far is obsidian, some of which has been sourced to Fergusson Island, and all of which probably came from there (Ambrose 1976). This material, in particular, has been used as a basis for arguing that the early ceramic sites were linked together by a long-distance exchange network, and it has also been used, to some extent, to strengthen the "Lapita connexion" (cf. Green 1979). Obviously, evidence of long-distance transport of one material does not tell us much about the mechanisms involved. For example, it is possible, although the stratigraphic evidence makes it unlikely, that all the obsidian described from south coast sites could have been brought in one canoe. For Irwin's four Mailu sites, the total quantity is about 1300 g* (G. Irwin, pers. comm. 1981); for the Port Moresby area and Yule Island sites the total is perhaps thirty small flakes ($<$ 50 g) (J. Allen 1972, 1977a:411; 1980; S. Bulmer 1978, 1979b). It is interesting to note that obsidian was most common in the earliest levels of the Mailu sites, forming about 80% of all the flaked stone, but it continued to occur in small quantities throughout the Early period, (i.e. to about 1000 years ago). The same lack of restriction to the earliest levels has been found in other sites and suggests a continuing, if small-scale, movement of materials along the coast.

No other materials can definitely be described as transported. However, trade or exchange continued along stretches of the coast, as is demonstrated by Rhoads' report (1980:132) that around 1200–1500 years ago (ANU-1963, 1480 $\pm$ 80 and several other dates) pottery from his Kulupuari site in the Gulf District was made using clay from sources 250–400 km east. This would mean that the clay, or more probably the pottery itself, came from the coast between Yule Island and Kerema (Lakekamu R.). The decoration is said to be very similar to that found at Nebira 4 and Oposisi at about the same period, although this information is difficult to check from the site reports. Nevertheless, the occurrence of trade or exchange seems secure, although what was given in return is not known. There is little evidence of sago trade, the basis of later large-scale trading systems, though this seems most likely *a priori*.

Whether the earliest pottery-making inhabitants came to the area as traders (Vanderwal 1978b) or migrants, it might be expected that their economy would have been strongly marine oriented. Vanderwal (1973:152–63) was able to identify 192 bones from the lowest level at

---

* Irwin (1977:Fig. 8.5) suggests that the total was about 500 g, but these data are incomplete. The number of chips is about 1700.

Oposisi, and he found roughly equal proportions of wallaby, pig, turtle and fish, along with a few specimens of dugong, crocodile and cassowary. Despite various sampling problems, we can at least recognize (a) that the economy was not entirely marine oriented and (b) that wallaby was of greater importance than is indicated by any subsequent level or site on the island. Vanderwal suggested (1973:162) that the presence of wallaby indicated exchange with people on the mainland coast, since it was not present on Yule Island in recent times. But if the island was previously unpopulated or was only lightly exploited, wallaby may have existed there, in which case the archaeological record would be of initial or increased human impact on a naive fauna. Shell samples from the site were not analysed in detail, but most are said to be from shallow reef species, with a minority from mangrove environments. Most of the fish were reef and estuary species; and one tiger shark tooth alone may suggest more open-water fishing, which was otherwise notable by its absence. However, there was little change in their subsistence between earlier and later periods.

A similarly mixed economy was recorded for Nebira 4 site, but during the 300–1400 years of debris accumulation (carbon dates at 2 s.d.), there was apparently a swing away from marine and freshwater foods towards a more land-based economy. This was shown in both fish and shellfish, absolute and relative numbers of which were about three times as great in the lowest levels as in the topmost (J. Allen 1972:118). About 85% of the fish are catfish, which could have been caught in the nearby Laloki River; the remainder are coastal reef dwellers, small numbers of which continued to be brought to the site throughout its history. Their numbers declined from 55% in the lower to 7.5% in the upper levels. Allen (1972:119) also referred to the "heavy occurrence" of turtle and dugong in earlier levels, but turtle was listed from only five of the nineteen excavated levels and dugong from only one, and all occurrences were in the middle and upper of Allen's three horizons (i.e. levels 1–8 and 9–15). Thirty-nine species of shellfish were identified, thirty-six of which came from reef, reef-flat or mangrove environments, and constituted about 99% of the total sample. Two genera, *Chama* sp.

and *Strombus* spp., accounted for 90% of the shell by weight, and for about 3000 shells in the excavation. As Allen noted, the presence of *Chama* so far inland is especially strange because of its low meat-to-shell weight ratio. Along with fish and shellfish, pig, macropod (wallaby) and other wild animals occurred throughout, although the relative quantities are not given.

At the Mailu and Selai sites the economies do seem to have been more marine oriented, with turtle, dugong, fish and shellfish occurring in quantity throughout. The only land animal present in any numbers was pig, which we may assume was kept on the island and fed with vegetables brought from mainland gardens. Wild land fauna was present only in very small amounts. Irwin (1977:343) notes that the data available from all excavated levels are consistent with economic patterns reported in the nineteenth century: there is no evidence of any changes in faunal exploitation. Given the tiny size of the island (1.3 km^2), this is not very surprising, though it does suggest that wild animals never developed into the major exchange item that they did over the last few hundred years in the Port Moresby region (J. Allen 1977c).

We have already mentioned that one of the few well-reported and dated early sites (Nebira 4) is in an inland location. In two coastal areas, around Port Moresby (S. Bulmer 1979b) and Mailu (Irwin 1977), surveys have been on a sufficiently large scale to allow us to discuss the pattern of site locations. It is difficult to identify initial settlements and distinguish them from those within the same ceramic tradition but later in time. If all that can be done is to attribute sites to an "Early" period, which may, and probably does, span up to 500 years, then we cannot say, for example, that initial settlements were on offshore islands or other defensible marine locations, with subsequent extension inland. With this caveat, the distribution of "Early" sites in the two regions are similar. In Port Moresby they occur on the coast and on riverine plains behind the low coastal ranges; in the Mailu area they occur on the coast, alluvial plains and offshore islands (Irwin 1977:385). In both cases sites judged later in time on the basis of their pottery occur much more frequently on hilltops. The distribution of "Early" sites has been taken to imply (a) that these settlers were agriculturalists and (b) that the coastal areas at this time were either sparsely or impermanently populated (J. Allen 1977b:37) or that the previous occupants were archaeologically almost invisible.

In attempting to decide between these options, the flaked and ground stone industries are of some assistance. At Mailu, an Early level of the Selai site produced one broken adze head of trapezoidal cross-section similar to those found by Vanderwal at Yule Island. More significant are the relative proportions of imported obsidian and local chert. The former comprised a majority of the raw material in the earliest levels, but then decreased rapidly to a virtual absence. This change was accompanied by a drop in the mean weight of obsidian pieces from between one and 2 g to about 0.5 g. Very similar industries were made with the two different raw materials. Apart from two drill-points, no obvious morphological types have been recognized, and functional edges of the tools are probably the best unit of analysis (Irwin 1977:313a). No changes in the formal or functional aspects of the industry are seen throughout the entire period.

At Nebira 4, Allen found only small quantities of obsidian, the basic raw material being a locally available, fine-grained chert. The mean size of all the material was very small, with retouched pieces averaging 2.1 g. As at Mailu, much of the utilized material was not shaped into clear morphological types, but Allen recognized, in particular, both awls (39, with bifacial use-wear flakes around the tip of flattish flakes) and drill-points (5, all on thicker blade-like flakes with heavy retouch (or wear?) around the tip). There were also sixty-four "scrapers" which can be divided into several forms. Technologically, the presence of "fabricators", probably bipolar cores despite their small size (cf. Vanderwal 1977; J. P. White 1968b), has not been noted elsewhere on the coast at this early date, and the use of this method of flaking is unusual on fine-grained raw materials. In so far as this raw material occurs widely in the area, and the industry is unlike that seen either at Kukuba or in the Highlands sites, it owes little to any previous local traditions.

At Oposisi the only formally patterned artefacts consisted of edge-notched flakes and cores, with most of the material consisting of flakes and pieces with edge-damage. Apart from two pieces of obsidian, stone in the early levels consisted of a low quality chert. Both in form and raw material it is very similar to the older stone industry found in Kukuba Cave, and Vanderwal specifically noted (1973:234) that in this aspect of technology the earliest levels of Oposisi site showed local rather than introduced ideas and forms. It was not until later levels that a finer quality chert appeared, probably imported from further away, and even then there was no change in the formal patterning of the industry.

It is now appropriate to attempt some evaluation of the first part of Allen's interpretation, given earlier. His suggestion that there appears to have been a migration of people to the Papuan coast seems relatively strong, and the wide range of Oceanic-style artefacts, including Lapita-like pottery at Oposisi, points to island Melanesia as the source of this, though not to a more precise location. The radiocarbon dates are consistent with the idea that all the earliest settlements took place "within a century or so of each other" (1977a:391), but they do not require this. They can equally be interpreted as documenting settlement over a period of several hundred years, 2000–1600 years ago. Such an interpretation would allow Oposisi to be the earliest site recovered so far, and its artefacts to be most like those of the Oceanic source. Nonetheless, the variations between sites — the bone and shell artefacts at Oposisi, the flaked stone industry and shell beads at Nebira 4, the stone assemblage indistinguishable from later levels at Mailu — and the range of subsistence practices shows that, despite ceramic similarities, local adaptations had already occurred in each area.

One argument which favours the synchrony of settlement at Port Moresby and Yule Island is the long-continued similarity in the sequence of pottery decoration. We have already pointed out that at Nebira 4 ceramic decorations were not stratigraphically well separated. Further, Rhoads has partially re-analysed Vanderwal's material from Yule Island. He draws attention to the fact that Vanderwal's attempt to define types has involved an artificial restriction of the apparent vertical distribution of decorative elements. This is because any decorated sherds found "out of sequence" have been explained as resulting from post-depositional treadage and scuffage. Rhoads comments (1980:137) that "while some decorative attributes dominate certain stratigraphic units, the danger implicit in Vanderwal's analysis is that of making a specific motif denote a particular age". In our view, it remains to be shown that a very close and continuous connection between the two areas must be posited; some continuing links are clear, but fuller analyses of larger, better dated samples are needed to support the claim of "close intra-cultural ties" (J. Allen 1977a:393).

Further data are also needed concerning the "disruption" which is claimed to have occurred at around 1000 AD. Allen's scenario mentions specifically the arrival of new groups of people in the Port Moresby and Yule Island areas.* However, the only major change recorded by Irwin (1978) at Mailu was in ceramics. He suggests (1978:411) that this change is not well dated, but it lies in the age range covered by radiocarbon dates ANU-1541 (780 ± 230) and ANU-1436 (710 ± 80) (Irwin 1977:66, 76). On the basis of five dates, an end to the "Early" pottery in the Gulf District sites is claimed by Rhoads (1980:140) to have occurred about 1200 years ago.

The markers of change in the Port Moresby and Yule Island areas include ceramic industries "which cannot be derived from [those] that preceded them" (J. Allen 1977b:39), a particular concentration of site locations along beach and hilltop areas and the cessation of obsidian use.

The clearest evidence for change comes from the Yule Island area where Vanderwal found two sites in which all the ceramics were distinctively different from those at his other sites. At one site, Uro'urina, a beach-side mound at least 80 × 35 m, three pits totalling about 4 m² were dug to about 60–90 cm depth. One date of 720 ± 105 bp (ANU-730) was obtained from the lowest level (Vanderwal 1973:52). Eight different decorative

attributes were distinguished on sherds from the site, the majority being executed with combs having between two and eight teeth. Shell-edge impressions and rows of holes punched with a single stick were also noted. The other noticeable difference was in the flaked stone tools: instead of high quality chert, the common material was quartz. Large flakes were often used, and bipolar flaking seems to have been the common flaking technique — a new one for this area, though not for the coast as a whole. Although the sample was very small, other artefacts suggested some continuity and similarity. These included stone adzes, bone spatulae, stone club-heads and a *Trochus* shell bracelet (Vanderwal 1973:194). In terms of subsistence, this site produced rather more marine fauna than others, not unexpected in view of its beach-side location. More importantly, this was the only site found which produced dog remains, though the absence from earlier sites was probably due to chance, since dog was found in levels 10–16 of the Nebira 4 site near Port Moresby (J. Allen 1972:117).

Vanderwal's account of this phase of Yule Island area prehistory notes particularly that the two younger sites were both at new locations and contained no earlier ceramics. Nor were sherds from this time found on even the surfaces of earlier sites. The major locational changes are perhaps the strongest evidence of some political or social changes in the area, though whether this necessarily involved large-scale immigration remains to be demonstrated. We must point out particularly that, although the radiocarbon dates can be interpreted as implying temporal continuity between Uro'urina and earlier sites, there may equally have been a considerable time gap. Finally, as Vanderwal (1973:195) noted, although the settlement locations, general economic patterns and many artefacts of the modern period are like those of Uro'urina, the modern pottery is not slipped, burnished or painted — it is decorated with little more than a potter's mark. This major change appears to have occurred without any noticeable "disruption" of other aspects of society.

In the Port Moresby area, changes in the last 1000 years or so are much less clearly defined. On the basis of her surface sites, dated by ceramic styles and somewhat tenuously linked to

* It must be stressed that, although Allen's scenario was written in 1975, it is the only published attempt at synthesis of the coastal material. Research and discoveries since then show that changes do occur in the Port Moresby region, and date to around 1200 AD, rather than 1000 AD. Some data for this period are becoming available (e.g. S. Bulmer 1978, 1979b). These suggest that the 1975 picture needs modification, but in what ways is not yet clear (J. Allen, pers. comm., 1982; see also J. P. White and Allen, 1980:732).

radiocarbon dates, S. Bulmer (1979b:13) suggests that this period saw the first occupation of coastal hills, but the number of sites involved is so small (4) that the change may be due to sampling error. We note that the relative proportions of sites on the coast and river plains remain unchanged. J. Allen (1977b:39) specifically instances the occupation of the hilltop site of Nebira 2, but as Bulmer points out (1978:132) and Allen elsewhere recognizes (1977a:411) pottery of the earlier "Red Slip Tradition" was also found there. In the Port Moresby region the most comprehensively excavated site is the islet of Motupore (1.6 ha). On the basis of twenty-two radiocarbon dates (some still unpublished), Allen (1978:51) claims that the site was occupied from about 750 until 300 years ago, with use being continuous. The earliest levels, some 4 m below surface, have been dated to 810 ± 105 (ANU-1211) and 740 ± 105 bp (I-5903), with a slightly higher level giving 715 ± 90 bp (I-5902); two dates from one metre down in the deposit are consistent (ANU-1177, 330 ± 55 and ANU-1212, 390 ± 65); and stratigraphically more recent levels have given "modern" readings (J. Allen 1977c:442–43; S. Bulmer 1975:52). Few other newly settled sites have been reported, though many are known.

The pottery from the earlier levels at Motupore was shell-impressed and combed, being similar in this respect to that from Uro'urina, and the same decorative attributes were involved. Allen (1977c:443) notes that, during the period of occupation, incised or stick-impressed decoration gradually replaced former methods, painting was used until the most recent levels and the final ceramics are very close to those made by the Motu potters who inhabit the area (but not the island) today. The origin of this ceramic tradition is obscure, but still unpublished material from Ava Garau, a coastal village site, dated to around 900–1200 years ago according to one radiocarbon date and various personal communications, has been seen as its ancestor (J. Allen, pers. comm., 1982; Swadling 1980).

In 1971 Bulmer claimed that there were a number of pot types found in the Port Moresby area which were similar to historic and prehistoric pottery known from the Milne Bay area, particularly pots recently made on Goodenough and the Amphlett Islands. She therefore labelled the style "Massim" (1971:57–60), claiming it to be distinct from the "Red Slip Tradition" in decorative methods and motifs. Pottery of this kind has been found at Nebira 2, Ava Garau and Taurama near Port Moresby, as well as at Uro'urina, but Egloff (1979:111) considers that the similarities to Massim wares are limited and, indeed, they have never been properly demonstrated. We note that Irwin (1977) saw no need to refer to other areas for the source of the major discontinuity in Mailu area pottery, and he drew attention to the considerable continuities in settlement pattern and technologies. Such, indeed, may also have been the case in the Port Moresby area, as S. Bulmer (1979b:22–24) later suggested.

The question of obsidian use in this later period is troublesome. None was found at Motupore, and in 1975 Allen was convinced that it did not reach the Port Moresby area (J. Allen 1977b:39). S. Bulmer now claims (1979b:19) that obsidian has been found in two of her later sites — at Eriama, where two flakes were bracketed by radiocarbon dates of 600 ± 125 (GX-3334) and 380 ± 120 bp (GaK-2668), and at Nebira 2, where ten flakes were bracketed by 660 ± 150 (GaK-2673) and 280 ± 80 bp (GaK-2672). (Note that the last two laboratory numbers quoted follow Bulmer 1978:130; in 1979b:19 they are reversed.) No obsidian was found at Taurama in levels clearly dated to less than 1000 bp (S. Bulmer 1978). Ambrose (1976:369) referred to one flake (out of 40,000 pieces of stone) found at Motupore, but because of its thick hydration rim, this appears to be an antique and does not refute the general statement (Allen 1977a:411). No obsidian was found by Vanderwal at his later sites, and very little by Irwin at Mailu. The extent of change in obsidian movement west of Mailu in the last millenium still seems to be unclear, but since the coastal sites have no obsidian, we wonder whether the few flakes found at inland sites are really obsidian and were in secure stratigraphic contexts.

To summarize, we believe that, while local discontinuites may have occurred between 800 and 1200 years ago, we do not think that these need to be explained by migrations of people on a large scale along the coast (J. Allen 1977b:39). Current knowledge is too localized for us to be confident that local developments could not have been the sources of change (for a modern analogue see Oram 1981).

Whatever its origins, the economy and technology of Motupore show something of the prehistoric background to the elaborate trading systems recorded in the nineteenth century. The following account is derived from J. Allen (1977a, 1977b, 1977c, 1978) whose complete excavation report is still being prepared.

Throughout the islet's history, two major industries appear to have been the manufacture of shell beads and pottery. The former is evidenced by many flaked stone drill-points (Fig 6.14), which account for nearly half the worked stone, and by hundreds of beads in all stages of manufacture. Misfires and other incomplete specimens of pottery abound, and analyses show that clay (perhaps as pots as well as raw material) came from several sources nearby on the mainland (J. Allen and Rye, in press). In the ethnographic record both beads and pots were

major units of exchange, the pottery from this area in particular being taken in very large quantities (up to 30,000 pots per year) several hundred kilometers to the west to exchange for sago.

So far, only a small sample of the faunal remains has been analysed, but this reveals some interesting patterns. Marine animals, including dugong, turtle and fish, are the most prolific. The fish consist almost entirely of shallow-reef and harbour species, which could have been caught by spearing, netting or poisoning. The presence of thousands of shell net sinkers and the absence of any fish-hooks is consistent with this picture, as it is with Motu ethnography. Swadling (1976, 1977) has made some examination of the shellfish and has shown that shell beds in the area were heavily exploited throughout the period of occupation. This is based on the fact that the shells of most specimens of *Strombus luhuanus* found on the site were shaped like juveniles, even though they are as large as shells with adult characteristics found in the area today. Such a situation suggests that all large *S. luhuanus*

FIGURE 6.14. Three chert drill-points from Motupore, near Port Moresby. The longest is 24.5 mm. Courtesy: J. Allen.

shellfish were being removed, which allowed younger animals to grow large before they became mature. Only two land animals occurred in the site — pig and agile wallaby. The small number of pig bones suggests that it was a minor resource. Wallaby occurred in large quantities, with a low proportion of very young and very old animals (J. Allen and Rye in press; note that earlier reports stressed the full range of the age sample). Allen argues strongly that, if Motuporeans were hunting for themselves, we would expect the presence of at least some other animals, such as cassowary and cuscus, as has been noted in all other sites in the area. He suggests that the nineteenth century accounts of the fire-driving of wallabies into nets and subsequent trading of them could readily have produced a population similar to that indicated by the excavated sample. The low number of very old animals is consistent with heavy predation, while the very young would not have been worth trading. The written records show that this hunting was done by inland dwellers who exchanged smoked carcasses for shell beads, armshells, pottery and even fish with people living on the coast.

Archaeological documentation of the range and kinds of trade found in the nineteenth century is limited. Allen (pers. comm., 1978) notes that at least seven of Renfrew's (1975) ten modes of trade were simultaneously practised by the closely inter-related groups around Port Moresby. Of these, no more than three can be shown in the archaeological record — the movement of pottery, shell beads and foodstuffs described above.

The origin of the best-known coastal trade system of the area, the *hiri*, is unclear. Oral traditions of the Motu people attribute it to an individual who lived perhaps ten generations ago (1750 AD?: Oram, in press), but there seems little doubt that some form of long-distance coastal trade is much older. For example, at his Ouloubomoto site Rhoads has recently found a few sherds which another analyst has said are similar to those found in the earliest levels of Motupore. They have been dated to 1050 ± 170 years ago (ANU-2236). On the other hand, he also notes that settlement patterns most congruent with intensive coastal trade have occurred only

twice, about 1500–1200 years ago and from about 300 years ago (Rhoads, in press).

The rationale behind the *hiri* voyages is also unclear (Allen 1977a, 1977c; Oram in press). Nineteenth century accounts stress the frequency of famines in the immediate area around Port Moresby, and recent scholars point out that the removal of several hundred men for several months would have alleviated the problem. But the situation is more complex. Why did people continue to live in such a "difficult" area? If food stress was the basic problem, why were other traders from villages east along the coast welcomed at times when local menfolk were away? Why was there not a greater attempt to acquire food from either inland or closer coastal sources? Because of these and similar problems with "utilitarian" explanations, some researchers have seen the *hiri* as reflecting the "conscious specialization" of trading. In other words, people such as the Motuporeans were not forced into trade but developed it over time as their way of acquiring valuables and status within their own society. Thus Allen (1977a:407) points out that in the nineteenth century "a successful *hiri* elevated the status of all who went ...", and suggests that it developed primarily for this reason. Our view is that the most recent trading systems derive from earlier ones, and we suggest that the *hiri* is simply the last of a series of similar status-acquiring trade systems which differed in scale, orientation and goods moved along the Papuan coast.

Irwin's interpretation of developments in the Mailu area also documents the gradual emergence of a specialized maritime trading system. As summarized by him (1978), the following features are notable.

1. During the last 800 years there has been a process of rapid change and standardization in pottery. Early in this period, pottery was highly variable in decoration and thickness, and the clay was being obtained from several sources. By the eighteenth century pottery had become much finer walled, it was so standardized that an individual's works could not be distinguished, and the clay was being obtained from only one source — Mailu Island. These changes are consistent with the development of Mailu as the focus of all known

trading networks. We may see these developments in ceramics as both economical for the pottery makers and as involving a degree of "planned obsolescence", even if the latter was not thought of in this way.

2. The spatial organization of settlements changed through time so that Mailu became the central place. Using connectivity analysis, Irwin has been able to show that Mailu's economic specialization coincided with a distinct locational advantage.

3. During the later period the movement of goods was on a larger scale and more extensive. Whereas 2000 years ago pottery was moved only about 6 km inland, this increased to 10 km by 800 years ago and to 40 km (the most remote interior of this part of Papua) by the nineteenth century. The movement of obsidian was not as straightforward, but there was a considerable increase in amount from about 800 to 400 years ago, followed by a decline. Irwin interprets this as resulting from obsidian being used to help establish the Mailu monopoly but, once acquired, "there would be no need for the Mailu to serve the requirements of customer villages beyond the level of their own interests" (1978:414).

As with the *hiri*, the Mailu trading system may be plausibly seen as one designed to give social as well as utilitarian rewards. There is no doubt that the trading of pots for food and stone axes provided the islanders with resources not locally available; but it is also clear that the long-distance trading, as well as their monopoly of pottery manufacture, was not necessary for day-to-day existence. Although the documentation is less complete than for the *hiri*, trading was the avenue to individual prestige among the Mailu people (Irwin 1977:26).

Changes and developments similar to those found along the Papuan coast may be posited for other areas of New Guinea, but in no case has a coherent study been produced. Among the more notable studies is one by Egloff (1978) in which he demonstrates that at least part of the famous *kula* exchange system is of relatively recent origin. Using both stylistic traits and X-ray

diffraction analyses of the clays, he has been able to show that whereas in the modern *kula* the Trobriand pottery supply is derived from the Amphlett Islands, 500–1000 years ago both Goodenough Island and communities on the mainland coast at Collingwood Bay were involved in the exchange network. Further investigations into the prehistory of the *kula* are still underway.

Egloff (1971a, 1979) has also investigated the prehistory of the north Papuan coast around Collingwood Bay. The earliest ceramics appear to be older than 1000 years bp and may be as much as 2000 years old. The majority were found on surface sites. They are notable for shallow bowls on pedestals (Group P) and jars with flat lips (Group J). The pedestaled bowls are decorated with cut-outs on the pedestals and shell-edge stamping and triangular cut-outs on the body (Fig. 6.15); the jars have unique decorations of criss-cross incisions and shell-edge impressions. This pottery cannot be readily related to other New Guinean or Melanesian traditions, though Egloff draws attention to the pedestals on some of the New Guinean stone mortars. Ceramic bowls of the type illustrated in Fig. 6.15 are common in several parts of South-East Asia. Egloff (1979:113–14) discusses other possible links between the two areas and suggests that a local origin for these ceramic forms seems to be unlikely. We would argue that we need to know much more about the prehistory of the area before favouring this interpretation.

The bulk of Egloff's material came from a series of midden mounds (HAC) on the coast at Wanigela. Diggings in these mounds earlier this century (Pöch 1907a, 1907b, and others unreported) revealed a variety of curious ceramic and shell artefacts (e.g. Fig. 6.16). Dates from the three mounds excavated showed that most of the accumulation occurred between 1000 and 500 years ago. Pottery in these mounds is only "tentatively related" (1971a:135) to earlier ceramics, and it is also dissimilar to historic pottery in the area. The mounds themselves were deposited over the same period of time and not in a sequence. Nonetheless, they produced very different proportions of both ceramic types and faunal remains. While the differences may be partly the result of sampling, they may also indicate that the mounds were the rubbish dumps of different social groups. Such social groups could have had access to different faunal resources, as well as rights to certain design elements and objects. They may also have been residentially segregated within the settlement (Egloff 1979: 104–106). These interesting suggestions are certainly worthy of further research, but Egloff's work at present stands very much in isolation.

We conclude this section on lowlands prehistory by quoting Irwin's conclusion concerning the Mailu evidence (1977:419). It is certainly more

widely applicable than he intended it.

... it has been possible to explain local prehistoric developments primarily in terms of local processes.... One cannot rely solely on apparently sudden typological change in artifacts to propose radical changes in local culture history such as migrations.... This interpretive bias ... is not to deny the existence... of frequent external contact and small-scale movement between areas, the diffusion of innovations, trade and the like. However the archaeological evidence is that the processes at work need not have been markedly different to those described ethnographically.

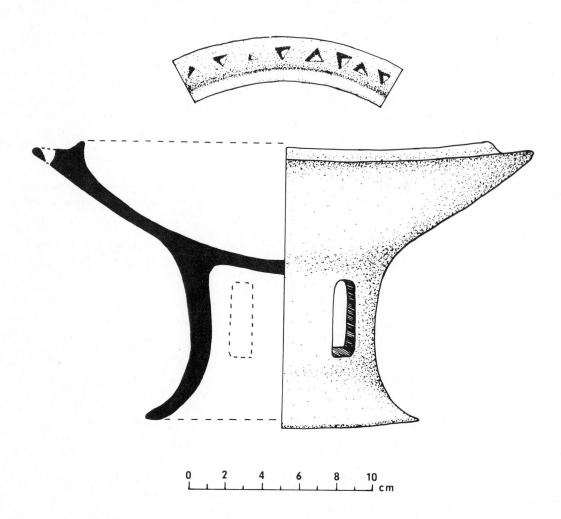

FIGURE 6.15. Pedestaled bowl from Wanigela, New Guinea. Source: Egloff (1971b).

FIGURE 6.16. Engraved conus shell from Wanigela, New Guinea. Australian Museum E15597. Height 105 mm. (J. P. White *et al.* 1970b). Courtesy: Trustees of the Australian Museum; photo: C. V. Turner.

7.1 Change in Prehistory

It is now some twenty-five years since professionalized archaeology began in Australia and twenty since it began in New Guinea. During this period a basic framework has been sketched and some interesting problems identified. The underlying premise of most interpretations has been that the prehistory of Sahul can be envisaged as a story of unidirectional evolution towards the ethnographic present. It has been widely, if usually implicitly, assumed that the particular forms, structures and even ethos of Sahul societies were established perhaps 30,000 years ago, and that since then they have been developed and modified but not substantially changed. According to this view the "Aboriginality" of the Australians and the "Niuginianization" of the northern Sahul inhabitants would have been recognizable more than 20,000 years ago. Such a view does not preclude change, but it does tend to suggest that basic subsistence patterns, the organization of people in the land, and the forms of social and religious life observed in the nineteenth century will not be grossly incongruent with the evidence from any past time.

We have suggested several times in earlier chapters, and others have been more explicit,

Chapter 7
Sahul: Internal Patterns and External Comparisons

that human life in Sahul has changed considerably during its history. There is both direct and indirect evidence of this. Within Australia, perhaps the most striking single piece of evidence is the 4000–7000-year-old cemetery at Roonka, South Australia (Pretty 1977). Many of the burials there were in forms unknown in the nineteenth century and were accompanied by a range of goods which included tooth chaplets, cloaks with fringes, pins and other regalia made from animal parts. These could be interpreted as status differences (cf. King 1979). A similarly spectacular find from the same period is the male burial from Lake Nitchie with its necklace of matched *Sarcophilus* teeth (Macintosh 1971). The implication of these finds is that not only the technology, but also the social and religious life, was very different from nineteenth century forms.

The occurrence of such a degree of change is supported by studies which suggest that the elaborate representation of beliefs and history in paint on rock surfaces may have occurred only during the last few thousand years. R. Edwards (1971) and, more elaborately, Maynard (1979) have shown that many carvings and engravings with a restricted range of motifs (animal tracks, circles) probably date from Pleistocene and early post-Pleistocene times and occurred throughout Australia, if not throughout all Sahul. However, there is only limited, directly dated support for this (Rosenfeld *et al.* 1981). Even if these designs and sites were vehicles for transmitting the same kinds of information as more recent paintings (which is quite uncertain), they must have done so in very different ways. Post-Pleistocene changes included the development of simple and complex figurative styles (Maynard 1979) which show wide regional variations. Attempts at seriating the various styles and techniques have a long history, but little record of success. Recently, Morwood (1979, 1980) has shown that in one area of the central Queensland highlands most paintings are almost certainly younger than 5000 years old, and that sequences in techniques and colour usages can be determined. There are hints, both here and

elsewhere (Bowdler 1981), that the development of these artistic traditions may be linked to the spread of the "small-tool tradition" and to economic changes. This would indicate that a very major change occurred in Australian history 4000–5000 years ago. (We should perhaps point out that we have not dealt with this class of prehistoric evidence in this book because its internal development and correlation with other aspects of prehistory is still only beginning to be explored (e.g. Clegg 1981).)

Changes in subsistence patterns and technologies are more widely recognized features of the archaeological record, the former especially in Pleistocene times. Twenty-five thousand years ago, seed grinding and eating was of little importance, if known at all; macrozamia starch was probably not processed; coastal shellfish almost certainly did not have the importance they later possessed, since coastlines were less stable; dogs were not present to give companionship, scare spirits and sometimes assist with hunting (Hamilton 1972; Hayden 1975a; Kolig 1973; I. M. White 1972; K. Gollan, in preparation). On the credit side, more and larger animals were available for hunting and, we have argued, were hunted. When interior lakes were fuller than at present, more fish, shellfish, waterbirds and plants would also have been available (Bowler and Jones 1979). We suspect it is no coincidence that the extinction of many animals occurred some time subsequent to the increasing aridity, for this would have been when major environmental stress was added to the continuing pressure of human hunting. It is also likely that faunal extinctions can be linked to the earliest evidence of seed grinding. Seeds, with their comparatively low return in relation to the effort expended in collecting and processing, would have been ignored as food when other kinds of food could be more effortlessly obtained.

We expect that evidence of subsistence changes of a similar kind will be found in northern Sahul, where late Pleistocene peoples also hunted large animals. Later, in the post-Pleistocene, roots and animals, some of South-East Asian origin, became of particular importance, but we suspect that local roots and fruits were first cultivated as basic foodstuffs.

While some technological changes can be linked to subsistence, and ultimately to the environment, the origin of others may well lie more directly in human relationships. We have already mentioned how the new artefacts which spread through Australia about 4000–5000 years ago were, in some areas, made in exotic stones not previously used. Gould (1977a, 1978a, 1980) has argued that these changes signify new and wider social linkages across the Central Desert, a development which it is tempting to link to the increase in aridity around this time. Although apparently minor elsewhere, it may have been of greater significance in desert areas. More broadly, Hamilton (1980) argues on the basis of ethnographic data that the new technology (including adzes) was exclusively used by males, was linked with new all-male rituals, and was used to establish (or reinforce) the structural and ideological dominance of men over women, a noticeable feature of traditional Australian societies. Similar changes have been suggested by Bowdler (1976) as a result of the introduction of fish-hooks along the south-east coast. In testing these suggestions, the Tasmanian and Cape York evidence, where the new technologies did not penetrate, is obviously vital. Jones' (1977a) argument is also relevant here, since it too suggests that the religious and social life of Tasmanian communities was cast in an older mould and had changed less than in mainland Australia. While these analyses are only suggestive, they draw attention not only to the fact of technological changes, but also to the economic and social consequences that can be considered by prehistorians.

The idea that Sahul society has changed throughout prehistoric times is not new. But we think that neither the depth nor the extent of the changes has been appreciated. This implies, in particular, that the ethnographic record is largely inadequate as a direct guide to more than the quite recent past, and that archaeological data must be looked at in terms of more general theories of human and material behaviour before the full story can be told.

7.2   Sahul in World Prehistory

For many years inhabitants of New Guinea, Australia and Tasmania have been important sources of information on which theoretical and empirical developments in cultural and social anthropology have been built. The Aboriginal Australians, in particular, have been of critical importance (cf. Burridge 1973). Partly due to ignorance of it, the prehistory of these peoples, and its implications, has not been of such import to world prehistory. But we can now recognize that there are some assumptions and discussions in world prehistory on which the Sahul data bears. We will here speculate broadly and generally on some of these themes.

During the last 100,000 years there has been an acceleration in the rate of change in human history. Although the suddenness of this has probably been over-emphasized, this period has seen signficant modifications to tool-kits, the occupation of higher latitudes in the continental Old World, the development of human burial, and a quantum increase in the decoration of artefacts, from jewellery to caves. An important aspect of this change was the wider use of marine environments, evidenced both by shells and fish bones in archaeological sites and by the occupation of Sahul. Whenever it occurred — and it was most probably 45,000–60,000 years ago — the crossing of Wallacea required watercraft capable of carrying several people. The navigator David Lewis (pers. comm., 1980) believes that these need have been no more sophisticated than bamboo rafts (cf. J. P. White and O'Connell 1979). Whatever kind they were, watercraft must have been part of the regular technology of any human societies using these tropical seas. We wish to suggest that watercraft need not have been restricted to these areas of the Pacific. If, for example, human material culture was adequate to allow people to live in the tundra, it is hard to believe that the island-strewn seas around China and Japan were not equally open to human exploitation. Direct evidence of marine exploitation in Japan appears to be only some 10,000 years old (Ikawa-Smith 1980), but considerably earlier use of watercraft is required by the distribution of technological traditions (V. Morlan 1971) and a 20,000-year-old obsidian trade (Aikens and Higuchi 1982: 94). As in Sahul, we may expect most earlier direct evidence of marine exploitation to have been destroyed by rising sea levels.

It is also worth considering the northward extension of this exploitation and the implication of this for the settlement of that other empty continent, the Americas (cf. Hallam 1977). The majority of current scenarios suggest that the first inhabitants moved rapidly overland, hundreds of kilometres along a narrow ice-free corridor from the north-west peninsula (see e.g. *Canadian Journal of Anthropology*, *1*, 1980). The possibilities of a marine-based migration have recently been persuasively argued by Fladmark (1979), but this clearly requires further research. We note in passing that this model would encourage us to accept that coastal settlement of western North America occurred in the late Pleistocene, a claim supported by some dated skeletal evidence.

The colonization process is also a topic which can benefit from comparative discussion. Sahul and the Americas are the only two continents that were settled by palaeotechnic humans, and yet the widely accepted models of their settlements could hardly be further apart. In Chapter 3 we discussed the lengthy process we consider Sahul colonization to have been, and the problems raised by the assumptions of coastal colonization, single-minded big-game hunters, and 3% p.a. population growth. Many Sahul prehistorians now suggest that modern population densities were not attained within a few millennia, and that the amount of evidence for the early settlement period one can thus expect to find will be very small, given the small numbers of people and the high probability that many of their sites are now under water. The belief in a slow rate of colonization — between 10,000 and 20,000 years for the coast and semi-arid zones, even ignoring the desert — derives strong support from both expectably low population growth-rates and, even more, from the time needed for environmental adaptation. Many plants of tropical lowland Sahul and seashore

animals would have been familiar to new arrivals, but new forms of plants and animals would have become evident as soon as they moved away from the tropic coasts. It would have been necessary for the new arrivals to learn the habits, occurrence and potentials of these new foods before they could be utilized. In moving to new environments people would also have had to discover the nature and locations of a full range of physical and spiritual resources necessary for life — a range of woods, fibres, animals and rocks for tools and clothing, the dreaming and totemic sites which gave them evidence of the fact that they were legitimate in the land. Further, these people were not "explorers"; they were not equivalent to those we know from the last few hundred years of industrial society. Rather, they were people who lived in and from an estate and whose moves were as small-scale and risk-free as they could manage.

If these views of the colonization process are applied to the Americas, we must believe that the northern continent, at least, was colonized no later than 20,000 years ago, and probably ten or more millennia earlier. There are certainly suggestions of this in the archaeological record (see MacNeish 1978 for a sympathetic review), especially from Meadowcroft shelter (but see Dincauze 1981) and dates on some Californian skeletons (Bischoff and Rosenbauer 1981). However, we think that stronger evidence is provided by the sites firmly radiocarbon dated to the early Holocene throughout South America, and the similar dates for developing plant cultivation (what Schoenwetter (1974:302) calls "the technical knowledge to support a farming economy") from the central Mexican highlands. The former imply that, by 10,000 years ago, people had traversed 17,000 km, from the sub-arctic to the sub-antarctic, and had learned to live off each environment encountered on the way. The latter imply not only this, but sufficient population growth and environmental knowledge to make experimentation necessary and worthwhile. We stress that, on the most conservative interpretation, the Central American highlands were occupied by 11,000 years ago, and experimental plant manipulation was occurring by 9000 years ago (see review by Bray 1980). It seems to us that chronologies of American prehistory have allowed totally insufficient time for a long-term, secure environmental understanding to be developed, and that the process of American colonization should be looked at from a wider perspective.

Similarly useful comparisons can be made in the case of faunal extinctions, for Sahul and the Americas are the only two cases where these occurred throughout large continents. We have already suggested that, although similar mechanisms may have been involved in different parts of Sahul, their importance may have varied. The same will probably be true of the Americas, although to date this has received less consideration because of the dominance of the "overkill" hypothesis. Whatever the "final solution", we suspect that a component of regional variability must be included.

On another level, the nature of the evidence from both areas is worth considering. In North America, it is clear that large animals were killed, butchered (and eaten?) in open-air locations (e.g. Haynes 1980; Saunders 1980). However, if Late Pleistocene diets were reconstructed on the basis of the material from caves and rock-shelters, there would be almost no indication that extinct animals were predated by humans, both because the numbers of bones are extremely small and there is often doubt about whether humans were responsible for depositing the bones in caves.* In Sahul no open kill-sites that are clearly the result of human activity have been reported, and discussion has concentrated especially on the dating of megafaunal extinction and on the degree of possible human involvement. Now that temporal overlap has been established, the nature of any interaction must be defined. The American evidence clearly suggests some appropriate depositional environments in which

research might be concentrated. Notice that most of the Sahul evidence is from shelters. Thus it is certainly not impossible that Sahulian and American megafaunal hunting patterns displayed close similarities.

Another aspect of human–environment relationships in which the Sahul situation is generally important is the development of a range of techniques designed to maintain or increase food production in a region. Throughout Australia, modern observations demonstrate that the classic hunter–gatherer continent was a partially managed landscape. The use of fire to increase the occurrence of certain plants, synchronize their seeding or attract animals to re-growth is perhaps the best documented single mechanism (Beaton 1977, 1982; A. M. Gill et al. 1981; Hallam 1975; D. R. Harris 1977; Jones 1969, 1975). Other manipulations include the care and transference of certain plants (Hynes and Chase 1982; Jones 1975; Kimber 1976), fish farming (Lourandos 1980a) and the like. These behaviours are similar to many documented in areas of North America, where regular field farming was unknown (see e.g. Lawton et al. 1976; Lewis 1977). In both areas there is a strong suggestion that "hunting and gathering" is an inadequate characterization of subsistence patterns, and a term such as "estate managers" might be more appropriate. This has wide-ranging implications for our models of hunter-gatherer societies, particularly as we seek to apply these to the past, and also for our ideas about the development of more intensive resource exploitation and population growth. As Lourandos points out, these Australian adaptations cannot be seen as static, as they were parts of "an overall drift towards a simpler ecosystem" (1980b:424). Over time, people came to depend more on a smaller range of more reliably available resources, so there was an increasing need for continuing management as the man-made aspects of the environment became more important. In this view, Australians are distinctive because of their position towards one end of a cline rather than because of any absolute differentiation from other societies.

The history of New Guinean subsistence, particularly in the highlands, must also be integrated with our general models of the past. There, it seems likely that intensive cultivation of

---

* In making these statements we are (a) considering data from Fort Rock and Connley Caves (Grayson 1980), Danger Cave (Jennings 1957), Wilson Butte Cave (Gruhn 1965), Smith Creek Cave (Tuohy and Randall 1979), Ventana Cave (Haury 1950 [1975]), Bonfire Shelter (Dibble and Lorrain 1968), Leonard Rockshelter (Heizer 1951) and Meadowcroft Shelter (Adovasio et al. 1978); and (b) noting the important comments on cave accumulations by McGuire (1980). The only comparable work we know of in Sahul is that of Balme (1980) and Archer et al. (1980).

root and tree crops was an indigenous development, with many exotic plants later incorporated into the system. What mechanisms can be envisaged for the development of this intensive land management, and how do these fit with more general theories of agricultural development of the kind reviewed and expounded by Cohen (1977)? On the present limited evidence, trade, population pressure, scheduling variations and similar explanations cannot be supported as mechanisms. What does occur at the same time as this development is environmental change, including increasing warmth, a rising treeline and perhaps increased cloudiness and rainfall between 11,000 and 9000 years ago (J. H. Hope and G. S. Hope 1976; Nix and Kalma 1972; Walker and Flenley 1979). What pressures this might have placed on people in the highland valleys remains to be determined. Another potential contributor to the need to bring some plant resources under closer control may have been the presence of a new competitor for them, namely pigs. In other parts of the world, the co-occurrence of plant and animal domestication may also be worth considering in competitive rather than cooperational terms.

We turn now to artefact studies. As Conkey (1980: 228) points out, one aspect of cultural evolution needing explanation is how material culture became rule-bound and elaborated in form, and often in function. With stone artefacts this occurred in much of the Old World and all of the New before or at the very end of the Pleistocene. In South-East Asia, Wallacea and Sahul this change occurred in only a few artefacts (e.g. axe and hatchet heads) before the later Holocene; in New Guinea and the Bismarck Archipelago it was restricted to these tools; and in Tasmania it never occurred at all. This poses an awkward problem for those who, like J. G. D. Clark (1970), M. Harris (1971) and Isaac (1972), see in stone tools a clear indicator of humanity's developing mastery of technology and increasing cultural complexity. As the evidence this book presents has indicated, it will hardly do to call Sahul "culturally backward" (see also J. P. White 1977b). It might be tempting to argue that the Late Pleistocene development of a ground-stone technology meant that flaked stone tools were, relatively and symbolically speaking, ignored (cf.

Hayden 1977b). But what do we then make of Japan, where ground stone *and* formalized flake tools have been found in Late Pleistocene sites? (Ikawa-Smith 1980). In our view, what has to be argued is that stone tools, like any other aspect of human behaviour, are *subject* to symbolization and formalization, but this is not necessary to their employment as tools. Nor does such formalization result in more operationally efficient or efficacious tools, as the New Guinea highlands situation in particular indicates. The consequence of accepting this view in other parts of the world is that relations between form and function need to be demonstrated rather than assumed. Function may be determinable by use-wear, association with other classes of artefacts, intra-site and inter-site distributions or other means; it may not be automatically determinable through form, even where this is quite tightly regulated.

Explaining why the Sahul stone industries display the patterns they do is more difficult. Other aspects of material culture such as burials or engravings and paintings indicate that highly symbolic behaviour has been common throughout prehistory. Why was it not applied to stone tools? The relative isolation of Sahul might be adduced, but this seems rather weak. A stronger explanation would be that the extraordinarily elaborate cosmologies of Australia, if prehistoric, reduced the employment of symbolism in other spheres of existence, but that explanation will serve less well in the New Guinea highlands, where cosmologies and other symbolic material behaviours seem less evident. The problem remains.

Relevant to the above, of course, is the widespread adoption of a series of highly formalized tools around 4000–5000 years ago. But a more important problem with these is to consider why small backed flakes and points were produced in so many parts of the world during the last 20,000 years. At present the oldest examples seem to be from Africa (J. D. Clark 1975) and Upper Palaeolithic sites in Western Europe. In the Holocene, they occurred in northern Europe, India, Sri Lanka and Sulawesi (Allchin 1966). They are often found in considerable numbers and range in shape from long, thinnish points to stumpy, trapezoid geometrics. The usual explanation for their occurrence and spread has been that they were barbs and heads for arrows, and that they are evidence of the invention and spread of this hunting tool (Allchin 1966). This has been directly confirmed in Holocene Europe by the finding of arrowheads (J. G. D. Clark 1963) and is implied for Africa both by ethnohistoric materials (J. D. Clark 1977) and the discovery of backed blades within the skeletons of slain humans (Wendorf 1968). Another experimentally verified minor use in Africa is as hafted knife blades in shredding vegetable fibres (J. D. Clark and Prince 1978). Neither explanation will serve for Australia, where, if used at all, they are most likely to have been spear points and barbs. As Kamminga (1980) points out, however, very few show any signs of use at all. We have also noted the very large numbers of these tools found in some locations. This rather tells against a purely functional interpretation. The absence of similar functions world-wide for backed blades, along with their variability in dating and the discontinuous nature of their occurrence, suggests that a single explanation for their development will not do. In the absence of clear temporal and technological links we cannot assume the Australian examples derive from Indian bows or Sulawesian traders. To insist that such links must be there obscures the problem (cf. Dortch 1981). We suggest that there is no particular link between the Australian and other occurrences, and perhaps not between several of the latter. We do not find the same technologies for manufacturing flakes or blades in all areas (punch-struck, polyhedral cores are only sometimes used), while backing itself may be done in various ways and is an extremely simple process (Dickson 1975). What we may be seeing, in fact, is a combination of diffusion in some areas (such as Europe and Africa), and invention in others. The fact that, despite their simplicity, none of these tools occurred until the Late Pleistocene may tell us more about general technological evolution and the increasing range of formal symbols in human technology than about the specific evolution of particular cultures.

Finally in this review we draw attention to a methodological problem of common concern to prehistorians. This is the nature and duration of relationships which may be expected between archaeologically or ethnographically derived material culture patterns, subsistence behaviour, languages and human physical attributes. The Sahul evidence suggests very little reason for believing in a long-term, regular link between any of these. At the most general level some correlation is obviously evident: throughout Australia and Tasmania all languages have a genetic unity (Dixon 1980:228) and are spoken by people of one broadly related physical type whose material culture can certainly be recognized as Australian. In each evidential class, the relationships within Australia are closer than any that can be found externally. Below this level, differences abound. In the north-west part of the continent (roughly, the Kimberleys and Arnhem Land), there are a number of languages, the grammars of which differ quite dramatically from those found over the rest of Australia. The latter, the Pama–Nyungan group, display a high degree of typological similarity. Physical diversity, as we have seen, appears to be much more environmentally related, at least in broad terms (Freedman and Lofgren 1981), and no aspect of it has so far displayed a more tightly defined geographical pattern (Kirk 1971). Material culture items, whether prehistoric stone tools or painting styles and motifs, or recent spears, spear-throwers, houses or musical instruments, cannot readily be shown to display correlated patterns of variation either with one another or with languages or other classes of evidence, except in cases where classes are related to the same environment. Thus fish-hooks are related to certain kinds of shorelines and their fish, house styles are primarily related to rain and cold, and grindstones to the extensive presence of seeds. But areas of similar art styles or the distribution patterns of stone hatchet heads cannot at present be correlated with other variables.

Within New Guinea the situation is different, but just as complex. Two comparatively unrelated language groups (Austronesian and Papuan) occur, but their inhabitants cannot be physically distinguished, nor is their material culture distinctive. There is some correlation between lower level, but large, language groups and aspects of material culture, but attempts to define elements of a continuing correlation have not been successful. Physical variation and, more so, material culture and subsistence activities are environmentally related, although within environmental zones some smaller scale cultural groupings can be observed. It is noticeable how 8000 years of separation have differentiated New Guineans from Australians and both from Tasmanians. However the environmental differences must also have been a major factor in this process.

Readers will, we hope, discover other problems where the prehistory of Sahul brings new considerations to bear on assumptions and models used in other parts of the world. It may be that we have overstressed the uniqueness of Sahul, although we do not think so, for the more research is done the greater it appears to be. Thus the prehistory of Sahul adds new dimensions to our models of humanity's history, and will continue to do so.

Chapter 8
Update

No book can hope to be completely up-to-date and report discoveries made and revisions published while it is in press. However, this chapter, added when the book was in proof, draws attention to recently published materials which bear on three sections of our discussion, in one case significantly modifying our argument.

Antiquity of Human Occupation (3.1)

Occupation of the south-west by 40,000 years ago is confirmed by the discovery of flakes and worked pieces, some with worn edges, along with many small chips, within a sandy clay terrace of the Swan River (Pearce and Barbetti 1981). Carbonized wood fragments in a patch at the same level as the flakes have been dated to 39,500 +2300/−1800 (SUA-1500). Associated carbonized nodules, possibly of naturally occurring resin, have given statistically similar dates. There are three reasons for believing the material was *in situ* or very nearly so. First, many very small chips of quartz and dolerite were found; second, nine sets of flakes and pieces could be fitted together; third, the dated samples are from different materials, 8 m apart at the same level. In addition to the flakes, a human cause is indicated by the fact that elsewhere the terrace contained no natural stones beyond occasional small quartz pebbles, and that 5% of the rocks collected were distinctive bryozoan chert. This chert may have come from a source now under the sea, and it certainly does not occur within the Swan drainage. We note that all the 968 artefacts collected over an area of 21 m^2 are small, the largest being less than 10 cm long. There are no large cores, pebble tools or large steep-edge scrapers of the kind found at Lake Mungo and some other early south-eastern sites. The Swan River material is more like that from Devil's Lair, 250 km away.

A claim for an antiquity of more than 40,000 years has been made by Lampert (1981) for some artefacts from Kangaroo Island, off the South Australian coast. Until 9300 years ago the island was Kangaroo Hill, overlooking the broad, well-watered Murray valley and estuary. On the hill, about 4400 km^2 in area, several thousand large stone artefacts have been found in about 160 places. More than 80% of the artefacts are "horse-hoof" cores and unifacially flaked beach pebbles, with an average weight of 500g. A few clear trimming (or re-sharpening) flakes and some quartz flakes and small tools have been found, but at no site was there the high proportion of small flakes and chips that one would expect to find at any workshop. None of the tools have been found in a directly dateable context, nor in association with fauna or other debris. The tools comprise the Kartan industry (Tindale 1937).

The Kartan is of Pleistocene age. We know this because of its formal similarities to assemblages dated to the Pleistocene (e.g. at Lake Mungo), and because it is not found on Recent (< 10,000 years) land surfaces. Nor is it concentrated near the present coastline. Further, two (of 11) sites with a quite different industry of much smaller tools have been radiocarbon dated to less than 16,000 years. Arguments that the Kartan was contemporaneous with this other industry, supposing it to be the result of different activities or activities in a different season, raise problems of various kinds.

Lampert's claim that the Kartan is very old relies essentially on an argument put forward by Lorblanchet and Jones (1979). They claim that "le sens de l'évolution typologique" within Sahul is from a small number of types of large tools to more types of smaller tools, and they draw on data from such sites as Lake Mungo and Rocky Cape to show this. Lampert points out that, since there are only two tool types, both very large, within the Kartan, whereas there are five, some of them small, at Lake Mungo, the Kartan must be older. This comparison assumes that the nature of the assemblages being compared is similar, but we do not think this has been clearly shown (O'Connell 1981; J. P. White 1981). Further, we think the original model is unsound, as it is based on a very selective use of data. For example, neither Devil's Lair nor the Swan River site reported above contained large tools, although both are at least as old as the Lake Mungo sites. Therefore, we are not convinced that the Kartan industry is older than 40,000 years, although some sites may turn out to be so.

The Kartan industry has also been found on the mainland opposite Kangaroo Island, and north into the Cooper Creek area (Lampert and Hughes 1980). A few tools have been found in geomorphic contexts likely to be 30,000–40,000 years old, and one in the Pooraka Formation, which has been dated to that age. However, unpublished radiocarbon dates show that nearly all the tools come from sediments dated to early Recent times, around 10,000–7000 years ago (R. J. Lampert, pers. comm., 1982). The Kartan thus covers a great range of time on the mainland, and we think on Kargaroo Island also.

The Colonization Process (3.2)

Horton (1981b) has proposed a three-phase model of Australian settlement. He suggests that, like the megafauna, early Australians were restricted to woodland areas, where water sources were sufficiently widespread to allow people to obtain drinking water every day. He thus believes that until about 25,000 years ago some two-thirds of Australia was utilized by people, with only the desert core remaining unoccupied. He argues that the high biomass of woodland areas would have attracted hunters, and that the desert areas were not used because carrying devices and artificial wells had not been developed.

Horton's second stage is between 25,000 and

12,000 years ago, when greatly increased aridity caused the extinction of many species of large animals and the movement of all human populations to coastal areas. This implies that sites throughout the interior of Australia will display no, or very little, evidence of use throughout this period. (The model takes no account of New Guinea or of Sahul as a unit.)

Finally, he believes that after 12,000 years ago conditions improved and that humans, aided by newly developed technology, started to utilize the whole of the Australian continent.

As Horton says, the model is open to archaeological testing, but we do not think there are sufficient data to do so fully. We note that archaeological evidence from such sites as Devil's Lair (see especially Balme 1980), Mt. Newman (Maynard 1980), Koonalda Cave (Wright 1971a), Lake Victoria (Kefous 1981) and Kenniff Cave (Mulvaney and Joyce 1965) shows that at least some parts of the interior were occupied during the arid period. Further, we think the model is deficient. Horton does not demonstrate why water storage and carrying devices should have been a late development, and he makes dubious assumptions about both human reliance on megafauna and the ease with which human groups could migrate.

Physical Anthropology (4.1)

Since section 4.1 was written, two important articles have appeared, one of which changes the nature of the debate about the physical anthropology of Australian Aboriginal people.

In 1979, Freedman and Lofgren described a skull from Cossack on the north-west coast, at 21°S, some 1300 km north of Perth. The fragmentary skull and some long-bone fragments were found eroding out of the seaward side of a 10 m high coastal sand-dune which itself cannot be more than 7000 years old. The skeleton, of course, may well be younger than this.

Because of missing parts, damage, distortion and friability, reconstruction of the cranium was difficult, but sufficient of it remained to piece together a passable individual. This done, the excavators were able to conclude (1979: 291): "the overall impression is of a massive, heavily constructed, dolichocephalic calvaria with a large, probably slightly prognathous face. The most striking feature is the markedly backward sloping forehead."

In both size and shape, especially the low frontal index and the length of the cranium, the Cossack skull parallels the robust or "primitive" skulls from Kow Swamp, Cohuna and Talgai. The same similarity is present in the mandible and teeth, which are large and heavy. Overall, the cranium and mandible are extremely robust and the cranial vault bones are very thick. The post-cranial material is robust, but not outside the range of modern Aboriginal Australian populations.

The date and location of the Cossack individual are its most important aspects. First, it is the youngest robust specimen that has been found, and may only be 2000–3000 years old. Second, its location strongly implies that the "robust" group did not consist of isolates or a population restricted to south-eastern Australia. If we accept that the Cossack skull does indicate a recent "robust" population, then the problems inherent within a two-population model are multiplied. These problems are not discussed by Freedman and Lofgren.

The second article, by Peter Brown (1981), provides us with a partial way out of the problem raised by Cossack, Kow Swamp and other "archaic-looking" people. He demonstrates that at least some of the "primitive" features on prehistoric skulls are almost certainly due to artificial cranial deformation.

The initial basis of Brown's argument is the comparison of two series of Melanesian skulls, one known to be artificially deformed, the other known not to be. The artificially deformed skulls come from Arawe people in New Britain, and the changes caused by head-binding include flattened and elongated frontal bones, low frontal curvature, greater parietal curvature, increased cranial height and some thickening of the diploë. Brown then examined two series of Australian skulls, one recent, and known to be undeformed, the other consisting of material from Kow Swamp, Cohuna and Coobool Crossing. This last site is some 120 km from Kow Swamp. The twenty-four skulls were dug up in 1950 without stratigraphic or detailed locational information, and they have not previously been described. They are very like the Kow Swamp individuals. Comparisons between the two Australian series showed the same differences as between the Melanesian groups, with the one significant difference being that the Australian "deformed" skulls were broad and not constricted. Brown suggests that this was because deformation was caused by the mothers' hands pressing on the infants' foreheads rather than by all-round binding. The pressing by mothers' hands is documented from Cape York in the nineteenth century.

Brown points out that within the apparently deformed series from Australia there is a range of shapes, from those obviously deformed to those apparently little changed. The degree of deformation, as well as its precise effects, is thus quite variable. This is to be expected with this technique. Crania which are clearly deformed include Kow Swamp 5 and 7 and Cohuna. In KS1 deformation is less clear.

What is not explained by Brown's analysis is the size and robustness of mandibles, palates and dentitions in the Coobool and Kow Swamp crania (or in any other crania). Thorne and Wolpoff (1981) suggest that these features are a

distinguishing aspect of Pleistocene and early Recent Australians, and Brown notes that neither Mungo 1 and 3 nor Keilor differs significantly from other Pleistocene humans in these features. If there is no clear difference (which has not yet been shown), then these characters cannot be used to support the idea of two Late Pleistocene populations. Why this orofacial region should decrease in size and robustness in Recent times remains a problem.

In our view, Brown's analysis is of basic importance because it undermines most of the argument in favour of two populations. If we accept his analysis, we no longer need to see morphologies like those from Kow Swamp as isolated, remnant or "archaic" in any way. Similarly, we can dismiss a scenario which brings a modern-looking *Homo sapiens sapiens* group to Sahul in the Late Pleistocene and then disperses it throughout the continent without considering the problems of genetic change, environmental adaptation and social conflict outlined in section 4.1. We do not think that the argument for two populations in Pleistocene Sahul has ever been a strong one, and Brown's article should allow us to dismiss it and turn our attention to other problems.

Appendixes

Appendixes

Appendix I

Uses of the Past: Tasmania

Different people interpret the past in different ways. The following articles and letters appeared in a leading Australian news magazine early in 1982. They demonstrate how important prehistory can be in present-day discussions. We reprint these pieces with the permission of the authors and the managing editor of the magazine.

Who Really Killed Tasmania's Aborigines?

By Patricia Cobern

The descendants of the early settlers of Tasmania have been branded as the children of murderers who were responsible for the genocide of the Tasmanian Aborigine. Is this really true?

The *Encyclopaedia Britannica* Research Service says " ... It is a reasonable assumption that had the island remained undiscovered and European settlement not attempted until the present day, the Aborigines of Tasmania would have already become extinct and their few relics mere bones of contention between differing schools of Pacific archaeology. Like the moa-hunters of New Zealand and the unknown race which erected the stone giants on Easter Island,

the fate of the Tasmanians would have been just another Polynesian mystery instead of a colonial tragedy ..."

What then was the cause of the extinction of Tasmanian Aborigines? Although the first people to settle in what was then called Van Diemen's Land were mainly convicts and soldiers there were some free settlers. These were peace-loving folks: farmers, bootmakers, shopkeepers and laborers who had been given free passage to Tasmania and land on which to settle. Only those of high moral character were given passage as settlers. They had to produce character references and be sponsored by some reputable person who had known them for many years. Few had used a gun or weapon of any kind and they knew nothing about hunting or fighting.

On the other hand, the Tasmanian Aborigines were war-like hunters. According to reports held at the Mitchell Library, Sydney, they were "fickle and unstable, and some unknown cause of offence would, in a moment, change their attitude from friendship to open hostility ..."

The reports of James Erskine Calder, who arrived in Tasmania on the *Thames* in November, 1829, and who remained in Tasmania for the rest of his life working as a surveyor, should be more accurate than the writings of moderns who have never lived there. Calder said ... "the natives had much the better of the warfare ..."

They had developed remarkable skill for surprise attacks. They would stealthily creep up on an isolated farm and surround it. After watching for hours, sometimes days, they would take the occupants by surprise, massacre them and burn their house and out-buildings. Then, they would move on to some pioneer family in another part of the island and repeat the massacre.

A trick frequently employed by the Tasmanian natives was to approach isolated settlers, apparently unarmed. They would wave their arms about in a friendly way and the naive settler, seeing no weapon, would greet them, often offering food or drink. When the natives were close enough to the house they would flick the spears from between their toes and plunge them into the hapless frontiersman and his wife and children. After that colonists learned to be wary of natives who walked through long grass, knowing that they could be dragging spears between their toes.

Naturally, after many of their neighbors had been massacred, settlers began to arm against attack but the superior fighting ability of the Aborigines was undeniable. More white people were killed in the so-called "black war" than Aborigines. The most Aborigines killed in any one melee was 41 of a force of several hundred who attacked the Royal Marines.

Reports of the number of natives living in Tasmania at the first white settlers' arrival in 1803 vary from 2000 to a mere 700. Some reports claim 700 would be the absolute maximum at the time of the first settlement and they were, even then, fast dying out.

The factors which killed the Tasmanian Aborigines become apparent after careful research. There were (1) their eating habits (2) hazards of birth (3) lack of hygiene (4) their marriage or mating customs (5) dangerous "magic" surgery (6) exposure to the harsh climate of Tasmania.

The eating habits of the Tasmanian natives alone were enough to wipe them out. It was their custom to eat everything that was available in one sitting. George Augustus Robinson, an authority on Aborigines, described their diet as "astounding." They ate every part of the carcass of any animal they found. Not a bone nor an organ was discarded. The hunters would sit around the fire chewing the half-cooked brain, eyes, and bones as well as the flesh of animals. The women, who were treated as less important than dogs, were thrown the worst parts of bone and gristle. Only the fur or feathers were uneaten. These were singed away on the fire.

Robinson reported seeing two men eat a whole seal. On another occasion, an Aboriginal woman was seen to eat 60 large eggs followed by a double ration of bread which had been given to her by Robinson. Even the babies consumed horrifying amounts of food. One baby of only eight months ate a whole kangaroo rat and then grabbed for more food.

Besides animals the Tasmanian natives ate mushrooms, birds' eggs, bracken, ferns, ants' eggs and shell fish of all kinds. But the eating of scaled fish was taboo to the Aborigines.

For the newly-born Tasmanian Aborigine and his/her mother life hung by a thread. When she was no longer able to keep up with the tribe the expectant woman was abandoned in the bush with a handful of food. If there was an old woman who could be spared she stayed with the mother-to-be and helped her at the delivery.

Usually, however, the woman coped alone. When the child was born she either chewed the umbilical cord or cut it with a sharp stone. The placenta was then reverently buried. The baby was cleaned with dry leaves or whatever vegetation was available and, as soon as she was able to walk, the mother slung the child over her shoulder and hurried after the tribe.

With such a primitive and undignified birth, the child often died before the mother could get up. If both mother and child survived it was fortunate, but their troubles did not end with a safe delivery. It might take days or weeks for the mother and child to overtake the tribe and during that time there were many perils.

Strange tribes coming upon the woman and her baby would kill and probably eat them. If she was able to avoid capture by hostiles there was still the problem of getting enough food to eat, with no hunter to provide and herself in a weakened state. More often, mother and child perished before rejoining the tribe.

Lack of hygiene was another hazard. Tasmania's climate is often cold and wet so bathing was something they never did. In spite of the rigors of the weather they went naked from birth to death, their bodies caked with mud, grease, charcoal and red ochre which was never removed.

Any cut or scratch would immediately become infected and the infection would spread. Lice and fleas multiplied.

When seeing Aborigines picking fleas off their bodies and cracking them in their teeth, Europeans were horrified and Robinson and his well-meaning associates made the natives bath. This hastened the death of those in the mission as it was a great shock to bath a body that had always sheltered behind a coating of mud and grease.

The marriage customs were hardly conducive to the survival of the race because only the elders of the tribe were permitted to take wives. For this reason, the young men would try to steal wives from another tribe and many met death in this way if caught. Naturally, the old men were not so fertile as the young bloods and few children were born to their women.

Charms and superstitious practices, although not so prevalent among these primitive people as with the more advanced Aborigines of the mainland, did exist and caused many deaths. Wounds caused by ritual slashing with stones to protect the person from harm often became infected.

Exposure to the weather was a common cause of death before the coming of the white man. As these Aboriginal people built no shelters and wore no clothes they were always battered by the weather. Some scientists believe that many died because of the exposure alone but others claim it was mainly a kind of melancholy death-wish due to an absence of strong religious beliefs to keep them going when life became intolerable.

Contrary to cherished beliefs held by modern society, the white men did not introduce venereal disease. This was already making inroads on the natives of Tasmania as well as the mainland when Europeans first landed.

Professor Manning Clark in his *Short History of Australia* says of the mainland … "Like their predecessors in the interior Sturt's men found the effect of syphilis amongst native tribes truly disgusting: many had lost their noses and all the glandular parts were considerably affected …"

This sort of thing obviously existed in Tasmania also and was the cause of many deaths as well as sterility among both men and women.

So we return to our original question: Who killed the Tasmanian Aborigines? My research has shown that the only massacres that were carried out were those on white people by the natives. The killer that stalked the Tasmanian Aborigine tribes was the traditions and customs of the race, its face was not white.

Tasmania's Aborigines

I must question Patricia Cobern's article "Who Really Killed Tasmania's Aborigines?"

I have been researching the Tasmanian Aborigines since 1970 and have recently published my findings (*The Aboriginal Tasmanians*, University of Queensland Press, 1981). They are diametrically opposed to Ms Cobern's. Here are some examples:

● The Tasmanian Aborigines did not die out — there are at least 4000 Tasmanians of Aboriginal descent in Tasmania now.

● At the height of the war between settlers and Aborigines, 1828–1832, 89 Europeans were killed by Aborigines and 150 Aborigines were killed by Europeans. The Europeans certainly had the better of the fight.

● There were at least five recorded massacres of Aborigines between 1804 and 1834. They are documented in my book.

I could go on. Why is [your journal] publishing such patent nonsense as stated in the article by Cobern? If the Tasmanian Aborigines haven't died out, why is [your journal] still so anxious to dehumanise and to exterminate them? Is it because [your journal] believes Aborigines are feral communists?

Dr Lyndall Ryan
Griffith University
Nathan Qld

Mere coincidence?

Aboriginal people have lived in Tasmania for at least 23,000 years and probably much longer. Within a mere 73 years after European settlement, the last full-blood Aborigine surviving in Tasmania had died.

Does Patricia Cobern, author of the strangely prejudiced and ill-informed article in [your journal], think this is a coincidence?

D. R. Gregg
Director
Tasmanian Museum and Art Gallery
Hobart Tas

Half-baked distortion

After reading your "Race" essay "Who Really Killed the Tasmanian Aborigines?" I find it hard to believe that Patricia Cobern is a serious researcher or that [your journal] would publish such a half-baked and distorted example of racist research. Unfortunately it is beyond the scope of this letter to correct the multiple errors in Cobern's essay. However it is worth mentioning that Tasmania has been inhabited for more than 20,000 years. If, for the sake of discussion, we accept Cobern's thesis that "the killer that stalked the Tasmanian Aborigine tribes (*sic*) was the traditions and customs of the race" one wonders why it took so long to get around to doing the job.

Scott Cane
The Research School of Pacific Studies
Australian National University
Canberra ACT

Nineteenth century thinking

I was shocked to read Patricia Cobern's piece on the Tasmanian Aborigines. Not only is it grossly ill-informed, it displays a racist attitude rarely encountered in responsible publications today. It appears to be based extensively on the Encyclopaedia Britannica's Research Service, and I can only think that this service is in a sad need of updating. Most of the information quoted is simply wrong and the rest is highly selective. None of it is scientifically based.

To take it paragraph by paragraph may be tedious but will illustrate the glaring errors. We open with "a reasonable assumption" that the Tasmanian people would have become extinct anyway. No evidence is given for the assumption, let alone its reasonableness.

The third paragraph is a eulogy of the early settlers and their peace-loving nature. In-dividually and in the bosoms of their families they may well have been gentle souls, but they came from a background which had firm ideas on the treacherous nature of "the native", founded on colonialist experiences in India, Africa and America, and, closer to home, in New South Wales. Blacks were characterised in the Press as cunning killers. One must not lose sight of the fact that these gentle folk were invaders, bent on depriving the Aboriginal people of their land and livelihood. I would also dispute Ms Cobern's claim that few of them knew how to use a gun. Added to their already established mistrust of black people was the understandable fear and tension brought about by being isolated in a strange and harsh environment.

The report held in the Mitchell Library (no reference) is apparently carefully selected to present a negative picture of the Tasmanians. Other reports are more positive. Labillardiere (1792) and Peron (1801) were both "delighted by the friendliness, kindness and generosity of the inhabitants" (Ryan, L. 1981 *The Aboriginal Tasmanians*: 61) and, offering no hostility, encountered none.

The following description of warfare may be accurate enough, but what point is it trying to make? That the Tasmanians were "naturally" or "instinctively" bloodthirsty? Written by a man who came to Tasmania 25 years after conflict began, and quoted without any attempt being made to examine the context in which such actions arose, it established nothing about the Tasmanians.

The paragraph beginning "Naturally ..." needs two comments. The implication is that white brutality was begun in defence against black treachery. The first recorded conflict took place eight months after the first European settlement, in 1804, when a panicky surgeon at Risdon fired on a group of Aborigines, setting off a general melee killing three (Ryan 1981:75). The first European was killed by an Aborigine in 1807 (Ryan 1981:77).

The second point that must be made on this matter is that the white settlers undeniably provoked bloodshed in other ways. By relying on kangaroo for fresh meat, they shot out Aboriginal hunting grounds. By 1816, the kidnapping of Aboriginal children to use as forced labor on farms, begun in the earliest years of the colony, was widespread (Ryan 1981:78). Whites failed to understand that the Aboriginal value system stressed reciprocity, that one made return for what one received. Thus many apparently unprovoked attacks were made upon the settlers when they failed to make return for use of the land, or for women. Abuse of women was also frequent. So the settlers were by no means the white-haired boys Ms Cobern would have us see.

To say that more white people were killed in the "black war" than Aborigines is plainly absurd, when Ms Cobern is also arguing that the entire Tasmanian Aboriginal population (numbering around 4000 by most estimates and not 700–2000, as she claims) was almost wiped out.

The reports she mentions are not cited, but the notion of a fast-dying population of 700 at the time of first settlement is not one held by any scholars working in this field.

Her "careful research" is nonsense if the six factors she then goes into are the result. The following discussion is an exercise in 19th-century Eurocentrism and racial prejudice. Since the population had survived for at least 23,000 years, according to the archaeological evidence, eating the same kinds of food and enduring even harsher climates (in the glaciated south-west 19,000 years ago at Fraser Cave), obviously these six factors cannot be of significance in their demise.

One could demolish the nonsense on diet, childbirth, lack of hygiene, etc, point by point, but it would take too long.

Suffice it to say that it is totally unscientific, racist in the extreme and not borne out by any of the evidence we have on the Aboriginal people of Tasmania.

A number of points, however, do need to be made:

• Cannibalism is not reliably reported anywhere in Tasmania and there is certainly no archaeological evidence for it.

• Labillardiere notes that the people he saw in 1792 had no trace of disease.

• What medical evidence is there that it is "a great shock" to bathe a formerly unwashed body? This sounds positively medieval to me.

• An elder is not necessarily an old man; he may be in his mid-thirties. I doubt his fertility is significantly lower than a man in his mid-twenties.

• "Melancholy death-wish due to the absence of strong religious beliefs ..." What rubbish! The little evidence collected during a time when no one cared to know about their religious beliefs, and before Aboriginal people either died or mistrusted Europeans, demonstrates the presence of a set of beliefs as important and logically consistent as ours were; in all probability they were of far more direct relevance to their lives than our beliefs are today to ours.

• I have never seen any evidence for venereal disease among Aboriginal populations prior to contact, nor any early reports noting its presence in Tasmania.

I do not know who Ms P. Cobern is but she is no scholar. The Tasmanian Aboriginal people at contact were a vigorous and healthy group with a successful culture, which showed signs in the archaeological record of development and change, of expansion into new niches and increasing sophistication in the use of ones already exploited.

There is no reason to think that the death of these 4000 people within 73 years of European contact was the end of an inevitable process.

Julia Clark
Curator of Anthropology
Tasmanian Museum and Art Gallery
Hobart Tas.

Tasmania's Aborigines

I have been engaged in research in the field of Tasmanian Aboriginal studies since 1973, and in that time I have read some pretty awful stuff, but never anything so spectacularly dreadful as the article by Patricia Cobern. It is unbelievably inaccurate, ill-informed and racist. If it were not for the racist implications, it would be hysterically funny.

My research has demonstrated that Aborigines have survived in Tasmania for more than 23,000 years despite their eating habits, hazards of birth, lack of hygiene, marriage "or mating" customs, dangerous "magic" sorcery, and exposure to the harsh climate of Tasmania — which was considerably harsher between 23,000 and 12,000 years ago.

A lot of Cobern's vilification is a matter of emphasis, but I would like to draw attention to some factual errors:

• The Tasmanians were hunters, but they were not warlike amongst themselves, nor is there any evidence that they ever practised any form of cannibalism.

• The description of Tasmanian marriage customs is quite incorrect, and seems to have been drawn from accounts of mainland Aboriginal marriage customs. The Tasmanian Aborigines were monogamous, and spouses were commonly of similar age to each other.

• Tasmanian Aborigines built bark huts and shelters, very substantial ones on the west coast, and often wore kangaroo skin coverings.

• There is no evidence whatsoever for the presence of syphilis or of gonorrhoea in any part of Australia or Tasmania before the arrival of Europeans. The quotation of Manning Clark is used quite improperly; the original implication was of the swiftness of the spread of syphilis across the continent after its introduction by Europeans, a well-documented fact.

• There are well-documented accounts of massacres carried out on Aborigines by Europeans in Tasmania, such as the incident at Victory Hill near Cape Grim in the north-west in which at least 30 Aborigines were killed by white shepherds in 1828.

Dr Sandra Bowdler
Balmain NSW

Distortion of history

Your article by Cobern entitled "Who really killed Tasmania's Aborigines?" appears to be a gross distortion of the historic evidence.

Cobern listed six factors which she claimed would have killed the Tasmanian Aborigines. The first five are largely speculative, dealing with diet, birth, hygiene, marriage and magic. However, there is ample evidence in the journals of George Augustus Robinson for the period 1829–1834 to refute all of Cobern's assertions (Plomley, 1966). The sixth factor relates to climate and it is this point I wish to address in the context of the west coast of Tasmania. I have chosen this region because it has the most extreme climate of coastal Tasmania, and yet has the highest density

of Aboriginal sites. The region enjoys a temperate maritime climate similar to the Mediterranean, with mild winters and cool summers. Along the coast mean monthly temperatures lie between 12–16°C in January and between 7–11°C in July. Rainfall averages about one to one-and-a-half metres per year. The region is occasionally exposed to high winds throughout the year (Bureau of Meteorology 1973 Climatic Survey, Northwest, Region 1, Tasmania).

In terms of extreme climates for man, these conditions are very mild. They could be compared to the much harsher conditions of the islands of Tierra del Fuego off South America (Bridges 1948 The Uttermost Part of the Earth), or those enjoyed by the people who lived in the Tasmanian west around 10,000 to 20,000 years ago when much of central Tasmania was covered by glacial ice sheets.

The climate of Tasmania now is not that different to that of our cultural homeland, the British Isles.

Jim Stockton
Turner ACT

Careful research?

After reading Patricia Cobern's article, I find myself a little incredulous that anyone could believe it was an article truly written "after careful research."

She cites their "astounding eating habits" as being "alone enough to wipe them out." She then goes on to describe quite a well-balanced diet of meat, liver, brains, eggs, bread, mushrooms, ferns *et cetera* that compares well to most staple diets eaten around the world today. She describes the quantities of food eaten as "horrifying" and then qualifies this by citing the example of an eight-month-old baby being fed a kangaroo rat — an animal which is, in fact, about half the size of a small guinea pig.

She cites lack of hygiene, infrequent bathing, lice and flea infestation, poor childbirth techniques and non-sterile surgical procedures as further evidence for her conclusions — yet quite similar charges could be laid against any white society of the time.

She cites as a myth that whites introduced syphilis to the Aborigines — this is simply not true. Syphilis was introduced by the new settlers, as was leprosy, tuberculosis, smallpox, measles, and numerous other diseases to which the Aborigines had no natural immunity.

Ms Cobern seems to completely ignore the role of the white settlers, pushing the blacks out of their traditional homes and hunting areas, destroying their natural food sources and limiting drastically their freedom of movement. She seems upset that blacks with spears would attack whites with guns using sneaky deceptions. She talks of the blacks' "superior fighting ability" and then goes on to tell how 41 were killed in one battle — a sizeable figure when she says in the next breath that the total population of the Tasmanian blacks at that time was 700, including women, children and those dirty old elders.

Does she really expect us to believe that it is coincidence when a society that has survived thousands of years, developed a complex tribal and traditional heritage, a reliable list of herbal medicines and treatments begins to die out just as the white settlers arrive?

Overall, after reading this article, with its highly emotive wording, shallow research and faulty, ill-thought-out argument, one is left with a sense of Ms Cobern's dislike of the simple tribal lifestyle of those Aborigines.

The conclusions reached are, it seems, much more likely to be a result of this writer's own cultural biases, socialisation and, perhaps, just a twinge of repressed guilt than any credible historical facts.

David A. Orth
Resident Medical Officer
Cherbourg Aboriginal
Reserve of Queensland

History, as Written by the Conquerors

By Charles Perkins

I am attempting to answer without anger what seems to be a racist and illogical article by one of your guest writers, Patricia Cobern.

Australian colonial history, as it has been compiled from early records, is proof of nothing more than the fact that history is always written by conquerors.

As such, the carefully sifted "facts" concerning Aborigines by white settlers and officials have been used as a foundation for all of the self-sustaining social myths that tend to justify the white man's dominance of Australia today.

However, official Australian history — even as it has been taught in schools — has never been as improvised as Patricia Cobern's article.

Certainly it has never been so hyperbolist as to try to conceal the systematic extermination of Tasmanian Aborigines.

How, then, does Patricia Cobern justify her claim that: "My research has shown that the only massacres that were carried out were those on white people by natives"? What research and where?

It seems that Ms Cobern read reports in the Mitchell Library (she mentions which library but not which report) and then wrote an article for [your journal].

Equally unsubstantiated is her claim that, "the factors which killed the Tasmanian Aborigines became apparent after careful research. There were (1) their eating habits (2) hazards of birth (3) lack of hygiene (4) their marriage or mating customs (5) dangerous "magic" surgery (6) exposure to the harsh climate of Tasmania."

The end result of an article based on such "careful research" is as flimsily propagandist as Hitler's claim that Shakespeare was German.

Ms Cobern claims that "reports of the number of natives living in Tasmania at the beginning of white settlement in 1803 vary from 2000 to a mere 700."

Ms Cobern settles conveniently for the figure of 700 " ... even then, fast dying out."

In refuting most of what Ms Cobern has to say I could quote many anthropologists, archaeologists and linguists as sources. However, we the Aboriginal people have been the sources for these academics in the first place. We, the Aborigines, are the experts and authorities on Aborigines. We can speak for ourselves and we do not need white experts to do it.

Ms Cobern's major source seems to be one George Augustus Robinson who, one assumes, was an early colonist and whom she describes as "an authority on Aborigines."

Robinson, it appears, is Ms Cobern's whole *raison d'être* — it is Robinson who seems to have supplied all those reasons why the extinction of Tasmanian Aborigines just happened to coincide with the arrival of the white man.

Her assertions about the eating habits of the Tasmanian Aborigines are far too histrionic to be taken with anything more than a good belly laugh. That "... an Aboriginal woman was seen to eat 60 large eggs followed by a double ration of bread ..." and that "even the babies consumed horrifying amounts of food. One baby of only eight months ate a whole kangaroo rat and then grabbed for more food" is preposterous.

Likewise, Ms Cobern demonstrates no understanding of the modes of childbearing practised in Aboriginal society. An extended family system which meant that all of a child's maternal aunts were treated as alternative mothers also meant that no woman was left to give birth alone.

Ms Cobern also claims that Aboriginal women were treated "as less important than dogs" and in so doing reflects the ethnocentricity of the inexact science of anthropology.

All that needs to be said on this score is that most anthropologists have so far been men: they have talked to other men when working with Aborigines rather than to Aboriginal women: and it is only now that women anthropologists are working in the field of Aboriginal affairs that the traditional role of Aboriginal women is beginning to be understood in Western society.

Ms Cobern's claims that a woman and her newborn babe would probably be killed and eaten is also quite unfounded and would be ludicrous if it was not likely to be believed by embryonic intellects among the readers.

The only time any form of cannibalism was practised by Aborigines it was purely symbolic — like Holy Communion.

Another factor of which Ms Cobern is blissfully unaware is that the practice of "walkabout" was as much, for most of Australia, a hygiene device as it was an economic device in a hunting economy.

Even with an abundance of flowing streams in places such as Tasmania it would have been still necessary for economic reasons for Aborigines to maintain their nomadic existence and their state of health, as a consequence, would have been far better than Ms Cobern would have us believe.

She also maintains that venereal disease was rife when the white man arrived and quotes Professor Manning Clark's *Short History of Australia*, the only documentation she gives for any of her claims.

But Professor Manning Clark is neither anthropologist, Aboriginal nor medicine man.

Aboriginal medicine men, called *wadiunguris*, were quite able to handle any indigenous diseases and it is a medically accepted fact today that venereal disease was introduced by white people.

Professor Fred Hollows, Professor of Ophthalmology at the Prince of Wales Hospital in Sydney, who led the National Trachoma and Eye Health Program, is but one Western doctor who, after many lengthy discussions with the *wadiunguris*, can confirm that there is every reason to believe venereal diseases were not indigenous diseases in Australia.

The only diseases that traditional Aboriginal healers could not handle were those that became rife when the rules for healthy living in a nomadic society broke down after Aborigines were herded into settlements and missions — often with no water supply.

This is still a problem on Aboriginal settlements and missions to this day and one factor Ms Cobern chooses to ignore is that, because of living conditions that have applied for the past 200 years and because of the bias in Western health care delivery, Aborigines have the highest rate of blindness in the world from curable eye diseases such as trachoma.

Interestingly, the cure for trachoma was discovered in Australia and no white Australian has gone blind from it in the past 30 years.

The rules for healthy living in a nomadic society are vastly different from the hygiene rules of a sedentary society, but Ms Cobern would seem not to understand any society that has not been moulded by the Judaeo-Christian ethic.

Ms Cobern knows nothing of the marriage or "mating" customs (as she calls them) of the Aborigines. It is pertinent to point out that a selective procreation system based on "skin" or genetic groupings was employed by Aborigines to ensure healthy reproduction.

Because Aboriginal words for "mother" were used in reference to maternal aunts and words for "brother" and "sister" were used to refer to certain cousins, Aboriginal society often appeared to be wantonly incestuous to early white settlers who reacted with shocked excitement as Ms Cobern does.

However, factors governing marriage in Aboriginal society related more to health and proper reproduction than they did to material acquisition, as is the case in Western society.

The study of genetics today bears witness to the wisdom of the marriage practices maintained in traditional Aboriginal Australia.

Ms Cobern lists one reason for the unexpected demise of Tasmania's Aborigines as being their "dangerous 'magic' surgery" but does not, fortunately, attempt to elaborate and, as such, indicates a wisdom one would not expect her to have from the tone of the rest of her article.

She has not been able to find evidence of this "magic" surgery because much of it was popular assumption.

Lastly, Ms Cobern maintains that after some 50,000 years, exposure to the harsh Tasmanian climate began to kill off the Aborigines — coincidentally, one assumes, just as the white man arrived.

Ms Cobern seems not to have heard of the practice among Aborigines — most notably the Kadaitcha men — of controlling their heart rate, breathing and body temperature.

Such things as telepathy, psycho-kinetics and bio-rhythmics are only just being investigated by Western science.

It is highly likely, therefore, that such practices on the part of Aborigines would have been seen by early settlers as so much mumbo-jumbo magic.

One thing is for sure, however, because of this so-called heathen magic the Aborigines of Tasmania did not die of the cold.

Australians today are fast becoming secure enough to accept the reality of this country's somewhat brutal beginnings as a Western nation and the fact that the continent did not pop out of the ocean just in time for Captain Cook.

Aborigines should be given some credit for having survived and also flourished in this country for 50,000 years as guardians of the land.

The Australia Day Council this year has adopted a three-wave theme which, although it suggests incorrectly that we, too, are migrants, nevertheless acknowledges that Australia has a pre-colonial as well as a post-colonial history.

However, biased public commentators do nothing to foster mutual understanding between Australians, both pre- and post-colonial.

Moreover, the propagation of racist misconceptions about the Aborigines makes more difficult the task of improving the lot of the Aboriginal people. It creates a white backlash and it places greater responsibility on senior Aboriginal politicians and bureaucrats such as myself to answer improperly based criticism.

Ms Cobern is far too subjective and ultra-defensive and her views are 200 years out of date. As a somewhat more notable public commentator (German or otherwise) would have put it: "Methinks the lady doth protest too much."

Appendix II
Journals

This book cites articles from a number of journals and newsletters which may be new to many readers. For convenience we list here the main journals and newsletters which publish material on Sahul prehistory.

Archaeology in Oceania (formerly *Archaeology and Physical Anthropology in Oceania*). Oceania Publications, Mackie Building, University of Sydney, NSW 2006.

Artefact. Archaeological and Anthropological Society of Victoria, GPO Box 328C, Melbourne, Vic. 3001.

Australian Archaeology. Publications, Department of Prehistory, Research School of Pacific Studies, Australian National University, PO Box 4, Canberra, ACT 2600.

Australian Institute of Aboriginal Studies, Newsletter. Australian Institute of Aboriginal Studies, PO Box 553, Canberra City, ACT 2601.

Indo-Pacific Prehistory Association, Bulletin. Secretary, IPPA, c/o Department of Prehistory and Anthropology, The Faculties, Australian National University, PO Box 4, Canberra, ACT 2600.

Mankind. Anthropological Society of NSW, c/o Australian Museum, 6–8 College Street, Sydney NSW 2000.

Terra Australis. Publications, Department of Prehistory, Research School of Pacific Studies, Australian National University, PO Box 4, Canberra, ACT 2600.

Victorian Archaeological Survey, Records. Victorian Archaeological Survey, 29–31 Victoria Avenue, Albert Park, Vic. 3206.

Appendix III
Selected Bibliography

The following books and articles are not referred to in the text, but may also be useful.

Barnett, G. L.
1978 *A Manual for the Identification of Fish Bones.* Department of Prehistory, Australian National University.

Bulmer, S.
1981 Human ecology and cultural variation in prehistoric New Guinea. *In* J. L. Gressitt (ed.), *Biogeography and Ecology in New Guinea,* pp. 153–190. W. Junk, The Hague.

Bowdler, S. (ed.)
In press *The Coastal Archaeology of Eastern Australia.* Department of Prehistory. Australian National University.

Connah, G. (ed.)
In press *Australian Archaeology: A Manual of Techniques.* Australian Institute of Aboriginal Studies, Canberra.

Haglund, L.
1976 *An Archaeological Analysis of the Broadbeach Aboriginal Burial Ground.* University of Queensland Press, Brisbane.

Haigh, C. and Goldstein, W. (eds)
1980 *The Aborigines of New South Wales.* National Parks and Wildlife Service, Sydney.

Kirk, R. L.
1981 *Aboriginal Man Adapting.* Oxford University Press, Melbourne.

Lofgren, M.
1975 *Patterns of Life: The Story of the Aboriginal People of Western Australia.* Western Australian Museum, Perth.

Merrilees, D. and Porter, J. K.
1979 *Guide to the Identification of Teeth and Some Bones of Native Land Mammals Occurring in the Extreme South-West of Western Australia.* Western Australian Museum, Perth.

Reynolds, H.
1981 *The Other Side of the Frontier: An Interpretation of the Aboriginal Response to the Invasion and Settlement of Australia.* James Cook University of North Queensland, Townsville.

Smith, B.
1980 *The Spectre of Truganini.* Australian Broadcasting Commission, Sydney.

Steensberg, A.
1980 *New Guinea Gardens: A Study of Husbandry with Parallels in Prehistoric Europe.* Academic Press, London.

Swadling, P.
1981 *Papua New Guinea's Prehistory.* National Museum and Art Gallery, Port Moresby.

Williams, N. W. and Hunn, E. S. (eds)
1982 *Resource Managers: North-American and Australian Hunter-Gatherers.* Westview Press, Boulder.

References

Abbie, A. A.
1968   The homogeneity of Australian Aborigines. *Archaeology and Physical Anthropology in Oceania* 3:223–231.
1976   Morphological variation in the adult Australian Aboriginal. *In* R. L. Kirk and A. G. Thorne (eds), *The Origin of the Australians*, pp. 211–214. Australian Institute of Aboriginal Studies, Canberra.

Adamson, D. A. and Fox, M. D.
In   Changes in Australasian vegetation since
press   European settlement. In J. Smith (ed.), *History of Australasian Vegetation*, Ch. 5. McGraw-Hill, Sydney.

Adovasio, J. M., Gunn, J. D., Donahue, J., and Stuckenrath, R.
1978   Meadowcroft Rockshelter 1977: An overview. *American Antiquity* 43:632–651.

Agogino, G. A.
1980   Review of Watson, V. D. and Cole, J. D. (1977). *Man* (n.s.) 14:756.

Aikens, C. M., and Higuchi, T.
1982   *Prehistory of Japan*. Academic Press, New York.

Akerman, K.
1975   The double raft or *kalwa* of the West Kimberley. *Mankind* 10:20–23.
1978   Notes on the Kimberley stone-tipped spear focusing on the point hafting mechanism. *Mankind* 11:486–489.
1979   Heat and lithic technology in the Kimberleys. *Archaeology and Physical Anthropology in Oceania* 14:144—151.

Aldiss, B. W.
1969   *Starship*. Avon Books, New York.

Allchin, B.
1966   *The Stone-tipped Arrow*. Phoenix, London.

Allen, H.
1968   Western plain and eastern hill. Unpublished B. A. (Honours) thesis, Department of Anthropology, University of Sydney.
1972   Where the crow flies backward. Unpublished Ph.D. thesis, Australian National University.
1974   The Bagundji of the Darling Basin: Cereal gatherers in an uncertain environment. *World Archaeology* 5:309–322.
1977   Archaeology of the East Alligator River region, Western Arnhem Land. Unpublished seminar paper, University of Auckland.
1979   Left out in the cold: Why the Tasmanians stopped eating fish. *Artefact* 4:1–10.

Allen, J.
1970   Prehistoric Agricultural Systems in the Wahgi Valley — A further note. *Mankind* 7:177–183.
1972   Nebira 4: An Early Austronesian site in Central Papua. *Archaeology and Physical Anthropology in Oceania* 7:92-124.
1977a   Sea traffic, trade and expanding horizons. *In* J. Allen, J. Golson and R. Jones (eds), *Sunda and Sahul: Prehistoric Studies in Southeast Asia, Melanesia and Australia*, pp. 387–417. Academic Press, London.

239

1977b Management of resources in prehistoric coastal Papua. *In* J. H. Winslow (ed.), *The Melanesian Environment*, pp. 35–44. Australian National University Press, Canberra.

1977c Fishing for wallabies: Trade as a mechanism for social interaction, integration and elaboration on the central Papuan coast. *In* J. Friedman and M. J. Rowlands (eds), *The Evolution of Social Systems*, pp. 419–455. Duckworth, London.

1978 The physical and cultural setting of Motupore Island, Central Province, Papua New Guinea. *Indo-Pacific Prehistory Association, Bulletin* 1:47–55.

1980 Correspondence. *New Zealand Journal of Archaeology* 2:169–170.

Allen, J., and Rye, O.
In press The importance of being earnest in archaeological investigations of prehistoric trade in Papua. *In* T. Dutton (ed.), *The Hiri in History*. Australian National University Press, Canberra.

Ambrose, W. R.
1976 Obsidian and its prehistoric distribution in Melanesia. *In* N. Barnard (ed.), *Ancient Chinese Bronzes and other Southeast Asian Metal and other Archaeological Artefacts*, pp. 351–378. National Gallery of Victoria, Melbourne.

Anderson, R. H.
1941 Presidential Address. *Proceedings of the Linnean Society of New South Wales* 66: v–xxiii.

Andresen, J. M., Byrd, B. F., Elson, M. E., McGuire, R. H., Mendosa, R. G., Staski, E., and White, J. P.
1981 The deer hunters: Star Carr reconsidered. *World Archaeology* 13:31–46.

Anon.
1977 Domestic animals gone bush. *Ecos* 13:10–18.
1980 *Annual Report*. Department of Prehistory, Research School of Pacific Studies, Australian National University.
1981 *Annual Report*. Department of Prehistory, Research School of Pacific Studies, Australian National University.

Aplin, K.
1981 The Kamapuk fauna. Unpublished B. A. (Honours) thesis, Department of Prehistory and Anthropology, Australian National University.

Archer, M., Crawford, I. M., and Merrilees, D.
1980 Incisions, breakages and charring, some probably man-made, in fossil bones from Mammoth Cave, Western Australia. *Alcheringa* 4:115–31.

Argyll, Duke of
1869 *Primeval Man*. Strahan & Co. London.

Arndt, W.
1961 The interpretation of the Delemere Lightning Painting and rock engravings. *Oceania* 32:163–177.

Bailey, G. N.
1975 The role of molluscs in coastal economies: The results of midden analysis in Australia. *Journal of Archaeological Science* 2:45–62.
1977 Shell mounds, shell middens and raised beaches in the Cape York Peninsula. *Mankind* 11:132–143.

Baldwin, J. A.
1976 Torres Strait: Barrier to agricultural diffusion. *Anthropological Journal of Canada* 14:10–17.

Balfour, H.
1925 The status of the Tasmanians among the stone-age peoples. *Proceedings of the Prehistoric Society of East Anglia* 5:1–15.

Balme, J.
1980 An analysis of charred bone from Devil's Lair, Western Australia. *Archaeology and Physical Anthropology in Oceania* 15:81–85.

Balme, J., Merrilees, D., and Porter, J. K.
1978 Late Quaternary mammal remains, spanning about 30,000 years, from excavations in Devil's Lair, Western Australia. *Journal of the Royal Society of Western Australia* 61:33–65.

Barker, G.
1976 The ritual estate and Aboriginal polity. *Mankind* 10:225–239.

Barrau, J.
1965 Witnesses of the past: Notes on some food plants of Oceania. *Ethnology* 4:282–294.

Bartstra, G.-J.
1977 Walanae formation and Walanae terraces in the stratigraphy of South Sulawesi (Celebes, Indonesia). *Quartär* 27/8:21–30.

Beaglehole, J. C. (ed.)
1955 *The Voyage of the "Endeavour" 1768–1771*, by Captain James Cook. Cambridge University Press, for the Hakluyt Society, Cambridge.

Beaton, J. M.
1977 Dangerous harvest. Unpublished Ph.D. thesis, Australian National University.
1982 Fire and water: Aspects of Australian Aboriginal Management of Cycads. *Archaeology in Oceania* 17:51–58.

Behrensmeyer, A. K.
1975 Taphonomy and palaeoecology in the hominid fossil record. *Yearbook of Physical Anthropology* 19:36–50.

Bellwood, P.
1978   *Man's Conquest of the Pacific.* Collins, Auckland.

Belshaw, J.
1978   Population distribution and the pattern of seasonal movement in northern New South Wales. *In* I. McBryde (ed.), *Records of Times Past,* pp. 65–81. Australian Institute of Aboriginal Studies, Canberra.

Bern, J. E.
1974   Blackfella business, whitefella law. Unpublished Ph.D. thesis, Macquarie University.

Berndt, R. M. and Berndt, C. H.
1964   *The World of the First Australians.* Ure Smith, Sydney.

Beveridge, W.
1889   *The Aborigines of Victoria and Riverina.* M. L. Hutchinson, Melbourne.

Bickford, R. A.
1966   The traditional economy of the Aborigines of the Murray Valley. Unpublished B.A. (Honours) thesis, Department of Anthropology, University of Sydney.

Binford, L. R.
1973   Interassemblage variability — The Mousterian and the "functional" argument. *In* C. Renfrew (ed.), *The Explanation of Culture Change: Models in Prehistory,* pp. 227–254. Duckworth, London.
1977   Forty-seven trips. *In* R. V. S. Wright (ed.), *Stone Tools as Cultural Markers. Change, Evolution, Complexity,* pp. 24–36. Australian Institute of Aboriginal Studies, Canberra.
1981   *Bones: Ancient Men and Modern Myths.* Academic Press, New York.

Binford, L. R. and Binford, S. R.
1966   A preliminary analysis of functional variability in the Mousterian of Levallois facies. *American Anthropologist* 68 (2), Part 2: 239–95.

Binford, S. R. and Binford, L. R.
1969   Stone Tools and Human Behavior. *Scientific American* 220(5), 70–84.

Binns, R. A., and McBryde, I.
1972   *A Petrological Analysis of Ground-edge Artefacts from Northern New South Wales.* Australian Institute of Aboriginal Studies, Canberra.

Birdsell, J. B.
1949   The racial origins of the extinct Tasmanians. *Records of the Queen Victoria Museum, Launceston* 2:105–22.
1953   Some environmental and cultural factors influencing the structuring of Australian Aboriginal populations. *American Naturalist* 87:171–207.
1957   Some population problems involving Pleistocene man. *Cold Spring Harbor Symposia on Quantitative Biology* 22:47–70.
1967   Preliminary data on the trihybrid origin of the Australian Aborigines. *Archaeology and Physical Anthropology in Oceania* 2:100–155.
1975   *Human Evolution,* 2nd edition. Rand McNally, New York.
1977   The recalibration of a paradigm for the first peopling of Greater Australia. *In* J. Allen, J. Golson, and R. Jones (eds), *Sunda and Sahul: Prehistoric Studies in Southeast Asia, Melanesia and Australia,* pp. 113–167. Academic Press, London.

Birmingham, J.
1969   "Fabricators" and "eloueras" in West Bengal. *Mankind* 7:153.

Bischoff, J. L. and Rosenbaer, R. J.
1981   Uranium series dating of human skeletal remains from the Del Mar and Sunnyvale Sites, California. *Science* 213: 1003–1005.

Black, S.
1978   Polynesian outliers: A study in the survival of small populations. *In* I. Hodder (ed.), *Simulation Studies in Archaeology,* pp. 63–76. Cambridge University Press, Cambridge.

Blackwood, B.
1939   The Technology of a modern stone age people in New Guinea. *University of Oxford, Pitt Rivers Museum, Occasional Papers on Technology,* 3.

Blackwood, B., and Danby, P. M.
1955   A study of artificial cranial deformation in New Britain. *Journal of the Royal Anthropological Institute* 85:173–191.

Blainey, G.
1975   *Triumph of the Nomads.* Macmillan, Melbourne.

Blurton Jones, N. and Sibly, R. M.
1978   Testing adaptiveness of culturally determined behaviour: Do Bushmen women maximise their reproductive success by spacing births widely and foraging seldom? *In* N. Blurton Jones and V. Reynolds (eds), *Human Behaviour and Adaptation,* pp. 135–158. Taylor and Francis, London.

Boaz, N. T.
1979   Hominid evolution in Eastern Africa during the Pliocene and early Pleistocene. *Annual Review of Anthropology* 8:71–86.

Bodmer, M., and Cavalli-Sforza, L. L.
  1976   *Genetics, Evolution and Man.* W. H. Free-
          man, San Francisco.
Bordes, F., Dortch, C., Raynal, J.-P., and Thibault, C.
  1980   Quaternaire et Préhistoire dans le bassin de
          la Murchison (Australie occidentale).
          *Comptes Rendus des Séances de l'Académie
          des Sciences, (Paris)* 291, Series D:39–42.
Boserup, E.
  1965   *The Conditions of Agricultural Growth: The
          Economics of Agrarian Change under Pop-
          ulation Pressure.* Allen and Unwin, London.
Bosler, W.
  1975   The Keilor archaeological sites: An histori-
          cal survey. Unpublished B.A. (Honours)
          thesis, Department of Prehistory and An-
          thropology, Australian National University.
Bowdler, S.
  1970   Bass Point: The excavation of a South East
          Australian shell midden showing cultural
          and economic change. Unpublished B.A.
          (Honours) thesis, Department of Anthro-
          pology, University of Sydney.
  1971   Ball's Head: The excavation of a Port
          Jackson rockshelter. *Records of the Aus-
          tralian Museum* 28:117–128.
  1974   An account of an archaeological recon-
          naissance of Hunter's Isles, north-west
          Tasmania, 1973/4. *Records of the Queen
          Victoria Museum, Launceston,* 54.
  1975   Further radiocarbon dates from Cave Bay
          Cave, Hunter Island, north-west Tasmania.
          Australian Archaeology 3:24–26.
  1976   Hook, line and dillybag: An interpretation of
          an Australian coastal shell midden. *Man-
          kind* 10:248–258.
  1977   The coastal colonisation of Australia. *In* J.
          Allen, J. Golson, and R. Jones (eds), *Sunda
          and Sahul: Prehistoric Studies in Southeast
          Asia, Melanesia and Australia,* pp. 205–246.
          Academic Press, London.
  1979   Hunter Hill, Hunter Island. Unpublished
          Ph.D. thesis, Australian National University.
  1980   Fish and culture: A Tasmanian polemic.
          Mankind 12:334–340.
  1981   Hunters in the Highlands: Aboriginal adap-
          tations in the eastern Australian uplands.
          Archaeology in Oceania 16:99–111.
  In   Prehistoric archaeology in Tasmania. *In* F.
  press   Wendorf (ed.), *Advances in World Archae-
          ology,* Vol. 1. Academic Press, New York.
Bowler, J. M.
  1971   Pleistocene salinities and climatic change:
          Evidence from lakes and lunettes in
          Southeastern Australia. *In* D. J. Mulvaney
          and J. Golson (eds), *Aboriginal Man and
          Environment in Australia,* pp. 47–65. Aus-
          tralian National University Press, Canberra.
  1976   Recent developments in reconstructing late
          Quaternary environments in Australia. *In* R.
          L. Kirk and A. G. Thorne (eds), *The Origin of
          the Australians,* pp. 55–77. Australian In-
          stitute of Aboriginal Studies, Canberra.
Bowler, J. M. and Jones, R.
  1979   Australia was a land of lakes. *Geographical
          Magazine* 51:679–685.
Bowler, J. M., and Thorne, A. G.
  1976   Human remains from Lake Mungo: Dis-
          covery and excavation of Lake Mungo III. *In*
          R. L. Kirk and A. G. Thorne (eds), *The Origin
          of the Australians,* pp. 127–138. Australian
          Institute of Aboriginal Studies, Canberra.
Bowler, J. M., Jones, R., Allen, H., and Thorne, A. G.
  1970   Pleistocene human remains from Australia:
          A living site and human cremation from
          Lake Mungo, western New South Wales.
          World Archaeology 2:39–60.
Bowler, J., Hope, G. S., Jennings, J. N., Singh, G., and
          Walker, D.
  1976   Late Quaternary climates of Australia and
          New Guinea. *Quarternary Research*
          6:359–394.
Branagan, D. F., and Megaw, J. V. S.
  1969   The lithology of a coastal Aboriginal settle-
          ment at Curracurrang, N.S.W. *Archaeology
          and Physical Anthropology in Oceania*
          4:1–17.
Brand, D. D.
  1971   The sweet potato: An exercise in metho-
          dology. *In* C. L. Riley, J. C. Kelley, C. W.
          Pennington and R. L. Rands (eds), *Man
          across the Sea,* pp. 343–365. University of
          Texas Press, Austin.
Bray, W.
  1980   Early agriculture in the Americas. *In* A.
          Sherratt (ed.), *Cambridge Encyclopaedia of
          Archaeology,* pp. 365–374. Cambridge Uni-
          versity Press, Cambridge.
Brennan, P.
  1979   The Enga Cultural Centre, Enga Province.
          Oral History VII(7):1–15.
Brew, J. O.
  1946   The Archaeology of Alkali Ridge, Southeas-
          tern Utah. *Papers of the Peabody Museum of
          American Archaeology and Ethnology, Har-
          vard University,* 21.
Bronstein, N.
  1977   Report on a replicative experiment in the
          manufacture and use of Western Desert
          microadzes. *Anthropological Papers of the
          American Museum of Natural History*
          54(1):154–157.

Brookfield, H. C.
1964 The ecology of Highland settlement: Some suggestions. *American Anthropologist* 66(4), Part 2:20–38.
1972 Intensification and disintensification in Pacific agriculture: A theoretical approach. *Pacific Viewpoint* 13:30–48.

Brookfield, H. C., and Hart, D.
1966 *Rainfall in the Tropical Southwest Pacific.* Department of Geography, Research School of Pacific Studies. Australian National University (Publication G/3, 1966).

Brookfield, H. C., with Hart, D.
1971 *Melanesia.* Methuen, London.

Brookfield, H. C., and White, J. P.
1968 Revolution or evolution in the prehistory of the New Guinea Highlands: A seminar report. *Ethnology* 7:43–52.

Brothwell, D.
1975 Possible evidence of a cultural practice affecting head growth in some Late Pleistocene East Asian and Australasian populations. *Journal of Archaeological Science* 2:75–77.

Brown, A. R. R.
1930 Former numbers and distribution of the Australian Aborigines. *Official Year Book of the Commonwealth of Australia* 23:686–696. Commonwealth Bureau of Census and Statistics, Canberra.

Brown, Paula
1978 *Highland Peoples of New Guinea.* Cambridge University Press, New York.

Brown, Peter
1981 Artificial cranial deformation: A component in the variation in Pleistocene Australian Aboriginal crania. *Archaeology in Oceania* 16:156–167.

Brown, T.
1976 Head size increases in Australian Aboriginals: An example of skeletal plasticity. *In* R. L. Kirk and A. G. Thorne (eds), *The Origin of the Australians*, pp. 195–209. Australian Institute of Aboriginal Studies, Canberra.

Brown, T. A.
1978 Experiments on possible functions of the pirri in Australia. Unpublished M. A. thesis, Department of Anthropology, Washington State University.

Bulmer, R. [N. H.]
1964 Edible seeds and prehistoric stone mortars in the highlands of east New Guinea. *Man* 64:147–150.
1976 Selectivity in hunting and in disposal of animal bone by the Kalam of the New Guinea Highlands. *In* G. de G. Sieveking, I. H. Longworth and K. E. Wilson (eds), *Problems in Economic and Social Archaeology*, pp. 169–186. Duckworth, London.

Bulmer, R. [N. H.], and S. [E.]
1962 Figurines and other stones of power among the Kyaka of central New Guinea. *Journal of the Polynesian Society* 71:192–208.

Bulmer, S. [E.]
1966 The Prehistory of the Australian New Guinea Highlands. Unpublished M. A. thesis, University of Auckland.
1971 Prehistoric settlement patterns and pottery in the Port Moresby area. *Journal of the Papua and New Guinea Society* 5(2):28–91.
1975 Settlement and economy in prehistoric Papua New Guinea: A review of the archaeological evidence. *Journal de la Société des Océanistes* 31(46):7–75.
1977a Waisted blades and axes. *In* R. V. S. Wright (ed.), *Stone Tools as Cultural Markers: Change, Evolution, Complexity*, pp. 40–59. Australian Institute of Aboriginal Studies, Canberra.
1977b Between the mountain and the plain: Prehistoric settlement and environment in the Kaironk Valley. *In* J. H. Winslow (ed.), *The Melanesian environment*, pp. 61–73. Australian National University Press, Canberra.
1978 Prehistoric culture change in the Port Moresby region. Unpublished Ph.D. thesis, University of Papua New Guinea.
1979a Archaeological evidence of prehistoric faunal change in Highland Papua New Guinea. Unpublished paper delivered to Australian and New Zealand Association for the Advancement of Science Congress, Section 25A, Auckland.
1979b Prehistoric economy and ecology in the Port Moresby Region. *New Zealand Journal of Archaeology* 1:5–27.

Bulmer S. [E.], and R. [N. H.]
1964 The Prehistory of the Australian New Guinea Highlands. *American Anthropologist* 66(4), Part 2:39–76.

Burridge, K.
1973 *Encountering Aborigines.* Pergamon Press, New York.

Bush, T.
1976 New Guinea Highlands arrows. Unpublished M.A. thesis, University of Sydney.

Byrne, D.
1980 Dynamics of dispersion: The place of silcrete in archaeological assemblages from the lower Murchison, Western Australia. *Archaeology and Physical Anthropology in Oceania* 15:110–119.

Calaby, J. H.
1976 Some biogeographical factors relevant to the Pleistocene movement of man in Australasia. *In* R. L. Kirk and A. G. Thorne (eds), *The Origin of the Australians*, pp. 23–28. Australian Institute of Aboriginal Studies, Canberra.

Callaghan, M.
1980 Some previously unconsidered environmental factors of relevance to south coast prehistory. *Australian Archaeology* 11:43–49.

Campbell, T. D., and Noone, N. V. V.
1943 South Australian microlithic stone implements. *Records of the South Australian Museum* 7:281–307.

Campbell, V.
1972 Some radiocarbon dates for Aboriginal shell middens in the lower Macleay River valley, New South Wales. *Mankind* 8:283–286.

Carnahan, J. A.
1978 Vegetation. *In* D. N. Jeans (ed.), *Australia: A Geography*, pp. 175–195. Sydney University Press, Sydney.

Carr, E. H.
1961 *What is History?* Macmillan, London.

Casey, D. A.
1939 Some prehistoric artefacts from the Territory of New Guinea. *Memoirs of the National Museum of Victoria* 11:143–150.

Cavalli-Sforza, L. L., and Bodmer, W. F.
1971 *The Genetics of Human Populations.* W. H. Freeman, San Francisco.

Chappell, J. [M. A.]
1964 Stone mortars in the New Guinea Highlands: A note on their manufacture and use. *Man* 64:146–147.
1966 Stone axe factories in the Highlands of East New Guinea. *Proceedings of the Prehistoric Society* 32:96–121.
1976 Aspects of late Quaternary palaeogeography of the Australian–East Indonesian region. *In* R. L. Kirk and A. G. Thorne (eds), *The Origin of the Australians*, pp. 11–22. Australian Institute of Aboriginal Studies, Canberra.
1982 Sea levels and sediments — Some features of the context of coastal archaeological sites in the tropics. *Archaeology in Oceania* 17.

Chappell, J. [M. A.], and Thom, B. G.
1977 Sea levels and coasts. *In* J. Allen, J. Golson and R. Jones (eds), *Sunda and Sahul: Prehistoric Studies in Southeast Asia, Melanesia and Australia*, pp. 275–291. Academic Press, London.

Chappell, J. [M. A.], and Veeh, H. H.
1978 Late Quaternary tectonic movements and sea-level changes at Timor and Atauro Island. *Geological Society of America, Bulletin* 89:356–368.

Chowning, A.
1973 *An Introduction to the Peoples and Cultures of Melanesia* (Addison-Wesley Module in Anthropology, 38). Addison-Wesley, Reading, Mass.

Christensen, O. A.
1975a A tanged blade from the New Guinea highlands. *Mankind* 10:37–39.
1975b Hunters and horticulturalists: A preliminary report of the 1972–4 excavations in the Manim Valley, Papua New Guinea. *Mankind* 10:24–36.

Christie, M. F.
1979 *Aborigines in Colonial Victoria 1835–86.* Sydney University Press, Sydney.

Clark, J. D.
1975 Africa in prehistory: Peripheral or paramount? *Man* (n.s.) 10:175–198.
1977 Interpretations of prehistoric technology from Ancient Egyptian and other sources. *Paleorient* 3:127–150.

Clark, J. D., and Prince, G. R.
1978 Use-wear on Later Stone Age microliths from Laga Oda, Haraghi, Ethiopia and possible functional interpretations. *Azania* 13:101–110.

Clark, J. G. D.
1963 Neolithic bows from Somerset, England, and the prehistory of archery in northwest Europe. *Proceedings of the Prehistoric Society* 29:50–98.
1970 *Aspects of Prehistory.* University of California Press, Berkeley.

Clark, P., and Barbetti, M.
1982 Fires, hearths and palaeomagnetism. Paper presented to the First Australian Archaeometry Conference, Sydney, February 1982.

Clark, R. L.
1981 The prehistory of bushfires. *In* P. Stanbury (ed.), *Bushfires*, pp. 61–73. Macleay Museum, University of Sydney.

Clay, R. B.
1974 Archaeological reconnaissance in central New Ireland. *Archaeology and Physical Anthropology in Oceania* 9:1–17.

Clegg, J. K.
1981 *Notes towards Mathesis Art.* Clegg Calendars, Balmain, NSW.

CLIMAP Project Members
1976 The surface of the Ice-Age Earth. *Science* 191:1131–1144.

Cody, M., and Diamond, J. M. (eds)
1975 *Ecology and Evolution of Communities.* Belknap Press, Harvard University, Cambridge.

Cohen, M. N.
1977 *The Food Crisis in Prehistory.* Yale University Press, New Haven.

Coleman, E.
1966 An analysis of shell samples from the West Point shell midden. Unpublished B.A. (Honours) thesis, Department of Anthropology, University of Sydney.

Coleman, J.
1978 The analysis of vertebrate faunal remains from four shell middens in the lower Macleay River district. Unpublished B.A. (Honours) thesis, Department of Prehistory and Archaeology, University of New England.
1980 Fish bones for fun and profit. *In* I. Johnson (ed.), *Holier than Thou,* pp. 61–75. Department of Prehistory, Australian National University.

Colinvaux, P.
1980 *Why Big Fierce Animals are Rare.* Pelican, Melbourne.

Collingwood, R. G.
1946 *The Idea of History.* Clarendon Press, Oxford.

Conkey, M. W.
1978 Style and information in cultural evolution: Toward a predictive model for the Paleolithic. *In* C. L. Redman, M. J. Berman, E. V. Curtin, W. T. Langhorne Jr., N. M. Versaggi and J. C. Wanser (eds), *Social Archaeology: Beyond Subsistence and Dating,* pp. 61–85. Academic Press, New York.
1980 Context, structure and efficacy in Paleolithic art and design. *In* M. Foster and S. Brandes (eds), *Symbol as Sense,* pp. 225–248. Academic Press, New York.

Connah, G.
1976 Archaeology at the University of New England, 1975–76. *Australian Archaeology* 5:1–6.

Corruccini, R. S.
1978 Morphometric analysis: Uses and abuses. *Yearbook of Physical Anthropology* 21:134–150.

Coutts, P. J. F.
1967 Pottery of Eastern New Guinea and Papua. *Mankind* 6:482–488.
1978a The Keilor Archaeological Project. *Records of the Victorian Archaeological Survey* 8:24–33.
1978b Victoria Archaeological Survey Activities

Report 1977/78. *Records of the Victorian Archaeological Survey* 8:1–23.
1981 Coastal Archaeology in Victoria. Part I: The morphology of coastal archaeological sites. *Proceedings of the Royal Society of Victoria* 92:67–80.

Coutts, P. J. F., and Witter, D. C.
1977 Summer Field Programme of the Victoria Archaeological Survey. *Australian Archaeology* 6:40–51.

Coutts, P. J. F., Witter, D., Cochrane, R. M., and Patrick, J.
1976a *Coastal Archaeology in Victoria.* Victoria Archaeological Survey, Melbourne.

Coutts, P. J. F., Witter, D., McIlwraith, M., and Frank, R.
1976b The Mound People of western Victoria: A preliminary statement. *Records of the Victorian Archaeological Survey* 1.

Coutts, P. J. F., Witter, D., and Parsons, D.
1977 Impact of European settlement on Aboriginal society in western Victoria. *Search* 8:194–205.

Coutts, P. J. F., Frank, R. K., and Hughes, P. J.
1978 Aboriginal engineers of the Western District, Victoria. *Records of the Victorian Archaeological Survey* 7.

Coutts, P. J. F., Henderson, P., and Fullager, R. L. K.
1979 A preliminary investigation of Aboriginal Mounds in north-western Victoria. *Records of the Victorian Archaeological Survey* 9.

Cowlishaw, G. K.
1979 Women's realm: A study of socialization, sexuality and reproduction among Australian Aborigines. Unpublished Ph.D. thesis, University of Sydney.

Crawford, M. H.
1973 Use of genetic markers of the blood in the study of the evolution of human populations. *In* M. H. Crawford and P. L. Workman (eds), *Methods and Theories of Anthropological Genetics,* pp. 19–38. University of New Mexico Press, Albuquerque.

Croll, P.
1980 An examination of backed tool assemblages from the south coast of New South Wales. Unpublished B.A. (Honours) thesis, Department of Anthropology, University of Sydney.

Crosby, E.
1973 A comparative study of Melanesian hafted edge tools and other percussive cutting implements. Unpublished Ph.D. thesis, Australian National University.
1977 An archaeologically oriented classification of ethnographic material culture. *In* R. V. S. Wright (ed.), *Stone Tools as Cultural Mar-*

kers: Change, Evolution, Complexity, pp. 83–96. Australian Institute of Aboriginal Studies, Canberra.

Curtain, C. C., von Loghem, E., and Schanfield, M. S.
1976   Immunoglobulin markers as indicators of popu- lation affinities in Australasia and the Western Pacific. In R. L. Kirk and A. G. Thorne (eds), The Origin of the Australians, pp. 347–364. Australian Institute of Aboriginal Studies, Canberra.

Dampier, W.
1688   Captain Dampier's Voyages. Edited by J.
[1906] Masefield. 2 Vols. E. Grant Richards, London.

Daniel, G. E.
1962   The Idea of Prehistory. Pelican, London.
1975   150 Years of Archaeology. Duckworth, London.

David, T. W. E., and Etheridge, R., Jr.
1889   Report on the discovery of human remains in the sand and pumice bed at Long Bay, near Botany. Records of the Geological Survey of New South Wales 1:9–15.

Davidson, D. S.
1935   Archaeological problems of northern Australia. Journal of the Royal Anthropological Institute 65:145–184.
1936   The spearthrower in Australia. Proceedings of the American Philosophical Society 76:445–483.

Davidson, J. M.
1979   New Zealand. In J. D. Jennings (ed.), The Prehistory of Polynesia, pp. 222–248. Harvard University Press, Cambridge.

Davies, J. L.
1978   The coast. In D. N. Jeans (ed.), Australia: A geography, pp. 134–151. University of Sydney Press, Sydney.

Deevey, E. S., Jr.
1960   The human population. Scientific American 203(3):194–205.

Deiley, R.
1979   The first Australians. Australian Playboy, September, pp. 50–56; October, pp. 112–118.

Diamond, J.
1977   Distributional strategies. In J. Allen, J. Golson and R. Jones (eds), Sunda and Sahul: Prehistoric Studies in Southeast Asia, Melanesia and Australia, pp. 295–316. Academic Press, London.
1978   The Tasmanians: The longest isolation, the simplest technology. Nature (London) 273:185–186.

Dibble, D. S., and Lorrain, D.
1968   Bonfire Shelter: A Stratified Bison Kill Site,

Val Verde County, Texas. Texas Memorial Museum, University of Texas at Austin, Miscellaneous Papers 1.

Dickson, F. P.
1971   Old glass from Kurnell. Mankind 8:60–61.
1972   Ground edge axes. Mankind 8:206–211.
1975   Bondi points. Mankind 10:45–46.
1976   Design and typology of stone hatchets. Mankind 10:259–263.
1977   Aboriginal relics at Boat Harbour and the adjoining reserve. Unpublished manuscript, National Parks and Wildlife Service, Sydney.
1978   Australian ground stone hatchets. Unpublished Ph.D. thesis, Macquarie University. [Published as Australian Stone Hatchets: A Study in Design and Dynamics, 1981, Academic Press, Sydney.]
1980   Making ground stone tools. Archaeology and Physical Anthropology in Oceania 15:162–167.

Dincauze, D. F.
1981   The Meadowcroft Papers. Quarterly Review of Archaeology 2:3–5.

Dixon, R. M. W.
1980   The Languages of Australia. Cambridge University Press, Cambridge.

Donovan, H. L.
1976   The Aborigines of the Nogoa Basin: An ethno-historical/archaeological approach. Unpublished B.A. (Honours) thesis, Department of Anthropology, University of Queensland.

Dortch, C. [E.]
1975   Geometric microliths from a dated archaeological deposit near Northcliffe, Western Australia. Journal of the Royal Society of Western Australia 58:59–63.
1976   Two engraved stone plaques of late Pleistocene age from Devil's Lair, Western Australia. Archaeology and Physical Anthropology in Oceania 11:32–44.
1977   Early and late stone industrial phases in Western Australia. In R. V. S. Wright (ed.), Stone Tools as Cultural Markers: Change, Evolution, Complexity, pp. 104–132. Australian Institute of Aboriginal Studies, Canberra.
1979a   Devil's Lair: An example of prolonged cave use in south-western Australia. World Archaeology 10:258–279.
1979b   33,000 year old stone and bone artifacts from Devil's Lair, Western Australia. Records of the Western Australian Museum 7:329–367.

1981   Recognition of indigenous development and external diffusion in Australian prehistory. *Australian Archaeology* 12:27–31.

In press   The Malimup middens: Evidence for mollusc eating in prehistoric south-western Australia. Paper presented to Xth International Congress of Archaeological and Ethnological Sciences, Poona, India.

Dortch, C., and Bordes, F.
1977   Blade and Levallois technology in Western Australian prehistory. *Quartär* 27/28:1–19.

Dortch, C., and Merrilees, D.
1973   Human occupation of Devil's Lair, Western Australia during the Pleistocene. *Archaeology and Physical Anthropology in Oceania* 8:89–115.

Downie, J. E., and White, J. P.
1978   Balof Shelter — Report on a small excavation. *Records of the Australian Museum* 31:762–802.

Draper, N.
1978   A model of Aboriginal subsistence and settlement in the Moreton Bay region of southeast Queensland. Unpublished B.A. (Honours) thesis, Department of Anthropology, University of Queensland.

Dury, C. H., and Langford-Smith, T.
1970   A Pleistocene Aboriginal camp fire from Lake Yantara, northwestern New South Wales. *Search* 1:73.

Easterlin, R. A.
1976   Population change and farm settlement in the northern United States. *Journal of Economic History* 36:45–83.

Edwards, R.
1971   Art and Aboriginal prehistory. *In* D. J. Mulvaney and J. Golson (eds), *Aboriginal Man and Environment in Australia*, pp. 356–367. Australian National University Press, Canberra.

Edwards, W. E.
1967   The Late-Pleistocene extinction and diminution in size of many mammalian species. *In* P. S. Martin and H. E. Wright (eds), *Pleistocene Extinctions*, pp. 141–154. Yale University Press, New Haven.

Egloff, B. J.
1971a   Collingwood Bay and the Trobriand Islands in recent prehistory: Settlement and interaction in coastal and island Papua. Unpublished Ph.D. thesis, Australian National University.

1971b   Archaeological research in the Collingwood Bay area of Papua. *Asian Perspectives* 14:60–64.

1978   The Kula before Malinowski: A changing configuration. *Mankind* 11:429–435.

1979   Recent Prehistory in Southeast Papua. *Terra Australis* 4.

Egloff, B., and Kaiku, R.
1978   An archaeological and ethnological survey of the Purari River (Wabo) Dam site and reservoir. *Purari River (Wabo) Hydroelectric Scheme* Vol. 5. Office of Environment and Conservation, Waigani.

Elkin, A. P.
1948   Pressure flaking in the northern Kimberley, Australia. *Man* 48:110–113.

Ellen, R. F., and Glover, I. C.
1974   Pottery manufacture and trade in the Central Moluccas, Indonesia: The modern situation and the historical implications. *Man* (n.s.) 9:353–379.

Etheridge, R., Jr.
1890   Has Man a geological history in Australia? *Proceedings of the Linnean Society of New South Wales* (series 2) 5:259–266.

1891   Notes on "rock-shelters" or "gibbagunyahs" at Deewhy Lagoon. *Records of the Australian Museum* 1:171–174.

1905   The further discovery of dugong bones on the coast of New South Wales. *Records of the Australian Museum* 6:17–19.

1908   Ancient stone implements from the Yodda valley goldfield, northeast British New Guinea. *Records of the Australian Museum* 7:24–28.

Etheridge, R., Jr., and Whitelegge, T.
1907   Aboriginal workshops on the coast of New South Wales, and their contents. *Records of the Australian Museum* 6:233–250.

Etheridge, R., Jr., David, T. W. E., and Grimshaw, J. W.
1896   On the occurrence of a submerged forest, with remains of the dugong, at Shea's Creek, near Sydney. *Journal and Proceedings of the Royal Society of New South Wales* 30:158–185.

Evans, R., Saunders, K., and Cronin, K.
1975   *Exclusion, Exploitation and Extermination.* A.N.Z. Book Co., Sydney.

Eyre, E. J.
1845   *Journal of Expeditions of Discovery into Central Australia, and Overland from Adelaide to King George's Sound, in the Years 1840–1; [etc.].* T. and W. Boone, London.

Feil, D. K.
1978   Enga women in the *Tee* exchange. *Mankind* 10:220–230.

Fenner, F. J.
1941   Fossil human skull fragments of probable

Pleistocene age from Aitape, New Guinea. *Records of the South Australian Museum* 6:335–356.

Ferguson, W. C.

1980 Edge-angle classification of the Quininup Brook implements: Testing the ethnographic analogy. *Archaeology and Physical Anthropology in Oceania* 15:56–72.

1981 Archaeological investigations at the Quininup Brook site complex, Western Australia. *Records of the Western Australian Museum* 8:609–637.

Fitzhardinge, L. F. (ed.)

1979 *Sydney's First Four Years*, by Captain Watkin Tench. Library of Australian History, Sydney.

Fladmark, K.

1979 Routes: Alternate migration corridors for Early Man in North America. *American Antiquity* 44:55–69.

Fletcher, R.

1981 People and space: A case study on material behaviour. *In* I. Hodder, G. Isaac and N. Hammond (eds), *Pattern of the Past*, pp. 97–129. Cambridge University Press, Cambridge.

Flood, J. M.

1970 A point assemblage from the Northern Territory. *Archaeology and Physical Anthropology in Oceania* 5:27–52.

1974 Pleistocene Man at Clogg's Cave — His toolkit and environment. *Mankind* 9:175–188.

1976 Man and ecology in the highlands of southeastern Australia: A case study. *In* N. Peterson (ed.), *Tribes and Boundaries in Australia*, pp. 30–49. Australian Institute of Aboriginal Studies, Canberra.

1980 *The Moth Hunters*. Australian Institute of Aboriginal Studies, Canberra.

Freedman, L.

1972 Human skeletal remains from Aibura Cave, New Guinea. *Terra Australis*, 2:153–159.

Freedman, L. and Lofgren, M.

1979 Human skeletal remains from Cossack, Western Australia. *Journal of Human Evolution* 8:283–299.

1981 Odontometrics of Western Australian Aborigines. *Archaeology in Oceania* 16:87–93.

Friedlaender, J. S.

1975 *Patterns of Human Variation*. Harvard University Press, Cambridge.

Gajdusek, D. C.

1964 Factors governing the genetics of primitive human populations. *Cold Spring Harbor Symposia on Quantitative Biology* 29:121–136.

Gallagher, J. P.

1972 A preliminary report on archaeological research near Lake Zuai. *Annales d'Ethiopie* 9:13–18.

Gallus, A.

1967 The excavations at Keilor. *Artefact*, No. 7:1–2.

1971 Excavations at Keilor, Report No. 1. *Artefact*, No. 24:1–12.

1972 Excavations at Keilor, Report No. 2. *Artefact*, No. 27:9–19.

1976 The Middle and Early Upper Pleistocene stone industries at the Dry Creek archaeological sites near Keilor, Australia. *Artefact* 1:75–108.

Gaughwin, D.

1978 A bird in the sand. Unpublished B.A. (Hons) thesis, Department of Prehistory and Anthropology, Australian National University.

Geyl, P.

1955 *The Use and Abuse of History*. Yale University Press, New Haven.

Giles, E.

1976 Cranial variation in Australia and neighbouring areas. *In* R. L. Kirk and A. G. Thorne (eds), *The Origin of the Australians*, pp. 161–172. Australian Institute of Aboriginal Studies, Canberra.

Giles, E., Wyber, S., and Walsh, R. J.

1970 Microevolution in New Guinea: Additional evidence for genetic drift. *Archaeology and Physical Anthropology in Oceania* 5: 60–72.

Gill, A. M.

1981 Adaptive responses of Australian vascular plant species to fires. *In* A. M. Gill, R. H. Groves and I. R. Noble (eds), *Fire and the Australian Biota*, pp. 243–272. Australian Academy of Science, Canberra.

Gill, A. M., Groves, R. H. and Noble, I. R. (eds)

1981 *Fire and the Australian Biota*. Australian Academy of Science, Canberra.

Gill, E. D.

1955 Aboriginal midden sites in western Victoria dated by radiocarbon analysis. *Mankind* 5:51–54.

1966 Provenance and age of the Keilor cranium: Oldest known human skeletal remains in Australia. *Current Anthropology* 7:581–584.

Gillespie, R., and Temple, R. B.

1976 Sydney University natural radiocarbon measurements III. *Radiocarbon* 18:96–109.

1977 Radiocarbon dating of shell middens. *Archaeology and Physical Anthropology in Oceania* 12:26–37.

Gillespie, R., Horton, D. R., Ladd, P., Macumber, P. G., Rich, T. H., Thorne, R., and Wright, R. V. S.
1978 Lancefield Swamp and the extinction of the Australian megafauna. *Science* 200:1044–1048.

Glover, E.
1974 Report on the excavation of a second rock shelter at Curracurrang Cove, New South Wales. *In* J. V. S. Megaw (ed.), *The Recent Archaeology of the Sydney District*, pp. 13–18. Australian Institute of Aboriginal Studies, Canberra.

Glover, I. [C.]
1967 Stone implements from Millstream Station, Western Australia: Newall's Collection reanalysed. *Mankind* 6:415–425.
1969 The use of factor analysis for the discovery of artefact types. *Mankind* 7:36–51.
1971 Prehistoric research in Timor. *In* D. J. Mulvaney and J. Golson (eds), *Aboriginal Man and Environment in Australia*, pp. 158–181. Australian National University Press, Canberra.
1973 Island Southeast Asia and the settlement of Australia. *In* D. E. Strong (ed.), *Archaeological Theory and Practice*, pp. 105–129. Seminar Press, London.
1976 Ulu Leang Cave, Maros: A preliminary sequence of post-Pleistocene cultural development in south Sulawesi. *Archipel* 11:113–154.
1978 Survey and excavation in the Maros district, South Sulawesi, Indonesia: The 1975 field season. *Indo-Pacific Prehistory Association Bulletin* 1:60–103.

Glover, I., and Glover, E. A.
1970 Pleistocene flaked stone tools from Timor and Flores. *Mankind* 7:188–190.

Glover, J. E.
1979 The provenance and archaeological significance of Aboriginal artefacts of Eocene chert in southwestern Australia. *Search* 10:188–190.

Goede, A., and Murray, P.
1977 Pleistocene man in south central Tasmania: Evidence from a cave site in the Florentine Valley. *Mankind* 11:2–10.
1979 Late Pleistocene bone deposits from a cave in the Florentine Valley, Tasmania. *Papers and Proceedings of the Royal Society of Tasmania* 113:39–52.

Goede, A., Murray, P., and Harmon, R.
1978 Pleistocene man and megafauna in Tasmania: Dated evidence from cave sites. *Artefact* 3:139–150.

Golding, W. G.
1954 *Lord of the Flies.* Faber and Faber, London.

Gollan, K.
In prep. Prehistoric dingo in Australia. Ph.D. thesis, Australian National University.

Golson, J.
1971 Australian Aboriginal food plants: Some ecological and culture-historical implications. *In* D. J. Mulvaney and J. Golson (eds), *Aboriginal Man and Environment in Australia*, pp. 196–238. Australian National University Press, Canberra.
1974 Both sides of the Wallace Line: New Guinea, Australia, Island Melanesia and Asian Prehistory. *In* N. Barnard (ed.), *Early Chinese Art and its Possible Influence in the Pacific Basin*, pp. 533–596. Authorised Taiwan Edition. Also published in USA by Intercultural Arts Press, New York.
1976 Archaeology and agricultural history in the New Guinea Highlands. *In* G. de G. Sieveking, I. H. Longworth and K. E. Wilson (eds), *Problems in Economic and Social Archaeology*, pp. 201–220. Duckworth, London.
1977a No room at the top: Agricultural intensification in the New Guinea highlands. *In* J. Allen, J. Golson and R. Jones (eds), *Sunda and Sahul: Prehistoric Studies in Southeast Asia, Melanesia and Australia*, pp. 601–638. Academic Press, London.
1977b The making of the New Guinea Highlands. *In* J. H. Winslow (ed.), *The Melanesian Environment*, pp. 45–56. Australian National University Press, Canberra.
1977c Simple tools and complex technology. *In* R. V. S. Wright (ed.), *Stone Tools as Cultural Markers: Change, Evolution, Complexity*, pp. 154–161. Australian Institute of Aboriginal Studies, Canberra.
In press The Ipomoean Revolution revisited: Society and the sweet potato in the Upper Wahgi valley. *In* A. Strathern (ed.), *Inequality in the New Guinea Highlands*. Cambridge University Press, Cambridge.

Golson, J., and Hughes, P. J.
1977 Ditches before time. *Hemisphere* 21(2):13–21.
In press The appearance of plant and animal domestication in New Guinea. *In* J. Garanger (ed.), *La Préhistoire Océanienne*. Centre National de la Recherche Scientifique, Paris.

Golson, J., Lampert, R. J., Wheeler, J. M., and Ambrose, W. R.
 1967 A note on carbon dates for horticulture in the New Guinea Highlands. *Journal of the Polynesian Society* 76:369–371.

Gorecki, P. P.
 1978 Further notes on prehistoric wooden spades from the New Guinea Highlands. *Tools and Tillage* 3:185–190.
 In prep. The archaeological record of modern agricultural systems in the Mt. Hagen area, Papua New Guinea. Ph.D. thesis, University of Sydney.

Gorman, C. [F.]
 1971 The Hoabinhian and after: Subsistence patterns in Southeast Asia during the late Pleistocene and early Recent periods. *World Archaeology* 2:300–320.
 1974 Modèles a priori et préhistoire de la Thailande. *Études rurales* 53–56:41–72.

Gorman, C. F., and Charoenwongsa, P.
 1976 Ban Chiang: A mosaic of impressions from the first two years. *Expedition* 18(4):14–25.

Gorter, J. D.
 1977 Fossil marsupials from the Douglas Cave, near Stuart Town, New South Wales. *Journal and Proceedings of the Royal Society of New South Wales* 110:139–145.

Gould, R. A.
 1969 Puntutjarpa Rockshelter: A reply to Messrs. Glover and Lampert. *Archaeology and Physical Anthropology in Oceania* 4:229–237.
 1971 The archaeologist as ethnographer: A case from the Western Desert of Australia. *World Archaeology* 3:143–177.
 1973 *Australian Archaeology in Ecological and Ethnographic Perspective* (Warner Modular Publications, Module 7). Warner, Andover, Mass.
 1977a Puntutjarpa Rockshelter and the Australian Desert Culture. *Anthropological Papers of the American Museum of Natural History* 54(1).
 1977b Ethno-archaeology; Or, where do models come from? *In* R. V. S. Wright (ed.), *Stone Tools as Cultural Markers: Change, Evolution, Complexity*, pp. 162–168. Australian Institute of Aboriginal Studies, Canberra.
 1978a Beyond analogy in ethnoarchaeology. *In* R. A. Gould (ed.), *Explorations in Ethnoarchaeology*, pp. 249–294. University of New Mexico Press, Albuquerque.
 1978b The anthropology of human residues. *American Anthropologist* 80:815–835.
 1980 *Living archaeology*. Cambridge University Press, Cambridge.

Gould, R. A., Koster, D. A., and Sontz, A. H. L.
 1971 The lithic assemblage of the Western Desert Aborigines of Australia. *American Antiquity* 36:149–169.

Grayson, D. K.
 1977 Pleistocene avifaunas and the overkill hypothesis. *Science* 193:691–693.
 1979 On the quantification of vertebrate archaeofaunas. *Advances in Archaeological Method and Theory*, 2:200–237. Academic Press, New York.
 1980 Mount Mazama, climatic change and Fort Rock Basin archaeo-faunas. *In* D. K. Grayson and P. D. Sheets (eds), *Volcanic Activity and Human Ecology*, pp. 427–457. Academic Press, New York.
 1981 The effect of sample size on some derived measures in vertebrate faunal analysis. *Journal of Archaeological Science* 8: 77–88.

Green, R. C.
 1979 Lapita. *In* J. N. Jennings (ed.), *The Prehistory of Polynesia*, pp. 27–60. Harvard University Press, Cambridge.

Gruhn, R.
 1965 The Archaeology of Wilson Butte Cave, South-central Idaho. *Idaho State College Museum, Occasional Paper* 6.

Guglielmino-Matessi, C. R., Gluckman, P., and Cavalli-Sforza, L. L.
 1979 Climate and the evolution of skull metrics in man. *American Journal of Physical Anthropology* 50:549–564.

Hale, H. H., and Tindale, N. B.
 1930 Notes on some human remains in the Lower Murray Valley, South Australia. *Records of the South Australian Museum* 4:145–218.

Hallam, S.
 1975 *Fire and Hearth*. Australian Institute of Aboriginal Studies, Canberra.
 1977 The relevance of Old World archaeology to the first entry of Man into New Worlds: Colonization seen from the Antipodes. *Quaternary Research* 8:128–148.
 1981 The first Western Australians. *In* W. Stannage (ed.), *A New History of Western Australia*, pp. 35–71. University of Western Australia Press, Perth.

Hallpike, C. R.
 1977 *Bloodshed and Violence in the Papuan Mountains*. Clarendon Press, Oxford.

Hamilton, A.
 1972 Aboriginal Man's best friend? *Mankind* 8:287–295.
 1980 Dual social systems: Technology, labour and

womens' secret rites in the eastern Western Desert of Australia. *Oceania* 51:4–19.

Harding, T. G.
1967   *Voyagers of the Vitiaz Strait.* University of Washington Press, Seattle.

Harlan, J. R.
1971   Agricultural origins: Centers and non-centers. *Science* 174:468–474.

Harris, D. R.
1977   Subsistence strategies across Torres Strait. *In* J. Allen, J. Golson and R. Jones (eds), *Sunda and Sahul: Prehistoric Studies in Southeast Asia, Melanesia and Australia,* pp. 421–464. Academic Press, London.

Harris, E. C., and Hughes, P. J.
1978   An early agricultural system at Mugumamp Ridge, Western Highlands Province, Papua New Guinea. *Mankind* 11:437–444.

Harris, M.
1971   *Culture, Man and Nature.* T. Y. Crowell, New York.

Hassan, F.
1981   *Demographic Archaeology.* Academic Press, New York.

Haury, E. W.
1950   *The Stratigraphy and Archaeology of Ven-*
[1975]   *tana Cave.* University of Arizona Press, Tucson.

Hawkes, K., Hill, K., and O'Connell, J. F.
In   Why hunters gather: Optimal foraging and
press   the Ache of eastern Paraguay. *American Ethnologist.*

Hayden, B.
1972   Population control among hunter/gatherers. *World Archaeology* 4:205–221.
1975a   Dingoes: Pets or producers? *Mankind* 10:11–15.
1975b   The carrying capacity dilemma: An alternate approach. *American Antiquity, Memoir* 30:11–21.
1977a   Stone tool functions in the Western Desert. *In* R. V. S. Wright (ed.), *Stone Tools as Cultural Markers: Change, Evolution, Complexity,* pp. 178–188. Australian Institute of Aboriginal Studies, Canberra.
1977b   Sticks and stones and ground edge axes: The upper palaeolithic in Southeast Asia? *In* J. Allen, J. Golson and R. Jones (eds), *Sunda and Sahul: Prehistoric Studies in Southeast Asia, Melanesia and Australia,* pp. 73–109. Academic Press, London.
1979a   *Palaeolithic Reflections.* Australian Institute of Aboriginal Studies, Canberra.

Hayden, B. (ed.)
1979b   *Lithic Use-Wear Analysis.* Academic Press, New York.

Hayden, B., and Kamminga, J.
1973   Gould, Koster and Sontz on "microwear": A critical review. *Newsletter of Lithic Technology* 2:3–15.

Haynes, C. V.
1980   The Clovis Culture. *Canadian Journal of Anthropology* 1:115–121.

Heider, K.
1967   Speculative functionalism: Archaic elements in New Guinea Dani culture. *Anthropos* 62:833–840.

Heizer, R. F.
1951   Preliminary report on the Leonard Rockshelter Site, Pershing County, Nevada. *American Antiquity* 17:89–98.

Hiatt, B.
1968   The food quest and the economy of the Tasmanian Aborigines. *Oceania* 38:99–133 and 190–219.

Hiscock, P.
1980   Review of R. V. S. Wright (ed.), "Stone Tools as Cultural Markers: Change, Evolution, Complexity". *Archaeology and Physical Anthropology in Oceania* 15:172–176.
1981   Comments on the use of chipped stone artefacts as a measure of "intensity of site usage". *Australian Archaeology* 13:30–34.

Hiscock, P., and Hughes, P. J.
1980   Backed blades in northern Australia: Evidence from northwest Queensland. *Australian Archaeology* 10:86–95.

Hodder, I. (ed.)
1978   *The Spatial Organization of Culture.* Duckworth, London.

Holland, R. C.
1976   Distribution and methods of construction of Aboriginal bark canoes. *Museum of Anthropology, University of Queensland, Occasional Papers in Anthropology* 6:69–83.

Hooijer, D. A.
1970   Pleistocene South-East Asiatic Pygmy Stegodonts. *Nature (London)* 225:474–475.

Hope, G. S., and Hope, J. H.
1976   Man on Mount Jaya. *In* G. S. Hope, J. A. Peterson, U. Radok and I. Allison (eds), *The Equatorial Glaciers of New Guinea,* pp. 225–240. A. A. Balkema, Rotterdam.

Hope, J. H., and Hope, G. S.
1976   Palaeoenvironments for man in New Guinea. *In* R. L. Kirk and A. G. Thorne (eds), *The Origin of the Australians,* pp. 29–54. Australian Institute of Aboriginal Studies, Canberra.

Hope, J. H., Lampert, R. J., Edmondson, E., Smith, M. J., and Van Tets, G. F.

1977   Late Pleistocene faunal remains from Seton rockshelter, Kangaroo Island, South Australia. *Journal of Biogeography* 4:363–385.

Horn, H. S.
1975   Optimal tactics of reproduction and life history. *In* M. Cody and J. M. Diamond (eds), *Ecology and Evolution of Communities*, pp. 411–429. Belknap Press, Harvard University, Cambridge.

Horne, G., and Aiston, G.
1924   *Savage Life in Central Australia.* Macmillan, London.

Horton, D. R.
1979a   The great megafaunal extinction debate:1879–1979. *Artefact* 4:11–25.
1979b   Tasmanian adaptation. *Mankind* 12:28–34.
1980   A review of the extinction question: Man, climate and megafauna. *Archaeology and Physical Anthropology in Oceania* 15:86–97.
1981a   Early thoughts on Early Man in Australia. *Artefact* 6:53–69.
1981b   Water and woodland: The peopling of Australia. *Australian Institute of Aboriginal Studies, Newsletter* 16:21–27.

Horton, D. R., and Wright, R. V. S.
1981   Cuts on Lancefield bones: Carnivorous Thylacoleo, not humans, the cause. *Archaeology in Oceania* 16:73–80.

Hossfeld, P. S.
1965   Radiocarbon dating and palaeoecology of the Aitape fossil human remains. *Proceedings of the Royal Society of Victoria* 78:161–165.

Howe, K. R.
1977   The fate of the "Savage" in Pacific historiography. *New Zealand Journal of History* 11:137–154.

Howell, N.
1976   The population of the Dobe area !Kung. *In* R. B. Lee and I. DeVore (eds), *Kalahari Hunter-Gatherers*, pp. 137–151. Harvard University Press, Cambridge, Mass.

Howells, W. W.
1973   *The Pacific Islanders.* A. H. and A. W. Reed, Wellington.
1976   Metrical analysis in the problem of Australian origins. *In* R. L. Kirk and A. G. Thorne (eds), *The Origin of the Australians*, pp. 141–160. Australian Institute of Aboriginal Studies, Canberra.

Howitt, A. W.
1890   The eucalypts of Gippsland. *Transactions of the Royal Society of Victoria* 2:81–120.

Hughes, D. R.
1968   Skeletal plasticity and its relevance in the study of earlier populations. *In* D. Brothwell (ed.), *Skeletal Biology of Earlier Human populations*, pp. 31–66. Pergamon, Oxford.

Hughes, I.
1977   New Guinea Stone Age Trade. *Terra Australis* 3.
1978   Good money and bad: Inflation and devaluation in the colonial process. *Mankind* 11:308–318.

Hughes, P. J.
1980   Thesis abstract. The geomorphology of archaeological sites on the south coast of New South Wales. *Australian Archaeology* 11:50–52.

Hughes, P. J., and Djohadze, V.
1980   Radiocarbon Dates from Archaeological Sites on the South Coast of New South Wales and the Use of Depth/Age Curves. *Department of Prehistory, Australian National University, Occasional Papers in Prehistory* 1.

Hughes, P. J., and Lampert, R. J.
In   Prehistoric population change in southern
press   coastal New South Wales. *In* S. E. Bowdler (ed.), *Coastal Archaeology of Eastern Australia.* Dept. of Prehistory, Australian National University.

Hughes, P. J., and Sullivan, M. E.
1981   Aboriginal burning and Late Holocene geomorphic events in eastern NSW. *Search* 12:277–278.

Hughes, P. J., Sullivan, M. E., and Lampert, R. J.
1973   The use of silcrete by Aborigines in southern coastal N.S.W. *Archaeology and Physical Anthropology in Oceania* 8:220–225.

Hughes, P. J., Sullivan, M. E., and Branagan, D. F.
1978   Are there prehistoric shell middens on Rottnest Island? *Australian Archaeology* 8:158–161.

Hynes, R. A., and Chase, A. K.
1982   Plants, sites and domiculture: Aboriginal influence on plant communities in Cape York Peninsula. *Archaeology in Oceania,* 17:38–50.

Ikawa-Smith, F.
1979   Technological traditions in late Pleistocene and early Holocene Japan. Paper presented to 14th Pacific Science Congress, Khabarovsk, 21–24 August.
1980   Current issues in Japanese archaeology. *American Scientist* 68:134–145.

Imbrie, J., and Imbrie, K. P.
1979   *Ice Ages.* Macmillan, London.

Irwin, G. J.
1977   The emergence of Mailu as a central place in the prehistory of coastal Papua. Un-

published Ph.D. thesis, Australian National University.

1978 The development of Mailu as a specialized trading and manufacturing centre in Papuan prehistory: The causes and the implications. *Mankind* 11:406–415.

1980 The prehistory of Oceania: Colonization and cultural change. *In* A. Sherratt (ed.), *The Cambridge Encyclopaedia of Archaeology*, pp. 324–332. Cambridge University Press, Cambridge.

Isaac, G. L.

1972 Early phases of human behaviour: Models in Lower Palaeolithic archaeology. *In* D. L. Clarke (ed.), *Models in Archaeology*, pp. 167–199. Methuen, London.

1977 Squeezing blood from stones. *In* R. V. S. Wright (ed.), *Stone tools as Cultural Markers: Change, Evolution, Complexity*, pp. 5–12. Australian Institute of Aboriginal Studies, Canberra.

Jacob, T., Soejono, R. P., Freeman, L. G., and Brown, R. H.

1978 Stone tools from Mid-Pleistocene sediments in Java. *Science* 202:885–887.

Jeans, D. N. (ed.)

1978 *Australia: A geography.* Sydney University Press, Sydney.

Jennings, J. D.

1957 Danger Cave. *Department of Anthropology, University of Utah, Anthropological Papers*, 27.

Johnson, D. L.

1980 Problems in the land vertebrate zoogeography of certain islands and the swimming powers of elephants. *Journal of Biogeography* 7:383–398.

Johnson, I.

1979 The getting of data. Unpublished Ph.D. thesis, Australian National University.

Jones, R.

1966 A speculative archaeological sequence for north-west Tasmania. *Records of the Queen Victoria Museum, Launceston* 25.

1968 The geographical background to the arrival of man in Australia and Tasmania. *Archaeology and Physical Anthropology in Oceania* 3:186–215.

1969 Firestick farming. *Australian Natural History* 16:224–228.

1971a Rocky Cape and the problem of the Tasmanians. Unpublished Ph.D. thesis, University of Sydney.

1971b The demography of hunters and farmers in Tasmania. *In* D. J. Mulvaney and J. Golson (eds), *Aboriginal Man and Environment in Australia*, pp. 271–287. Australian National University Press, Canberra.

1972 Tasmanian Aborigines and dogs. *Mankind* 7:256–271.

1973 Emerging picture of Pleistocene Australians. *Nature (London)* 246:278–281.

1974 Tasmanian tribes. *In* N. B. Tindale, *Aboriginal Tribes of Australia*, pp. 319–354. University of California Press, Berkeley.

1975 The Neolithic, Palaeolithic and the hunting gardeners: Man and land in the Antipodes. *In* R. P. Suggate and M. M. Cresswell (eds), *Quaternary Studies*, pp. 21–34. Royal Society of New Zealand, Wellington.

1976 Tasmania: Aquatic machines and off-shore islands. *In* G. de G. Sieveking, I. H. Longworth and K. E. Wilson (eds), *Problems in Economic and Social Archaeology*, pp. 235–263. Duckworth, London.

1977a The Tasmanian paradox. *In* R. V. S. Wright (ed.), *Stone Tools as Cultural Markers: Change, Evolution, Complexity*, pp. 189–204. Australian Institute of Aboriginal Studies, Canberra.

1977b Man as an element of a continental fauna: The case of the sundering of the Bassian bridge. *In* J. Allen, J. Golson and R. Jones (eds), *Sunda and Sahul: Prehistoric Studies in Southeast Asia, Melanesia and Australia*, pp. 317–386. Academic Press, London.

1978 Why did the Tasmanians stop eating fish? *In* R. Gould (ed.), *Explorations in Ethnoarchaeology*, pp. 11–48. University of New Mexico Press, Albuquerque.

1979 The fifth continent: Problems concerning the human colonization of Australia. *Annual Review of Anthropology* 8:445–466.

1980 Cleaning the country: The Gidjingali and their Arnhemland environment. *BHP Journal* 1.80:10–15.

1981 Hunters in the Australian coastal savanna. *In* D. Harris (ed.), *Human Ecology in Savanna Environments*, pp. 107–146. Academic Press, London.

Joyce, E. B., and Anderson, J. R.

1976 Late Quaternary geology and environment at the Dry Creek archaeological sites near Keilor in Victoria, Australia. *Artefact* 1:47–74.

Joyce, T. A.

1912 Notes on prehistoric pottery from Japan and New Guinea. *Journal of the Royal Anthropological Institute of Great Britain and Ireland* 42:545–546.

Kamminga, J.

1977 A functional study of use-polished eloueras.

In R. V. S. Wright (ed.), *Stone Tools as Cultural Markers: Change, Evolution, Complexity*, pp. 205–212. Australian Institute of Aboriginal Studies, Canberra.

1978   Journey into the microcosms. Unpublished Ph.D. thesis, University of Sydney.

1979   The nature of use-polish and abrasive smoothing on stone tools. *In* B. Hayden (ed.), *Lithic Use-Wear Analysis*, pp. 143–158. Academic Press, New York.

1980   A functional investigation of Australian microliths. *Artefact* 5:1–18.

Kamminga, J., and Allen, H.
1973   *Report of the Archaeological Survey, Alligator Rivers Environmental Fact-Finding Survey.* Australian Government, Darwin.

Keast, A. L.
1966   *Australia and the Pacific Islands.* Random House, New York.

1981   *Ecological Biogeography in Australia.* W. Junk, The Hague.

Keast, A. L., Crocker, R. L., and Christian, C. S. (eds)
1959   *Biogeography and Ecology in Australia.* W. Junk, The Hague.

Keeley, L. H.
1980   *Experimental Determination of Stone Tool Uses.* University of Chicago Press, Chicago.

Kefous, K. C.
1977   We have a fish with ears, and wonder if it is valuable? Unpublished B.A. (Honours) thesis, Department of Prehistory and Anthropology, Australian National University.

1981   The chronology of Lake Victoria lunette — Some recent evidence. *Australian Archaeology* 13:8–11.

Kennedy, E.
1934   Excavating a rock-shelter at Brown's Bay, Pittwater, N.S.W. *Mankind* 1:200–201.

Kennedy, G.
1978   *Bligh.* Duckworth, London.

Key, C. A.
1969   The identification of New Guinea obsidians. *Archaeology and Physical Anthropology in Oceania* 4:47–55.

1972   The mineralogy of the pottery finds at Aibura. *Terra Australis* 2:160–161.

Kimber, R. G.
1976   Beginnings of farming? Some man–plant–animal relationships in Central Australia. *Mankind* 10:142–150.

King, T. F.
1979   Don't that beat the band? Non-egalitarian political organization in prehistoric California. *In* C. L. Redman, M. J. Berman, E. V. Curtin, W. T. Langhorne Jr., N. M. Versaggi and J. C. Wanser (eds), *Social Archaeology:*

Beyond Subsistence and Dating, pp. 225–248. Academic Press, New York.

Kirch, P. V.
1979   Subsistence and ecology. *In* J. D. Jennings (ed.), *The Prehistory of Polynesia*, pp. 286–307. Harvard University Press, Cambridge.

1982   Ecology and the Adaptation of Polynesian Agricultural Systems. *Archaeology in Oceania* 17:1–6.

Kirk, R. L.
1971   Genetic evidence and its implications for Aboriginal prehistory. *In* D. J. Mulvaney and J. Golson (eds), *Aboriginal Man and Environment in Australia*, pp. 326–343. Australian National University Press, Canberra.

1976   Serum protein and enzyme markers as indicators of population affinities in Australia and the Western Pacific. *In* R. L. Kirk and A. G. Thorne (eds), *The Origin of the Australians*, pp. 329–346. Australian Institute of Aboriginal Studies, Canberra.

Kirk, R. L., and Thorne, A. G.
1976   Introduction. *In* R. L. Kirk and A. G. Thorne (eds), *The Origin of the Australians*, pp. 1–8. Australian Institute of Aboriginal Studies, Canberra.

Klein, R. G.
1975   The relevance of Old World Archaeology to the first entry of Man into the New World. *Quaternary Research* 5:391–394.

1977   The ecology of early man in Southern Africa. *Science* 197:115–126.

1980   Environmental and ecological implications of large mammals from upper Pleistocene and Holocene sites in southern Africa. *Annals of the South African Museum* 81:223–283.

Koettig, M.
1976   Rising damp. Unpublished B.A. (Honours) thesis, Department of Anthropology, University of Sydney.

Kolig, E.
1973   Aboriginal Man's best foe? *Mankind* 9:122–123.

Krebs, C. J.
1978   *Ecology: The Experimental Analysis of Distribution and Abundance*, 2nd edition. Harper and Row, New York.

Ladd, P. G.
1976   Past and present vegetation in the Lancefield area, Victoria. *Artefact* 1:113–128.

Lampert, R. J.
1966a   An excavation at Durras North, New South Wales. *Archaeology and Physical Anthropology in Oceania* 1:83–118.

1966b Archaeological Reconnaissance in Papua and New Guinea: 1966. Manuscript, Department of Anthropology, Australian National University.

1967 Horticulture in the New Guinea Highlands: C14 Dating. *Antiquity* 41:307–308.

1971a Burrill Lake and Currarong. *Terra Australis* 1.

1971b Coastal Aborigines of Southeastern Australia. *In* D. J. Mulvaney and J. Golson (eds), *Aboriginal Man and Environment in Australia* pp. 114–132. Australian National University Press, Canberra.

1972 Hagen Axes. Manuscript, Department of Prehistory, Australian National University.

1975 A preliminary report on some waisted blades found on Kangaroo Island, South Australia. *Australian Archaeology* 2:45–47.

1977 Kangaroo Island and the antiquity of Australians. *In* R. V. S. Wright (ed.), *Stone Tools as Cultural Markers: Change, Evolution, Complexity*, pp. 213–218. Australian Institute of Aboriginal Studies, Canberra.

1979a The Great Kartan Mystery. Unpublished Ph.D. thesis, Australian National University.

1979b Aborigines. *In* M. J. Tyler, C. R. Twidale and J. K. Ling (eds), *Natural History of Kangaroo Island*, pp. 81–89. Royal Society of South Australia, Adelaide.

1980 Variation in Australia's Pleistocene Stone Industries. *Journal de la Société des Océanistes* 36(68):190–206.

1981 The Great Kartan Mystery. *Terra Australis* 5.

Lampert, R. J., and Hughes, P. [J.]
1974 Sea level change and Aboriginal coastal adaptation in southern New South Wales. *Archaeology and Physical Anthropology in Oceania* 9:226–235.

1980 Pleistocene archaeology in the Flinders Ranges: Research prospects. *Australian Archaeology* 10:11–20.

Latz, P. K., and Griffin, G. F.
1978 Changes in Aboriginal land management in relation to fire and to food plants in Central Australia. *In* B. S. Hetzel and H. J. Frith (eds), *The Nutrition of Aborigines in Relation to the Ecosystem of Central Australia*, pp. 77–85. Commonwealth Scientific and Industrial Research Organisation, Melbourne.

Lawton, H. W., Wilke, P. J., De Decker, M., and Mason, W. M.
1976 Agriculture among the Paiute of Owens Valley. *Journal of California Anthropology* 3:13–50.

Lawrence, R.
1969 Aboriginal Habitat and Economy. *Department of Geography, School of General Studies, Australian National University, Occasional Paper* 6.

Leahy, M., and Crain, M.
1937 *The Land that Time Forgot.* Hurst and Blackett, London.

Leask, M. F.
1943 A kitchen midden in Papua. *Oceania* 13:235–242.

Lee, R. B.
1980 *The !Kung San.* Cambridge University Press, Cambridge.

Lewis, H. T.
1977 Masuta: The ecology of Indian fires in northern Alberta. *West Canadian Journal of Anthropology* 7:15–52.

Lilley, I. A.
1978 Prehistoric subsistence and settlement in the sub-coastal zone of the Moreton region, southeast Queensland. Unpublished B.A. (Honours) thesis, Department of Anthropology, University of Queensland.

Little, M. A., and Morren, G. E. B., Jr.
1976 *Ecology, Energetics and Human Variability.* Wm. C. Brown Company, Dubuque, Iowa.

Long, A., and Rippeteau, B.
1974 Testing contemporaneity and averaging radiocarbon dates. *American Antiquity* 39:205–214.

Lorblanchet, M., and Jones, R.
1979 Les premières fouilles à Dampier, (Australie occidentale), et leur place dans l'ensemble australien. *Bulletin de la Société Préhistorique Française* 76:463–487.

Lourandos, H.
1970 Coast and hinterland: The archaeological sites of Eastern Tasmania. Unpublished M.A. thesis, Australian National University.

1976 Aboriginal settlement and land use in south-western Victoria: a report on current field work. *Artefact* 1:174–193.

1977 Aboriginal spatial organization and population: South-western Victoria reconsidered. *Archaeology and Physical Anthropology in Oceania*, 12:202–225.

1980a Change or stability?: Hydraulics, hunter-gatherers and population in temperate Australia. *World Archaeology* 11:245–266.

1980b Forces of change. Unpublished Ph.D. thesis, University of Sydney.

Lubbock, J.
1865 *Prehistoric Times, as Illustrated by Ancient Remains, and the Manners and Customs of*

Modern Savages. Williams and Norgate, London.

Luebbers, R. A.

1975 Ancient boomerangs discovered in South Australia. *Nature (London)* 253:39.

1978 Meals and menus: A study of change in prehistoric coastal settlements in South Australia. Unpublished Ph.D. thesis, Australian National University.

Luedtke, B. E.

1979 Quarrying and quantification: Estimates of lithic material demand. *Mid-Continental Journal of Archaeology* 4:255–265.

Lynch, T. F.

1974 The antiquity of Man in South America. *Quaternary Research* 4:356–377.

Mabbutt, J. A.

1971 The Australian arid zone as a prehistoric environment. *In* D. J. Mulvaney and J. Golson (eds), *Aboriginal Man and Environment in Australia*, pp. 66–79. Australian National University Press, Canberra.

McArthur, A. G.

1973 Plotting ecological change. *In* D. Dufty, G. Harman and K. Swan (eds), *Historians at Work*, pp. 27–48. Hicks Smith and Sons, Sydney.

McArthur, N.

1976 Computer simulations of small populations. *Australian Archaeology* 4:53–57.

McArthur, N., Saunders, I. W., and Tweedie, R. L.

1976 Small population isolates: A microsimulation study. *Journal of the Polynesian Society* 85:307–326.

MacArthur, R. H.

1972 *Geographical Ecology.* Harper and Row, New York.

MacArthur, R. H., and Wilson, E. O.

1967 *The Theory of Island Biogeography.* Princeton University Press, Princeton.

McBryde, I.

1974 *Aboriginal Prehistory in New England.* Sydney University Press, Sydney.

1976 Subsistence patterns in New England prehistory. *University of Queensland, Occasional Papers in Anthropology* 6:48–68.

1977 Determinants of assemblage variation in New England prehistory. *In* R. V. S. Wright (ed.), *Stone Tools as Cultural Markers: Change, Evolution, Complexity*, pp. 225–250. Australian Institute of Aboriginal Studies, Canberra.

1978a *Records of Times Past.* Australian Institute of Aboriginal Studies, Canberra.

1978b *Wil-im-ee Moor-ring:* Or, where do axes come from? *Mankind* 10:354–382.

1979 Petrology and prehistory: Lithic evidence for exploitation of stone resources and exchange systems in Australia. *Council for British Archaeology, Research Report* 23:113–126.

McBurney, C. B. M.

1967 *The Haua Fteah (Cyrenaica) and the Stone Age of the South-East Mediterranean.* Cambridge University Press, Cambridge.

MacCalman, N. R., and Grobbelaar, B. J.

1965 Preliminary report on two stone-working Ova Tjimba groups in the northern Kaokoveld of South-West Africa. *Cimbebasia* 13.

McCarthy, F. D.

1948 The Lapstone Creek excavation: Two culture periods revealed in eastern New South Wales. *Records of the Australian Museum* 22:1–34.

1964 The archaeology of the Capertee Valley, New South Wales. *Records of the Australian Museum* 26:197–246.

1977 The use of stone tools to map patterns of diffusion. *In* R. V. S. Wright (ed.), *Stone Tools as Cultural Markers: Change, Evolution, Complexity*, pp. 251–262. Australian Institute of Aboriginal Studies, Canberra.

1978 New light on the Lapstone Creek excavation. *Australian Archaeology* 8:49–60.

McCarthy, F. D., and Setzler, F. M.

1960 The archaeology of Arnhem Land. *In* C. P. Mountford (ed.), *Records of the American–Australian Scientific Expedition to Arnhem Land*, Vol. 2, pp. 215–296. Melbourne University Press, Melbourne.

McCarthy, F. D., Bramell, E., and Noone, H. V. V.

1946 The stone implements of Australia. *Memoirs of the Australian Museum* 9.

McCoy, P. C.

1979 Easter Island. *In* J. D. Jennings (ed.), *The Prehistory of Polynesia*, pp. 135–166. Harvard University Press, Cambridge.

McGuire, K. R.

1980 Cave sites, faunal analysis, and big-game hunters of the Great Basin: A caution. *Quaternary Research* 14:263–268.

Macintosh, N. W. G.

1951 Archaeology of the Tandandjal Cave, southwest Arnhem Land. *Oceania* 31:178–204.

1965 The physical aspect of man in Australia. *In* R. M. Berndt and C. H. Berndt (eds), *Aboriginal Man in Australia*, pp. 29–70. Angus and Robertson, Sydney.

1971 Analysis of an Aboriginal skeleton and a pierced tooth necklace from Lake Nitchie, Australia. *Anthropologie* 9:49–62.

Macintosh, N. W. G., and Barker, B. C. W.
1965   The osteology of Aboriginal Man in Tasmania. *Oceania Monographs* 12.

Macintosh, N. W. G., and Larnach, S.
1976   Aboriginal affinities looked at in world context. *In* R. L. Kirk and A. G. Thorne (eds), *The Origin of the Australians*, pp. 113-126. Australian Institute of Aboriginal Studies, Canberra.

McIntyre, M. L., and Hope, J. H.
1978   *Procoptodon* fossils from the Willandra Lakes, Western New South Wales. *Artefact* 3:117–132.

Macknight, C. C.
1976   *The Voyage to Marege'*. Melbourne University Press, Melbourne.

MacNeish, R.
1978   Late Pleistocene adaptations: A new look at early peopling of the New World as of 1976. *Journal of Anthropological Research* 34:475–496.

Macphail, M. K.
1975   Late Pleistocene environments in Tasmania. *Search* 6:295–300.
1979   Vegetation and climates in southern Tasmania since the last glaciation. *Quaternary Research* 11:306–341.
1980   Regeneration processes in Tasmanian forests. *Search* 11:184–190.

Macumber, P. G., and Thorne, R.
1975   The Cohuna Cranium site — A reappraisal. *Archaeology and Physical Anthropology in Oceania* 10:65–70.

Maddock, K.
1972   *The Australian Aborigines*. Allen Lane, The Penguin Press, London.

Main, A. R.
1978   Ecophysiology: Towards an understanding of Late Pleistocene marsupial extinction. *In* D. Walker and J. C. Guppy (eds), *Biology and Quaternary Environments*, pp. 169–184. Australian Academy of Science, Canberra.

Malinowski, B.
1922   *The Argonauts of the Western Pacific*. Routledge and Kegan Paul, London.

Marshall, L.
1973   Fossil vertebrate faunas from the Lake Victoria region, south west New South Wales, Australia. *Memoirs of the National Museum of Victoria* 34:151–173.

Martin, H. A.
1973   Palynology and historical ecology of some cave excavations in the Australian Nullarbor. *Australian Journal of Botany* 21:283–316.

Martin, P. S.
1967   Prehistoric overkill. *In* P. S. Martin and H. E. Wright, Jr. (eds), *Pleistocene Extinctions*, pp. 75–120. Yale University Press, New Haven.
1973   The discovery of America. *Science* 179:969–974.

Marun, L. H.
1974   The Mirning and their predecessors on the Coastal Nullarbor Plain. Unpublished Ph.D. thesis, University of Sydney.

Matthews, J. M.
1965   Stratigraphic disturbance: The human element. *Antiquity* 39:295–298.
1966   The Hoabinhian affinities of some Australian assemblages. *Archaeology and Physical Anthropology in Oceania* 1:5–22.

Maynard, L.
1979   The archaeology of Australian Aboriginal art. *In* S. M. Mead (ed.), *Exploring the Visual Art of Oceania*, pp. 83–110. University Press of Hawaii, Honolulu.
1980   A Pleistocene date from an occupation deposit in the Pilbara region, Western Australia. *Australian Archaeology* 10:3–8.

Meehan, B.
1971   The form, distribution and antiquity of Australian Aboriginal mortuary practices. Unpublished M.A. thesis, University of Sydney.
1977a Man does not live by calories alone: The role of shellfish in a coastal cuisine. *In* J. Allen, J. Golson and R. Jones (eds), *Sunda and Sahul: Prehistoric Studies in Southeast Asia, Melanesia and Australia*, pp. 493–531. Academic Press, London.
1977b Hunters by the seashore. *Journal of Human Evolution* 6:363–370.

Megaw, J. V. S.
1965   Excavations in the Royal National Park, New South Wales: A first series of radiocarbon dates from the Sydney district. *Oceania* 35:202–207.
1966   Report on excavations in the South Sydney district. *Australian Institute of Aboriginal Studies Newsletter* 2(3):4–15.
1968   A dated culture sequence for the South Sydney region of New South Wales. *Current Anthropology* 9:325–329.
1969   Captain Cook and bone barbs at Botany Bay. *Antiquity* 43:213–216.
1974   *The Recent Archaeology of the Sydney District. Excavations 1964–1967*. Australian Institute of Aboriginal Studies, Canberra.

Megaw, J. V. S., and Wright, R. V. S.
1966   The excavation of an Aboriginal rockshelter

on Gymea Bay, Port Hacking, N.S.W. *Archaeology and Physical Anthropology in Oceania* 1:23–50.

Merrilees, D.
1968 Man the destroyer: Late Quaternary changes in the Australian marsupial fauna. *Journal of the Royal Society of Western Australia* 51:1–24.
1979 The prehistoric environment in Western Australia. *Journal of the Royal Society of Western Australia* 62:109–128.

Meyer, O.
1907 Funde prähistorischer Töpferei und Steinmesser auf Vuatom, Bismarck-Archipel. *Anthropos* 4:251–252 and 1093–1095.

Milham, P., and Thompson, P.
1976 Relative antiquity of human occupation and extinct fauna at Madura Cave, southeastern Western Australia. *Mankind* 10:175–180.

Miller, T. O., Jr.
1979 Stonework of the Xêtá Indians of Brazil. *In* B. Hayden (ed.), *Lithic Use-Wear Analysis*, pp. 401–407. Academic Press, New York.

Modjeska, C. N.
1977 Production among the Duna. Unpublished Ph.D. thesis, Australian National University.

Moore, D. R.
1978 Cape York Aborigines: Fringe participants in the Torres Strait trading system. *Mankind* 11:319–325.
1979 *Islanders and Aborigines at Cape York.* Australian Institute of Aboriginal Studies, Canberra.

Moresby, J.
1876 *Discoveries and Surveys in New Guinea and the D'Entrecasteaux Islands.* John Murray, London.

Morlan, R. E.
1979 A stratigraphic framework for Pleistocene artefacts from Old Crow River, northern Yukon Territory. *In* R. L. Humphrey and D. Stanford (eds), *Pre-Llano Cultures of the Americas: Paradoxes and Possibilities*, pp. 125–145. Anthropological Society of Washington, D.C.

Morlan, V. J.
1971 The Preceramic Period of Japan: Honshu, Shikoku, and Kyushu. *Arctic Anthropology* 8:136–170.

Morren, G. E. B.
1977 From Hunting to herding: Pigs and the control of energy in montane New Guinea. *In* T. P. Bayliss-Smith and R. G. Feachem (eds), *Subsistence and Survival: Rural Ecology in the Pacific*, pp. 273–316. Academic Press, London.

Morse, K.
1981 Prehistoric Aboriginal midden deposits in south-western Australia: An appraisal of some new archaeological evidence. Unpublished B.A. (Honours) thesis, Department of Anthropology, University of Western Australia.

Morwood, M. J.
1979 Art and stone: Towards a prehistory of central western Queensland. Unpublished Ph.D. thesis, Australian National University.
1980 Time, space and prehistoric art: A principal components analysis. *Archaeology and Physical Anthropology in Oceania* 15:98–109.
1981 Archaeology of the central Queensland highlands: The stone component. *Archaeology in Oceania* 16:1–52.

Mosimann, J. E., and Martin, P. S.
1975 Simulating overkill by Paleoindians. *American Scientist* 63:304–313.

Mount, A. B.
1969 Eucalypt ecology as related to fire. *Proceedings of the Annual Tall Timbers Fire Ecology Conference* 9:75–108. Tallahassee, Florida.
1979 Natural regeneration processes in Tasmanian forests. *Search* 9:180–186.

Mountain, M.-J.
1979 The rescue of the ancestors in Papua New Guinea. *Institute of Archaeology, University of London, Bulletin* 16:63–80.
1981 Digging into yesterday. *Paradise* 27:25–29 (Air Niugini, Port Moresby).

Mulvaney, D. J.
1958 The Australian Aborigines 1606–1929: Opinion and fieldwork, Parts I and II. *Historical Studies Australia and New Zealand* 8:131–151 and 297–314.
1960 Archaeological excavations at Fromm's Landing on the lower Murray River, South Australia. *Proceedings of the Royal Society of Victoria* 72:53–85.
1961 The Stone Age of Australia. *Proceedings of the Prehistoric Society* 27:56–107.
1962a Advancing frontiers in Australian archaeology. *Oceania* 33:135–138.
1962b Archaeological excavations on the Aire River, Otway Peninsula, Victoria. *Proceedings of the Royal Society of Victoria* 75:1–15.
1964 Australian archaeology 1929–1964: Problems and policies. *Australian Journal of Science* 27:39–44.
1966a Fact, fancy and Aboriginal Australian ethnic origins. *Mankind* 6:299–305.

1966b The prehistory of the Australian Aborigine. *Scientific American* 214(3):84–93.

1969 *The Prehistory of Australia.* Thames and Hudson, London.

1971a *Discovering Man's Place in Nature.* Sydney University Press for Australian Academy of the Humanities, Sydney.

1971b Aboriginal social evolution: A retrospective view. *In* D. J. Mulvaney and J. Golson (eds), *Aboriginal Man and Environment in Australia,* pp. 368–380. Australian National University Press, Canberra.

1975 *The Prehistory of Australia,* 2nd edn. Pelican, Melbourne.

1976 "The chain of connection": The material evidence. *In* N. Peterson (ed.), *Tribes and Boundaries in Australia,* pp. 72–94. Australian Institute of Aboriginal Studies, Canberra.

1977 Classification and typology in Australia: The first 340 years. *In* R. V. S. Wright (ed.), *Stone Tools as Cultural Markers: Change, Evolution, Complexity,* pp. 263–268. Australian Institute of Aboriginal Studies, Canberra.

1978 Australian backed blade industries in perspective. Paper presented to the Indo-Pacific Prehistory Association, Poona, India, December.

1979 Blood from stones and bones. *Search* 10:214–218.

Mulvaney, D. J., and Joyce, E. B.
1965 Archaeological and geomorphological investigations on Mt. Moffatt Station, Queensland, Australia. *Proceedings of the Prehistoric Society* 31:147–212.

Mulvaney, D. J., and Soejono, R. P.
1970 The Australian–Indonesian archaeological expedition to Sulawesi. *Asian Perspectives* 13:163–178.

Mulvaney, D. J., Lawton, G. H., and Twidale, C. R.
1964 Archaeological Excavation of Rock Shelter No. 6, Fromm's Landing, South Australia. *Proceedings of the Royal Society of Victoria* 72:479–516.

Murray, P. F.
1978 Australian megamammals: Restorations of some Late Pleistocene fossil marsupials and a monotreme. *Artefact* 3:77–100.

Murray, P. F., Goede, A., and Bada, J. L.
1980 Pleistocene human occupation at Beginner's Luck Cave, Florentine Valley, Tasmania. *Archaeology and Physical Anthropology in Oceania* 15:142–152.

Murray, T., and White, J. P.
1981 Cambridge in the bush? Archaeology in Australia and New Guinea. *World Archaeology,* 13:255–263.

Newton, D.
1979 Prehistoric and Recent art styles in Papua New Guinea. *In* S. M. Mead (ed.), *Exploring the Visual Art of Oceania,* pp. 32–57. University Press of Hawaii, Honolulu.

Ninkovich, D., and Burckle, L. H.
1978 Absolute age of the base of the hominid-bearing beds in Eastern Java. *Nature (London)* 275:306–308.

Nix, H. [A.]
1981 The environment of *Terra Australis. In* A. Keast (ed.), *Ecological Biogeography in Australia,* pp. 103–134. W. Junk, The Hague.

Nix, H. A., and Kalma, J. D.
1972 Climate as a dominant control in the biogeography of northern Australia and New Guinea. *In* D. Walker (ed.), *Bridge and Barrier,* pp. 69–92. Department of Biogeography and Geomorphology, Australian National University (Publication BG/3, 1972).

Noone, H. V. V.
1943 Western Australian Stone Implements. *Records of the South Australian Museum* 7:271–280.

O'Connell, J. F.
1977 Aspects of variation in central Australian lithic assemblages. *In* R. V. S. Wright (ed.), *Stone Tools as Cultural Markers: Change, Evolution, Complexity,* pp. 267–281. Australian Institute of Aboriginal Studies, Canberra.

1981 Review of R. J. Lampert, "The Great Kartan Mystery". *Australian Archaeology* 13:97–100.

O'Connell, J. F., and Hawkes, K.
1981a Alyawara plant use and optimal foraging theory. *In* B. Winterhalder and E. A. Smith (eds), *Hunter-Gatherer Foraging Strategies: Ethnographic and Archaeological Analyses,* pp. 99–125. University of Chicago Press, Chicago.

1981b Dropping reds in the desert: Patch choice among modern Alyawara hunters. Paper presented to the American Anthropological Association, Los Angeles, December.

Oda, S., and Keally, C. T.
1973 Edge-ground stone tools from the Japanese preceramic culture. *Busshitsu Bunka [Material Culture]* 22:1–26. (Tokyo, Japan).

Ohtsuka, R.
1977 The sago eaters: An ecological discussion

with special reference to the Oriomo Papuans. *In* J. Allen, J. Golson and R. Jones (eds), *Sunda and Sahul: Prehistoric Studies in Southeast Asia, Melanesia and Australia*, pp. 465–492. Academic Press, London.

O'Neill, G.

1980   New light on the origins of Australia's flora. *Ecos* 24:3–9.

Oram, N.

1977   Environment, migration and site selection in the Port Moresby coastal area. *In* J. H. Winslow (ed.), *The Melanesian Environment*, pp. 74–99. Australian National University Press, Canberra.

1981   The history of the Motu-speaking and the Koita-speaking peoples according to their own traditions. *In* D. Denoon and R. Lacey (eds), *Oral Tradition in Melanesia*, pp. 207–230. University of Papua New Guinea, Port Moresby.

In   Pots for sago: Economic aspects of the Hiri
press   trading network. *In* T. E. Dutton (ed.), *The Hiri in History*. Australian National University Press, Canberra.

Orchiston, D. W., and Glenie, R. C.

1978   Residual Holocene populations in Bassiania: Aboriginal man at Palana, northern Flinders Island. *Australian Archaeology* 8:127–141.

Paijmans, K.

1976   Vegetation: *In* K. Paijmans (ed.), *New Guinea Vegetation*, pp. 23–105. Australian National University Press, Canberra.

Palter, J. L.

1977   Design and construction of Australian spearthrower projectiles and hand-thrown spears. *Archaeology and Physical Anthropology in Oceania* 12:161–172.

Parsons, P. A., and White, N. G.

1976   Variability of anthropometric traits in Australian Aboriginals and adjacent populations: Its bearing on the biological origin of the Australians. *In* R. L. Kirk and A. G. Thorne (eds), *The Origin of the Australians*, pp. 227–246. Australian Institute of Aboriginal Studies, Canberra.

Pearce, R. H.

1973   Uniformity of the Australian backed blade tradition. *Mankind* 9:89–95.

1974   Spatial and temporal distribution of Australian backed blades. *Mankind* 9:300–309.

1975   Reply. *Mankind* 10:46.

1977   Investigations of backed blade problems by statistical specification of distinctive features. *In* R. V. S. Wright (ed.), *Stone Tools as Cultural Markers: Change, Evolution, Complexity*, pp. 282–287. Australian Institute of Aboriginal Studies, Canberra.

Pearce, R. H., and Barbetti, M.

1981   A 38,000-year-old archaeological site at Upper Swan, Western Australia. *Archaeology in Oceania* 16:173–178.

Peterson, N.

1971   Open sites and the ethnographic approach to the archaeology of hunter-gatherers. *In* D. J. Mulvaney and J. Golson (eds), *Aboriginal Man and Environment in Australia*, pp. 239–248. Australian National University Press, Canberra.

1972   The structure of two Australian Aboriginal ecosystems. Unpublished Ph.D. thesis, University of Sydney.

1973   Camp site location amongst Australian hunter-gatherers: Archaeological and ethnographic evidence for a key determinant. *Archaeology and Physical Anthropology in Oceania* 8:173–193.

1976   The natural and cultural areas of Aboriginal Australia: A preliminary analysis of population groupings with adaptive significance. *In* N. Peterson (ed.), *Tribes and Boundaries in Australia*, pp. 50–71. Australian Institute of Aboriginal Studies, Canberra.

Pietrusewsky, M.

1973   A multivariate analysis of craniometric data from the Territory of Papua and New Guinea. *Archaeology and Physical Anthropology in Oceania* 8:12–23.

Plane, M. D.

1972   Fauna from the basal clay at Kafiavana. *Terra Australis* 2:168.

Plomley, N. J. B. (ed.)

1966   *Friendly Mission: The Tasmanian Journals and Papers of George Augustus Robinson 1829–1834*. Tasmanian Historical Research Association, Hobart.

Pöch, R.

1907a   Ausgrabungen alter topfscherben in Wanigela (Collingwood Bay). *Mitteilungen der Anthropologischen Gesellschaft in Wein* 37:137–139.

1907b   Einige bemerkenswerte Ethnologika aus Neu-Guinea. *Mitteilungen der Anthropologischen Gesellschaft in Wein* 37:57–71.

Poiner, G.

1976   The process of the year among Aborigines of the central and south coast of New South Wales. *Archaeology and Physical Anthropology in Oceania* 11:186–206.

Powell, J. [M.]

1974   A note on wooden gardening implements of the Mt. Hagen region, New Guinea. *Records of the Papua New Guinea Public Museum and Art Gallery* 4:21–28.

1976   Ethnobotany. *In* K. Paijmans (ed.), *New Guinea Vegetation*, pp. 106–183. Australian National University Press, Canberra.

1977   Plants, man and environment in the Island of New Guinea. *In* J. H. Winslow (ed.), *The Melanesian Environment*, pp. 11–20. Australian National University Press, Canberra.

1982   Plant resources and palaeobotanical evidence for plant use in the Papua New Guinea Highlands. *Archaeology in Oceania* 17:28–37.

Powell, J. M., Kulunga, A., Moge, R., Pono, C., Zimike, F., and Golson, J.

1975   Agricultural Traditions of the Mount Hagen area. *Department of Geography, University of Papua New Guinea, Occasional Paper* 12.

Pretty, G. L.

1977   The cultural chronology of the Roonka Flat. *In* R. V. S. Wright (ed.), *Stone Tools as Cultural Markers: Change, Evolution, Complexity*, pp. 288–331. Australian Institute of Aboriginal Studies, Canberra.

Pullar, E. M.

1953   The wild (feral) pigs of Australia: Their origin, distribution and economic importance. *Memoirs of the National Museum of Victoria* 18:7–24.

Ranson, D.

1978   A preliminary examination of prehistoric coastal settlement at Nelson Bay, west coast of Tasmania. *Australian Archaeology* 8:149–157.

Rathje, W.

1979   Modern material culture studies. *Advances in Archaeological Method and Theory*, 2:1–37. Academic Press, New York.

Read, K. E.

1954   Cultures of the Central Highlands, New Guinea. *Southwestern Journal of Anthropology* 10:1–43.

Reber, G.

1965   Aboriginal carbon dates from Tasmania. *Mankind* 6:264–268.

Renfrew, C.

1975   Trade as action at a distance: Questions of integration and communication. *In* J. Sabloff and C. C. Lamberg-Karlovsky (eds), *Ancient Civilization and Trade*, pp. 3–60. University of New Mexico Press, Albuquerque.

Reynolds, H.

1980   The land, the explorers and the Aborigines. *Historical Studies* 19:213–26.

Rhoads, J. W.

1980   Through a glass darkly: Present and past land-use systems of Papuan sago-palm users. Unpublished Ph.D. thesis, Australian National University.

1982   Sago palm management in Melanesia: An alternative perspective. *Archaeology in Oceania* 17:20–27.

In   Prehistoric Papuan exchange systems: The
press *hiri* and its antecedents. *In* T. Dutton (ed.), *The Hiri in History*. Australian National University Press, Canberra.

Ride, W. D. L.

1958   The edge-ground axes of south-western Australia. *Western Australian Naturalist* 6:162–170.

Riesenfeld, A.

1950   *The megalithic culture of Melanesia.* E. J. Brill, Leiden.

Robbins, R. G.

1963   Correlations of plant patterns and population migration into the Australian New Guinea Highlands. *In* J. Barrau (ed.), *Plants and the Migrations of Pacific Peoples*, pp. 45–60. Bishop Museum Press, Honolulu.

Roberts, D. F.

1978   *Climate and Human Variation.* Benjamin-Cummings, Palo Alto.

1979   Genetic evolution in an isolated population. *Journal of Anthropological Research* 35:1–17.

Rosenfeld, A.

1975   The Early Man sites: Laura 1974. *Australian Institute of Aboriginal Studies, Newsletter* 3:37–40.

Rosenfeld, A., Horton, D. R., and Winter, J. W.

1981   Art and archaeology in the Laura area, North Australia. *Terra Australis* 6.

Ross, A.

1981   Holocene environments and prehistoric site patterning in the Victorian Mallee. *Archaeology in Oceania* 16:145–154.

Ross, A., and Specht, J.

1976   An archaeological survey on Port Jackson, Sydney. *Australian Archaeology* 5:14–17.

Roth, W. E.

1904   Domestic implements, arts and manufactures. *North Queensland Ethnography Bulletin* 4. (Home Secretary's Department, Brisbane).

Rowland, M. J.

1980   The Keppel Islands — Preliminary investigations. *Australian Archaeology* 11:1–17.

Rowley, C. D.
1970   *The Destruction of Aboriginal Society.* Australian National University Press, Canberra.

Ryan, L.
1972   Outcasts in White Tasmania. *Mankind* 8:249–254.
1981   *The Aboriginal Tasmanians.* University of Queensland Press, Brisbane.

Sanders, B.
1975   Scrapers from Ingaladdi. Unpublished M.A. (Qualifying) thesis, Department of Prehistory and Anthropology, Australian National University.

Sanson, G. D.
1978   The evolution and significance of mastication in the Macropodidae. *Australian Mammalogy* 2:23–28.

Satterthwait, L. D.
1980   Aboriginal Australia: The simplest technologies? *Archaeology and Physical Anthropology in Oceania* 15:153–156.

Sauer, C. O.
1952   *Agricultural Origins and Dispersals.* M.I.T.
[1969] Press, Cambridge, Mass.

Saunders, J. J.
1980   A model for Man–mammoth relationships in Late Pleistocene North America. *Canadian Journal of Anthropology* 1:87–98.

Schiffer, M. B.
1976   *Behavioral Archaeology.* Academic Press, New York.

Schmitz, C. A.
1966   Steinerne, Schalenmörser, Pistille und Vogelfiguren aus Zentral-Neuguinea. *Baessler-Archiv* (n.f.) 14:1–60.

Schoenwetter, J.
1974   Pollen records of Guila Naquitz Cave. *American Antiquity* 39:292–303.

Schrire, C.
1972   Ethno-archaeological models and subsistence behaviour in Arnhem Land. *In* D. L. Clarke (ed.), *Models in Archaeology*, pp. 653–670. Methuen, London.
1980   An analysis of human behaviour and animal extinctions in South Africa and Australia in late Pleistocene times. *South African Archaeological Bulletin* 35:3–12.

Schrire, C., and Steiger, W. L.
1974   A matter of life and death: An investigation into the practice of female infanticide in the Arctic. *Man* (n.s.)9:161–184.

Seligmann, C. G., and Joyce, T. A.
1907   On prehistoric objects in British New Guinea. *In* W. H. R. Rivers, R. R. Marett and N. W. Thomas (eds), *Anthropological Essays presented to E. B. Tylor*, pp. 325–341. Oxford University Press, Oxford.

Shapiro, H.
1968   *The Pitcairn Islanders.* Simon and Schuster, New York.

Sharpe, C. E., and Sharpe, K. J.
1976   A preliminary survey of engraved boulders in the Art Sanctuary of Koonalda Cave, South Australia. *Mankind* 10:125–130.

Shawcross, F. W. and Kaye, M.
1980   Australian archaeology: Implications of current interdisciplinary research. *Interdisciplinary Science Reviews* 5:112–128.

Sheridan, G.
1979   Tulas and Triodia. Unpublished M.A. (Qualifying) thesis, Department of Prehistory and Anthropology, Australian National University.

Sillitoe, P.
1978   Ceremonial exchange and trade: Two contexts in which objects change hands in the Highlands of Papua New Guinea. *Mankind* 11:265–275.
1979   *Give and Take.* Australian National University Press, Canberra.

Simmons, R. T.
1976   The biological origin of Australian Aboriginals: An examination of blood group genes and gene frequencies for possible evidence in populations from Australia to Eurasia. *In* R. L. Kirk and A. G. Thorne (eds), *The Origin of the Australians*, pp. 307–328. Australian Institute of Aboriginal Studies, Canberra.

Simmons, S., and Ossa, P. P.
1978   Interim report on the Keilor Excavation, May 1978. *Records of the Victorian Archaeological Survey* 8:63–66.

Simpson, G. G.
1977   Too many lines: The limits of the Oriental and Australian zoogeographic regions. *Proceedings of the American Philosophical Society* 121:107–120.

Singh, G., Kershaw, A. P., and Clark, R.
1981   Quaternary vegetation and fire history in Australia. *In* A. M. Gill, R. H. Groves and I. R. Noble (eds), *Fire and the Australian Biota*, pp. 23–54. Australian Academy of Science, Canberra.

Smith, B.
  1960   *European Vision and the South Pacific, 1768–1850.* Clarendon Press, Oxford.
Smith, I. E. M., Ward, G. K., and Ambrose, W. R.
  1977   Geographic distribution and the characterization of volcanic glasses in Oceania. *Archaeology and Physical Anthropology in Oceania* 12:173–201.
Smith, L. R.
  1976   Aboriginal demography. Unpublished Ph.D. thesis, University of New South Wales. [Published as *The Aboriginal Population of Australia*, 1981, Australian National University Press, Canberra.]
Solheim, W. G., II.
  1979   Irian Jaya origins. *Australian Natural History* 19:324–327.
Sollas, W. J.
  1911   *Ancient Hunters and their Modern Representatives.* Macmillan, London.
Sorenson, E. R.
  1972   Socio-ecological change among the Fore of New Guinea. *Current Anthropology* 13:349–383.
  1976   *The Edge of the Forest.* Smithsonian Institution Press, Washington.
Sorenson, E. R., and Kenmore, P. E.
  1974   Proto-agricultural movement in the Eastern Highlands of New Guinea. *Current Anthropology* 15:66–73.
Souter, G.
  1963   *New Guinea: The Last Unknown.* Angus and Robertson, Sydney.
Specht, J.
  1979   Rock art in the western Pacific. *In* S. M. Mead (ed.), *Exploring the Visual Art of Oceania*, pp. 58–82. University Press of Hawaii, Honolulu.
  1980   Preliminary report on archaeological research in West New Britain Province, 1979–80. *Oral History* 8(8):1–10.
Specht, R. L.
  1970   Vegetation. *In* G. W. Leeper (ed.), *The Australian Environment*, pp. 44–67. Melbourne University Press, Melbourne.
Spencer, B.
  1904   *The Northern Tribes of Central Australia.* Macmillan, London.
Spencer, J. E.
  1963   The migration of rice from mainland Southeast Asia into Indonesia. *In* J. Barrau (ed.), *Plants and the Migrations of Pacific Peoples*, pp. 83–90. Bishop Museum Press, Honolulu.
Spriggs, M.
  1982   Taro cropping systems in the Asian–Pacific

region: Archaeological evidence. *Archaeology in Oceania* 17:7–15.
Stanner, W. E. H.
  1977   "The history of indifference thus begins". *Aboriginal History* 1:3–26.
Statham, E. J.
  1892   Observations on shell-heaps and shell-beds. *Journal of the Royal Society of New South Wales* 26:304–314.
Stewart, G. R.
  1949   *Earth Abides.* Fawcett, Greenwich, Conn.
Stocker, G. C.
  1966   Effects of fires on vegetation in the Northern Territory. *Australian Forestry* 30:223–230.
Stockton, E. D.
  1970   An archaeological survey of the Blue Mountains. *Mankind* 7:295–301.
  1971   Investigations at Santa Teresa, central Australia. *Archaeology and Physical Anthropology in Oceania* 6:44–61.
  1973   Shaw's Creek Shelter: Human displacement of artefacts and its significance. *Mankind* 9:112–117.
  1977   Review of Early Bondaian Dates. *Mankind* 11:48–51.
Stockton, E. D., and Holland, W.
  1974   Cultural sites and their environment in the Blue Mountains. *Archaeology and Physical Anthropology in Oceania* 9:36–65.
Story, R.
  1969   Vegetation of the Adelaide–Alligator area, Lands of the Adelaide–Alligator area, Northern Territory. *CSIRO Land Research Series*, 25:109–134.
  1976   Vegetation of the Alligator Rivers area, Lands of the Alligator Rivers area, Northern Territory. *CSIRO Land Research Series* 38:89–111.
Strathern, M.
  1969   Stone axes and flake tools: Evaluations from two New Guinea highlands societies. *Proceedings of the Prehistoric Society* 35:311–329.
Stringer, C. B.
  1978   Some problems in Middle and Upper Pleistocene hominid relationships. *In* D. J. Chivers and K. A. Joysey (eds), *Recent Advances in Primatology*, Vol. 3, *Evolution*, pp. 395–418. Academic Press, London.
Sullivan, H.
  1977   Aboriginal gatherings in south-east Queensland. Unpublished B.A. (Honours) thesis, Department of Prehistory and Anthropology, Australian National University.

Sullivan, M. E.
  1975   An archaeological survey of Montagu Is-
          land. *Australian Archaeology* 2:37–43.
  1976   Archaeological occupation site locations on
          the south coast of New South Wales.
          *Archaeology and Physical Anthropology in
          Oceania* 11:56–69.
  1981   Ninety years later: A re-survey of shell
          middens on Wagonga Inlet and Pambula
          Lake, New South Wales. *Archaeology in
          Oceania* 16:81–86.
Sutherland, F. L.
  1972   The classification, distribution, analysis and
          sources of materials in flaked stone imple-
          ments of Tasmanian Aborigines. *Records of
          the Queen Victoria Museum, Launceston* 42.
Swadling, P. L.
  1973   *The Human Settlement of the Arona Valley,
          Eastern Highlands District, Papua New
          Guinea.* Papua New Guinea Electricity
          Commission, Boroko.
  1976   Changes induced by human exploitation in
          prehistoric shellfish populations. *Mankind*
          10:156–162.
  1977   Central Province shellfish resources and
          their utilisation in the prehistoric past of
          Papua New Guinea. *Veliger* 19:293–302.
Swadling, P., Aitsi, L., Trompf, G., and Kari, M.
  1977   Beyond the early oral traditions of the
          Austronesian speaking people of the Gulf
          and Western Central Provinces. *Oral His-
          tory* 5(1):50–80.
  1980   Decorative features and sources of selected
          potsherds from archaeological sites in the
          Gulf and Central Provinces. *Oral History*
          8(8):101–125.
Tatz, C.
  1980   Aboriginality as civilization. *Australian
          Quarterly* 52:352–362.
Taylor, G.
  1950   Migrations of the Tasmanians. *Mankind*
          4:145–147.
Tedford, R. H.
  1967   The Fossil Macropodidae from Lake Menin-
          dee, New South Wales. *University of Cali-
          fornia, Publications in Geological Sciences*
          64.
Terrell, J., and Fagan, J.
  1975   The savage and the innocent: Sophisticated
          techniques and naive theory in the study of
          human population genetics in Melanesia.
          Yearbook of Physical Anthropology 19:
          2–18.
Thompson, J. P.
  1892   *British New Guinea.* George Philip, London.

Thomson, D. F.
  1933   The hero cult, initiation and totemism on
          Cape York. *Journal of the Royal Anthro-
          pological Institute* 63:453–537.
  1934   Notes on a hero cult from the Gulf of
          Carpentaria, North Queensland. *Journal of
          the Royal Anthropological Institute*
          64:217–235.
  1939   The seasonal factor in human culture,
          illustrated from the life of a contemporary
          nomadic group. *Proceedings of the Pre-
          historic Society* 5:209–221.
  1949   Arnhem Land: Explorations among an
          unknown people. *Geographical Journal*
          53:1–8 and 54:53–67.
  1964   Some wood and stone implements of the
          Bindibu tribe of Central Western Australia.
          Proceedings of the Prehistoric Society
          30:400–422.
Thorne, A. G.
  1971   Mungo and Kow Swamp: Morphological
          variation in Pleistocene Australians. *Man-
          kind* 8:85–89.
  1976   Morphological contrasts in Pleistocene Aus-
          tralians. *In* R. L. Kirk and A. G. Thorne (eds),
          The Origin of the Australians, pp. 95–112.
          Australian Institute of Aboriginal Studies,
          Canberra.
  1977   Separation or reconciliation? Biological
          clues to the development of Australian
          society. *In* J. Allen, J. Golson and R. Jones
          (eds), *Sunda and Sahul: Prehistoric Studies
          in Southeast Asia, Melanesia and Australia*,
          pp. 187–204. Academic Press, London.
  1980   The longest link: Human evolution in
          Southeast Asia. *In* J. J. Fox, R. G. Garnaut, P.
          J. McCawley and J. A. C. Mackie (eds),
          Indonesia: Australian Perspectives, pp.
          35–43. Research School of Pacific Studies,
          Australian National University.
Thorne, A. G., and Macumber, P. G.
  1972   Discoveries of late Pleistocene Man at Kow
          Swamp, Australia. *Nature (London)*
          238:316–319.
Thorne, A. G., and Wilson, S. R.
  1977   Pleistocene and Recent Australians: A
          multivariate comparison. *Journal of Human
          Evolution* 6:393–402.
Thorne, A. G., and Wolpoff, M. H.
  1981   Regional continuity in Australasian Pleis-
          tocene Hominid evolution. *American Jour-
          nal of Physical Anthropology* 55:337–341.
Thorpe, W. W.
  1932   Ethnological notes, No. 4. *Records of the
          Australian Museum* 18:302–311.

Tichelman, G. L.

1963 Ethnographical bronze objects from the Lake Sentani district. *6eme Congrès International des Sciences Préhistorique et Protohistorique*, Vol. 2, Part 1, pp. 645–651. Musée de l'Homme, Paris.

Tindale, N. B.

1937 Relationship of the extinct Kangaroo Island culture with cultures of Australia, Tasmania and Malaya. *Records of the South Australian Museum* 6:39–60.

1957 Culture succession in south-eastern Australia from Late Pleistocene to the present. *Records of the South Australian Museum* 13:1–52.

1959 The ecology of primitive man in Australia. *In* A. L. Keast, R. L. Crocker and C. S. Christian (eds), *Biogeography and Ecology in Australia*, pp. 36–51. W. Junk, The Hague.

1961 Archaeological excavation of Noola rock shelter: A preliminary report. *Records of the South Australian Museum* 14:193–196.

1963 Preface. *In* J. Greenway, *Bibliography of the Australian Aborigines, and the Native Peoples of Torres Strait to 1959*. Angus and Robertson, Sydney.

1965 Stone implement making among the Nakako, Ngadadjara and Pitjandjara of the Great Western Desert. *Records of the South Australian Museum* 15:131–164.

1968 Nomenclature of archaeological cultures and associated implements in Australia. *Records of the South Australian Museum* 15:615–640.

1977a Further report on the Kaiadilt people of Bentinck Island, Gulf of Carpentaria, Queensland. *In* J. Allen, J. Golson and R. Jones (eds), *Sunda and Sahul: Prehistoric Studies in Southeast Asia, Melanesia and Australia*, pp. 247–273. Academic Press, London.

1977b Adaptive Significance of the Panara or grass seed culture of Australia. *In* R. V. S. Wright (ed.), *Stone Tools as Cultural Markers: Change, Evolution, Complexity*, pp. 345–349. Australian Institute of Aboriginal Studies, Canberra.

Tuohy, D. L., and Randall, D. R.

1979 The archaeology of Smith Creek Canyon, eastern Nevada. *Nevada State Museum, Anthropological Papers* 17.

Tyndale-Biscoe, H.

1973 *Life of Marsupials*. Edward Arnold, London.

Underwood, A. J.

1979 The ecology of intertidal gastropods. *Advances in Marine Biology*, 16:111–210. Academic Press, London.

Urquhart, A.

1978 A critique of some faunal analytical methods used in an examination of fish remains from NSW coastal Aboriginal middens. Unpublished B.A. (Honours) thesis, Department of Anthropology, University of Sydney.

van Balgooy, M. M. J.

1976 Phytogeography. *In* K. Paijmans (ed.), *New Guinea Vegetation*, pp. 1–22. Australian National University Press, Canberra.

Vanderwal, R. L.

1973 Prehistoric studies in central coastal Papua. Unpublished Ph.D. thesis, Australian National University.

1977 The "fabricator" in Australia and New Guinea. *In* R. V. S. Wright (ed.), *Stone Tools as Cultural Markers: Change, Evolution, Complexity*, pp. 350–353. Australian Institute of Aboriginal Studies, Canberra.

1978a Adaptive technology in southwest Tasmania. *Australian Archaeology* 8:107–126.

1978b Exchange in prehistoric coastal Papua. *Mankind* 11:416–428.

van Heekeren, H. R.

1972 The Stone Age of Indonesia, 2nd edition. *Verhandeligen van het Koninklijk Instituut voor Taal-, Land- en Volkenkunde* 61.

Virili, F. L.

1977 Aboriginal sites and rock art of the Dampier Archipelago, Western Australia: A preliminary report. *In* P. J. Ucko (ed.), *Form in Indigenous Art*, pp. 439–451. Australian Institute of Aboriginal Studies, Canberra.

Volman, T. P.

1978 Early archaeological evidence for shellfish collecting. *Science* 201:911–913.

Walker, D. (ed.)

1972 *Bridge and Barrier: The Natural and Cultural History of Torres Strait*. Department of Biogeography and Geomorphology, Australian National University (Publication BG/3, 1972).

Walker, D., and Flenley, J. R.

1979 Late Quaternary vegetational history of the Enga Province of upland Papua New Guinea. *Philosophical Transactions of the Royal Society of London*, series B, 286:265–344.

Wallace, A. G., and Doran, G. A.

1976 Early Man in Tasmania: New skeletal evidence. *In* R. L. Kirk and A. G. Thorne (eds), *The Origin of the Australians*, pp. 173–182. Australian Institute of Aboriginal Studies, Canberra.

Wallace, A. R.
1860 On the zoological geography of the Malay Archipelago. *Zoological Journal of the Linnean Society, London* 4:172–184.

1869 *The Malay Archipelago: The Land of the Orang-utan and the Bird of Paradise.* 2 vols. Macmillan, London.

Walters, I. N.
1980 Vertebrate remains from two sites on Moreton Island, Queensland. *Australian Archaeology* 11:28–32.

Watson, J. B.
1964 New Guinea: The central highlands. *American Anthropologist* 66(4), Part 2.

1965a From hunting to horticulture in the New Guinea Highlands. *Ethnology* 4:295–309.

1965b The significance of a recent ecological change in the Central Highlands of New Guinea. *Journal of the Polynesian Society* 74:438–450.

1967 Horticultural traditions of the Eastern New Guinea Highlands. *Oceania* 38:81–98.

1977 Pigs, fodder and the Jones Effect in post-ipomoean New Guinea. *Ethnology* 16:57–70.

Watson, V. [D.]
1955 Pottery in the Eastern Highlands of New Guinea. *Southwestern Journal of Anthropology* 11:121–128.

1979 New Guinea Prehistory: A model of regional comparison. *Archaeology and Physical Anthropology in Oceania* 14: 83–98.

Watson, V. D., and Cole, J. D.
1977 *Prehistory of the Eastern Highlands of New Guinea.* University of Washington Press, Seattle.

Webb, L. J.
1968 Environmental relationships of the structural types of Australian rainforest vegetation. *Ecology* 49:296–311.

Webby, E.
1980 The Aboriginal in early Australian literature. *Southerly* 40(1): 45–63.

Webster, P. J., and Streten, N. A.
1978 Late Quaternary Ice Age climates of tropical Australasia: Interpretations and reconstructions. *Quaternary Research* 10:279–309.

Weiner, A.
1976 *Women of Value, Men of Renown.* University of Queensland Press, Brisbane.

Wells, R. T.
1978 Fossil mammals in the reconstruction of Quaternary environments with examples from the Australian fauna. *In* D. Walker and J. C. Guppy (eds), *Biology and Quaternary Environments*, pp. 103–124. Australian Academy of Science, Canberra.

Wendorf, F.
1968 Site 117: A Nubian Final Paleolithic graveyard near Jebel Sahaba, Sudan. *In* F. Wendorf (ed.), *The Prehistory of Nubia*, vol. 2, pp. 954–995. Southern Methodist University Press, Dallas.

White, C.
1967 Plateau and plain. Unpublished Ph.D. thesis, Australian National University.

1971 Man and environment in northwest Arnhem Land. *In* D. J. Mulvaney and J. Golson (eds), *Aboriginal Man and Environment in Australia*, pp. 141–157. Australian National University Press, Canberra.

White, C., and Peterson, N.
1969 Ethnographic interpretations of the prehistory of western Arnhem Land. *Southwestern Journal of Anthropology* 25:45–67.

White, I. M.
1972 Hunting dogs at Yalata. *Mankind* 8:201–205.

White, J. P.
1967a Taim bilong bipo: Investigations towards a prehistory of the Papua New Guinea Highlands. Unpublished Ph.D. thesis, Australian National University.

1967b Ethnoarchaeology in New Guinea: Two examples. *Mankind* 6:409–414.

1968a Ston naip bilong tumbuna. *In* De. de Sonneville-Bordes (ed.), *La Préhistoire: Problèmes et tendances*, pp. 511–516. Centre National de la Recherche Scientifique, Paris.

1968b Fabricators, outils écaillés or scalar cores? *Mankind* 6:658–666.

1969 Typologies for some prehistoric flaked stone artefacts of the Australian New Guinea highlands. *Archaeology and Physical Anthropology in Oceania* 4:18–46.

1971 New Guinea and Australian prehistory: The "Neolithic Problem". *In* D. J. Mulvaney and J. Golson (eds), *Aboriginal Man and Environment in Australia*, pp. 182–195. Australian National University Press, Canberra.

1972 Ol Tumbuna: Archaeological excavations in the Eastern Central Highlands, Papua New Guinea. *Terra Australis* 2.

1973 Archaeological sites in the Lake Kopiago region. Manuscript on file with Papua New Guinea Archaeological Survey.

1977a *Axes and aré: Stone tools of the Duna.* Extension Media Center, University of California, Berkeley.

1977b Crude, colourless and unenterprising? Prehistorians and their views on the stone age of Sunda and Sahul. *In* J. Allen, J. Golson and R. Jones (eds), *Sunda and Sahul: Prehistoric Studies in Southeast Asia, Melanesia and Australia*, pp. 13–30. Academic Press, London.

1977c *The Christensen Axe Collection.* Department of Prehistory, Australian National University, Canberra.

1981 Review of R. J. Lampert, "The Great Kartan Mystery". *Quarterly Review of Archaeology* 2(4):1–2.

In Notes on some stone tools from Passis-
press manua, New Britain. *Indo-Pacific Prehistory Association Bulletin.*

White, J. P., and Allen, J.
1980 Melanesian prehistory: Some recent advances. *Science* 207:728–734.

White, J. P., and Dibble, H.
In Inter- and intra-group variation in stone
press tools. *In* P. Callow and G. Bailey (eds), *Festschrift for C.B.M. McBurney* (title to be announced).

White, J. P., and Modjeska, N.
1978a Where do all the stone tools go? *In* I. Hodder (ed.), *The Spatial Organization of Culture,* pp. 25–38. Duckworth, London.

1978b Acquirers, users, finders, losers: The use axe blades make of the Duna. *Mankind* 11:276–287.

White, J. P., and O'Connell, J. F.
1979 Australian prehistory: New aspects of antiquity. *Science* 203:21–28.

White, J. P., and Thomas, D. H.
1972 What mean these stones? Ethnotaxonomic models and archaeological interpretations in the New Guinea Highlands. *In* D. L. Clarke (ed.), *Models in Archaeology,* pp. 275–308. Methuen, London.

White, J. P., and White, C.
1964 Rock art in Papua New Guinea. *Illustrated London News* 245(6537):775–777.

White, J. P., Crook, K. A. W., and Ruxton, B. P.
1970a Kosipe: A late Pleistocene site in the Papuan Highlands. *Proceedings of the Prehistoric Society* 36:152–170.

White, J. P., Disney, H. J. de S., and Yaldwyn, J. C.
1970b Prehistoric Papuan engraving. *Australian Natural History* 16:344–345.

White J. P., Modjeska, N., and Hipuya, Irari
1977 Group definitions and mental templates: An ethnographic experiment. *In* R. V. S. Wright (ed.), *Stone Tools as Cultural Markers: Change, Evolution, Complexity,* pp. 380–

390. Australian Institute of Aboriginal Studies, Canberra.

White, J. P., Downie, J. E., and Ambrose, W. R.
1978 Mid-recent human occupation and resource exploitation in the Bismarck Archipelago. *Science* 199:877–879.

White, N. G.
1976 A preliminary account of the correspondence among genetic, linguistic, social and topographic divisions in Arnhem Land, Australia. *Mankind* 10:240–247.

Wieneke, C., and White, J. P.
1973 Backed blades: Another view. *Mankind* 9:35–38.

Williams, E.
1979 A fishy tale: "Anomalous" cases of storage, sedentism and environmental manipulation. Unpublished B.A. (Honours) thesis, Department of Anthropology, University of Sydney.

Williams, P. W., McDougall, I., and Powell, J. M.
1972 Aspects of the Quaternary geology of the Tari-Koroba area, Papua. *Journal of the Geological Society of Australia* 18:333–347.

Winterhalder, B.
1981 Optimal foraging strategies and hunter-gatherer research in anthropology: Theories and models. *In* B. Winterhalder and E. A. Smith (eds), *Hunter-Gatherer Foraging Strategies: Ethnographic and Archaeological Analyses,* pp. 13–35. University of Chicago Press, Chicago.

Witter, D. C.
1978 Late Pleistocene extinctions: A global perspective. *Artefact* 3:51–66.

Witter, D. C., and Simmons, S.
1978 Interim report on excavations at the Keilor archaeological area, November 1977 and January 1978. *Records of the Victorian Archaeological Survey* 8:34–62.

Wolpoff, M. H.
1980 *Paleoanthropology.* A. A. Knopf, New York.

Wright, R. V. S.
1971a *The Archaeology of the Gallus Site, Koonalda Cave.* Australian Institute of Aboriginal Studies, Canberra.

1971b Prehistory in the Cape York Peninsula. *In* D. J. Mulvaney and J. Golson (eds), *Aboriginal Man and Environment in Australia,* pp. 133–140. Australian National University Press, Canberra.

1974 Significance tests and archaeological importance. *Mankind* 9:169–174.

1976 Evolutionary process and semantics: Australian prehistoric tooth size as a local adjustment. *In* R. L. Kirk and A. G. Thorne (eds), *The Origin of the Australians*, pp. 265–274. Australian Institute of Aboriginal Studies, Canberra.

1977   Introduction and two studies. *In* R. V. S. Wright (ed.), *Stone Tools as Cultural Markers: Change, Evolution, Complexity*, pp. 1–4. Australian Institute of Aboriginal Studies, Canberra.

Wurm, S. A.
1964   Australian New Guinea Highlands languages and the distribution of their typological features. *American Anthropologist* 66(4), Part 2: 77–97.

Wyrwoll, K.-H., and Dortch, C.
1978   Stone artifacts and an associated Diproto-dontid mandible from the Greenough River, Western Australia. *Search* 9:411–413.

Yen, D. E.
1974   The Sweet Potato and Oceania. *Bernice P. Bishop Museum, Bulletin* 236.

1977   Hoabinhian horticulture: The evidence and the questions from northwest Thailand. *In* J. Allen, J. Golson and R. Jones (eds), *Sunda and Sahul: Prehistoric Studies in Southeast Asia, Melanesia and Australia*, pp. 567–600. Academic Press, London.

Yen, D. E., and Wheeler, J. M.
1968   Introduction of taro into the Pacific: The indications of the chromosome numbers. *Ethnology* 7:259–267.

Index of Names

A

Abbie, A. A., 77
Adamson, D. A., 16
Adovasio, J. M., 53, 217
Agogino, G. A., 173
Aikens, C. M., 216
Aiston, G., 84, 87
Akerman, K., 44, 86
Aldiss, B. W., 158, 170
Allchin, B., 121, 218, 219
Allen, H., 19, 20, 33, 35, 39, 59, 70, 78, 100, 118, 119, 121, 142, 159
Allen, J., 19, 30, 68, 84, 86, 175, 197–208
Ambrose, W., 189, 202, 206
Anderson, J. R., 39, 40
Anderson, R. H., 14
Anon., 16, 184, 188
Aplin, K., 176
Arabanoo, 17
Archer, M., 40, 90, 91, 217
Argyll, Duke of, 158
Arndt, W., 2
Attenbrow, V., 109

B

Bailey, G. N., 24, 154, 155, 156
Baldwin, J. A., 19
Balfour, H., 163

Balme, J., 40, 41, 50, 52, 91, 217, 223
Banks, J., 17, 145
Barbetti, M., 105, 221
Barker, B. C. W., 81
Barker, G., 20
Barrau, J., 191
Bartstra, G. J., 45
Bates, D., 84
Baudin, N., 157
Bayliss-Smith, T., 183
Beaglehole, J. C., 17, 19
Beaton, J. M., 64, 100, 104, 217
Behrensmeyer, K., 79
Bellwood, P., 48, 184, 191, 192
Belshaw, C. S., 153
Bern, J. E., 20
Berndt, C. H., 18
Berndt, R. M., 18
Beveridge, W., 141
Bickford, A., 141
Binford, L. R., 2, 40, 88, 124
Binford, S. R., 124
Binns, R. A., 129, 130
Birdsell, J. B., 19, 45, 46, 48, 50, 54, 75–77, 82, 100
Birmingham, J., 121
Bischoff, J. L., 216
Black, S., 47
Blackwood, B., 80, 191
Blainey, G., 30, 39, 98
Blurton Jones, N., 47, 50
Boaz, N. T., 43

Bodmer, W. F., 75, 76, 83
Bordes, F., 42, 106
Bosler, W., 40
Bowdler, S. E., 21, 50, 51–53, 64, 70, 92, 104, 117, 134, 147–148, 157, 159, 162, 166, 214, 215, 232
Bowler, J., 15, 16, 33, 34, 35–37, 39, 40, 42, 49, 54–55, 65–66, 78, 99, 157, 175, 214
Bramell, E., 28
Branagan, D. F., 85
Brand, D. D., 183
Bray, W., 216
Brennan, P., 190
Brew, J. O., 85
Bridges, E. L., 232
Bronstein, N., 85
Brookfield, H. C., 6, 12, 13, 16, 19, 94, 170, 174, 183–185, 196
Brothwell, D., 80
Brown, A. R., 29, 56
Brown, Paula, 18, 175
Brown, Peter, 223, 224
Brown, T., 75
Brown, T. A., 85
Bulmer, R. [N. H.], 30, 57, 186, 190, 191, 192
Bulmer, S. [E.], 30, 57, 65, 67, 68, 175–176, 187, 189–192, 199, 200–203, 205, 206
Burckle, L. H., 43
Burridge, K. O., 18, 215

Bush, T., 194
Byrne, D., 65, 85

C

Calaby, J., 88, 93, 95
Calder, J. E., 227
Callaghan, M., 99
Campbell, T. D., 106
Campbell, V., 154
Cane, S., 230
Carnahan, J. A., 12, 13, 15
Carr, E. H., 2
Casey, D. A., 30
Cavalli-Sforza, L. L., 75, 76, 83
Chappell, J. [M. A.], 15, 45, 49,
    55, 99, 190, 191
Charoenwongsa, P., 184
Chase, A., 217
Chowning, A., 18
Christensen, O. A., 68, 69, 175,
    176, 185, 189
Christie, M. F., 17
Clark, J., 231
Clark, J. D., 218, 219
Clark, J. G. D., 83, 218, 219
Clark, M., 229, 232
Clark, P., 105
Clark, R. L., 14, 42
Clarke, D. L., 2
Clay, R. B., 173
Clegg, J., 214
CLIMAP Project Members, 35
Cobern, P., 227–235 passim
Cody, M., 46
Cohen, M. N., 218
Cole, J. D., 56, 84, 175–176,
    185–186, 189, 190, 197
Coleman, E., 166
Coleman, J., 99, 151, 157
Colinvaux, P., 46
Collingwood, R. G., 30
Collins, D., 148
Conkey, M. W., 100, 218
Connah, G. 99, 154, 157
Cook, J., 17, 19
Corruccini, R. S., 77
Coutts, P. J. F., 40, 138, 139, 140,
    141, 176, 190
Cowlishaw, G. K., 47
Craig, B., 84
Crain, M., 18, 21
Crawford, M. H., 76
Croll, P., 106
Crosby, E., 68

Curtain, C. C., 76

D

Dampier, W., 17
Danby, P. M., 80
Daniel, G. E., 22, 83
David, T. W. E., 23
Davidson, D. S., 29, 124
Davidson, I., 51
Davidson, J. M., 183
Davies, J. L., 12
Deevey, E. S., 54
Deiley, R., 79
Diamond, J. M., 46, 159
Dibble, D. S., 217
Dibble, H., 175
Dickson, F. P., 67, 68, 86, 121,
    123, 125, 128–129, 219
Dincauze, D. F., 53, 216
Dixon, R. M. W., 219
Djohadze, V., 99, 117, 143, 147,
    157
Donovan, H. L., 100
Doran, G. A., 81
Dortch, C. E., 40, 42, 59, 61, 62,
    71, 91, 106, 112, 115, 117, 118,
    157, 219
Downie, J. E., 188
Draper, N., 135, 136
Dun, J. W., 25
Dury, C. H., 36

E

Easterlin, R. A., 46
Edwards, R., 71, 214
Edwards, W. E., 95
Egloff, B. J., 173, 206, 209, 210,
    211
Elkin, A. P., 29, 86, 87
Ellen, R. F., 173
Etheridge, R. Jr., 23, 24, 25, 28,
    120, 128, 195
Evans, R., 17
Eyre, E. J., 23

F

Fagan, J., 82
Feil, D. K., 21
Fenner, F., 82
Ferguson, W. C., 61

Fison, L., 23
Fitzhardinge, L. F., 17
Fladmark, K., 53, 216
Flenley, J. M., 175, 218
Flood, J. M., 50, 64, 65, 66, 84, 91,
    104, 118, 121, 123
Freedman, L., 82, 177, 219, 223
Friedlaender, J. S., 82
Fox, M. D., 16

G

Gajdusek, D. C., 49
Gallagher, J. P., 87
Gallus, A., 40, 49
Gaughwin, D., 166, 168
Geyl, P., 2
Giles, E., 76, 81, 82
Gill, A. M., 14, 93, 217
Gill, E. D., 29, 39, 49
Gillen, F. J., 23
Gillespie, R., 16, 90, 94, 119, 143,
    154
Glenie, R. C., 158
Glover, E., 45, 151
Glover, I. [C.], 43, 45, 84, 106,
    116, 121, 173, 188
Glover, J. E., 61, 85
Goede, A., 91, 157
Golding, W., 158
Gollan, K., 104, 214
Golson, J., 14, 30, 42, 67–68, 71,
    177, 178, 179, 180–181,
    183–184
Gorecki, P. P., 181, 182
Gorman, C. [F.], 184
Gorter, J. D., 90
Gould, R. A., 29, 30, 65–66, 70,
    85, 87–88, 106, 117, 120, 121,
    123, 131, 215
Grayson, D. K., 89, 151, 161, 217
Green, R. C., 202
Gregg, D. R., 230
Griffin, G. F., 15, 93
Grobbelaar, B. J., 87
Groube, L. M., 197
Gruhn, R., 217
Guiglielmino-Matessi, C. R., 82

H

Hale, H. M., 26, 27, 28, 84, 106,
    120, 124

Hallam, S., 15, 53, 55, 93, 94, 123, 125, 216–217
Hallpike, C. R., 20
Hamilton, A., 103, 104, 214, 215
Harding, T. G., 19
Harlan, J. R., 184
Harris, D. R., 19, 20, 133, 217
Harris, E. C., 177, 178, 180
Harris, M., 83, 218
Hart, D., 6, 12, 13, 16, 19, 94, 174, 183, 184, 185, 196
Hassan, F., 105
Haury, E. W., 217
Hawkes, K., 71, 93, 95
Hayden, B., 47, 63, 65, 66, 67, 85, 87, 88, 104, 131, 169, 170, 214, 218
Haynes, C. V., 217
Heider, K., 187
Heizer, R. F., 217
Hiatt, B., 168
Higuchi, T., 216
Hiscock, P., 87, 105, 112
Hodder, I., 100
Holland, R. C., 44
Holland, W., 64
Hollows, F., 234
Hooijer, D. A., 45
Hope, G. S., 15, 59, 173, 175, 176, 218
Hope, J. H., 15, 35, 59, 89, 90, 91, 173, 176, 218
Horn, H. S., 46
Horne, G., 84, 87
Horton, D. R., 22, 28, 40, 84, 90, 92, 94, 103, 124, 159, 168, 169, 170, 222, 223
Hossfeld, P: S., 82
Howe, K. R., 18
Howell, N., 47
Howells, W. W., 49, 76, 77, 82
Howitt, A. W., 14, 23
Hughes, D. R., 75, 76
Hughes, I. M., 18, 19, 20, 21, 189, 190
Hughes, P. J., 42, 85, 99, 105, 112, 117, 120, 143, 147, 157, 177, 178, 180, 181. 222
Hunter, G., 17
Hynes, R. A., 217

I

Ikawa-Smith, F., 67, 215, 218
Imbrie, J., 15

Imbrie, K. P., 15
Irwin, G. J., 19, 86, 184, 198, 199, 200–206, 208–210
Isaac, G. L., 72, 83, 86, 121, 218

J

Jacob, T., 43
Jeans, D. N., 6
Jennings, J. D., 217
Johnson, D. L., 43
Johnson, I., 64, 104, 106, 117, 120
Jones, R. M., 15, 18, 22, 23, 36, 42, 44, 50, 56, 65, 66, 70, 79, 84, 85, 86, 90, 92, 93, 94, 98, 99, 104, 105, 117, 124, 133, 157, 158, 159, 160, 161, 162, 163, 166, 167, 168, 169, 170, 214, 215, 217, 222
Joyce, E. B., 39, 40, 50, 64, 66, 84, 106, 117, 118, 120, 125, 133, 223
Joyce, T. A., 30, 195

K

Kaiku, R., 173
Kalma, J. D., 15, 49, 52, 218
Kamminga, J., 59, 65, 66, 70, 85, 86, 106, 116, 118, 119, 121, 123, 131, 142, 147, 219
Kaye, M., 33
Keally, C. T., 67
Keast, A. L., 6, 14
Keeley, L. H., 85
Kefous, K., 35, 36, 223
Kenmore, P. E., 175
Kennedy, E., 28
Kennedy, G., 48
Kenyon, A. S., 138
Key, C. A., 189, 190
Kimber, R. G., 217
King, T. F., 214
Kirch, P. V., 183
Kirk, R. L., 75, 76, 77, 81, 82, 219
Klein, R. G., 53, 92, 94, 95
Koettig, M., 19
Kolig, E., 214
Krebs, C. J., 47
Kroeber, A. L., 100

L

Labillardiere, J., 230, 231
Ladd, P. G., 94
Lampert, R. J., 63, 64, 65, 66, 68, 69, 84, 85, 105, 120, 123, 124, 125, 136, 143, 144, 145, 146, 147, 148, 149, 150, 152, 157, 173, 177, 190, 222
Langford-Smith, T., 36
Larnach, S. L., 78
Latz, P. K., 15, 93
Lawrence, R., 18
Lawton, H. W., 217
Leahy, M., 18, 21
Leask, M. F., 30
Lee, R. B., 100, 133
Lewis, D., 215
Lewis, H. T., 217
Lightning Brothers, 2
Lilley, I. A., 136, 137
Little, M. A., 170
Lofgren, M., 219, 223
Long, A., 199
Lorblanchet, M., 65, 66, 84, 86, 117, 154, 222
Lorrain, D., 217
Lourandos, H., 19, 20, 52, 102, 105, 124, 137, 138, 140, 159, 168, 169, 170, 217
Lubbock, J., 23, 158
Luebbers, R. A., 99, 102, 124, 137, 138, 154, 168, 170
Luedtke, B., 88
Lyell, C., 2
Lynch, T. F., 53

M

Mabbutt, J. A., 15
McArthur, A. G., 14
McArthur, N., 47
MacArthur, R. H., 46
McBryde, I., 18, 29, 64, 67, 100, 102, 104, 120, 121, 124, 125, 129, 130, 131, 132, 151, 153
McBurney, C. B. M., 43
MacCalman, N. R., 87
McCarthy, F. D., 22, 23, 28, 66, 70, 106, 112, 116, 117, 121, 125, 128, 131, 156
McCoy, P. C., 183
McGuire, K. R., 217
Macintosh, N. W. G., 29, 77, 78, 81, 214

McIntyre, M. L., 35, 90
Macknight, C. C., 18
MacNeish, R., 53, 216
Macphail, M. K., 99, 157, 166
Macumber, P. G., 78
Maddock, K., 18
Main, A. R., 95
Malinowski, B., 19
Marshall, L., 90
Martin, H., 62
Martin, P. S., 53, 54, 92, 95
Marun, L. H., 50, 62
Mathew, R. H., 23
Matthews, J. M., 69, 70, 117
Maynard, L., 50, 71, 104, 194, 214, 223
Meehan, B., 39, 100, 103, 133, 156
Megaw, J. V. S., 70, 85, 117, 125, 136, 145, 150, 151
Menzies, J. L., 57
Merrilees, D., 40, 54, 89, 90, 92
Meyer, O., 30
Milham, P., 16, 91, 104
Miller, T. O., 87
Modjeska, C. N., 20, 21, 87, 103, 129, 181, 183, 190
Moore, D. R., 19, 20
Moresby, J., 19
Morgan, L. H., 83
Morlan, R. E., 53
Morlan, V., 216
Morren, G. E. B., 170, 183, 189
Morse, K., 157
Morwood, M. J., 64, 84, 100, 103, 104, 117, 120, 121, 125, 194, 214
Mosimann, J. E., 92
Mount, A. B., 14
Mountain, M. J. 57, 59, 91
Mulvaney, D. J., 18, 20, 22, 23, 24, 28, 29, 30, 50, 54, 64, 65, 66, 71, 72, 78, 83, 84, 86, 104, 106, 117, 118, 120, 121, 122, 123, 124, 125, 131, 133, 223
Mumford, W., 58, 69
Murray, P. F., 64, 89, 91, 94, 157, 167
Murray, T., 22, 29

N

Newton, D., 190, 191, 192
Ninkovich, D., 43

Nix, H. [A.], 11, 15, 49, 52, 218
Noone, H. V. V., 28, 106, 125

O

O'Connell, J. F., 30, 71, 85, 93, 95, 124, 131, 215, 222
Oda, S., 67
Ohtsuka, R., 19
O'Neill, G., 12
Oram, N., 196, 198, 207, 208
Orchiston, D. W., 158
Orth, D. A., 233
Ossa, P., 40

P

Paijmans, K., 12, 195
Palter, J. L., 124
Parsons, P. A., 77
Pearce, R. H., 84, 106, 121, 221
Perkins, C., 233
Peron, L., 230
Peterson, N., 100, 101, 102, 124, 133, 141, 142, 156
Philip, A., 17, 22
Pietrusewsky, M., 82
Plane, M. D., 91
Plomley, N. J. B., 17, 87, 168
Pöch, R., 30, 195, 209
Poiner, G., 52, 100, 134, 135, 136, 137, 143, 148
Powell, J. M., 177, 181, 184, 185, 195
Pretty, G. L., 16, 78, 103, 214
Prince, G. R., 219
Pullar, E. M., 188

R

Randall, D. R., 217
Ranson, D., 167
Rappaport, R., 84
Rathje, W., 2
Read, K. E., 175
Reber, G., 157
Renfrew, C., 208
Reynolds, H., 18
Rhoads, J., 19, 87, 196, 200, 202, 204, 205, 208
Ride, W. D. L., 125
Riesenfeld, A., 22, 30, 192

Rippeteau, B., 199
Robbins, R., 185
Roberts, D. F., 48, 49, 82
Robinson, G. A., 87, 138, 168, 169, 228, 229, 232, 233
Rosenbaer, B. J., 216
Rosenfeld, A., 71, 214
Ross, A., 50, 99, 105, 134
Roth, H. L., 23
Roth, W. E., 87
Rousseau, J. J., 17
Rowland, M. J., 151
Rowley, C. D., 17
Roy, P., 128
Ryan, L., 17, 158, 168, 229, 230, 231
Rye, O., 207, 208

S

Sanders, B., 121
Sanson, G. D., 94
Satterthwait, L., 18
Sauer, C., 43, 184
Saunders, J. J., 217
Schiffer, M. B., 2, 88
Schoenwetter, J., 216
Schmitz, C. A., 192
Schrire, C., 18, 47, 92, 94, 118, 142
Seligmann, C. G., 30, 195
Setzler, F. M., 116, 131, 156
Shapiro, H., 48
Sharpe, C. E., 62
Sharpe, K. J., 62
Shawcross, F. W., 33
Sheridan, G., 123, 131
Sibly, R. M., 47, 50
Sillitoe, P., 190
Simmons, R. T., 76
Simmons, S., 40
Simpson, G. G., 12, 44
Singh, G., 16, 42
Smith, B., 17, 18
Smith, I. E. M., 189
Smith, L., 56, 77
Soejono, R. P., 121
Solheim, W. G., 30, 173
Sollas, W. J., 22
Sorenson, E. R., 20, 175, 176, 187
Souter, G., 18
Specht, J., 134, 173, 190, 192
Specht, R. L., 15
Spencer, J. E., 184

Spencer, W. B., 23, 44
Spriggs, M., 184
Stanner, W. E. H., 17, 21
Statham, E. J., 24, 25, 154
Steiger, W. L., 47
Stewart, G. R., 170
Stocker, G. C., 14
Stockton, E. D., 64, 104, 116, 117, 123
Stockton, J., 232
Story, R., 94
Strathern, M., 66, 84
Streten, N. A., 49
Stringer, C. B., 80
Sturt, C., 229
Sullivan, H., 104, 136
Sullivan, M. E., 30, 52, 105, 133, 134, 153
Sutherland, F. L., 85
Swadling, P. L., 175, 176, 185, 186, 196, 206, 207

T

Tasman, A. J. van, 17
Tatz, C., 17
Taylor, G., 50
Tedford, R. H., 90
Temple, R. B., 119, 143, 154
Tench, W., 17
Terrell, J., 82
Thom, B. G., 15, 49, 55
Thomas, D. H., 66, 87, 175
Thompson, J. P., 191
Thompson, P., 16, 91, 104
Thomson, D. F., 20, 85, 87, 133
Thorne, A. G., 34, 35, 37, 39, 75, 76, 78, 79, 80, 81, 224

Thorne, R., 78
Thorpe, W. W., 151
Tichelman, G. L., 173
Tindale, N. B., 23, 26, 27, 28, 29, 30, 44, 64, 69, 71, 84, 87, 92, 106, 117, 120, 124, 125, 222
Tjabuindji, 2
Tuohy, D. L., 217
Turner, C. V., 211
Tylor, E. B., 23, 83
Tyndale-Biscoe, H., 14

U

Underwood, A. J., 133, 148
Urquhart, A., 151, 153

V

van Balgooy, M. M. J., 14
Vanderwal, R. L., 159, 167, 168, 196, 197, 198, 199, 201, 202, 203, 204, 205, 206
van Heekeren, H. R., 42
Veeh, H. H., 45
Virili, F. L., 155
Volman, T. P., 43
von Blandowski, W., 23

W

Walker, D., 12, 14, 19, 175, 218
Wallace, A. G., 81
Wallace, A. R., 12, 43, 187, 188
Watson, J. B., 175, 183, 186, 189

Watson, V. D., 56, 84, 175, 176, 185, 186, 189, 190, 197
Webb, L. J., 12
Webby, E., 17
Webster, P. J., 49
Weiner, A., 21
Wells, R. T., 90, 94
Wendorf, F., 219
Wheeler, J. M., 184
White, C., 59, 60, 65, 67, 99, 100, 116, 118, 119, 121, 123, 125, 141, 142, 157, 197
White, I. M., 104, 214
White, J. P., 19, 22, 29, 30, 56, 57, 65, 66, 67, 68, 83, 84, 86, 87, 93, 106, 113, 121, 124, 129, 145, 168, 173, 175, 176, 181, 183, 186, 187, 188, 189, 190, 194, 197, 200, 204, 205, 211, 215, 218, 222
White, N. G., 77, 82
Whitlegge, T., 24, 120
Wieneke, C., 106
Williams, E., 20
Williams, P. W., 91
Wilson, S. R., 46, 78
Winterhalder, B., 93
Witter, D. C., 40, 95, 140
Wolpoff, M. H., 80, 224
Wright, R. V. S., 40, 61, 63, 67, 80, 84, 90, 131, 150, 163, 223
Wurm, S. A., 175
Wyrwoll, K. H., 42

Y

Yagdjabula, 2
Yen, D. E., 181, 183, 184

Index of Places

Numbers refer to pages, *f* to figures, and *t* to tables

A

Aibura (NAE), 172*f*, 185*f*, 186*t*, 189, 194*f*
Africa, 67, 92, 94, 218, 219, 230
Aibala, 20
Aitape, 82
Albatross Bay, 155, 156
Alice Springs, 116
Amazon Bay, 172*f*, 198
Amazon R, 6
America (Americas), 6, 24, 33, 53, 54, 94, 95, 124, 133, 216, 217, 230
Amphlett Is, 172*f*, 196, 206, 209
Andaman Is, 81
Arafura Plain, 49, 52, 54, 56, 59, 67, 98
Arafura Sea, 49
Armstrong Bay, 138
Arnhem Land, 16, 44, 59, 67, 68, 71, 82, 93, 98*f*, 99, 104, 112, 116, 118, 119, 120, 121, 125, 129, 131, 141, 155, 156, 157, 184, 219
Aroma Coast, 197
Arona Valley, 172*f*, 176
Aseurica, 6, 42, 43
Asia (see also South-East Asia), 12, 14, 42, 67, 68, 157, 184
Australian Museum, 23

Australian National University, 29, 230
Ava Garau, 206
Ayers Rock, 42

B

Baldina Ck, 108*f*,
Bali, 42
Baliem Valley, 172*f*, 174
Ballina, 24, 25*f*,
Barcoo R, 104
Bassian Plain, 98
Bass Pt, 32*f*, 64, 70, 98*f*, 117, 128, 145, 146*f*, 147*t*, 148, 151, 153
Bass Strait, 170
Batari (NBY), 172*f*, 189
Beecroft Peninsula, 143
Beginner's Luck Cave, 32*f*, 91
Beginner's Luck Cave (Site P), 64
Belfast Lough, 140
Belgium, 24
Berrambool, 132*f*,
Bismarck Archipelago, 190, 218
Blackman's Cave, 98*f*, 166
Blue Mountains, 64, 120
Blyth R, 156
Boera, 172*f*
Bomaderry Ck, 136

Bonfire Shelter, 217
Botany Bay, 24, 128, 146*f*
Bougainville, 82
Brazil, 53
Bridgewater Caves, 140
Brisbane, 98, 135*f*, 136, 153
Brisbane R, 136
British Isles, 232
Burrill Lake, 32*f*, 64, 70, 98*f*, 117

C

Cairns, 76
California, 216
Cambridge University, 29
Canberra, 42, 230
Cannon Hill, 60*f*, 98*f*, 116*f*
Cape Grim, 232
Capertee, 70, 98*f*
  Site 3, 117
Cape York, 8, 16, 19, 50, 67, 71, 76, 98*f*, 102, 104, 112, 116, 131, 155, 171, 172*f*, 184, 189, 215, 224
Cape Zone (South Africa), 92
Carlton, 164*f*
Carnarvon Ranges, 64, 103, 104
Cave Bay Cave, 32*f*, 64, 158*f*, 166

Central America, 216
Central Desert, 19, 65, 117, 215
Chile, 53
Chimbu–Asaro divide, 190
China, 215
Clarence R, 129, 153
Clogg's Cave, 32*f*, 64, 91
Cohuna, 78*t*, 80, 223
Collingwood Bay, 209
Colo R, 126*f*
Connley Cave, 217
Coobool Crossing, 223, 224
Cooper Ck, 222
Coorong, 102
Cossack, 74*f*, 223
Curracurrang, 70, 98*f*, 117, 125,
   136, 146*f*, 152*f*
   1CU, 151
   2CU, 151
Curracurrang Ck, 151
Currarong, 98*f*, 136, 143, 144*f*,
   145, 147, 148
   Currarong 1, 117, 157

D

Dampier, 117, 154, 155
Dampier Is, 154
Danger Cave, 217
Darling R (see also
   Murray–Darling), 33, 39, 64,
   70, 74*f*, 129
Darwin, 15
Deep Ck, 109*f*
Delamere, 2, 29
Devil's Lair, 32*f*, 40, 41*f*, 42, 52,
   59, 61, 62*f*, 70, 71, 91, 222, 223
Devon Downs, 24, 26–27*f*, 28, 29,
   84, 98*f*, 106, 117, 120
Durras North, 98*f*, 136, 148*t*,
   149*f*, 150

E

Easter Is, 81, 227
East Indies, 17
England, 24
Eriama (ACV), 172*f*, 201, 206
Etpiti (MJW), 172*f*, 176*t*
Europe, 22, 24, 67, 83, 84, 97,
   100, 218, 219

F

Falmouth, 164*f*
Fanning Is, 48
Fergusson Is, 172*f*, 189, 197, 202
Flinders Is, 158*f*
Flores, 45, 46
Fort Rock, 217
France, 24
Fromm's Landing, 98*f*, 117, 120
Furneaux Is, 48

G

Garden of Eden, 42
Glenelg R, 138
Goodenough Is, 172*f*, 206, 209
Gragrin Peak, 130*f*
Great Australian Bight, 98
Great Barrier Reef, 45
Greater Australia, 6
Green Gully, 74*f*, 78*t*
Greenland, 53
Greenough R, 42
Griffith University, 229
Gulf District (see also Gulf of
   Papua), 172*f*, 196, 197, 200,
   202, 205
Gulf of Carpentaria, 55, 76
Gulf of Papua (see also Gulf
   District), 172*f*, 197
Gymea Bay, 152*f*

H

Hawaii, 53, 183
Henderson Is, 48
Hunter Hill, 64, 157
Hunter Is, 64, 158*f*, 166, 168
Hobart, 230, 231
Hopkins R, 141
Howqua, 132*f*
Huon Peninsula, 196, 197

I

India, 24, 184, 213, 218, 230
Indo-China, 67
Indonesia, 17, 18, 30, 42, 121,
   183
Ingaladdi, 98*f*, 118
Ireland, 24

Irian Jaya, 30, 173, 175
Italy, 6

J

Japan, 6, 67, 215, 218
Java, 42, 43, 45, 46

K

Kafetu, 172*f*, 190
Kafiavana (NBZ), 32*f*, 67, 172*f*,
   187*t*, 189, 190
Kalimantan, 42, 67
Kamapuk (MKK), 172*f*, 176*t*
Kangaroo Hill, 65, 222
Kangaroo Is, 29, 32*f*, 58*f*, 63, 68,
   90, 91, 105, 222
Keilor, 32*f*, 39, 40, 49, 74*f*, 78*t*,
   79, 90
Kenniff Cave, 32*f*, 64, 84,
   98*f*, 117, 119, 120, 223
Kerema, 202
Kikori, 172*f*, 200
Kimberley, 98*f*, 112, 115*f*, 116,
   118, 125, 219
King George Sound, 157
King Is, 158*f*
King's Table, 32*f*, 64
Kiowa (NAW), 32*f*, 68, 172*f*,
   187*t*, 189, 190
Koonalda Cave, 32*f*, 61, 63*f*, 71,
   223
Kosipe (AER), 32*f*, 56*f*, 57*f*, 58*f*,
   67, 68, 172*f*, 197
Kow Swamp, 32*f*, 71, 74*f*, 77,
   78*t*, 79, 80, 223, 224
Kuk (MAB), 32*f*, 42, 172*f*,
   177–178, 178*f,t*, 179*f*, 179–182,
   182*f*, 183, 184, 185
Kukuba Cave (ADL), 172*f*, 196,
   197, 204
Kulupuari, 172*f*, 202
Kurnell, 98*f*, 120, 128, 136, 146*f*,
   152*f*

L

Lachlan R, 34*f*, 35
Lake Bolac, 138
Lake Condah, 98*f*, 138, 139*f*
Lake Eyre, 110*f*

Lake George, 32*f*, 42
Lake Illawarra, 109*f*
Lakekamu R, 202
Lake Kopiago, 172*f*, 192
Lake Menindee, 90
Lake Mulurulu, 32*f*, 70
Lake Mungo, 32*f*, 33, 34*f*, 34–39,
 42, 49, 59, 70, 71, 78*t*, 79, 80,
 90, 94, 157, 222
Lake Nitchie, 74*f*, 78*t*, 79, 214
Lake Nitchie South, 78*t*
Lake Sentani, 173
Lake Tandou, 32*f*, 70, 74*f*, 78*t*
Lake Torrens, 123
Lake Victoria, 223
Lake Yantara, 36
Laloki R, 203
Lancefield, 16, 90, 91, 94
Lapstone Ck, 28, 29*f*, 84, 98*f*,
 125
Laura, 32*f*, 67, 71
Leichhardt Site, 98*f*, 119
Leonard Rockshelter, 217
Lindner Site, 98*f*, 119
Little Swanport, 158*f*, 168
Long Bay, 23
Lou Is, 189
Louisa Bay, 167

M

Maatsuyker Is, 158*f*, 167, 168
Macassar, 121
Macassar Well, 156
Macleay R, 153, 154
Madagascar, 53
Madang, 190
Mailu, 19, 172*f*, 197, 198, 200,
 202–206, 208–210
Malangangerr, 98*f*, 118, 119,
 142*f*
Malaya, 42
Malden Is, 48
Mallee, 105
Mammoth Cave, 32*f*, 40, 91
Manim Site, 172*f*, 176
Manim Valley, 176
Manly, 17
Manton (MCS), 172*f*, 177, 180,
 181
Manus Is, 172*f*, 189
Maribyrnong Ck, 39
Markham R, 172*f*, 175, 190
Markham Valley, 12, 82, 176

Maros, 122*f*
Massim, 206
Mauritius, 95
Meadowcroft, 53, 54, 216, 217
Melanesia, 86, 173, 174, 183, 197,
 200, 204
Melbourne, 39, 158*f*
Mexico, 53
Micronesia, 183
Milingimbi, 155
Milingimbi Is, 156
Miriwun, 59, 61*f*, 70, 71, 98*f*,
 115*f*, 117, 118
Milne Bay, 172*f*, 206
Mitchell Library, 227, 230, 233
Mojokerto, 43
Montagu Is, 98*f*, 153
Moore Ck, 98*f*, 129, 130
Mossgeil, 74*f*, 78*t*, 79
Motupore (AAK), 172*f*, 198, 206,
 207*f*, 208
Mt Burr, 104
Mt Camel, 132
Mt Cameron West, 158*f*, 167*f*
Mt Hagen, 42, 57, 172*f*, 176, 177
Mt Jaya, 172*f*, 173
Mt Lamington, 56, 57*f*
Mt Newman, 223
Mt Wilhelm, 172*f*, 175
Mt William, 138
Mugumamp Ridge, 172*f*, 177,
 178, 180*f*
Murchison R, 42, 65
Murramurrang, 107*f*, 109*f*
Murray R, 16, 19, 24, 63, 74*f*, 78,
 103, 106, 117, 118, 119, 124,
 140, 141, 222
Murray–Darling river system, 8,
 9, 16, 79, 81, 120

N

N 145 (site), 32*f*, 62
Native Well I, 98*f*, 117, 120
Nawamoyn, 98*f*, 118, 119
Nebira 2 (ACJ), 200, 206
Nebira 4 (ACL), 172*f*, 197, 200,
 201*t*, 201, 202, 203, 204, 205
Nelson Bay, 167
New Britain, 68, 80, 172*f*, 189,
 196, 223
New England, 6
New South Wales, 23, 33, 35, 42,
 80, 99, 104, 116, 117, 119, 120,

 124, 125, 129, 131, 134, 151,
 157, 230
New World, 218
New Zealand, 53, 81, 95, 183,
 227
NFB (site), 172*f*, 190, 192
NFX (site), 32*f*, 56, 57
Ngandong, 43
Ngarradj Warde Djobkeng, 98*f*,
 119
Nile R, 6
Nillipidji, 87
Nombe (NCA), 32*f*, 57, 58*f*, 91,
 176*f*, 189, 190
Noola, 32*f*, 64
Norah Beach, 164*f*
North America, 53, 89, 92, 100,
 216, 217
North Bosworth, 110*f*
Northcliffe, 98*f*, 117, 118*t*
Northern Territory, 29, 123
North-West Territories, 53
Nullarbor Plain, 98*f*, 116
Nyah, 141

O

Oenpelli, 59, 60*f*, 67, 98*f*, 116*f*,
 141, 142*f*
Old Crow, 53
Old World, 43, 218
Oposisi, 172*f*, 197, 198–200, 201,
 202, 203, 204
Ord R, 59, 74*f*
Oriomo Plateau, 171, 172*f*
Ouloubomoto, 208

P

Pacific Ocean, 3, 6, 8, 42, 55, 67,
 68, 181, 184, 215
Pacific islands, 6, 48, 200
Palmerston Is, 48
Pam Is, 189
Papua, 86, 173, 192*f*, 196,
 197–208, 209
Papua New Guinea, 173, 175
Penrith, 126*f*
Perth, 125, 223
Philippine Is, 183
Pier Lake, 127*f*
Pitcairn Is, 48
Polynesia, 47, 183, 227

Platypus Shelter, 136
Port Essington, 15
Port Fairy, 98f, 140
Port Hedland, 8
Port Macquarie, 151
Port Moresby, 172f, 195, 197,
    198, 201, 202, 203, 204, 205,
    206, 208
Potter Pt, 128
Puntutjarpa, 32f, 70, 98f, 117,
    120

Q

Queensland, 15, 76, 100, 116,
    117, 118, 119, 120, 124, 151,
    214
Quininup, 71
Quininup Brook, 70

R

Ramu R, 172f, 175
Ramu Valley, 176
Reamur Rocks, 140
Richmond R, 98f, 129, 153, 154,
    156
Risdon, 230
Rocky Cape, 32f, 158f, 159f,
    160–163t, 161, 162, 163, 166,
    170, 222
Rocky Cape North, 159, 160,
    162, 163, 166
Rocky Cape South, 159, 160, 163
Rocky R, 91
Roonka, 16, 74f, 78t, 103, 104,
    214
Rupo, 172f, 197

S

Samoa, 200
Seal Point, 138
Selai, 172f, 201, 203, 204
Sepik Hills, 192
Sepik R, 12, 172f, 190
Seton, 90
Shea's Ck, 24, 25f, 128
Siassi Is, 172f, 196
Siberia, 150
Sicily, 46

Skew Valley, 98f, 117, 154, 155,
    157
Smith Creek Cave, 217
Snowy Mountains, 35
Sogeri, 197
Solo R, 43
South America, 53, 54, 183, 216,
    232
South Australia, 29, 69, 76, 85,
    116, 119, 123, 125, 137, 214,
    222
South-East Asia, 22, 28, 30, 31,
    42, 43, 69, 81, 173, 184, 209,
    214, 218
Southern Ocean, 61
Spirit Cave, 184
Sri Lanka, 121, 218
Strait of Malacca, 187
Strickland R, 172f, 175
Stuart's Point, 154
Sulawesi, 43, 45, 121, 122f, 218,
    219
Sundaland, 42, 43, 45
Suwarrow Is, 48
Swan R, 221, 222
Sydney, 17, 21, 24, 28, 42, 64,
    108f, 120, 123, 125, 126f, 134,
    143, 146f, 147, 148, 150, 151,
    152t, 153, 227

T

Talasea, 172f, 189, 190
Talgai, 74f, 78t
Tambar Springs, 38f, 126f, 128f
Tandandjal, 29
Tasmania, 6, 8, 9, 12, 14, 17, 18,
    23, 45, 55, 56, 64, 66, 81, 82,
    85, 91, 94, 95, 98, 99, 103, 124,
    125, 156, 157–170, 215, 218,
    219
Tasmanian Museum, 230, 231
Taurama (AJA), 172f, 200, 201,
Taurama (AJA), 172f, 200, 210,
    202, 206
Telefomin, 184
Thailand, 184
The Craigs, 140
The Tombs, 98f, 120
Tierra del Fuego, 232
Timor, 43, 45, 46, 121
Tirrikiba, 109f
Titan's Shelter, 91
Toolondo, 138

Torres Strait, 19, 20, 54, 82, 171,
    172f, 188
Tower Hill, 140
Townsville, 9
Tristan da Cunha, 48
Trobriand Is, 193f, 209
Tropic of Capricorn, 12, 141
Tugeri (MJX), 172f, 176t
Tyimede I, 60f, 98f, 119, 142
Tyimede II, 119, 121, 123, 142

U

Ulu Leang, 122f
Umboi Is, 172f, 196
University of Melbourne, 29
University of New England, 29
University of Sydney, 29
Uro'urina (ADG), 172f, 200, 205,
    206

V

Ventana Cave, 217
Victoria, 29, 48, 50, 90, 91, 102,
    105, 125, 129, 131, 137, 140,
    141, 157, 169, 170
Victory Hill, 232
Vietnam, 42
Vitiaz Strait, 172f, 196

W

Wahgi Valley, 172f, 174, 176,
    177, 181, 183
Waigani Swamp, 200
Wallacea, 12, 31, 42, 43, 44f, 45t,
    46, 50, 67, 184, 187, 215, 218
Wanigela (HAC), 172f, 209, 210f,
    211f
Wañlek (JAO), 172f, 190, 192
Warrego R, 104
Washington Is, 48
Wattamolla, 150, 151
WB (site), 150
Weipa 98f, 155, 156, 157
Western Australia, 40, 52, 65,
    70, 71, 76, 154, 155
Western Desert, 20, 87
Western Europe, 218
West Point, 158f, 166, 167

Willandra Lakes, 16, 34*f*, 35, 36*t*,
    51, 54, 55, 65, 80, 90, 92, 94,
    105
Willeroo, 29
Wilson Butte Cave, 217
WL (site), 150

WT (site), 150

Y

Yambuk Heads, 140

Yarar, 98*f*, 118, 121, 123
Yuku (MAH), 32*f*, 57, 67, 68,
    172*f*, 176, 187*t*, 189, 190
Yule Is, 172*f*, 196, 197, 198, 202,
    203, 204, 205

Subject Index

A

Abalone, 162, 166
Aborigines, 17–18, 22–29, 33, 48–49, 100
  culture areas, 100–102, 131, 219–220
  numbers of, 55–56
  physical nature of, 75–83, 223–224
  population density, 55
Acacias, 12, 13*f*, 14
Acheulean hand-axes, 69
Adzes (see also Axe-adzes)
  Australian, 59, 61, 66, 70, 88*t*, 121, 125, 127*f*, 128–133, 147
  New Guinean, 200–201, 204
Africans, 82, 95
Agriculture, 19–20, 173–186, 217–218
  development of, 177–187, 218
  implements, 68, 173
Alyawara (people), 85
Anbara (people), 100, 156
Andesite, 45
Anthropometry, 75, 76, 78, 82
Anvil, 150
Arawe (people), 80, 223
Archaeological visibility, 92, 197
Argillite, 163

Armshells, 197, 208
Arrows, 19, 194, 219
Artificial cranial deformation, 80, 223
Aspartic acid racemization date, 91
Axe-adzes (see also Axes), 68, 181, 190
Awls, 145, 201, 204

B

Backed blades, 84, 85, 106, 107*f*, 108*f*, 112, 116–122*f*, 123–125, 147, 218–219
  Kimberley type, 117
Bananas, 183–184, 195
Bandicoot, 64, 89, 140, 143, 161
Barramundi, 155
Basalt, 56, 131, 138, 153, 200
Bats, 12, 57
Batissa cf. *violacea*, 156
Beech (*Nothofagus*), 12
Bergmann's rule, 82
Bogong moths, 104
Bondi points, see Backed blades
Bone artefacts, 161–162*t*, 199–200
  adzes, 199
  bipoints, 84, 145, 146*f*, 147, 150

beads, 61–62*f*, 70–71, 200
  chaplets, 103, 214
  cranial bone tablets, 200
  pins, 103, 214
  points, 61–62*f*
  unipoints, 145, 146*f*, 147, 150, 162
Boomerangs, 168
Bounty (ship), 48
Bows, 19, 219
Brainerd-Robinson coefficient, 176
Bream, 145, 148, 151
Bronze, 30, 173, 192
Buffalo, 16, 93
Bunya pine nuts, 104, 136
Burial (see also Cremation), 22, 27*f*, 37, 39, 71, 103, 214
Burin, 83, 86, 124

C

Carpentarians, 76
Cassowary, 187, 200, 203, 208
Casuarina, 181
Catfish, 155, 203
Ceramics, see Pottery
Cemeteries, see Burial
Chama sp., 203
Chauvenet's criterion, 199

Chert, 8, 43, 61, 68, 153, 163, 166, 196, 204, 205, 222
  Bryozoan, 222
Chisels, 128f, 129, 147
Circumcision, 87
Climate, climatic change (see also Environment), 8–9,14–15, 49, 54–56, 94–95, 97–99, 134, 222–223
Cloaks, capes, 103, 162, 168, 214, 232
Clothes, 17, 216, 229
Clovis points, 124
Clubs, 173, 177, 190, 191, 192f, 193f, 205
Coasts
  Australia, 18, 45, 49, 50–52, 54, 55, 63, 65, 69, 97–99, 102, 125, 128, 133–137, 140–141, 143–157
  New Guinea, 12, 49, 59, 172–173, 194–210
Cockles (*Anadara* spp.), 154, 155, 156, 189
Colonization, 46–54, 216–217, 222–223
  coastal, 50–52, 203, 216
Connectivity analysis, 198, 209
Cone shell (*Conus*), 21, 200, 211f
Cores (see also Horse-hoofs), 37, 39, 43, 63, 65, 66, 69, 84, 86, 106, 120, 121, 140, 163, 196, 200, 204, 219, 222
Core-tool-and-scraper tradition, 65, 67
Cost-benefit criteria, 51, 145, 148, 157, 183
Cowries (*Cypraea*), 21, 189
Crabs, 143, 155, 156, 201
Crania (see also Skeletons), 27, 77, 78, 79, 82, 223
  Cohuna, 78, 80, 224
  Cossack, 223
  Keilor, 39, 78, 79, 224
  Kow Swamp, 77–81, 223–224
  Lake Mungo, 78, 79–80
  Lake Nitchie, 78, 79
  Melanesian, 223
  modern, 82
  Mossgeil, 78, 79
  Talgai, 78
Crayfish, 137, 141
Cremation (see also Burial), 37–39
Crocodile, 200, 203
Culture period, 28

Cycas, 64, 104, 214

D

Dasyurids, 90, 161
Demography, 46–48, 50
Dentition, see Teeth
Desert, 14, 19, 20, 33, 50, 54–56, 59, 70, 71, 85, 87, 88, 105, 116–117, 131, 222
Diffusion, diffusionism, 22, 30, 210, 219
Digging sticks, 18, 88t, 181
Dingo (see also Dog), 16, 104, 168
Diprotodon, 88–91, 94
Djetis fauna, 43
Dog (see also Dingo), 200, 205, 214, 228
Dolerite, 131, 221
Donacella nitida, 140
Drainage, see Water control
Drill points, 201, 204, 207f
Dugong (*Dugong dugon*), 24, 128, 136, 203, 207
Duna (people), 20

E

Ecological theory, 46–47
Edge-notched flakes ("saws"), 70, 125, 204
Eels, 105, 137, 138, 169, 170
Eggshell, 36, 59, 141, 228, 232
Elephants, 43, 45
Elouera, 84, 85, 106, 109f, 116f, 120, 121, 131, 147, 200
Emu, 36, 50
Engravings, 61, 63f, 71, 72, 103, 104, 155, 167f, 192–194, 197, 214, 218
  Panaramitee style, 71
Environment, environmental change, 14–17, 24, 35–36, 49, 51–54, 59, 75, 82, 94, 133–134, 136–137, 175–176, 218
Environmental management, 133, 137–138, 170, 216–217
Ethnographic records, 20–21, 23, 48, 100–102, 138, 168–170, 196, 208, 215
Eucalypts, 12, 13, 14, 15
Eurocentrism, 22, 231
European contact, 20–22, 169,

227–235
Evolution, 46, 75, 81–82
Exchange, trade, 18–21, 72, 86, 124–128, 173, 188–190, 196–197, 202, 207–210
Extinct animals (see also specific names of animals), 28, 40, 42, 45, 59, 74, 83, 88–95, 157
Extinction, 45, 88–95, 214, 217

F

Fabricators, 145, 204
Faunal analysis, 161
Feathers, 21, 103
Feral animals, 16, 188–189
Figurines, 173, 190, 191
Fire, 14, 15, 42, 92, 93, 94, 141, 166, 185, 217
Fish, 134–170 *passim*, 203, 207–208
Fish eating, 157–170 *passim*
Fish farming, 217
Fish-hooks, 36, 48, 105, 125, 145, 147, 148, 150, 151, 152f, 155, 168, 207, 215, 219
Fish-hook files, 145, 148, 150, 151, 152f
Fish traps, 137, 138, 139f, 151, 155
Fish weirs, 18, 136, 137, 138, 141
Fishing, 36, 136, 140, 141, 151, 153, 197, 207
Flathead, 151
Flint, 8, 61, 65f, 68, 69, 140
Food production, see Agriculture
Food storage, 183
Fore (people), 20
Forest clearance, 176, 177, 181, 185

G

Genyornis, 89, 90
Geology, 6, 8, 23–24, 28, 35, 42, 45, 73
Geomorphology, 35, 99
Glaciers (see also Ice Age), 53–55, 64, 157, 175
Glass tools, 112, 114f, 125
Golden perch, 36
Golgol unit, 34f, 35, 36t, 42
Gouges, 200

Grassland, 12, 13, 54, 93–94, 186, 195
Grave goods, 103
Greenstone, 102, 129, 131, 132*f*
Greywacke, 130*f*
Grindstones, 18, 39, 70–71
Groper, 148, 151
Gum (see also Resin), 61, 123, 145, 147

H

Hafting (see also Gum; Resin), 68, 121, 123, 150
Hakea, 14
Hatchets (see also Axes; Axe-adzes), 59, 60, 67, 68, 102, 105, 124, 125, 126*f*, 128–132, 145, 168, 218, 219
Hearths, 33, 36–39, 61, 64, 105, 141, 157, 159, 166, 173, 196
Highlands, 15, 56, 100
    Australian, 8, 15, 50, 64, 65, 70, 91, 99–100, 104–105, 116, 125, 131, 214
    New Guinean, 6, 12, 15, 18, 19, 20, 21, 42, 52, 56–59, 68, 81, 84, 88, 91, 172–194
Hiri, 196, 208, 209
History of archaeological research, 22–30, 83–84, 171, 173, 195
Homo erectus, 43, 81
Homo modjokertensis, 43
Homo sapiens (see also Crania; Skeletons), 37–39, 224
Honey, 67, 145
Hornfels, 129
Horse-hoofs (see also Cores), 37, 38*f*, 63, 65–66, 222
Horticulture, *see* Agriculture; Gardens
Houses, 17, 18, 19, 56, 133, 137, 138, 139, 153, 176, 177, 181, 219, 232
Human antiquity (see also Colonization), 2, 6, 42, 83, 221–222
Hunting, 50–53, 92, 93, 95, 104, 133, 141, 142, 145, 157, 168, 173, 185, 189, 197, 208, 214, 217, 219
Huxley's line, 44*f*

I

Ice Age, 15, 64, 76
Igneous rocks, 128, 153
Igneous/metamorphic rocks, 67, 121
Indurated claystone, 128
Infanticide, 47
Intensity of site use, 105

J

Jasper, 43
Jewellery, 200, 215
"Jones effect", 189

K

Kabuh beds, 43
Kalam (people), 186
Kangaroos (see also Macropods; Wallabies), 89, 92
Karta, 63
Kartan, 63, 222
Kawelka (people), 181
Kitchen middens, *see* Shell middens
Koala, 64, 90
K-selection, 46
Kula ring, 174, 209

L

Lakes, 34, 35, 36, 78, 137, 138
Languages, 82, 100, 175, 194, 219
    Austronesian, 192, 197, 219
    Pama-Nyungan, 219
    Papuan, 219
Lapita, 133, 197, 202, 204
Leatherjacket (*Aluteridae*), 147, 148, 151, 168
Lelira blades, 106, 111*f*
Limestone, 8, 27, 61, 62, 186, 196, 197
Limpets, 140, 150
Linnean Society, 23, 24
Lithic, *see* Stone
Littoral resources, 49, 51, 52, 55, 59, 214
Lydekker's line, 44*f*

M

Macropods (see also Kangaroos; Wallabies), 12, 14, 57, 61, 64, 88, 90, 94–95, 161*t*, 186*t*
Macropus titan, 90, 91, 94
Macrozamia, see *Cycas*
Male bias, 21, 23
Male–female relations, 47–48, 148, 215, 228, 234
Mallee, 12
Mammals (see also Marsupials) 16, 43
Mandible
    animal, 186*t*
    human, 78–80, 223–224
Mangrove, 12–13, 49, 154–156, 203
Mangrove clams, 156
Marsupials, (see also Mammals), 4, 16, 24, 64
Megafauna (see also Extinction), 40, 42, 53, 80, 88–95, 217, 222, 223
Metal Age, 192
Metamorphic rock (see also igneous/metamorphic), 59, 128
Microliths, see Backed blades
Middens, see Shells; Middens
Migration (see also Colonization), 28, 43–45, 53, 73–77, 79, 82, 197–198, 205–206, 216
Mining, 61, 63*f*
Mirryn-yong mounds, 140–141
Molluscs, see Shellfish
Mortars, 71, 173, 177, 190, 191*f*, 192, 209
Motu (people), 196, 198, 206–208
Mullet, 151, 154
Mungo unit, 34*f*, 35, 36*t*, 37, 90
Murrayans, 76
Mussel (*Mytilus edulis*), 147, 148, 156, 168
    freshwater, 36, 64
Mutton bird (*Puffinus tenuirostris*), 136, 143, 145, 150, 151, 153, 166

N

Neolithic, 23, 24, 28, 67
Nerite shell, 189

Nets, 18, 36, 138, 141, 151, 168, 207, 208
New Guineans, 17–19, 22, 33, 49, 220
  physical nature of, 75–83
Ngandong fauna, 43, 46
Notopuro beds, 43

O

Obsidian, 85, 86, 173, 189, 197, 202–209 *passim*, 216
  hydration dating, 216
Oceanic Negritos, 76
Ochre, 37, 39, 71, 191
Olive shell, 189
Oysters, 145, 154, 157, 168, 189

P

Palaeo-Indian, 53
Palaeolithic, 23, 28, 83, 124
Palaeomagnetism, 105
Palate, 79, 80, 224
Palorchestes, 94
Pandanus, 12, 56, 185
Panicum, 39, 70
Pebble tools, 45, 63, 69, 105, 125, 128, 222
Penguin, 153
Perch, 151, 154
Pestles, 71, 173, 177, 190, 191
Pets, 188
Phalangers
  cuscus, 12, 57, 186t, 187, 208
  possum, 12, 57, 64, 67, 140, 145, 161, 186
Phascolarctos, 90
Phascolomys, 90
Phascolonus, 89
Phyllite, 56
Pig (*Sus scrofa*), 16, 21, 48, 57, 183, 187t, 188f, 200, 203, 208, 218
  wallows, 177
Pine (*Araucaria*), 12
Plaques, 61, 71
Platypus, 136
Plebidonax deltoides, 140
Pleistocene coastline, 15, 153
Points, 83, 84, 106–125, 142, 218
  backed, 86, 112, 115f
  bifacial, 106, 112f, 113f, 116, 123, 125

Kimberley, 86–87, 112, 116, 125
  Levallois, 106
  Maros, 121
  pirri, 84, 106, 119–120
  trigonal, 106
  unifacial, 106, 110f, 111f, 116, 119, 125
  Woakwine, 106
Pollen, 36, 54, 64, 99, 175, 177, 180, 181, 183, 185
Polynesians, 47–48
Pooraka formation, 222
Population
  aggregation, 100, 135–136
  decline, 169, 173
  density, 5, 19, 20, 52, 54, 55–56, 64, 71–72, 100, 105, 131, 138, 153, 168–169, 173–175, 183, 185, 190, 195, 216
  distribution, 70, 173
  growth, 31, 47–51, 53–54, 102, 105, 157, 176, 183, 186, 216–218
  replacement, 76–77, 79–80, 82, 231
Portulacca, 70
Possum, see Phalanger
Potassium argon dating, 43
Pottery, 18, 30, 133, 173, 176, 190–209 *passim*
  classification of, 198–199, 209
  decoration, 194, 198, 199, 200, 201t, 202, 204, 205, 206, 210
  manufacture, 196, 201
  "Massim" style, 206
  Red slip, 200, 202, 206
  rims, 199
  style, 197, 199, 205
Predation, 93, 95
Procoptodon, 89f, 90, 94
Protemnodon, 89, 91, 94
  P. anak, 94
Pueraria lobata, 184
Putjangan beds, 43

Q

Quartz, 35, 36, 40, 61, 121, 123, 125, 141, 145, 147, 153, 163, 205, 221, 222
Quartzite, 39, 63, 90, 119, 121, 147, 163

R

Radiocarbon dates (specific), 29, 35, 36t, 37, 39, 40, 41f, 52, 56, 57f, 59, 62, 64, 67, 70, 78, 90, 91, 99, 105, 117, 118t, 119, 120, 125, 128, 140, 143, 147t, 148, 150, 151, 154, 155, 156, 157, 160t, 166, 167, 168, 173, 175, 176, 181, 186, 187t, 189, 190, 196, 197, 199, 201, 202, 204, 205, 206, 208, 216, 219, 221, 222
Radiocarbon dating, 4, 30, 83–85, 123
Rainfall, 5, 8–9, 10f, 12, 14, 35, 36, 49, 52, 54, 55, 71, 82, 99, 100, 133, 134, 136, 153, 155, 174, 175, 195, 218, 232
Rainforest, 12, 13, 14, 15, 18, 51, 52, 53, 59, 75, 76, 82, 93, 94, 112, 195
Regalia, 214–215
Religion, 31–33, 100, 104, 124, 125, 168–169, 186, 215, 229, 231
r-selection, 46
Resin (see also Gum), 68, 70, 123, 131, 145, 150, 221
Rhyolite, 147
Rice, 184
Rock art (see also Engravings), 33, 61–62, 71, 100, 102–104, 167, 173, 177, 192–194f, 195f, 197, 214, 218, 219
Rock cod, 147
Rock platforms, 99, 133, 140, 145, 148, 150, 151
Rock-shelters, 33, 90, 142, 150, 151, 153, 157, 166, 173, 176, 177, 196, 201, 217
Rodents, 12, 43, 57, 166, 186t
Roots, 71, 136, 138, 183
Root crops, 138, 173, 182–184, 195, 214, 218
Royal Society of NSW, 23

S

Saccharum spp., 183–184
Sago, 12, 19, 87, 173, 195, 197, 200, 202, 207
  pounders, 87
Salmon, 133

Sampling, 3, 75, 79–80, 134, 145, 151, 154, 160, 175–176, 203, 206

Sand dunes, 35, 36, 42, 55, 63, 78, 153, 154, 166, 223

Sandstone, 59, 64, 70, 143, 148, 150

Sarcophilus, 16, 90, 91, 214

Savages, 3, 17, 22–23

Scavengers, 64

Scrapers, 45, 63, 66, 70, 83, 84, 116, 131, 162, 204

  bone, 199

  concave, 66

  concave and nosed, 84, 163

  end, 84, 121

  end and side, 66

  flake, 131

  flat, straight-edge, 66, 84, 163

  nosed, 66

  notched, 84, 163

  reniform slate, 85

  round-edge, 163

  steep-edge, 63, 66, 84, 163, 222

Sea levels, 9*f*, 29, 43, 45–46, 49, 52–55, 98, 99

  change in, 15, 45*f*, 97, 157, 184, 216

Seal, 138, 140, 143, 161, 162, 166, 167, 168, 170

  elephant seal, 161, 166

  fur seal, 151, 153, 161

Seasonality, seasonal variation, 14*f*, 134, 136, 138, 141, 142, 143, 148, 153, 155, 166, 170, 175, 185, 195

Seeds (see also Grindstones), 70–71, 95, 191, 214, 219

Settlement patterns, 19, 31, 39, 197, 206, 208, 209

Shag (*Phalocrocorax* sp.), 161

Shale, 8, 56

Shells, 35, 144*f*, 150, 173–174, 189, 215

  artefacts, 103, 204, 209

  beads, 201, 204, 207, 208

  beds, 24

  bracelets, 197, 200, 205

  heaps, 137, 155

  impressions on pottery, 202

  lenses, 149, 160

  middens, 24, 29, 37, 64, 92, 99, 118, 119, 134, 140, 142*f*, 143, 147*t*, 150, 151, 153, 154, 155, 157, 159, 162, 166, 167, 209

  mounds, 25*f*, 154–156

  necklaces, 168

  tools, 124, 136, 142

Shellfish, 12, 20, 21, 23, 35–36, 52, 99, 120, 133–167 *passim*, 199, 200, 203, 214, 228

  eating, 157

  gathering, 100, 157, 168

  growth lines, 137, 143

Shields, 168

Shrubland, 12, 13

Silcrete, 8, 65, 120, 128, 153

Silicified wood, 128

Sites

  destruction, 28, 134

  intra-site use, 33, 134, 186

  locations (see also Settlement patterns), 30, 133, 197, 203, 205

Site types

  base camps, 138

  butchering, 39

  camp, 155, 157

  ceremonial, 62, 105

  cooking, 37, 39, 92, 105, 141

  hunting, 176

  kill, 39, 50, 217

  long-term, 140

  open, 33, 90

  residence, 177

  rubbish dumps, 24, 196, 210

  shell middens, etc., see Shells, middens

  short-term, 138, 140

  task-specific, 88

  workshop, 37, 39

Skeletons (see also Crania), 23, 36, 37, 39, 75, 77, 78*t*, 79, 80, 81, 82, 177, 216, 219, 223, 224

  Green Gully, 78

  Kow Swamp, 78, 79, 80, 81, 224

  Lake Mungo, 34*f*, 37, 39, 78, 79, 224

  Lake Tandou, 78

  Roonka, 78

Skin working, 66, 70, 85, 87, 145

Skulls, see Crania

Small-tool tradition (see also Backed blades; Points), 86, 102, 106–125, 214

  origin of, 102, 121–122

Snapper, 145, 147, 148, 150, 151

Social life, 20, 31, 81, 99, 100, 104, 138, 175, 186, 190, 210, 213, 214, 215, 224

Spades, wooden, 18, 181

Spanish voyages, 183

Spatulae, 200, 205

Spears, 19, 36, 74, 88*t*, 105, 124, 136, 141, 142, 145, 150, 151, 155, 207, 219, 228

  barbs, 123–124, 145, 147, 219

  bone-tipped, 142, 150

  death, 123, 145

  fish, 105, 145, 168

  hand-thrown, 124

  heads, 124

  points, 123, 147, 150, 219

Spear thrower, 19, 88*t*, 124, 125, 168, 219

Spondylus shell, 201

Steel tools, 20

Stegodon, 45, 46

Sthenurus, 89*f*, 91, 94

Stone artefacts (see also Stone tools, specific tool names), 29, 30, 33, 36, 40, 42, 43, 45, 55, 56, 57, 62, 64, 65, 83, 90, 91, 118, 142, 143, 153, 154, 155, 163, 177, 181, 196, 201, 218–219, 221, 222

  bipolar flaking, 61, 86, 147, 204–205

  discard, 86–88, 123

  "exotic" raw materials, 85, 86, 102, 106, 120, 121, 123, 124, 145, 163*t*, 166, 170, 177, 215, 222

  heat treatment, 86

  loss, 129, 181, 190

  percussion flaking, 106

  pressure flaking, 106

  raw materials, 30, 85–87, 124, 125, 128, 129–131, 163

  rejuvenation flakes, 140

  technology, 86, 103, 105–133 *passim*, 136, 142, 170, 189, 216, 219

Stone tools (see also Stone artefacts, specific tool names), 21, 23, 28, 36, 37, 39–40, 57, 59, 61, 63, 64, 68, 70, 73, 83, 85, 88*t*, 90, 102, 103, 105, 106, 157, 161, 162–166, 168, 173, 175, 176, 200, 204, 205, 216, 218, 219

  ad hoc, 84, 87

  blunting retouch, 106

  classification, 28, 65–67, 73, 88–85, 86, 163, 210, 218, 222

  curated, 88

ethnographic, 65, 84, 87–88
function, 85, 86, 87, 123, 175
ground, 59, 60*f*, 67–68, 124, 204, 218
manufacture, 39, 65, 67, 87
resharpening, 129
sequence, 28–29
spatial patterning, 73
use-wear, 65, 85, 87, 123, 131, 147, 196, 204, 218
Strombus sp., 203, 207
Sub-incision, 87
Subninella undulata, 140
Subsistence, 18–20, 23, 31, 39, 51, 55, 59, 64, 68–71, 102, 103, 133–157 *passim*, 166, 168, 170, 173, 175, 177, 187, 198, 202, 204, 205, 213, 217, 219–220
change, 70, 170, 176, 214–215
general models, 134–143
Sugar cane, see *Saccharum*
Sumatralith, 69
Swamp (see also Wetland), 13, 137, 138, 141, 153, 155, 169, 171, 177, 180, 181, 183, 185, 195
Sweet potato (*Ipomoea batatas*), 19, 174, 181, 183, 186, 189, 192
Syphilis, 229, 231, 232, 233, 234

T

Tapes hiantina (Diama), 156
Taro (*Colocasia esculenta*), 19, 176, 184
Tasmanian Aborigines, 17, 18, 19, 22, 28, 29, 49, 81, 82, 124, 157–170, 220, 227–235
numbers of, 168–169
Tauade (people), 20
Tectonic movements, 45
Teeth, 27, 80, 94, 223
Terebralia palustris, 155
Termite nests, 105
Tern, 153
Tertiary, 8, 93

Thylacinus, 16, 90
Thylacoleo, 89*f*, 90
Tiger cat, 64
Tiger shark, 203
Tortoise, 136, 142
Toys, 129
Trade, see Exchange
Treadage and scuffage, 117
Tree crops, 195, 218
Tree rings, 137
Trema, 181
Trihybid theory, 76–77
Trinil fauna, 43, 46
Triton, 147, 148
Trochus (*Trochus* sp.), 189, 197, 200, 205
Trumpet shell, 189
Tubers, see Root crops
Turban shell (*Ninella torquata*), 145, 147, 148, 150
Turtle, 200, 203, 207
Typha, 71

U

Ungulates, 43
Uniformitarianism, 1, 23
Upper Palaeolithic, 100, 218

V

Vegetables, 87, 156, 183, 219
Vegetation, 12, 13*f*, 14–16, 93, 175, 186, 195
introduced, 16, 218
Villages, 19, 133, 137, 138, 184, 196
Volcanics, volcanic ash, 8, 42, 43, 56, 57, 59, 177, 180, 181

W

Waisted blades (see also Axes; Axe-adzes), 56, 57, 58*f*, 59, 63, 67, 68, 69*f*, 70

Wallaby (see also Macropods), 12, 64, 92, 140, 155, 161*t*, 170, 200, 203, 208
Wardaman (people), 2
Warfare, 82, 178, 196, 228, 230, 233
Warrener shell, 162
Watercraft, 31, 43–47, 215
canoes, 44, 162
canoe-rafts, 166, 168
rafts, 44, 215
sailing vessels, 197
Water control systems,
Australian, 137–138
New Guinean, 177–183
Wetlands (see also Swamps), 170, 177, 178, 181, 183–184
Whales, 92, 143
Whelks, 21, 145, 156, 189
Wombat (*Vombatus*), 64, 89*f*, 90, 91, 161
Woodland, 12, 13*f*, 14
Wooden artefacts, 64, 87, 181, 216
Woodworking, 66, 68, 70, 87, 88*t*, 200
Woomera, see Spearthrower
Wrasses ("parrot fish"), 145, 147, 148, 151, 155, 161

X

X-Ray diffraction analysis, 209

Y

Yam (*Dioscorea*), 19, 104, 184, 195
Yam daisy (*Microseris scapigera*), 138

Z

Zanci unit, 34*f*, 35, 36*t*
Zebra finches, 14
Zygomaturus, 89*f*, 91

2 3 4 5 6 7 8 9 0 1
A B C D E F G H I J